Mortals and Immortals

Mortals and Immortals

COLLECTED ESSAYS

JEAN-PIERRE VERNANT

Froma I. Zeitlin, Editor

❖

PRINCETON

UNIVERSITY PRESS

PRINCETON, NEW JERSEY

Copyright © 1991 by Princeton University Press
Published by Princeton University Press, 41 William Street,
Princeton, New Jersey 08540
In the United Kingdom: Princeton University Press, Oxford

Library of Congress Cataloging-in-Publication Data

Vernant, Jean Pierre.
Mortals and immortals : collected essays / Jean-Pierre Vernant ;
edited by Froma I. Zeitlin.
p.   cm.
Includes index.
1. Greece—Religion. 2. Greece—Civilization—To 146 B.C.
I. Zeitlin, Froma I. II. Title.
BL782.V45   1991   938—dc20   90-46651

ISBN 0-691-06831-3 (cloth)

Publication of this book has been aided by the Magie Publication Fund
of the Classics Department of Princeton University

This book has been composed in Linotron Times Roman

Princeton University Press books are printed on acid-free paper,
and meet the guidelines for permanence and durability of the
Committee on Production Guidelines for Book Longevity of the
Council on Library Resources

Printed in the United States of America by Princeton University Press,
Princeton, New Jersey

3 5 7 9 10 8 6 4 2

CONTENTS

PART FOUR: *Divinity*

PART FIVE: *Theory*

ABBREVIATIONS

ABSA	*Annual of the British School at Athens*
AC	*L'antiquité classique*
AJA	*American Journal of Archaeology*
Anc. Soc.	*Ancient Society*
ArchEph	*Archaiologike Ephemeris*
ARW	*Archiv für Religionswissenschaft*
ASNSP	*Annali della Scuola Normale Superiore di Pisa, Cl. di Lettere e Filosofia*
BICS	*Bulletin of the Institute of Classical Studies* (University of London)
CP	*Classical Philology*
DK	Diels, H., and W. Kranz, eds. *Die Fragmente der Vorsokratiker*. 3 vols. 6th ed. Berlin, 1951.
FGrHist	Jacoby, F., ed. *Die Fragmente der griechischen Historiker*. Berlin and Leiden, 1923–1958.
HSCP	*Harvard Studies in Classical Philology*
JHS	*Journal of Hellenic Studies*
KR	Kirk, G. S., and J. E. Raven, eds. *The Presocratic Philosophers*. Cambridge, 1957.
LIMC	*Lexicon Iconographicum Mythologiae Classicae*. Zurich, 1981–.
Mnem.	*Mnemosyne*
PMG	Page, D. L., ed. *Poetae Melici Graeci*. Oxford, 1962.
QS	*Quaderni di storia*
QUCC	*Quaderni urbinati di cultura classica*
REA	*Revue des études anciennes*
REG	*Revue des études grecques*
Rev. Arch.	*Revue archéologique*
RhM	*Rheinisches Museum für Philologie*
RHR	*Revue de l'histoire de religions*
RPh.	*Revue de Philologie*
SIFC	*Studi italiani di filologia classica*
YClS	*Yale Classical Studies*

Translations of Greek Texts: Translations of Greek texts without attribution are by the translator(s). Translations with authors' names only are from the Loeb Classical Library editions.

Transliteration of Greek Names: Names of authors, place names, and familiar personages are given in the standard Latinate usage. Elsewhere, and when possible, Greek orthography is followed. The inevitable inconsistencies remain.

ACKNOWLEDGMENTS

I WOULD like to thank Andrew Szegedy-Maszak and Deborah Lyons, who contributed articulate translations of several of the essays. François Lissarrague and Jesper Svenbro read the earlier versions of my other translations with care and discernment. Mary Margaret MacKenzie passed a philosophical eye over "The Birth of Images" and offered many helpful suggestions. Georgia Nugent, Anthony Grafton, David Quint, William Levitan, and Lucette Valensi read the Introduction in its various forms and shared their perceptions and counsel with me. Thanks also to Jane Taylor for her sensitive and intelligent handling of a cumbersome manuscript, to Ronald Cluett for his accuracy and acumen, and to Carolyn Fox who could always be counted upon to smooth the path from here to the Press. Joanna Hitchcock of Princeton University Press supported this project from the beginning with her special combination of enthusiasm, cooperation, good counsel, and tact. Everyone should have an editor like her.

I also wish to express my gratitude to the National Endowment for the Humanities for a Research Fellowship in 1988–90, which I used in part to work on this project in Paris. Finally, I acknowledge with deepest thanks the generous financial assistance of the Magie Publication Fund of the Department of Classics at Princeton University, which inaugurated its new series with this distinguished volume of essays by a sometime and welcome visitor to this side of the Atlantic.

Mortals and Immortals

INTRODUCTION

Froma I. Zeitlin

As it appears in Vernant's previous work (and in the pages that follow), the landscape of Greece is a territory of a special kind. It ranges across mountains, rivers, and cultivated fields down to marshlands and the sea. It features places of sacrifice and divination and sites of cult, and it takes in communities of all sizes, from the precincts of Sparta and the acropolis at Athens to those numberless out-of-the-way places mentioned, among many others, by the indefatigable tourist Pausanias and that figure of erudition, Plutarch. The territory also extends to zones of the mythic imagination: the emerging features of the physical world in Hesiod's *Theogony*, the ends of the earth visited by Perseus in his quest of the Gorgon, and the regions of Olympos, Hades, and Tartaros, above and below the solid foundations of mundane life.

The spaces over which Vernant travels are well marked. They have boundaries and limits, levels and planes, and paths that bifurcate, leading now in one direction, now in another, and often, against all expectation, converging or shifting elevation into other domains or fields. Along the way some paths may veer off to take a different course without ever obscuring entirely the familiar landmarks that link them, in part, to more ancient or parallel routes. And then there are indications of potential highways, still only dimly glimpsed, roads—as we know from our later vantage—that have not yet been taken, to stopping points not yet imagined, not in this era, not in this place. Above all, routes that at first seemed to be trivial or to wander off in random confusion turn out to have a broad and sure destination. The intricate journey is bound to end in perceptions of structure, coherence, and order, and for all the detours, all the subtle gradations, the result is a map of criss-crossing lines that make up a network of intelligible signs for those who know how to read them.

It is, finally, this map that commands our attention, this translation into and out of the region of the mind that configures the territory of an ancient culture in both space and time, through a wide-angled prospect over new frontiers and a gift for discerning unsuspected layers and levels of meaning in familiar ground. It thus reshapes the topography we are used to thinking of as Greece and, in so doing, gives us a guide that passes beyond the diagram and chart to bring a society vividly to life—dynamic, inventive, dialectically articulated, haunted by questions of its own mortality, and addicted to building structures, both of institutions and of the mind itself.

I use "mind" as a two-sided affair: first, it is the agile and resourceful mind of the interpreter that ranges over disparate data, finding the questions to ask and the techniques to use in order to construct a set of cultural models and codes. This mind gathers up details—the word, the anecdote, the myth, the telltale gesture or action, the image; it looks for clusters of symbolic associations, semantic fields, narrative patterns, and significant themes, and situates them in the frame of an organized conceptual whole. All these elements are then sorted into relations of identity and difference, correspondence and contrast, so that what initially seemed paradoxical, ambiguous, or out of place can be shown to belong to a complex system (or systems) with a logic that is peculiarly its own.

The quest of this mind is to enter into the mind of the other—into the "architecture of the mind," as Vernant puts it—to discover those mental and psychological categories "beyond texts and documents," those "forms of thought and sensibility, modes of organization of will and acts," those techniques of knowledge and systems of beliefs and values that we, as heirs of this culture, often assume to be automatically and transparently our own. Thus, the big concepts we take for granted—time, space, memory, the body, death, sexuality, the idea of work, even the notion of the individual—are relative categories. They are defined and shaped as particular creations and expressions of a particular mind in a particular setting, not universal givens, fixed and immutable in some timeless state.

This other mind, this Greek mind, has a context; that context is historical, and this means, first, taking account of the great turning points that usher in changes and new formations, such as the invention of philosophy or the inauguration of legal institutions or the birth of the image as an imitation of appearance. All these events may be taken as evidence of shifts in mentality with psychological and cognitive implications that extend far beyond the facts and details of their specific achievements. But, second and even more to the point, this abstraction we are calling "mind" belongs, of course, to human subjects, and human subjects are in turn rooted in the society they have fabricated and continue to maintain in the course of their history. For Vernant, mind can at no time be separated from its society; every mental fact is also and always a social fact (and the inverse), and its presence is discernible in the multiple and multidimensional workings of that society. "Whether it is a question of religious facts: myths, rituals, and figural representations—or of philosophy, science, art, social institutions, technical or economic facts, we always consider them as works created by men, as an expression of an organized mental activity." The quest for mind as revealed through these works is therefore a first and necessary stage along the route of the ultimate quest, which is "to investigate what man was himself, this ancient Greek man who cannot be detached from the social and cultural context of which he is both its creator and product."[1]

---

[1] Introduction to *Mythe et pensée chez les Grecs: Études de psychologie historique* (Paris, 1965), 9.

Mind and society, mind in society, and society in historical context: these indissociable pairings account for the stereoscopic gaze that surveys a territory it always envisions simultaneously from two or more points of view. Thus, a polytheistic organization of divinities is understood both "as a divine society with its own hierarchy, in which each god enjoys his or her own particular attributes and privileges, bearing a more or less close, more or less direct relation to the structure of human society; and secondly as a classificatory system, a symbolic language with its own intellectual ends."[2] Or, to take another, more limited example, divination (as discussed in this volume) is treated as a mode of thought, an intellectual operation, and as an affair of social actors, whose oracular expertise competes with other forms of knowledge and other practitioners (bards, physicians), who also participate in decision making within the body politic.

In the case of the dramatic genre of tragedy, the aim is to take account of its three different historical aspects, none of which can be reduced to the other, but which "hinge together and combine to constitute a unique human achievement." Tragedy is a social and public phenomenon, sponsored by the *polis* in fifth-century Athens; it is a new type of aesthetic production with its own formal shape and internal concerns. It also reflects a new psychological state of mind, concerned with developing notions of the agent, the will, individual responsibility, and choices in action, that represents a turning point in the history of the self.[3]

Different angles of approach to a single problem are not mutually exclusive. Each can shed light on one facet of the question, and in so doing, better elucidate the relations between them. This principle is especially true in the case of a long-standing mythic tradition when faced with the facts of evolving social realities. The institution of marriage is an excellent case in point. It can be studied historically as the changing customs of a social institution and also as a subject for mythological analysis, without any divorce between the two on grounds of incompatibility. Quite the contrary; it was Marcel Detienne's work on the relevant corpus of myths that stimulated Vernant's interest in the historical project. In Vernant's view, "these are two aspects of a single piece of research," whose double aim "is to distinguish more clearly the reciprocal effects of society and myth and to define both the similarities and . . . divergencies between these two levels which illuminate one another and which now reinforce, now check and counterbalance, one another."[4]

Vernant's approach has a name, several names in fact: historical anthropol-

---

[2] Introduction to *Myth and Society in Ancient Greece*, trans. Janet Lloyd (Atlantic Highlands, N.J., 1980), ix (originally published as *Mythe et société en Grèce ancienne* [Paris, 1974]).

[3] Preface to *Tragedy and Myth in Ancient Greece*, with Pierre Vidal-Naquet, trans. Janet Lloyd (Atlantic Highlands, N.J., 1981), ix (originally published as *Mythe et tragédie en Grèce ancienne* [Paris, 1973]).

[4] Ibid.

ogy is one. It too has a history and a context reaching back to the anthropological and sociological tradition founded in France in the early years of this century by Emile Durkheim and Marcel Mauss, among others, and incorporating the later shifts in historical method and outlook exemplified by the work of the *Annales* school of historiography.

In his own writings, Vernant credits two figures as his mentors: Louis Gernet, the Hellenist, historian (especially of juridical institutions), and pioneer in the application of anthropological methods to the study of ancient Greece, and the other, Ignacy Meyerson, who developed the field known as historical psychology, which takes the range of psychological and cognitive functions to be historically determined and operative in every type of cultural and social activity. To these can be added the work and theories of two scholars in Indo-European studies. The first is Georges Dumézil, who revitalized the comparatist study of myth through his use of linguistic and sociological techniques. His aim was to identify an ideological continuum underlying the structures of these mythic traditions and to determine how these permanent patterns are to be understood in the historical frame of actual social organizations.[5] The second is Emile Benveniste, who turned to comparative linguistic phenomena and focused on the study of semantic fields in order to pinpoint the cultural meanings of significant concepts, values, and institutions. Finally, we should single out the structuralist anthropologist, Claude Lévi-Strauss, who treats myth as a logical system of classification consisting of sets of binary oppositions that, like a language, may be combined in different ways, and undergo certain rule-governed transformations that can be identified and deciphered only in the light of all the versions of a given myth and only according to the cultural categories of a given society. In this emphasis on the formal structures and codes underlying the surface of the mythic narrative, myth assumes a function and meaning as a provisional problem-solving device; it is a kind of "logical tool" that each time aims to find some middle term to mediate "between contradictions that, in life, are actually insoluble," the most persistent of these being the variance between nature and culture.[6]

The foregoing is, of course, only the most cursory sketch of the shaping influences on Vernant's own intellectual development, and it could also have included the names and accomplishments of still other scholars who have made their distinctive contributions to the study of ancient Greece. It is not my intention, however, to trace in any detail the theoretical principles and individual achievements of these other pioneers in their respective fields, nor to specify their and others' relevance to Vernant's own work and outlook. On these interrelated topics Vernant himself has, on more than one occasion, writ-

---

[5] See "The Reason of Myth," in *Myth and Society*, 225–26.

[6] For a useful summary, see ibid., 226–33. For a trenchant critique, see Renate Schlesier, "Lévi-Strauss' Mythology of the Myth," *Telos* 77 (1988): 143–57.

ten with clarity and spirit, and no more so than in two pieces included in this volume. The first is a paper he presented on history and psychology in 1965 before an audience of historians, and the second is his inaugural lecture for the Chair in Comparative Studies of Ancient Religions at the Collège de France (which he held from 1975 until his retirement in 1984). I want, rather, to take my cue from Vernant's insistence on cultural context, this time not with respect to the society under scrutiny, but as seen from the other side, that of the observer. And as the representative of another, if related, culture, who is in a position to observe the observer, I want to raise another issue, based on Vernant's frequent assertions that Greek culture cannot serve as a mirror in which we unreflectively view ourselves and our own habits of thought and through which we translate back into another time and place those cognitive assumptions we have absorbed and ourselves transformed in the course of our own history.

To attempt to reach into the mind of that other whom Vernant calls "ancient Greek man" requires therefore a special mental effort on our part, a conscious process of disengagement that drives a wedge between what we are and think and what we have inherited. And yet, in the objective stance we cultivate, are we not also and always subjects? Even in the name of historical anthropology, can one ever cross that mental boundary over distant reaches of space and time without considering how the self and the other are bound into some kind of symbiotic relation, some perceivable affinity? Is there, in fact, a mirror that Vernant holds up to the study of ancient Greece in which he himself is inevitably reflected, revealed as a bearer, just like the other, of his own cultural baggage? And to what extent can he gaze in that mirror, and, as in the case of the uncanny mirror hung on the wall of a temple in Arcadia, see not his own image therein but that of those others, the gods whose statues are placed in that shrine? At one level, Vernant himself provides the answer that states his position and justifies his own optimism:

> The works ancient Greece created are different enough from that of our mental universe to give us a sense of disorientation from ourselves, to give us, along with the feeling of a historical distance, the consciousness of a change in the person. At the same time, they are not as foreign to us as others are. They are transmitted to us without a loss of continuity. They are still living in our cultural tradition to which we continue to remain attached. Remote enough from us to study him as an object and as any other object to which our modern psychological categories do not entirely apply, Greek man is nevertheless close enough for us to be able, without too many obstacles, to enter into communication with him.

Vernant wrote these words more than twenty-five years ago in the introduction to *Mythe et pensée chez les Grecs* (p. 10), his first collection of eye-opening essays (since issued with additions and corrections in ten editions and translated into numerous languages), and, although current critical opinion would tend to reassess the idea of continuity as a series of historical reinventions of the past, I think it likely that he would not substantially modify this general view. That his confidence was not misplaced, however, is borne out by the broad range of work he then produced, often in collaboration with others, in the growth and success of the center he helped found for comparative research on ancient societies, and in the increasing diffusion of the concepts and principles identified with his name in a number of different intellectual spheres. But it is precisely the success of his enterprise, even if challenged at times or modified by the work of others, that leads me to question again the relation between Vernant in his French-speaking culture and that other with whom he feels able to establish an easy communication. To put it somewhat differently, what does Vernant mean when he speaks of the continuities within ''our'' tradition, and how might these be defined in the present context? Here, playing the ''other'' to Vernant's ''self,'' I propose that perhaps there is indeed a special affinity, not just between the Greek tradition and some larger category called Western tradition, but some distinctive ''meeting of minds'' when French culture encounters the Hellenic world in this anthropological perspective by which the emphasis falls on the entwined concern with mind and society that is expressed in the very notion of ''les sciences humaines.''

There is no exact English equivalent for this term that joins together what we usually separate into two domains. In the current climate in French intellectual life, which has witnessed a remarkable period of ferment in an atmosphere of both heated debates and cordial collaborations, ''les sciences humaines'' have come to fulfill their two underlying premises in an intense preoccupation with theory, method, and principle, on the one hand, and in a continuing engagement with the social dimensions of history, on the other. Despite the obvious differences in their work, all the various figures I mentioned earlier could be analyzed from this dual perspective (with the addition of others such as Roland Barthes and Michel Foucault, both also former professors at the Collège de France). What I see as the common thread that binds them is the responsiveness in their work to the ideological bent of their formalist rule-governed culture and its demand for cognitive coherence. The emphasis on reason, logic, and exacting analysis speaks to a certain passion for order, system, and intelligibility that is not limited to philosophical contexts but philosophically extends to the study of society itself. Vernant's vision of an ''organized mental activity'' is matched by the corresponding shared conviction that society is indeed intelligible. With the proper conceptual framework and sufficiently rigorous techniques of analysis, society can be made to reveal its underlying structures and forms as well as its salient points of stress and strain. Social processes, if not always reasonable, in the Cartesian sense of the word, can at least be deciphered and understood when viewed through the optic of an organizing focus. The persistent search for those underlying principles that would make sense of the diversity and contradictions of human life accounts for the widespread tendency to emphasize the social aspects of human psychology, and corresponds to the challenge of interpreting the particular and the peculiar within a constructed frame of established social norms. Depth psychology, along with Freud, is a latecomer, as we know, to the French scene. If it is embraced more warmly as a result of the cerebral transformations worked on it by a figure like Jacques Lacan, it is in part because to be accepted, the politics of the family romance seemed to require a symbolic and social level of analysis that would transcend a stay-at-home Oedipus and the tyrannical role he has exercised in the literal scenario of psychic formations. Oedipus in France is also the Oedipus of Lévi-Strauss, an exemplar of the human dilemma of "born from one, born from two," or the "anti-Oedipe" of capitalist society as promoted by Deleuze and Guatarri, where for Vernant, of course, the original Oedipus is "sans complexe," a figure of the theater who reflects his society in the ritual role of the scapegoat (*pharmakos*) and the political institution of ostracism.

But the name of Oedipus leads me to shift to the other side of the argument, namely, the contention that there is some vital bond between classical French attitudes and concerns and the heritage of classical culture, which seems to have penetrated deeply and silently into the mental practices of French society and is, in part, replicated there in its modes of discourse. All the general trends and habits enumerated above can be found, I think, in the cultural tradition of the other that serves as the fundamental and enduring model: the emphasis on mind from the *noos* of the *Odyssey* to Anaxagoras's deified *Nous* to Platonic and Aristotelian notions of intellection, the demand for reason and intelligibility, the gift for theory and formal categories of thought, the preoccupation with the analysis of society and social norms, endlessly debated, and the curiosity about human nature and what is often sentimentally called "the human condition."

Even rhetorical habits, inculcated over centuries of French educational practices, show affinities with the binary thought characteristic of Greek language and expression with the familiar oscillation between "on the one hand" and "on the other." There is the insistence on a triadic form of argument with a beginning, a middle, and an end, or the division of a problem into three component parts, and the high value placed on the achievement of an aesthetic style of form and balance. This fondness for balance also reveals itself in the desire to station oneself in a position neither too remote nor too close to the object in question. Both an intellectual and an aesthetic stance, the concept of a "bonne distance," reflected in the thought of Pascal and evident too in structuralist ideas about mediation between opposites through a middle term, owes not a little to Aristotle's notion of the mean, and fits more generally with Greek concerns about geometrically defined limits and boundaries.

These generalizations are far too broad and there are, of course, many other trends and pressures in the French intellectual and humanist tradition. Never-

theless, for Vernant in particular, trained originally in philosophy before he
turned to anthropology and the study of religion and society, there is a remarkable consonance between his style, thought, and strategies of analysis
and those of the very culture he is exploring. Especially revealing in this respect is a remark Vernant made criticizing the usual historical approach to
Greek myth that treats it as an aggregate of random particulars rather than "as
a whole system with its own vocabulary and general framework, its own rules
and inherent constraints." Refusing to accept the idea of "a scattered and
heterogeneous pantheon, a mythology of bits and pieces," he asks: "If this
was the polytheism of the Greeks, how could these men, whose exacting rigor
in the realms of intellectual consistency is extolled, have lived their religious
life in a kind of chaos?"[7] Vernant's attraction to myth and the structured logic
he has found in its modes of expression, which constitutes perhaps his most
enduring achievement, exemplifies the passion of that philosophical mind to
turn the most tangled, the most recalcitrant bundle of stuff into the warp and
weft of an elegant fabric with intricate but regular folds.

If I have pointed to some of the mirroring, even mimetic, effects that account for the intimate relationship between the observer and the observed
(which is not entirely immune to a certain critique that the modes of inquiry
are enmeshed in the very system they aim to explicate),[8] the issue is one less
of theoretical purity than of the practical results of Vernant's work, which has
helped shape and direct a field that bears the distinctive impression of his vir-
tuoso mind and that, in its details, has proved so accurate in contexts he never
even addressed. It is finally this encompassing power that, beyond all the de-
terminants of his cultural milieu, beyond his rare combination of the qualities
of an exceptional scholar, decisively places him in a pantheon of preeminence
shared by the very few.

George Steiner's admiration for another remarkable scholar of our era applies precisely also, in my opinion, to Vernant:

> No less than the master translator or actor or performer of music, the truly great
> scholar becomes as one with his material, however abstruse, however recondite.
> He melts the strength of his own personality and technical virtuosity into the his-
> torical epoch, the literary or philosophic text, the sociological fabric that he is
> analyzing and presenting to us. In turn, that fabric, that set of primary sources,
> will take on something of its interpreter's voice and style. It will become his with-
> out ceasing to be itself. . . . Yet in each case the alchemy reinstates the strength
> of the material.

Steiner is speaking of Gershom Scholem, the towering figure who through his
study of Kabbalistic works transformed our understanding of Hebrew thought

---

[7] "Greek Religion, Ancient Religions," below, chap. 16.
[8] See Robert Pogue Harrison, "The Ambiguities of Philology," *Diacritics* 16 (1986): 14–20.

and left a lasting heritage in other fields of endeavor. In support of his judgment on the special character of Scholem's "life-giving scholarship," Steiner
points to those others in whom the fusion of the self and the material has
achieved a kind of memorable transcendence. "There is now an ancient
China," he says, "that is Joseph Needham's, a Hellenistic civilization that
speaks in the accents of the late Arnaldo Momigliano, a mapping of grammars
which will for a long time to come carry the imprint of Roman Jakobson."[9]
To these attributions I would add that there is a distinctive territory of archaic
and classical Greece, which is the one I earlier attempted to describe, and it
most assuredly belongs to Jean-Pierre Vernant.

II

The majority of the essays in this volume represent the work of the last decade,
both published and unpublished. A substantial number of these have now been
gathered in Vernant's most recent book, *L'individu, la mort, l'amour* (Paris,
1989). A few were published earlier as parts of other collections in French,
and in one case, the work appeared independently as a short book (*La mort
dans les yeux*). Of the reports of the year's work published in the *Annuaire du
Collège de France*, I have taken one in its entirety to complement the other
pieces on the goddess Artemis and have excerpted another for use as additional
notes.[10] For the sake of convenience, I have grouped the essays into five sections: Mortality, Gender, Image, Divinity, and Theory. These divisions are
meant to function not as rigorous lines of demarcation, but rather as a way of
emphasizing certain salient features of the individual pieces, which may in
fact spill over the boundaries I have established to guide the way. In general,
these essays could be said to revolve about certain recurrent themes: the relations between mortals and immortals, death, the body, the soul, the individual;
the mask, the mirror, the image, and the imagination; the self and the other,
and more broadly, the concept of otherness or "alterity."

Part 1, "Mortality," is concerned particularly with those most enduring
questions that preoccupied the Greek imagination and were essential in constructing its distinctive cultural values: death, the gods, and the status of the
body. The opening piece, which in part gives its title to the volume, "Mortals
and Immortals: The Body of the Divine," addresses the whole notion of a

---

[9] The entire quote is excerpted from George Steiner's piece, "The Friend of a Friend," a review of *Correspondence of Walter Benjamin and Gershom Scholem: 1932–1940*, trans. Gary
Smith and André Lefevere, *New Yorker* (January 23, 1990): 133–36.

[10] One lengthy study, "A la table des hommes," which returns to the subject of Prometheus
and Pandora that has been central to Vernant's work on Hesiod and to his analysis of the relations
among sacrifice, marriage, and agriculture, was omitted because it has just appeared in the translation by Paula Wissing of the volume *La cuisine de sacrifice en pays grec*, ed. M. Detienne and
J.-P. Vernant (Paris, 1979), under the title *The Cuisine of Sacrifice among the Greeks* (Chicago,
1989), and hence is now readily available to an English-speaking audience.

polytheistic system of divinities and its relation to the human world through the paradox of gods who are endowed with bodies and yet are beyond corporeal limitations. They may eat but have no need of food, sleep but yet their eyes are open, and a blood courses through them that is not blood. At stake is a distinction between mortals and immortals described as that between a "sub-body" and a "super-body," the first incomplete and evanescent, given over to decrepitude and death, the second sublimated, radiant, and impervious to negation. Vernant argues against the traditional view that the "anthropomorphism of the Greek gods means that they were conceived in the image of human beings" to propose the reverse, that in its physical and psychological dynamism, it is the human body that "reflects the divine model as the inexhaustible source of vital energy when, for an instant, the brilliance of divinity happens to fall on a mortal creature."

That brilliance is most often encountered in the heroic milieu of epic (or epinician poetry), and "A 'Beautiful Death' and the Disfigured Corpse in Homeric Epic" investigates the ideology of heroic honor in Homeric poetry, which aims through death to transcend death, first through the treatment of the body after death, then in the funeral rites that include the erection of a memorial stone, and finally through the memory enshrined in epic itself. Every detail here takes its place in the aesthetics of death, in the opposition between the beauty of the fallen warrior that previews his transfiguration into the collective memory of epic and the terror of possible outrage visited on the body that, once disfigured, maimed, a prey for dogs and birds, is doomed to dishonor and oblivion.

With this system of values in place, the next essay, "India, Mesopotamia, Greece: Three Ideologies of Death," broadens the horizons both to locate Greek ideas of death in a comparative context and to raise the discussion to a more general level by considering funeral ideology as one that "defines the entire effort that makes use of the social imagination to develop an acculturation of death, to assimilate it by civilizing it, and to assure its 'management' on the institutional level." In exploring the pervasive contrasts between Mesopotamian and Brahmanic Indian practices that reflect the differences between "intraworldly" and "extraworldly" orientations, Vernant does not take Greece as the third or mediating term, although it shares characteristics with each of the other two cultures. Rather, he views the Greek way of death as a distinctive and original development in that it uses a collective epic tradition not limited to a specific time and place and creates a "living biography of an exemplary man," who is known not for his social status but because of his deeds and exploits, and thus becomes available as a "social symbol" and "a communal model" in the generations that follow.

The last piece in this section, "*Panta Kala*," returns to the notion of a "beautiful death" but traces the transformation of the ideal from the Homeric warrior to the citizen of the city-state as reflected in an important fragment of the poet Simonides. The virtues that had characterized the warrior have, under the pressures of historical and political change, passed on to the citizen, who can now be praised during his lifetime and not only after his death. No longer an objectified figure of epic song, this new man may, as in this case, be a personal friend of the poet, not a hero but a man of good sense and civic rectitude. Excellence or *aretē* is adjusted now to the city's standards of value and finds its eulogy in behavior that is displayed, not on the epic battlefield of long ago, but in the complex daily rounds of the *polis*, in life and not, as in Homer, in death.

The ideological glow that surrounds a "beautiful death" and aims to turn death into a glorious affirmation of the "ideal type" of life is both countered and paradoxically intensified by the grimmer and more realistic side of what it means to "leave the light of the sun": that is, to descend into the darkness of Hades and confront there the powers of horror and fear and the experience of radical loss and privation. This is the side that in the Greek social imagination is identified not with Thanatos, brother of Sleep, and a worthy adversary, but with feminine forces, who may be emblems of the cruelty and terror that accompany the bloodshed and mayhem of battle, or tempting lures of seduction who entice men to the doom of oblivion. In part 2, which I have called "Gender," the essay "Feminine Figures of Death in Greece" examines this latter category in which Death seems inseparable from Eros, whether in the intimacy of male warrior bodies locked in mortal combat, or more particularly, in encounters with such mythic females as Harpies, Sphinxes, and Sirens for whom "the dead are both their victims and their lovers." Kalypso, too, is included, this time as the figure who offers an immortality that amounts to a nonlife, to which Odysseus in the end would prefer the alternative of death and mortality.

In the second and longer essay, "Death in the Eyes," Vernant examines the monstrous figure of Gorgo, who, with the mesmerizing potency of her frontal gaze, confronts man with an image of absolute otherness, of a pure supernatural terror that is finally the very incarnation of the power of death. Vernant starts from the idea of the mask that is the Gorgon's head and explores the entire psychological repertory of radical fear as expressed in Medusa's iconography and myth. In addition to the uncanny impact of a disembodied head, a monstrous face composed of hybrid elements, and an associated bestiary of dog, horse, and snake, Gorgo works through visual and auditory effects: wide staring eyes and gaping mouth, clacking of teeth and hissing of serpents, groans and shrieks as well as piercing sounds of the war cry and trumpet accompanied by the blinding gleam of bronze. The flute in particular occupies a special place in this list, both for the wild music it produces and for the resemblance between the facial distortions of the one who blows into it and those of the Gorgon's mask. Above all, the sequence of events in the myth of Perseus, who, with the aid of magic instruments, vanquishes the Gorgon, brings into play the interrelations of mask and mirror, of the game of seeing and being seen. The Gorgon's mask is finally the monstrous double of the self, who possesses you and alienates you from yourself but also induces a reciprocal relation of intimacy and repulsion. This piece stands out, in my opinion, in Vernant's work, not only for the intricacy and range of the evidence he marshals, but for its articulation of a feeling state and emotional disposition.

Turning away from the emphasis on death and the feminine through the medium of the mask, the next essay, "In the Mirror of Medusa," which heads the section I have called "Image," takes up the same myth of Perseus and Medusa, this time to focus on the detail of the shield used as a mirror to deflect the monster's deadly gaze. Considering first the wider context of ancient ideas about mirrors, especially their ambiguous status between the real and the reflection, between the self and the double, Vernant shows how the shield-mirror, although a later addition to the story, is integrally related to the myth of Perseus, which, in each and every episode, turns on some problematic of seeing and being seen. The mirror serves as the most striking emblem of this interaction, related both to the archaic magic of mirror reflections and to intellectual developments of the fifth and fourth centuries B.C.E. among artists (the uses of perspective), philosophers (the status of imitation), and scientists (experiments in optics). This essay therefore stands as an excellent introduction to the pieces that follow, which are preoccupied with the aesthetic, psychological, and ontological status of the image, imagination, and imitation as these concepts develop and take shape in Greek culture.

Broadly speaking, this interest follows the wider trajectory that passes from the religious orientation of the archaic age to the one that evolves under the social and political pressures of the new institution of the city-state in the classical period, culminating in the philosophical explorations of Plato that will remain dominant until yet another turning point in the career of the image takes place in late antiquity.

Vernant treats this evolution from two different perspectives. In the piece "From the 'Presentification' of the Invisible to the Imitation of Appearance," he argues that in the archaic period the function of the image is not to represent a recognizable similitude to any model but rather to incarnate a religious reality, a means of mediating between two worlds, ours and the one beyond, whether that of the gods in the ancient idol called the *xoanon* or that of the dead in the uninscribed brute stone erected as a memorial. Surveying the special properties of the *xoanon* as a magic talisman of a closed social group, family, or clan, which is animated in the game of "hide and reveal," he suggests that only with the appearance of the temple and the institution of public cult does the image become the exterior representation of the god and an object of public appearance that all are entitled to view. The way is opened that will lead to the idea of the image, properly speaking, an "imitative artifice reproducing, in the form of a counterfeit, the external appearance of real things."

The transformation of the solid funeral stele into sculptured representations of the deceased, endowed with names and epigrams, is based on different kinds of evidence. But here too, in the notion that the figure represents the corporeal beauty of the dead person, that it is made to stand "in place of," "instead of," the concept of a copy "imitating a model and giving the spectator an illusion of reality" takes over from the earlier religious values of mysterious incarnation and muted sign.

Once the image has arrived at its status of artifice and appearance, the stage is set for the next act of the drama that places the image, the imaginary, and the imagination at the center of a mental universe organized around the distinctions between the visible and invisible, illusion and reality, being and nonbeing. In this next, closely argued essay, "The Birth of Images," Vernant discusses the importance of imitation or *mimēsis* in Plato's work, which acquires "a more precise, even a technical value" and comes to serve as the "common and characteristic feature of all figurative or representational activities," whether pictorial or verbal, applicable to painters, poets, and sophists. In Plato, Vernant contends, the status of the image (*eikōn, eidōlon,* and *phasma*) is the key to understanding the philosophical hierarchy established between the entire sensible world of appearances and that of the permanent, the ideal, and the "authentically" real. Related to conjecture (*eikasia*), sight/knowledge (*eidenai*), and seeming (*phainein*), the vocabulary of the image attests to its emblematic representation of all those forms of knowledge Plato devalues, including *doxa,* opinion, which typifies only what "seems" rather than what "is." At the same time, the image gains a "paradoxical status as an intermediary between nonbeing and being," since it is not a "pure nothing but yet not a something," and is therefore comparable to the epistemological status of *doxa* when contrasted with true science and knowledge (*epistēmē*). Given Plato's negative views about "seeming" and "appearance" (*phainein*), it is not surprising that he does not view the imagination (*phantasia*) as "a faculty," as the "power of constructing or using mental images," but rather as that "uncritical state of thought in which spontaneous assent is given to the appearance of things in the form in which they are viewed." It is not until the second century of our era that *phantasia* comes into its own as the inspiration for creative work and is deemed superior to *mimēsis* precisely because it sees not appearances, but what is in the mind's eye. Imagination and the power of art, as Vernant sagely concludes, now seem to gain "the same power of contemplating the invisible and of passing beyond appearance by acceding to the superior world of Forms that Plato had previously reserved for philosophy."

Concomitant with this world of Forms in Platonic thought is the well-known distinction between body and soul, between the material and spiritual aspects of the individual. The next essay, "Psuche: Simulacrum of the Body or Image of the Divine?" briefly addresses the evolution of this relationship between body and soul, again through the three formative moments in the archaic, classical, and late antique periods. Here too the image or *eidōlon* is a central concern, as are the uses of *mimēsis*, for in Homer the *psuchē* is represented as a little body, an *eidōlon* or phantom image of the corporeal form of the deceased, while in Plato, the *psuchē* is a permanent and interior attribute of the living individual. In the Platonic inversion of values, it is the body now that "is made to look like the semblance of the soul." The result is that, as Vernant observes, "we have passed from the soul, ghostly double of the body, to the body as a ghostly reflection of the soul," conceived as both an immaterial and an immortal entity. Thus represented, the human soul, in turn, is the image, the "simulacrum of the divine, of Being, and the all-encompassing One." What Plato only sketches out is made explicit in the second-century philosopher Plotinus, for whom philosophy affords the passport that would allow the self, now identical to itself, to enter into full identification with the divine beyond the limits of *mimēsis*. Thus, Plato remains the touchstone of theory, whether for the arts, as in the case of Philostratus, who "rewrites" Platonic notions to validate the concept of artistic creativity, or with Plotinus, who extends and develops the uses of the *eidōlon* and of *mimēsis* with the aim of achieving the dream of an immortal and interiorized self.

The next group of essays, under the rubric "Divinity," all concern a single figure in the Greek pantheon, the goddess Artemis. The study of her roles and functions and her characteristic features and modes of intervention was the task that occupied Vernant for a number of years in his seminars at the Collège de France, in the context of the broader questions he was posing about images, idols, masks, and ways of representing the divine. Along with Dionysos and Gorgo, Artemis completes the triad of divinities associated with the mask, which, as Vernant sees it in general terms, is the emblem of an "otherness" that intrudes on the world of here and now. The first essay is a general survey of Artemis's roles and functions that was originally published as the preliminary section to the discussion of Gorgo in *La mort dans les yeux*. Given the number of other pieces on Artemis, it seemed best to place it here with the other essays on Artemis that enlarge and develop themes and concepts only touched on in the first brief overview. These four pieces range widely over the evidence for the worship of Artemis, in myth and cult, in literary and historical documents, and in social and religious contexts. Throughout, Vernant challenges the usual depiction of Artemis as a goddess of fertility and the untamed world (animal, vegetal, and territorial, as well as the young of all species) to demonstrate the underlying unity and coherence of all the manifold ways in which the Greeks represented the manifestations of her power.

Briefly put, Artemis is a goddess of boundaries, of border zones, particularly at home in indeterminate spaces where sea and land meet, or in uncultivated lands at the borders of fields. The essential point is that Artemis does not operate as an alternative to the civilized, but is located rather on the frontiers, where wild and cultivated exist side by side, opposed to one another and yet also in precarious contact. Artemis's role is a double one: she keeps watch over the lines of demarcation, ensuring that the boundaries remain intact, yet she also facilitates passage between the two zones at the right time and under the proper auspices. Whether it is a matter of the hunt or of war, or of the general rearing of children, or of the protection of women in childbirth, Vernant demonstrates again and again the active function Artemis assumes in her twofold aspect as guardian of boundaries and agent of transitions. In this sense, she is continually shown as an intermediate figure, herself betwixt and between, associated with the wild, with strangeness and otherness, and yet contributing to successful integration in the community or warding off uncontrolled eruptions of otherness into normal life. At Brauron and Mounychia, where little Athenian girls are sent to be "tamed" in preparation for marriage; at Patras where, under the title of Triklaria (and together with Dionysos), she sanctions the proper rules for marriage; as Orthia in Sparta, who presides over the famous initiatory rites of Laconian youth that, in addition to the interesting use of masks, include flagellation and other bodily ordeals, Artemis sees to the strict demarcation between the worlds of young and adult, and at the same time escorts the young over to the other side.

In war and combat, Artemis is invoked only in special circumstances and not with a military end in mind. Rather, "Artemis goes into action when one of the combatants violates the limits set either on the use of violence during battle or on the treatment of the defeated party afterward," when the "civilized" rules for warfare have been or are in danger of being breached. Thus, through supernatural interventions, she muddles the boundaries for those who have offended against these principles, leading them astray and putting them at the mercy of their adversaries, while concomitantly giving special vision to those she favors, bringing them through snow and fog to discern the outlines of enemies and landmarks. Preliminary sacrifices are made to her, not so much to achieve victory in war, but to ensure in advance that the army in question will not cross the boundary that will plunge them into a war of annihilation and total destruction. Like her role in the hunt, Artemis's function in war is to preserve this thin and fragile line between civilization and savagery in circumstances where violence threatens to sweep away the usual limits. As a barbarian goddess, taken from the land of Taurians and brought to Greece, she too is "civilized" and "tamed." She gives up her literal demand for human sacrifice in favor of substitutional practices and becomes, in turn, a figure who transforms the "other" into the "same," escorting those who are marginal, whether aberrant individuals or a cohort of age-mates, into the official community.

The various essays in the final section are included under the title "Theory," since each approaches a general problem from a theoretical point of view. The first, "History and Psychology," is an early essay (1965) that,

meant originally for oral presentation before a group of historians, gives a
succinct and lucid account of what is meant by historical psychology and how
the disciplines of history and psychology may fruitfully interact. The second,
"Greek Religion, Ancient Religions," is the broadest in scope in that it explores an entire field of inquiry and is perhaps the most comprehensive statement Vernant has made about the principles, concerns, and general orientation
that stamp all his work with his special signature. It was the inaugural lecture
delivered at the Collège de France in the fall of 1975, when he took up his
chair in Comparative Religions in the Ancient World; the occasion offered
Vernant the opportunity both to situate himself intellectually in the context of
the field of comparative religion—taking up a "frontier post, this center of a
crossroads . . . the point of focus where, through me, many divergent and
radiating strands are collected and woven together"—and to elucidate his past
and future programs of study. A prime illustration he uses to demonstrate his
comparative method is to juxtapose Greek and Vedic sacrificial rituals and,
through the observation of their contrasting forms and goals, to highlight the
specific nature of Greek sacrifice in its religious and social contexts.

This essential feature of Greek religion is one to which Vernant has returned
a number of times, as in the case of the next essay, which was his contribution
to a collective exploration of Greek sacrifice and its meanings by a diverse
group of scholars. This piece, "A General Theory of Sacrifice and the Slaying
of the Victim in the Greek *Thusia*," also exemplifies Vernant's principle of
looking at a widespread phenomenon within the context of a particular religion
and society to determine how that group constructs its culturally specific version of the scenario in question. Here the choice falls on the *thusia*, the nor-
mative type of sacrifice meant for human consumption (by contrast to the kind
that is wholly destroyed) and, as the title indicates, it focuses on the most
dramatic and contested aspect of the rite. Disputing the emphasis on violence
and murder that other scholars, such as Walter Burkert and René Girard, have
seen as the hidden unrecognized core of the sacrificial act, Vernant argues that,
in both language and image, the Greeks scrupulously distinguish between
murder (*phonos*) and the sacrifice (*thusia*), which, together with rules for marriage and for agriculture, is a central component of their idea of civilized life.
Readers familiar with Vernant's earlier work and that of his associates will
recognize this fundamental triad of cultural activities, which they identified
and explored across many different aspects and sectors of Greek life. Here
Vernant again emphasizes the role of sacrifice in determining the proper relations among beast, human, and divine, but he does so through an analysis of
the myth and ritual of the Bouphonia, an archaic Athenian ritual, which, as he
argues, actually confronts the idea of murder in sacrifice, and "transcends it
so it may enter into culture and found the religious, civic, and human order."
The story the Greeks themselves tell about the origins of this ritual shows they
acknowledge the problem but regard it "as a subversive threat" that the or-

ganization of the rite is meant to control and distinguish from an outright murder of the victim.

In speaking of sacrifice as a cross-cultural phenomenon, Vernant rejects the idea of "a general theory of sacrifice" in favor of a "comparative typology of different sacrificial systems." The same principle is at work in the approach to divination, considered one of the most "widely distributed commodities in the world," which is treated in the next essay, "Speech and Mute Signs," originally published as the introduction to a comparative volume entitled *Divination et rationalité*. The aim of the project was to treat divination from two points of view: as a "mental attitude" implying a certain kind of intelligence at work in oracular consultation, possessing its own logic, rules, and type of rationality, and as a "social institution," involving the relative status and function of oracular knowledge and its practitioners, compared with other ways of knowing and other social actors who are also entrusted with the power of decision making in any given society. Framed in a cross-cultural perspective of societies both ancient and modern, the case of ancient Greece appears quite atypical in its reliance on the importance given to speech in preference to other kinds of divinatory signs and modes of augury. Furthermore, divination is not the highest-rated form of decision making, nor are its practitioners at the top of the social ladder. Reserved for the most part for matters of religious importance and relegated to the margins of the city in Panhellenic sanctuaries like Delphi, divination was a special form of knowledge, contrasted with the rational discourse developed in the city. At the same time, its favorite mode of consultation bears a marked resemblance to the uses of debate in political assemblies. In the literary texts, divination is most often represented as the uttering of enigmatic words (such as in the *Oedipus Rex*), but the historical record shows that in practice, most consultations, both public and private, were conducted on a yes or no basis that answered a specific question put to the oracle, not unlike the political decisions based on the choice of one or the other alternative course of action put before the citizens of the city-state. Yet the literary evidence must not be dismissed as some imaginative construct; rather it is a " 'theoretical' representation of divinatory activity . . . that implies a true omniscience, founded on the gift of double sight and on a direct contact with the invisible and the world beyond," which allows the seer control of "what was, what is, and what will be." In this context, divination has a theological value and attains the status of an enigmatic word, a " 'spoken' that functions like a sign, but an obscure sign, as difficult for human intelligence to decode as the events about which they came to consult."

The last essay, "The Individual within the City-State," is both the most ambitious and the most explicit effort to address a topic of perennial interest and vital historical importance: the category of the person, the individual identity, and what we would call the "self." For a historical psychologist, this is the underlying question that governs the principles of research. The idea of the person does not constitute a universal given; it is strictly conditioned by cultural and historical contexts, and it undergoes transformations in the course of time. From the beginning of his work, Vernant has been preoccupied with this issue, starting with a piece published in *Mythe et pensée* on ''Aspects of the Person in Greek Religion''; over the years, his outlook has been modified as he has come to realize the essential role played by those defined as ''others'' in the project of self-definition. As he himself says:

> In a face-to-face society, a culture of shame and honor where competition for glory leaves little room for the sense of duty and does not know that of sin, everyone's existence is continually placed under the regard of someone else. It is in the eyes of the one who faces you, in the mirror it presents you that the image of the self is constructed. There is no consciousness of one's identity without this other who, in facing you, reflects you and yet is opposed to you. Self and other, identity and alterity go together, are reciprocally constructed.

In addition to the standard forms of the Other (animals, slaves, barbarians, children, women), ''three,'' as Vernant observes,

> stand out . . . as particularly significant: the figure of the gods, the face of death, and the visage of the beloved. Because they mark the frontiers within which the human individual is inscribed, because they emphasize one's own limitations and yet, by the intensity of emotions they arouse, also awaken the desire to overcome them, these three types of encounter with the other serve as touchstones for the testing of identity as the Greeks understood and adopted it.[11]

The essay in question, however, frames the problem in dialogue with the work of two social philosophers, Louis Dumont and Michel Foucault, who both tried to theorize the historical conditions that were necessary for an individual identity to emerge from the social and collective matrix. Vernant proposes a different classification that distinguishes among three categories: the ''individual'' (situated in his social environment and the limitations imposed on his autonomy), the ''subject'' (expressed through the use of the first person, which endows him or her with a ''unique being''), and finally, the ''ego'' or person (*le moi*), defined as ''the ensemble of psychological practices and attitudes that give an interior dimension to the subject and a sense of wholeness.'' For Vernant, the evolution of the self is always firmly attached to social practices, however numerous and various these may be. The category of the individual depends on the heroic code that validates exemplary individuals, the uses of spiritual exercises for controlling the self practiced as early as the end of the archaic period by figures called ''mages'' or wise men, the development of the *sumposion* as a meeting ground for personal friends, the shift in

---

[11] Introduction to *L'individu, la mort, l'amour: Soi-même et l'autre en Grèce ancienne* (Paris, 1989).

funerary practices in the elaboration of the grave stele with its image and inscription, participation in the mysteries for individual salvation as well as adherence to special sects and religious groups, the role of the law court in developing new ideas about agency and personal responsibility, and the changes in wills and testaments to reflect private and optional choices. For the second category, the subject, Vernant points to the uses of first-person narrative, especially as used by the lyric poets from Archilochus on, both to give expression to personal experience and to introduce the notion of time that is no longer cosmic or social, but rather subjectively lived as phases in the life cycle of the individual with all its vicissitudes and uncertainties. With regard to the last and most complex category, the "ego," Vernant considers the philosophers from Plato on, the uses of memory, and the techniques of self-mastery, but like Foucault, he sees this moment as one that finds its specificity only in late paganism when the "concern" and the "care" for the self reach new levels of intimacy and self-consciousness, and like Peter Brown, he recognizes the importance of the Christian "holy man," who may search for the self in relation to God but still, like his forebears, remains deeply attached to the world here below. Having insisted in his first essay on the idea of the person as indissociably linked to the context of Greek polytheism, Vernant returns, as by a "ring composition," to religion as a determining factor when he concludes his assessment of this long development.

It is fitting perhaps that this last essay places the emphasis on the growth of the individual as an entirely masculine affair, for throughout, when I have used the term "Greek man" or have quoted Vernant himself, there is little doubt that what he means is "*l'homme grec*"—*anēr* and not *anthrōpos*—because, as he says in the essay on Gorgo, the Greeks represented as other "all those whom, for the purposes of reflection, they ranked under different headings in the category of difference, and whose representations always appear deformed because these figures—barbarian, slave, stranger, youth, and woman—are always constructed with reference to the same model: the adult male citizen." From a prescriptive point of view, this general statement is not likely to be challenged, and it provides a convenient point of reference and an often reiterated norm, which he has done much to elucidate, especially in his brilliant and by now classic article on the conception of space as mediated through the interaction of the two opposing masculine and feminine figures of Hermes and Hestia. Yet having established the fundamentally androcentric position, there is perhaps more to question, especially with regard to the configuration of the feminine as the logical opposite possessing a more dramatic threat and allure than any of those other "others," constituted from the beginning both in the linguistic fact of gender and in a world inhabited by gods of both sexes. Vernant will end his analysis, as he generally does, when the features of a given system are firmly in place, the lines are clearly drawn, and the dynamic movement among the operative terms he sets in motion has played itself out. But others, as some have already done, may want to probe further into the reasons for, the psychology behind, these pervasive and problematic confrontations between male and female. They will also want to question the workings of a masculine imagination that reflects itself and on itself in the phantasmic mirror of the other, who conversely is barred by the social rules from any reciprocity of gaze. To what extent is masculine identity compromised as well as enhanced when the lines are blurred or redefined? Is there such a category as feminine subjectivity, and if so, what are the means for finding it? I raise these issues here in the context of those already implicitly raised by Vernant's essays in this volume, especially on the figures of Gorgo and of Artemis, but evident too in many other passing details, in which their feminine attribution goes unremarked in the structure of the argument.

III

It remains only to offer some more personal thoughts on Vernant and his work and the roles he has played in others' lives.

In speculating earlier on the special affinities between Vernant and the approaches he takes to his objects of study, I deferred one last point for discussion until I had completed the summary of essays included in this volume. I did so because I could then rely on the brief synopses to highlight what is perhaps the feature most characteristic of Vernant's intellectual position but which I suggest is also ultimately revealing of the man himself.

At the heart of his enterprise is the belief in the idea of relatedness as the way to understand any given phenomenon, large or small, whether an institution, a figure, a concept, or even an entire ideology. This emphasis is a natural corollary of the insistence on system and structure, on a network of interlocking parts, each indispensable to the other. It goes well too with the conviction that cultural facts can and must be interpreted on a number of different planes since, by his own definition, they participate in more than one sphere of interest—political, social, religious, cognitive, aesthetic, and so forth. Whether that relationship is one of sameness or difference, of similitude or opposition, no one feature or fact is permitted to exist in isolation, extracted from its context and left to stand all alone. It is always a question of relative position through which some constitutive element can be defined and situated in its proper place. This principle extends from a single immediate context to the larger cultural sphere and operates all the way up to the level of culture itself as it is compared with other cultures that share relevant points of contact in respect to some given theme, such as an ideology of death, sacrificial rites, religious beliefs, or the concept of the individual.

But beyond this habit of comparison and contrast and the inclusiveness of data and method, Vernant's integrative approach to his object of study has another, more human dimension; it is matched and enhanced by his interest in how a society integrates the outsider, the stranger, into its civic and religious structures, able to accommodate even the presence of a barbarian goddess like Taurian Artemis, transposed to Greece and finally Hellenized. To bring an other into the group is what he admires; this is best expressed perhaps in one of his very few editorializing remarks:

> In making the goddess of the margins into a power of integration and assimilation, as when they take Dionysos, who incarnates the figure of the Other in the Greek pantheon, and install him at the center of the social system, right out front in the theater, the Greeks pass on an important lesson. They invite us, not to become polytheists, to believe in Artemis and Dionysos, but to construe the idea of civilization as giving each his or her place. They invite us to an attitude of mind that not only has moral and political value, but that is properly intellectual and is called tolerance.[12]

The spatial metaphor of map and territory, boundaries and divisions, juxtaposition and distance, as I have used it, is a convenient way to describe Vernant's entire undertaking and indeed is a frequent idiom in his work that it was also my intention to imply. But if we shift the angle of vision, we might reread this entire complex ensemble as a sign of a certain sociability implicit in the work that, beyond theoretical principles, turns out to depend for its scope on a host of relations with many others. It is true, of course, that to compare one's own sphere with another's obviously requires the contacts of collective ventures, some of which are represented in this assortment of essays. It is also true that the demand for multiple levels of analysis and for the integration of many disparate facts into a single frame means that the work can best be done in collaboration with others, who all contribute their special funds of knowledge and whose own inquiries can corroborate and also expand the prior fields of reference. These are the practical factors, and the availability of many hands and many minds has made it possible to produce a large and substantial body of work that covers many areas and addresses many different concerns. But beyond their utilitarian value, these factors attest to Vernant's own situation within a group, his emplacement always in relation to others with whom he shares a cooperative enterprise. Speaking of comparatist study, he comments that "each project, each team working together on it, thus takes on a slight tinge of joint adventure in which open-mindedness, intellectual empathy, and friendship, quite apart from competence, have always had and will always have their place."[13] No small part of the success of what has been called "l'école de Paris" and its group of Vernantiens[14] has been due to the formal establishment of the Centre de Recherches Comparées sur les Sociétés

---

[12] "The Figure and Functions of Artemis in Myth and Cult," below, chap. 11.
[13] "Greek Religion, Ancient Religions," below, chap. 16.
[14] *Libération* (April 13, 1989).

Anciennes in Paris (now called Centre Louis Gernet)[15] and to those who jointly participated in seminars or shared the fruits of their research. Vernant may have been the guiding star here until his retirement, but he was also one element in a web of reciprocal relations, both intellectual and social, involving other colleagues in France and elsewhere, those in his own field as well as those in other disciplines.[16] I am thinking here particularly of Pierre Vidal-Naquet, a cofounder of the Centre, as well as Marcel Detienne, Nicole Loraux, Françoise Frontisi-Ducroux, François Lissarrague, Alain Schnapp, Claude Mossé, François Hartog, and others too numerous to mention. The Centre at 10 rue Monsieur le Prince extended (and still extends) its hospitality to all comers, welcoming outsiders of every sort and attuned to a babel of many accents and tongues. In those days it was always Vernant who, by the magnetic force of his personality and that innate sociability—that deep concern for and interest in the other—brought people together, myself included, into a sheltering society of diverse relations. And it was Vernant whose home, like his mind, was always a crossroads, a hospitable meeting place, for those whose persons and ideas he so generously entertained.

There are, of course, other valid points of contact between the man and the work, his ideas and his ideals. But one in particular is appropriate for the end, and that is the link between Vernant's emphasis on the civic order as the central focus of mind in action and Vernant himself in the role of the citizen, not only as a "speaker of words" but also as a "doer of deeds" in the heroic manner. In France, if Vernant has won renown for his intellectual feats and oratorical skills, he has also won *kleos* in the annals of the Resistance as the famous "Colonel Berthier" who at Toulouse ran a military network of the FFI in the region of the Midi-Pyrénées, and whose daring exploits earned him the cherished title of "Compagnon de la Libération."

In civilian life, however, even as he ascended the ranks of academe, he has always been affectionately known as Jipé to all and sundry. A man of courage and simplicity, generous in spirit, wise of counsel, a born raconteur, and possessed of a deep kindness and sympathy for others. The work on this volume was truly a labor of love for me and a very small tribute to that honest and radiant human being who is Jean-Pierre Vernant.

[15] This group is under the auspices of the Ecole des Hautes Etudes.

[16] See for example the lists of contributors in *Poikilia: Etudes offertes à Jean-Pierre Vernant* (Paris, 1987), and in *Texts and Contexts: American Classical Studies in Honor of J.-P. Vernant*, guest editors Ann Bergren and Froma I. Zeitlin, *Arethusa* 15 (1982).

Mortality

Chapter 1

MORTALS AND IMMORTALS: THE BODY
OF THE DIVINE

THE BODY of the gods. How does this expression pose a problem for us? Can gods who have bodies—anthropomorphic gods like those of the ancient Greeks—really be considered gods? Six centuries before our era, Xenophanes already protested the possibility of such a thing, denouncing the foolishness of mortals who believe they can measure the divine by the yardstick of their own nature: "Men believe that, like themselves, the gods have clothing, language, and a body."[1] An identical body for gods and men? "The Ethiopians claim that their gods are flat-nosed and black-skinned; the Thracians, that they are blue-eyed and have red hair."[2] Why not an animal's body, then, Xenophanes ironically asks: "If oxen, horses, and lions had hands with which to draw and make works like men, horses would represent the gods in the likeness of a horse, oxen in that of an ox, and each one would make for them a body like the one he himself possessed."[3]

These remarks made by the Greek poet and philosopher are conveyed to us by Clement of Alexandria in his *Stromata*, written in the second century C.E. Clement wishes to show that through the light of reason the wisest of the ancients were able to recognize the vanity of idolatry and to mock the gods of Homer—those puppets invented by man in his own image, with all his faults, vices, passions, and weaknesses.

It is perhaps only fair play that in his polemic against "false gods" a Church Father should make use of criticisms voiced by a pagan philosopher who stands apart from the collective beliefs of a religion in which divinity occasionally appears in too human a light. But it is certainly neither the most reliable nor the most suitable way by which to approach the problem of the body of the gods in ancient Greece. To do this, one must put oneself in the framework of polytheism itself and adopt its perspective.

Under the title, "Corps obscur, corps éclatant," the French text appeared in *Corps des dieux*, ed. Charles Malamoud and Jean-Pierre Vernant, *Le temps de la réflexion* 7 (Paris, 1986), 19–45, and was republished as "Mortels et immortels: Le corps divin" in *L'individu, la mort, l'amour: Soi-même et l'autre en Grèce ancienne* (Paris, 1989): 7–39. The original English version was translated by Anne M. Wilson and appeared in *Fragments for a History of the Human Body*, ed. Michel Feher, *Zone* 3 (1989) 19–47. It has been revised in several places by Froma I. Zeitlin.

[1] Frag. 14, Clem. Alex., *Strom.* 5.109.2 = fr. 170 KR.
[2] Frag. 16, Clem. Alex., *Strom.* 7.22.1 = 171 KR.
[3] Frag. 15, Clem. Alex., *Strom.* 5.109.3 = 172 KR.

Would the Greeks, in representing the gods to themselves, really have attributed to them the form of corporeal existence that is proper to all perishable creatures here on earth? To pose the question in these terms would be to admit from the outset that for human beings "the body" is a given, a fact, something immediately evident, a "reality" inscribed in nature and, as such, beyond question. In the case of the Greeks, the difficulty arises only because they apparently projected the notion of a body onto beings who, insofar as they are divine, are situated outside the body's legitimate sphere of application, since gods are, by definition, supernatural and belong to the other world, the one beyond ours.

But we can also approach the problem from the opposite angle and direct our inquiry to the body itself, no longer posited as a fact of nature, a constant and universal reality, but rather viewed as an entirely problematic idea, a historical category, steeped in the imagination (to use Le Goff's expression), and one which must, in every case, be deciphered within a particular culture by defining the functions it assumes and the forms it takes within that culture. The real question, therefore, can be formulated as follows: what did the body mean to the Greeks? For us, the concept of the body gives the illusion of being self-evident, for essentially two reasons: first, because of the definitive opposition between soul and body, spiritual and material, that has established itself in our Western tradition. And consequently and correspondingly, because the body, once reduced entirely to matter, depends on positivistic study; in other words, it has acquired the status of a scientific object defined in anatomical and physiological terms.

The Greeks contributed to this "objectification" of the body in two ways. First, within the religious context of the sectarian cults (whose teaching was later taken up and transposed by Plato into the field of philosophy), they elaborated a new notion of the soul, an immortal soul that man must isolate and purify in order to separate it from a body whose role has now become nothing more than that of a receptacle or tomb. Then through medical practice and medical writings, the Greeks investigated the body, observing, describing, theorizing about its visible aspects, its parts, the internal organs that compose it, their functioning, and the diverse humors that circulate in it and control its state of health or illness.

But like the naturalistic approach to the body, the affirmation of the presence of a noncorporeal element within us, which is related to the divine and which is also "our selves," marks more than just a turning point in Greek culture: it marks a kind of rupture.

In this respect and despite Clement of Alexandria, Xenophanes is a good witness to that which we might perhaps call (in reference to the most ancient Greek philosophers) the pre-Socratic body. Xenophanes, it is true, lampoons that heterogeneous and restless troop of Homeric gods so as to propose a more rigorous and refined conception of divinity, akin to the spherical One of Parmenides (who some believe was his student).[4] Yet he does not radically dissociate divine nature from corporeal reality. Just as he does not postulate the existence of a unique god when he writes "one god, the greatest among gods and men," he also does not affirm that the gods do not have bodies. Xenophanes merely claims that the body of a god is not like that of a mortal. It is dissimilar for precisely the same reason that a god's capacity for thought (*noēma*)—with which gods are abundantly endowed—is dissimilar to human thought.[5] Dissimilarity of both body and thought are jointly proclaimed in the unitary formula that states that gods' bodies and thoughts are linked by virtue of their common difference from human beings.[6] Like everybody and anybody, a god sees, hears, and understands. But for all that, a god does not require specialized organs like our eyes and ears. A god is "wholly" seeing, hearing, understanding.[7] He (or she) moves without effort or fatigue; without having to budge, without even changing position, divinity introduces motion and shakes everything up.[8] In order to cross the gulf that separates god and man, Xenophanes does not end up by opposing the corporeal to the noncorporeal, the immaterial, a pure Spirit; it is enough for him to acknowledge the contrast between that which is constant and that which changes, between the immutable and the mutable, the perfection of that which remains eternally complete in the plenitude of itself, and the incompleteness and imperfection of that which is divided, dispersed, partial, transitory, and perishable.

The fact is that in the archaic period Greek "corporeity" still does not acknowledge a distinction between body and soul, nor does it establish a radical break between the natural and the supernatural. Man's corporeality also includes organic realities, vital forces, psychic activities, divine inspirations or influxes. The same word can refer to each of these various domains. On the other hand, there is no term that designates the body as an organic unity that supports the individual in the multiplicity of his vital and mental functions. The word *sōma*, translated as body, originally designated a corpse—that is to

---

[4] Arist., *Met.* A5.986b21 = 177 KR; Diog. Laert. 9.21–23 = 28A1 DK.

[5] Frag. 23, Clem., Alex., *Strom.* 5.109.1 = 173 KR.

[6] *Outi demas thnētoisin homoiïos oude noēma*: "like mortals neither in body nor in thought."

[7] Frag. 24, Sex., *Adv. math.* 9.144 = 175 KR: "Wholly [*oulos*] he sees, wholly he understands, wholly he hears."

[8] Frags. 26 + 25, Simpl., *Phys.* 23.11 + 23.20 = 174 KR. The text specifies that, without becoming fatigued, without difficulty, and without moving, the god makes everything shake through the "desire of his intellection [*noou phreni*]." The association of the terms *noos* and *phrēn* is reminiscent of the Homeric expression *noein phresi*, to have a thought, or a project, in one's *phrenes* (*Il.* 9.600 and 22.235). What are the *phrenes*? A part of the body: the lungs or the membrane of the heart, and an interior place of thought, since it is through the *phrenes* that one knows; but also a site of feeling or of passion—in effect, the *thumos* (ardor, anger, and also breath, vapor) can, like intellection, be situated in the *phrenes* (*Il.* 8.202; 13.487; 22.475; 24.321). Let us add that the *noos*, the intelligence, insofar as it perceives, understands, or projects, may itself be localized in the *thumos* (*Od.* 14.490).

say, what remains of an individual after his incarnated life and physical vitality have left him, reducing him to a purely inert figure: an effigy. He becomes an object of exhibition and lamentation for others before he disappears—whether cremated or buried—into invisibility. The term *demas*, used only in the accusative, designates not the body but an individual's stature, his size, his build made up of assembled pieces. (The verb *demō* signifies the erecting of a construction through superimposed rows, as in a brick wall.) It is often used in connection with *eidos* and *phuē*: the visible aspect, the carriage, the imposing appearance of what has grown to full stature. Nor is *chrōs* the body; rather, it is the external envelope, the skin, the surface where there is contact between oneself and another; it also means flesh tint or complexion.

To the extent that a human being is alive, inhabited by force and energy, susceptible to drives that move and stir him (or her), his body is plural. Greek vocabulary of the corporeal is characterized by multiplicity, even when it comes to expressing it in its totality. The Greeks use the word *guia*—the bodily members in their suppleness, their articulated mobility—or *melea*, the limbs as bearers of force.

They also use the word *kara*, the head, with a metonymic value: a part for the whole. Even in this case, the head is not equivalent to the body; it is a way of saying "a man himself," as an individual. In death, men are called "heads," but they are heads shrouded in night, enveloped in darkness, faceless. Among the living, heads have a countenance, a face, a *prosōpon*; they are there, present before your eyes just as you are present to their eyes. The head, the face is what one sees first in a human being, what is revealed of him (or her) on the surface; it is what identifies him and makes him recognizable when he (or she) is present to the gaze of others.

When one wishes to speak of the body in terms of its vitality, its life force, its emotions, as well as its ability to reflect and know, a host of terms is available: *stēthos*, *ētor*, *kardia*, *phrēn*, *prapides*, *thumos*, *menos*, *nous*. The values of these words are closely related. They designate, without always distinguishing very precisely, bodily parts or organs (heart, lungs, diaphragm, chest, guts); breaths, vapors, liquid juices; feelings, drives, desires; and thoughts, concrete operations of the intellect such as comprehension, recognition, naming, and understanding.[9] This intertwining of the physical and the psychological in a self-consciousness that involves the parts of the body is summarized in James Redfield's striking remark that for the Homeric heroes, "the interior I is none other than the organic I."[10]

---

[9] On this vocabulary as a whole and the problems it raises concerning psychology, the person, and self-consciousness in Homer, see James Redfield, "Le sentiment homérique du Moi," *Le genre humain* 12 (1985): 93–111, whose penetrating study contains a useful bibliography of the principal books and articles dealing with these questions.

[10] Ibid., 100; and further, "organic consciousness is self-consciousness," 99; or, in speaking of the epic character, "his consciousness of himself is also a consciousness of his 'me' as an organism," 98.

This vocabulary of the body—or more precisely, the various dimensions or aspects of the corporeal—constitutes in its entirety the code that allowed a Greek to express and think about his relation to himself, his presence to himself, which, depending on the circumstances, was greater or smaller, more or less unified or diffused. But it connotes equally his relations to others, to whom he is bound by all forms of bodily appearance; face, size, bearing, voice, gestures—what Mauss calls "techniques du corps" (body techniques)—as well as what relates to the olfactory and tactile senses. This vocabulary also encompasses the relation to the divine or supernatural, whose presence within oneself, in and through one's own body, like the external manifestations in the case of a god's apparitions or epiphanies, expresses itself in the same symbolic register.

To pose the problem of the body of the gods is thus not to ask how the Greeks could have equipped their gods with human bodies. It is rather an investigation of how this symbolic system functions, how the corporeal code permits one to think of the relations between man and god under the double figures of the same and the other, of the near and the far, of contact and separation. Such an investigation of this system will also mark that which associates the poles of human and divine through a play of similitudes, mutual advances, overlapping areas, and that which dissociates them through the effects of contrast, opposition, incompatibility, and mutual exclusion.

From this symbolic system that codifies the relation to oneself, to others, and to the divine, I would like to draw attention to certain elements that are pertinent to our subject. Roughly speaking, the problem consists of deciphering all the signs that mark the human body with the seal of limitation, deficiency, and incompleteness, and that make it a sub-body. This sub-body cannot be understood except in reference to what it presupposes: corporeal plenitude, a super-body, the body of the gods. We will therefore examine the paradox of the sublimated body, of a divine super-body. By taking to an extreme all the qualities and bodily values that are present in humans in a form that is always diminished, derivative, faltering, and precarious, we can endow the divinities with a set of traits that, even in their epiphanic manifestations here below, when they are present among mortals, still locates them in an inaccessible region beyond our ken. The result is that gods actually transgress the strict corporeal code by means of which they are represented in their relations to humans.

II

Man and his body are embedded in the course of nature, *phusis*, which causes all that is born here below to rise, mature, and disappear according to the rhythm of the days, seasons, years, and life span proper to each species.[11] Man

[11] Cf. *Il*. 6.146ff.: "As with the generations of leaves, so with the generations of men: the wind

and his body, therefore, bear the mark of a congenital infirmity; like a stigma, the seal of the impermanent and evanescent is branded on them. In order to exist, they must, like plants and other creatures living on this earth, pass through successive phases of growth and decline: after childhood and youth, the body matures and expands in the strength of manhood (or womanhood), and then, when old age comes, it changes, weakens, and becomes ugly and dilapidated, until it is engulfed forever in the night of death.

It is this inconstant body, vulnerable to the vicissitudes of time flowing on without return, that makes human beings the creatures the Greeks have named "the ephemeral ones," in order to contrast them with "those who exist eternally."[12] Humans are beings whose lives unfold in the quotidian, the day-to-day, in the narrow limits of a changing and unstable "now" whose continuity and future is always uncertain.

The human body is ephemeral. This does not merely signify that, no matter how beautiful, strong, or perfect it may appear to be, it is still destined for decrepitude and death; in a more essential way, it means that since nothing in it is immutable, the vital energies it deploys and the psychological and physical forces it puts into play can remain only for a brief moment in a state of plenitude. These bodies are exhausted as soon as they become active. Like a fire that consumes itself as it burns, and that must continuously be fed in order to keep from going out, the human body functions in alternating phases of expenditure and recuperation. It does not function along a continuous line or at a constant level of intensity, but in cycles punctuated by more or less complete or lasting eclipses, pauses, or fade-outs. Sleep follows waking as its necessary counterpart; every effort brings on lassitude and demands time for rest. When in any particular activity the body is tasked or strained, it must restore the inner loss, the decrease in energy that hunger soon signals and that finds only a provisional remedy in the satiety of a meal. If in order to survive, the human being must continually sit down to a meal and eat in order to abate his (or her) depleted forces, it is because these forces weaken with use. The more intense and arduous an activity, the more serious and difficult it is to overcome the consequent weakness.

In this way, death not only stands out in the lives of mortals as the end that unremittingly limits the horizon of their existence: it is there every day, every moment, ensconced in life itself, like the hidden face of a condition of existence in which the two opposing positive and negative poles—being and its

---

scatters the leaves over the ground and the burgeoning forest makes them grow again when the spring season returns. Thus it is with men: one generation is born at the very instant that another disappears" [trans. Richmond Lattimore (Chicago, 1951)].

[12] The gods are defined as *hoi aei ontes*, "those who exist forever." On the value of *aei* and its relation to the *aiōn*, the continuity of being that characterizes divine vitality, cf. E. Benveniste, "Expression indo-européenne de l'éternité," *Bulletin de la Société de linguistique* 38, fasc. 1 (1937): 103–13.

privation—are again inextricably intertwined: no birth without death, no waking without sleep, no lucidity without unconsciousness, no tension without relaxation. The other side of a luminous youthful body is an ugly faded one. The body is the agent and instrument of actions, powers, and forces that can only deploy themselves at the price of a loss of energy, a failure, and a powerlessness caused by a congenital weakness. Death, Thanatos, might borrow the mask of his twin brother Sleep, Hupnos, or assume the appearance of some of his sinister associates—Ponos, Limos, Gēras—who incarnate the human ills of fatigue, hunger, and old age. (Through their mother *Nyx*, the Dark Night, these associates are all children of the same lineage, and like Death himself, they are the issue of Chaos, the original Chasm, the dark, primordial Abyss that existed before anything had form, solidity, and foundation.)[13] But it is always Death, in person or by delegation, who sits within the intimacy of the human body, like a witness to its fragility. Linked to all the nocturnal powers of confusion that mark a return to the indistinct and unformed, Death, companionate with the tribe of his kin—Sleep, Fatigue, Hunger, Old Age— proclaims the failure, the incompleteness of a body, whose visible aspect—its contours, radiance, external beauty—and inner forces of desire, feeling, thoughts, and plans can never be found in a perfectly pure state. These are never radically separated from the part of darkness and nonbeing that the world inherited from its ''chaotic'' origins and that, even in the cosmos organized and now presided over by Zeus, remains alien to the luminous domain of divinity, to its constant, inexhaustible vitality.

Thus, for the Greeks of the archaic period, man's misfortune is not that a divine and immortal soul finds itself imprisoned in the envelope of a material and perishable body, but that his body is not fully unified. It does not possess, completely and definitively, the set of powers, qualities, and active virtues that bring to an individual being's existence a constant, radiant, enduring life in an unmixed, totally vital state—a life that is imperishable because it is free from any seed of corruption and divorced from what could darken, wither, and annihilate it, from within or without.

III

Although they belong to the same universe as human beings, the gods are of a different race: they are the *athanatoi*, the nonmortals, the *ambrotoi*, the ones who do not perish. This designation is paradoxical because, by comparison with human beings, it defines those beings whose bodies and lives possess complete positivity—without lack or defect—through negation and absence. The paradox is instructive because it implies that in order to think of the divine

[13] Cf. Hes., *Theog.* 220ff., and Clemence Ramnoux, *La nuit et les enfants de la nuit dans la tradition grecque* (Paris, 1959; reprint, 1986).

life and body, the required reference or point of departure for the Greeks is this defective body—this mortal life, which they themselves experienced each day. To be sure, the mortal body is the gods' point of departure so that they might better disengage themselves from it, break free from it and, through a series of deviations and successive denials, constitute a kind of purified body. This ideal body incarnating divine efficiencies and sacred values will forever appear as the source, the foundation, the model of that which is only its poor reflection, its feeble, deformed, paltry image on this earth: those phantoms of the body and of life that are at a mortal's disposal in the course of his (or her) brief existence.

In the human body, blood is life. But when it gushes out of a wound,[14] flows over the ground, mixes with earth and dust,[15] coagulates and becomes putrid, then blood means death. Because the gods are alive, there is undoubtedly blood in their bodies. Yet even when it trickles from an open wound, this divine blood cannot tip the scales toward the side of death. A blood that flows, but does not mean the loss of life; a blood that does not hemorrhage, that is always intact, incorruptible; in short, an "immortal blood," *ambroton haima*—is it still blood? Since the gods bleed, one must admit that their bodies have blood in them, but it must immediately be added that this is so only on the condition that this blood is not really blood, since death, the other side of life, is not present in it. Bleeding blood that is not blood, the gods simultaneously appear to have "immortal blood" and to be "bloodless."

The same oscillation, the same wavering back and forth, occurs with respect to meals. The gods dine just as men do. Men are mortal because their bodies, inhabited by a hunger that is endlessly renewed, cannot survive without eating. Men's vitality and blood are nourished by a sustenance that, whether meat, bread or wine, can be defined as "ephemeral food"[16] because it is itself marked by death, decomposition, decay. Meat is the dead flesh of an animal slaughtered during sacrifice and offered to the gods. Its life has departed, leaving the field open to the internal forces of corruption in those parts of the animal reserved for man (i.e., all that is edible). Bread represents human nourishment par excellence: it is the symbol of civilized life; men are "bread eaters," and for the Greeks, "to eat bread," "to live off the fruit of the plowed earth," is another way of saying "to be mortal." If the Ethiopians, living at the edge of the world in the little island of the golden age that they are privi-

[14] On the interplay of *brotos*, mortal, and *brotos*, the blood that flows from a wound, cf. the analysis of Nicole Loraux, "Le corps vulnérable d'Arès," in Malamoud and Vernant, *Corps des dieux*, 335.

[15] On *to luthron*, blood mixed with dust, cf. J.-P. Vernant, "The Pure and the Impure," in *Myth and Society in Ancient Greece*, trans. Janet Lloyd (Atlantic Highlands, N.J., 1980), 121–41 (originally published as *Mythe et société en Grèce ancienne* [Paris, 1974]).

[16] Cf. Apollod. 1.6.3 on the monstrous Typhon, weakened and conquered by Zeus after having eaten the *ephēmeroi karpoi*, the "ephemeral fruits," instead of the drug of immortality.

leged to inhabit, are closest of all humanity to the gods by virtue of their striking physical beauty, the fragrance they exude, and their exceptional longevity, it is because their diet knows no cereals, and they consider wheat to be a kind of manure.[17] Even wine, that ambiguous and disturbing drink, is worked on by fermentation, so that it too is the result of corruption.

According to the Homeric formula, to enjoy imperishable life, to possess immortal blood (or not to have blood at all), implies "not to eat bread, not to drink wine." To include Hesiod, one must add that this also means not to touch the flesh of the sacrificial victim, to keep for oneself only the aroma of the herbs burned on the altar, the emanations of the charred bones that rise in smoke toward heaven. The gods are always observing a fast.

Under these conditions, why do the gods sit down to a meal? The first answer: they assemble as guests for the pleasure of it, for the splendor of the celebration and the radiant joy of the banquet. They do not gather in order to appease their appetites, to satisfy their stomachs, or to fill up that belly, that *gastēr*, the cause of man's misfortune that dooms him to death.[18] The second answer: just as there is ephemeral nourishment, so is there immortal food and drink. Whoever eats and drinks or succeeds in procuring such repast for himself becomes a god, if he is not one already. But jealous of their privileges, the gods are careful to keep exclusively for themselves this nourishment that is "ambrosian" like their own bodies. Thus, once the table is set at the summit of Mount Olympos, the gods are those who, nourished by nectar and ambrosia, eat the dishes of immortality, and at the same time, those whose immortal bodies know no hunger and have no need at all to eat.

These paradoxes are not really perverse. Beneath their contradictory appearance, the propositions they enunciate are really saying the same thing: whatever positive forces, such as vitality, energy, power, and luster, the human body may harbor, the gods possess these forces in a pure and unlimited state. In order to conceive of the divine in its plenitude and permanence, it is therefore necessary to subtract from the human body all those traits that bind it to its mortal nature and betray its transitory, precarious, and unfulfilled character.

It is also necessary to correct the commonly held view that the anthropomorphism of the Greek gods means they were conceived in the image of human beings. It is rather the reverse: in all its active aspects, in all the components of its physical and psychological dynamism, the human body reflects the

---

[17] Herod. 3.22.19. Having learned what wheat is and how it grows, the Ethiopian Long-Life (*makrobios*) observes "that he is not at all surprised if others [the Persians], nourished on manure [*kopros*], lived a short span of years."

[18] On the *gastēr kakoergos* (the evildoing belly), *stugerē* (odious), *lugrē* (despicable), and *oulomenē* (baneful), cf. J.-P. Vernant, "A la table des hommes," in *La cuisine de sacrifice en pays grec*, ed. Marcel Detienne and J.-P. Vernant (Paris, 1979), 94ff.; trans. Paula Wissing, under the title "At the Table of Men" in *The Cuisine of Sacrifice among the Greeks* (Chicago, 1989).

divine model as the inexhaustible source of a vital energy when, for an instant, the brilliance of divinity happens to fall on a mortal creature, illuminating him, as in a fleeting glow, with a little of that splendor that always clothes the body of a god.

IV

Splendor of the gods. That is what shows through in all the *dunameis*, the powers that the body manifests when it is as it should be: radiating youth, vigor, and beauty, "similar to a god, like to the Immortals."[19] Let us look, with the *Homeric Hymns*, at the Ionians on the island of Delos, as they engage in dance, song, wrestling, and in the Games to please Apollo: "An unexpected visitor would think them immortal and forever free from old age for he would see grace in all of them" (*Hom. Hym. Apollo* 1.151–53). Grace, *charis*, makes the body shine with a joyful luster that is like the emanation of life itself, like the charm that continually wells up from it. First and foremost, then, there is *charis*, and together with it there is stature, breadth, presence, speed of leg, strength of arm, freshness of complexion, and a relaxation, suppleness, and agility of the limbs. All these are no longer perceived through someone else's eyes but are grasped by everyone within himself, in his *stēthos*, *thumos*, *phrenes*, *nous*, fortitude, enthusiasm for combat, the warrior's frenzy, and the momentum of anger, fear, desire, self-mastery, prudent intellection, and subtle guile. These are some of the powers for which the body is the repository, powers that can be read upon it like marks that attest to what a man is and what he is worth.

The Greek body of antiquity does not appear as a group morphology of organs fitted together in the manner of an anatomical drawing, nor in the form of physical particularities proper to each human being, as though in a personal portrait. Rather, it appears like a coat of arms, and through emblematic traits presents the multiple "values" concerning the life, beauty, and power with which an individual is endowed, values he bears and which proclaim his *timē*, his dignity and rank. To designate the nobility of soul, the generosity of the hearts of the best men, the *aristoi*, the Greeks used the phrase *kalos kagathos* in order to emphasize the indissoluble bond linking physical beauty and moral superiority. The latter trait can be evaluated only through a comparison with the former. Through a combination of its qualities, powers, and "vital" values, which are always sacralized with reference to their divine model, and which each individual has in varying amounts, the body assumes the form of a sort of heraldic picture on which each person's social and personal status is inscribed and can be deciphered: the admiration, fear, longing, and respect he inspires, the esteem in which he is held, the honors to which he is entitled—in short, his value, his price, his place on a scale of "perfection" that rises as

---

[19] Cf. Elena Cassin, *La splendeur divine* (Paris, 1968).

high as the gods encamped on its summit, and whose lower rungs, at various levels, human beings share.

V

Two orders of remarks will complete this preliminary outline. The first concerns the body's frontiers. The human body is, of course, strictly delimited. It is circumscribed like the figure of a distinct being, separate and singular, with its own inside and outside: its skin marks the surface of contact, while its mouth, anus, and genitals are the orifices that assure communication with the outside. Nevertheless, it is not closed in on itself, isolated, or cut off from the outside, like an empire within an empire. On the contrary, it is fundamentally permeable to the forces that animate it; it is accessible to the intrusion of the vital powers that make it act. When a man feels joy, irritation, or pity, when he suffers, is bold, or feels any emotion, he is inhabited by drives that he senses within himself, in his "organic consciousness," but which, breathed into him by a god, run through and across him like a stranger coming from the outside. By touching the two Ajaxes with his staff, Poseidon "fills them both with a powerful passion [*meneos krateroio*]; he makes their limbs agile, first the legs, then the arms, as they rise" (*Il.* 13.59–61). *Menos*, vital ardor, *alkē*, fortitude, *kratos*, the power of domination, *phobos*, fear, *erōs*, the impetus of desire, and *lussa*, the warrior's frenzy, are all localized in the body, bound to the body they invest; but as "powers," these exceed and surpass every individual carnal shell. They can abandon it just as they invaded it. In the same way, when a man's spirit is blinded or enlightened, it is most often because, in the intimate recesses of his *nous* or his *phrenes*, a god intervenes to inspire the aberration of error, *atē*, or its contrary, a wise resolve.

The powers that, in penetrating the body, act upon the inner scene in order to move and animate it, find on its outside—in what a man wears or handles (clothing, garb, adornments, weapons, tools)—extensions that permit them to enlarge their field of action and to reinforce their effects. For example, the ardor of *menos* burns in the warrior's breast; it shines in his eyes. Sometimes, in exceptional cases when it becomes incandescent, as with Achilles, this *menos* bursts into flames above his head. But it also manifests itself in the dazzling brilliance of the bronze worn by the warrior. Rising skyward, the gleam of weapons that incites panic in the enemy's ranks is like an exhalation of fire that burns in the warrior's body. The hero's accoutrements, the prestigious arms that represent his career, his exploits, and his personal value, are a direct extension of his body. They adhere to him, form an alliance with him, are integrated into his remarkable figure like every other trait of his bodily armor.[20]

---

[20] Cf. the description of Achilles putting on the warrior's equipment that Hephaistos forged for him: "And brilliant Achilleus tried himself in his armor, to see if it fitted close, and how his

What military panoplies are to the body of a warrior, jewelry, iridescent fabrics, breast ribbons, ointments, and rouge are to a woman's body. The grace and seductiveness, the power to attract that are part of these adornments, emanate from them like magical charms whose effect on others is no different than that exercised by the charms of the feminine body itself.

When the gods create Pandora, so that she, this "marvel to behold," will become the deep, inextricable trap where men will be caught, they create in the same gesture a virgin's body and the vestmental trappings that will make this body "operative"—dress, veil, belt, necklaces, tiara. . . .[21] This provisioning of Pandora's clothing is integrated into her anatomy to compose the bodily physiognomy of a creature one cannot behold without admiring and loving because in the femininity of her appearance she is as beautiful as an immortal goddess. The lion's skin that Herakles wears on his shoulders, Ajax's bow, Peleus's javelin in Achilles' hand, the scepter of the Atreides carried by Agamemnon, and, among the gods, the aegis on Athena's breast, the dogskin cap worn by Hades, the thunderbolt brandished by Zeus, the caduceus that Hermes flourishes—all these precious objects are efficacious symbols of powers held, of functions exercised. Serving as a support or link to the inner energies with which a person is endowed, they belong to his (or her) "appurtenances," like his (or her) arms or legs, and, together with the other parts of the body, define that person's bodily configuration.

We must go one step further. Physical appearance itself, with all that it entails and that seems to our eyes genetically determined—size, stature, bearing, complexion, the brightness of eyes, the liveliness and elegance of movements: in brief, a person's beauty—can be, on occasion, "poured" from the outside onto the body in order to modify, revivify, and embellish his appearance. These "salves" of youth, grace, power, and radiance that the gods sometimes give their protégés by suddenly "clothing" them in supernatural beauty, and that operate on a more modest level in the activities of grooming, bathing, and applying oils, function to transfigure the body through cleansing and purifying, ridding it of everything that makes it blemished or dirty, of anything that pollutes, disfigures, defiles, or soils it.[22] Suddenly made unrecognizable, as if he had exchanged his sordid old rags for sumptuous apparel, the individual, newly clothed in strength and grace, appears radiant in the bloom of youthful vitality.

Thus when Nausikaa discovers Odysseus on the beach where he has been

---

glorious limbs ran within it, and the armor became as wings and upheld the shepherd of the people" (*Il.* 19.384–86) [trans. Richmond Lattimore (Chicago, 1951)].

[21] Hes., *Theog.* 570–85; *WD* 70–75.

[22] The care lavished on a god's statue, of course, falls into the same category: at its fabrication, an incorruptible material is selected and it is enhanced with precious stones and metals to make it shine with a thousand fires; as part of its upkeep, its decayed parts are replaced and it is anointed with oil to increase its brilliance.

deposited by the tide, his naked body swollen from the sea, Odysseus is fearful, terrible to look at (*smerdaleos*, *Od*. 6.137). The hero washes himself, rubs himself with oil, and puts on new clothes. Athena makes him "taller and more massive, with his hair curling down over his forehead." When Nausikaa sees him again, "he is radiant with charm and beauty" (*Od*. 6.227–37). The same scenario, the same metamorphosis takes place in Odysseus's meeting with Telemachos. Odysseus is in the courtyard, like an old beggar with a withered body, bald and bleary-eyed (*Od*. 13.429–35). Athena, touching him with her golden wand, "gives him back his handsome bearing and his youth"; his skin becomes ruddy, his cheeks fill out, his beard grows back blue-tinged on his skin. When Telemachos sees him like this, he is afraid, and turns his eyes away for fear of looking on a god. "Stranger, how you have changed," he confides to Odysseus. "A moment ago I saw you in other clothes and with a completely different skin [*chrōs*]. Are you perhaps some god, a lord of the heavens?" (*Od*. 16.173–83).

One may contrast this sudden beautification of the body through the exaltation of its positive qualities and the effacing of what taints and darkens it with mourning rituals and the brutalities leveled against the enemy's corpse, procedures that pollute the body, make it dirty, and commit outrage on it. Here it is a matter of destroying all the values the body incarnates, all the vital, aesthetic, social, and religious qualities it once bore, to make it ugly and to dishonor it by sending it, deprived of form and vitality, to the dark world of the formless.

For a Greek, therefore, of this period, to conceive of the category of the body is less a matter of precisely determining its general morphology or the particular form nature bestows on one individual or another than it is a matter of situating the body between the opposite poles of luminosity and darkness, beauty and ugliness, value and foulness. And it must be situated all the more rigorously because, when it does not have a definitively fixed position, it tends to oscillate between extremes, moving from one pole to another. Not that in such a case a person would actually change bodies. Frightful or splendid, Odysseus always has the same body. But corporeal identity lends itself to these sudden mutations and changes in appearance. The young, strong body that becomes old and weak with age, that moves in action from enthusiasm to dejection, can also, without ceasing to be itself, rise or descend in the hierarchy of life's values, which it reflects and to which it bears witness, from the darkness and ugliness of disgrace all the way to the brilliant beauty of glory.

VI

This leads us to the second order of our remarks. Epic characters are often represented as being perfectly sure of their powers in the hour of combat. They overflow with confidence and enthusiasm or, as we would say today, they are in great shape, all keyed up. They express this feeling of corporeal plenitude and strength by saying that their *menos* is *atromon*, unshakable (*Il.* 17.157), that, similar in its inflexible ardor "to blazing iron, [*aithōni sidērōi*]" (*Il.* 20.372), it remains *empedon*, unalterable (*Il.* 5.527), secure in its powers. *Héroisme oblige!* In reality, like everything human, like strength, suppleness, or speed, the ardor of *menos* is subject to vicissitudes: it relaxes, wavers, weakens, and disappears with death. In Hades, the dead form the troops of the *amenēna karēna*, the heads that are without *menos* (*Od.* 10.521). With age, the physical and psychic qualities that make a man complete leave the body, delivering the old man up to nostalgia for his lost strength, his extinguished ardor: "Why isn't your strength intact [*biē empedos*]," Agamemnon says to Nestor, who is overwhelmed by the weight of years (*Il.* 4.314); the old man, in an extended litany, voices his regret at no longer being what he was: "My strength today is no longer the same as that which once inhabited my supple limbs. Oh! If only I were young now, if only my strength were still intact [*biē empedos*]" (*Il.* 11.668–70). And again: "No, my limbs no longer have the same sureness [*empeda guia*], neither do my feet, nor my arms—no longer do you see them thrust out rapidly to the right and the left of my shoulders. Oh! If only I were young again, if only my strength were intact [*biē empedos*]" (*Il.* 23.627–29).

The nature of the bronze sky is, in fact, *empedos*, unshakable above our heads like the gods who live there. No hero can change the fact that everything in the human body is consumed and destroyed, and decays. This exhaustion of vital forces that must fade with time is translated by the root *phthi* in the verbs *phthinō*, *phthiō*, *phthinuthō*. In order, therefore, to make himself *empedos*, the hero cannot count on the body or anything connected with it. Whatever his strength, passion, or valor may have been, he too, when the day comes, will become one of those heads emptied of *menos*. His corpse, his *sōma*, would rot as carrion if the funeral ritual, in consuming his flesh on the pyre, did not previously dispatch it into invisibility, its skin intact and smooth as in the case of the young warrior fallen as a hero on the field of battle, the bloom of his virile beauty still upon him.

When his body disappears, vanishes, what remains of the hero here below on earth? Two things: first, the *sēma*, or *mnēma*, the stele, the funeral memorial erected on his tomb, which will remind the generations of men to come of his name, his renown, his exploits. As the *Iliad* puts it, "once set up on the tomb of a man or a woman, the stele is immutable [*menei empedon*]" (17.434–35). The grave stele is a permanent witness to the identity of a being who, together with his body, finds his end in definitive absence—and even, it would seem, somewhat more than a witness. In the sixth century, when the stele began to bear a figurative representation of the deceased, or when a funeral statue—a *kouros* or *korē*—was erected on the tomb, this *mnēma* appeared as a kind of corporeal substitute that expressed in an immutable form the values of beauty and life that the person incarnated during his or her brief existence. Second, parallel to the funeral monument, there is the song of praise that faithfully remembers high deeds of the past. Endlessly preserved and revivified in the oral tradition, the poetic word, in celebrating the exploits of the warriors of yesteryear, snatches them from the anonymity of death, from the darkness of Hades where the common man disappears. Their constant remembrance in the course of epic recitation makes these vanished ones "shining heroes" whose figures, always present to the spirit of the living, radiate a splendor that nothing can dim, the splendor of *kleos aphthiton*, "imperishable glory" (*Il.* 9.413).

The mortal body must return and lose itself in the nature to which it belongs, a nature that only made the body appear in order to swallow it up again. The permanence of immortal beauty, the stability of undying glory: in its institutions, culture alone has the power to construct these by conferring on ephemeral creatures the status of the illustrious, the "beautiful dead."[23] If the gods are immortal and imperishable, it is because, unlike men, their corporeality possesses, by nature and even in the very heart of nature, the constant beauty and glory that the social imagination strives to invent for mortals when they no longer have a body to display their beauty or an existence that can win them glory. Living always in strength and beauty, the gods have a super-body: a body made entirely and forever of beauty and glory.

VII

Though I cannot claim to be able to offer an answer, there is one last question that cannot be avoided. What is a super-body; how does the splendor of a divine body manifest itself?

First of all, it is manifested by what one might call its superlative effects: the magnification or multiplication of all values that appear by comparison in the human body as diminished, paltry, even ridiculous. The gods are much larger and "a hundred times stronger" than men. When they confront one another in hand-to-hand combat on the battlefield of Troy in order to settle their partisan differences, the entire world trembles, shaken to its foundations; in the depths of his subterranean dwelling, Hades leaps from his throne and is alarmed. Will the earth break open, revealing the ghastly dwelling place of death and corruption hidden in its bowels (*Il.* 20.54–65)? When Apollo advances in front of the Trojans, with a simple playful kick of his foot he causes the collapse of the embankment that the Achaeans have built to protect their ships. Then, effortlessly, he pulls down their wall: "As a child by the seashore makes childish playthings out of the sand and then wrecks them with a kick or a punch to amuse himself, in the same way, Phoebus, you destroy what cost

[23] See "A 'Beautiful Death' and the Disfigured Corpse in Homeric Epic," below, chap. 2.

the Argives so much pain and toil" (*Il.* 15.361–65). To Kalypso, who takes pride in being equal in the beauty of her body and appearance (*demas, eidos*) to the human wife Odysseus longs to see again, the hero answers that, in fact, next to the goddess, as perfect as Penelope may be, she would seem "inferior in appearance and size [*eidos, megethos*] by comparison, because she is only human and you are free from death and old age [*athanatos, agērōs*]" (*Od.* 5.217–18).[24]

But the difference between the body of the gods and that of men is not essentially on the order of "more" as opposed to "less." The way the gods manifest themselves to mortals when they decide personally to intervene in their affairs varies greatly. It depends on whether the god concerned is a Power, like Hades, whose status requires that he must always remain hidden and invisible to human eyes; or whether, like Pan and the Nymphs, he is given to appearing in broad daylight, or during the night in a dream, like Asklepios; or whether it is a god who, like Hermes, normally enjoys human company and commerce; or finally, whether, like Dionysos, he is one who appears by surprise, when it pleases him, so that his presence may be recognized as an imperious and baffling epiphany. Furthermore, the nature of our documents adds to this diversity: divine apparitions do not follow a single standard scenario, nor do they obey the same model in an epic narrative, a religious hymn, or a scene of a tragedy.

Nevertheless, one might venture a typological schema of the forms assumed by the gods when they make corporeal appearances. The gamut of possibilities runs from complete incognito to the god's revelation in full majesty. There are two kinds of incognito: the first is for the god or goddess to hide the self by clothing the body in a fog, enveloping it in a mist so that it becomes (or remains) invisible. Master of the situation, he (or she) acts with all the more power and efficiency as the spectators, blind to his (or her) presence, neither see nor understand what is happening right under their noses. When Aphrodite wishes to save Paris from Menelaos's impending blow, she makes him vanish from the closed space where the two men are pitted against each other and deposits him in Helen's room. Everyone, both Greek and Trojan, is deceived. Paris is already resting next to his beloved while the Greek warriors are still searching the ranks of the enemy to see where on earth that Trojan could have hidden himself (*Il.* 3.373–82).

The gods, therefore, have a body that they can at will make (or keep) totally invisible to mortal eyes—and it does not cease to be a body. The visibility that defines the nature of the human body (inasmuch as it necessarily has a form, *eidos*), is flesh colored (*chroiē*), and has a covering of skin (*chrōs*) that takes

---

[24] In the same way, when Alkinous wonders if Odysseus might not be a god who has come to visit him and his people, Odysseus answers: "Do not harbor this thought. I have nothing, neither stature nor presence [*demas, phuē*] in common with the Immortals, masters of this vast sky; I am but a simple mortal" (7.208–10).

on a completely different meaning for the gods. In order to manifest his presence, the divinity chooses to make himself visible in the form of a body, rather than *his* or *her* body. From a divine perspective, the opposition visible/invisible is no longer entirely pertinent. Even within the frame of an epiphany, the god's body may appear to be perfectly visible and recognizable to one of the spectators while remaining, at the same time and in the same place, completely hidden to the eyes of others. Before the assembled Greek army, Achilles ponders in his heart whether to draw the sword and strike Agamemnon. Immediately, Athena dashes down from the heights of heaven. She stops short behind the son of Peleus and puts her hand on his fair hair, "visible to him alone; no one else sees her. The hero turns around and immediately recognizes Pallas Athena" (*Il.* 1.197–200).[25]

The second type of incognito appearance occurs when a god gives his or her body a strictly human appearance. This frequently used trick, however, has its limits. As well-camouflaged as a god may be in the skin of a mortal, there is something "off," something in the otherness of the divine presence that remains strange and disconcerting even when the god is in disguise. Rising from the sea, Poseidon gives himself the stature and voice of Kalchas, the diviner. He approaches the two Ajaxes, exhorts them, and with his words gives them confidence and an ardor that wells up in their breasts. His mission accomplished, he turns and departs. But the son of Oileus is not deceived. It is a god who has come to us in the guise of Kalchas, he confides to his companion: "No, that is not Kalchas the seer. Without difficulty, I recognized from behind the trace of his feet and legs, while he was going away. The gods are recognizable" (*Il.* 13.70–72). One detects a god by his trace, just as a hunter recognizes the marks of the game he pursues. In spite of his disguise, the imprint left by the god as he walks on the ground undoubtedly reveals the disorienting, paradoxical, and prodigious character of a body that is "other," because in the very effort to look as though nothing were wrong, it reveals itself to be both the heaviest and lightest of bodies. When Athena climbs into her chariot, it creaks and buckles under her weight. But when she leaps from one place to another, the same goddess does not even touch the ground. Poseidon left the two Ajaxes while in the human appearance of Kalchas, imitating his gait, but his step was like that of "a quick winged falcon pursuing a bird across the plain" (*Il.* 13.62–65). The divine body, in all the concentrated mass of its being, weighs as much as the marble or bronze statue located in the god's temple: yet it is aerial, ethereal, impalpable, and as weightless as a ray of light.

In order not to be recognized when they mingle with the crowd of fighters, the gods take the precaution of casting a mist over the warriors' eyes to prevent

---

[25] On the episode as a whole and the problems that Athena's appearance poses in the text of the *Iliad* itself, see the excellent analysis by Pietro Pucci, "Epifanie testuali nell' *Iliade*," *SIFC* 78 (1985): 170–83.

them from distinguishing the divine from the human. To support Diomedes, Athena is not content to inspire him with a passion three times greater than his usual ardor, to make his legs, then his arms and whole body supple from top to bottom: she takes away the mist that covered his eyes so he can discern whether a god or man is before him, and thus will not run the risk of hand-to-hand combat with immortal divinities.

The blindfold of darkness that covers their eyes and causes them to confuse mortals and immortals not only gives men a disadvantage because it hides the divine presence from them, but also protects them. To see a god face to face, as he or she is authentically in his (or her) uncovered body, is far more than human strength can bear. For the experience of seeing Artemis bathing in the nude, Actaeon pays with his life; for seeing Athena, Tiresias pays with his sight. After having slept with the immortal Aphrodite, but without fully knowing that he has been with a goddess (*ou saphra eidōs, Hom. Hym. Aph.* 167), the mortal Anchises is understandably frightened when, on waking, he sees the deity. Her head touches the roof of the room; her body is dressed in all its best finery; her cheeks are "radiant with immortal beauty" (*kallos ambroton,* 172–75). It is enough to see Aphrodite's "neck and lovely eyes." He turns his gaze away in terror, hides his face under the covers, and begs for mercy (181–90): may the goddess spare him, may he not be made *amenēnos,* deprived forever of *menos,* the fire of his vital ardor, for having approached too brilliant a flame. Metaneira also feels her knees weaken and is speechless, prostrate, and terror-stricken when Demeter, shedding the guise of an old woman, reveals herself in all her majesty to Metaneira: tall and noble of stature, radiant with beauty, breathing forth a lovely perfume, "the immortal body of the goddess gave out a light that spread far; her fair hair fell over her shoulders and the stronghold was illuminated as if by a bolt of lightning" (*Hom. Hym. Dem.* 275–80).[26]

The body of the gods shines with such an intense brilliance that no human eye can bear it. Its splendor is blinding. Its radiance robs it of visibility through an excess of light in the way that darkness causes invisibility through a lack of light. Between the shadows of death where they finally must lose themselves and the pure luminosity of the divine which remains inaccessible to them, human beings live in a middle world, divided between day and night. Their perishable bodies stand out clearly in the light of the sun. Their mortal eyes are made to recognize that which, through the combination of light and shadow, presents a precise form with its own shape, color, and solidity. The paradox of the divine body consists in the fact that in order to appear to mor-

---

[26] Even animals react to the terrible strangeness of a divine presence: in Eumaios's hut, Athena stands before the door in the guise of a tall and beautiful woman, a skilled craftswoman. She is invisible to the eyes of Odysseus; Telemachos faces her without seeing her; but, like Odysseus, the dogs have perceived the goddess. Growling, but without barking, they take refuge in fright in a corner of the hut (*Od.* 16.157–63).

tals, it must cease to be itself; it must clothe itself in a mist, disguise itself as a mortal, take the form of a bird, a star, a rainbow. Or, if the god chooses to be seen in all majesty, only the tiniest bit of the splendor of the god's size, stature, beauty, and radiance can be allowed to filter through, and even this is already enough to strike the spectator with *thambos*, stupefaction, to plunge him into a state of reverential fear. But to show themselves openly, as they truly are—*enargēs*—is a terrible favor the gods accord to no one.[27] Herakles himself, who very much wanted to see Zeus, was unable to look at the god's face. Zeus, "who did not want to be seen by him," hid his face behind an animal skin (Herod. 2.42).

More than any other part of the body, the face, like a mirror, reveals what an individual is and what he stands for. When a human being disappears in death, he loses his face at the same instant that he loses his life. The dead, their heads covered with darkness, immersed in shadow, are "faceless" as they are "without *menos*." On the other hand, for a god to show his or her face openly would be to surrender divinity: the face-to-face encounter implies a relationship of parity between partners who look one another in the eyes. Looking away, lowering one's eyes to the ground, covering one's head: mortals have no other way to acknowledge their unworthiness and to avoid the risk of confronting the unequaled, unbearable splendor of the divine countenance.

VIII

A body invisible in its radiance, a face that cannot be seen directly: the apparition, rather than revealing the being of a god, hides it behind the multiple disguises of a "seeming to be" that is adapted to feeble human vision. If a god's body can take on so many forms, it is because not one of them can encompass within itself a power that surpasses each of them and would impoverish itself if it were to be identified with any one of the figures that lend it its appearance. It is not important that Athena, in her struggle against the suitors with Odysseus, initially approaches him in the guise of a very young boy taking his herd to pasture (*Od.* 13.221), only to take on a little later the appearance of a tall and beautiful woman (13.288). As boy or woman, Athena's visible body fails equally to express what the goddess authentically is. It fails to designate that invisible body made of undying energy, power, and vitality, and, in the case of Athena, a sovereign mastery of the art of cunning intelligence, ingenious stratagems, skillful know-how, shrewd lies. These are capacities that all belong to her, that constitute her attributes and define her

[27] *Il.* 20.131; *Od.* 16.161. If Alkinous on his Phaeacian isle can claim that his people's ancestors in the past saw the gods appear *enargeis* a hundred times—in flesh and blood—it is because in contrast to other men, the Phaeacians, like the Cyclopes and the Giants, are of the same origin, the same family of the gods, who therefore do not need to "hide themselves from them" (*Od.* 7.201–5).

power among the gods, just as they are Odysseus's lot and glory among mankind. Confronted with a goddess who lies to "take all manner of shapes,"[28] the only authentic criterion the hero has, however cunning he may be, by which he can ascertain whether it is Athena in person who is really facing him, is to admit that in the game of cunning, in craftiness, in deceptive discourse, he is not her match and that he must take a backseat to one who, in divine Olympos, is intelligence incarnate (13.295–99).

One of the functions of the human body is that it precisely positions every individual, assigning him (or her) one and only one location in space. A god's body escapes this limitation to no less an extent than it does that of form. The gods are here and there at the same time. They are on earth where they show themselves by exercising their actions, and in the heavens where they reside. When Poseidon goes to the Ethiopians to feast with them in the land of the rising and setting sun, he travels, in the same movement, to the two opposite extremities of the earth (*Od.* 1.22–25). Certainly, each god is attached to a particular domain of action depending on his or her type of power: the underworld for Hades, the ocean depths for Poseidon, cultivated land for Demeter, woods, forests, and peripheral wilderness for Artemis. Thus, the gods do not enjoy absolute ubiquity any more than any one of them possesses omniscience or omnipotence. But by traveling at a speed as swift as thought, the constraints imposed by the externality of the divisions of space are child's play to them, just as, through the independence they enjoy from natural cycles and their successive phases, they do not know the externality of the divisions of time as they relate to one another. In a single impulse, the gods' corporeal vitality extends across past, present, and future, in the same way that its energy is deployed to the ends of the universe.

IX

If the nature of the gods, therefore, seems to belie rather than to exalt the traits that define the corporeal in human existence, why speak of the body of the gods? First, because the Greeks of the archaic period, in order to conceive of a being of whatever kind, had no alternative but to express that being within the framework of the body's vocabulary, even though it meant skewing this code through procedures of distortion and denial, contradicting it at the very moment they used it. We have observed that the gods have blood that is not blood; that they eat the food of immortality while continuing to go without; and that sometimes they even sleep without closing their eyes or letting their vigilance fall completely into a state of slumber.[29] Should we then not add: they have a body that is not a body?

---

[28] "Goddess," Odysseus declares to Athena, "what mortal, however quick-witted he may be, could recognize you at once when he met you: you take on all manner of shapes" (13.312–14).

[29] Zeus's eye is always open, his vigilance is faultless. Nevertheless, when Zeus is asleep,

We may indeed, as long as we specify that in the traditional religious system the step that would finalize the rupture between the divine and the corporeal is never taken—the step that at the same time would sever the continuity between gods and humans established by the presence of the same vital values, the same qualities of force, radiance, and beauty whose reflection invests the bodies of both mortals and immortals. Moreover, all the activities of cult presuppose the incorporation of the divine: how could humankind institute regular exchange with the gods in which homages and benefits balance out, unless the Immortals appear in this world in a visible and specific form, in a particular place and at a particular time?

But another reason, one that relates to the very nature of polytheism, must also be taken into consideration. For the Greeks, the divine world is organized into a society of the world beyond, with its hierarchies of rank, its scale of grades and functions, its distribution of competencies and specialized abilities. Thus, it gathers together a multiplicity of particular divine figures, with each having its place, role, privileges, signs of honor, and particular mode of action—a domain of intervention reserved for each alone: in short, each one has an individual identity.

Individual identity has two aspects: a name and a body. The proper name is that particular social mark attributed to a subject in order to consecrate its uniqueness within the species to which it belongs. Generally, things and animals do not have proper names. Each human being—as a human being—has one, because each person, even the most unknown, has a form of individual existence. As Alkinous reminds Odysseus when he invites him to tell who he is, "there has never been a man without a name; whether he is noble or a peasant, everyone receives one at the time of his birth" (*Od*. 8.552–54). Similarly, it is the body that gives a subject his or her identity, by distinguishing that person from all of his (or her) peers through appearance, physiognomy, clothing, and insignia. Like human beings, the gods have proper names. Like them too, gods have bodies—that is to say, a set of specific characteristics that make them recognizable by differentiating them from the other supernatural Powers with whom they are associated.

The divine world is multiple and therefore divided within itself by the plurality of beings composing it. Gods, each one of whom has his (or her) own

---

Typhon takes advantage of the occasion to try to steal his thunderbolt. The attempt goes badly for Typhon; before he is able to lay a hand on the royal weapon, Zeus's eyes have already struck him with lightning. On the gods' sleep as a substitute for the death they cannot undergo, one can also invoke the case of Kronos who, once having been dethroned by Zeus, is plunged, according to some traditions, into sleep and dreams. Especially noteworthy is the *kakon kōma*, the cruel torpor that, for the duration of a great year, envelops the gods who are at fault, who are guilty of perjury, "hiding" them (*kaluptei*) as death hides humans. For these gods, there is no more council, no more banquet, no more nectar or ambrosia, no more contact, communication, or exchange of words with other divinities. Without being dead—since they are immortal—those who are guilty are put into parentheses, as it were; they are out of the game (Hes., *Theog*. 793–804).

name and individual body, partake of a limited and particular form of existence: this conception has not failed to arouse questions, reservations, or rejection in certain marginal religious currents and sects, as well as among philosophers. These hesitations, which have been expressed in widely divergent ways, proceed from a single conviction: the presence of evil, misfortune, and negativity in the world results from the process of individuation to which it has been subjected and which has given rise to beings who are separate, isolated, and individual. Perfection, plenitude, and eternity are the exclusive attributes of totally unified Being. Every fragmentation of the One, every dispersion of Being, every distinction among parts signifies death's entrance on the stage, together with a multiplicity of individual existences and the finitude that necessarily delimits each of them. To rid themselves of death, to fulfill themselves in the permanence of their perfection, the gods of Olympos would therefore have to renounce their individual bodies, dissolve themselves in the unity of a great cosmic god, or be absorbed into the person of the orphic Dionysos—the god who is divided up and later reunified by Apollo. Dionysos is the guarantor of the return to primordial indistinctness and the reconquest of a divine unity that must be found again after having been lost.[30]

Hesiod's orthodox *Theogony* gives the corporeal nature of the gods its theological foundation by categorically rejecting this perspective: it places the complete, perfect, and immutable not in the confusion of an original unity, in the obscure indistinctness of chaos, but rather in its opposite, in the differentiated order of a cosmos whose parts and constitutive elements have bit by bit become separate, delimited, and located. Here, the divine Powers that were at first included in vague cosmic forces took on in the third generation definitive form as celestial gods living in a constant ethereal light, with their particular personalities and figures, their functions articulated each in relation to the others, their powers balanced and adjusted under the unshakable authority of Zeus. If the gods possess plenitude, perfection, immutability, it is because at the end of the process that led to the emergence of a stable, organized, and harmonious cosmos, each divine person's individuality is clearly fixed.

The divine being is one who, endowed with an existence that, like human existence, is individual, nevertheless knows neither death nor what is associated with it, because in its very particularity it has the value of a general, atemporal essence, of a universal, inexhaustible power. Aphrodite is *one* beauty: she is that particular goddess whose appearance makes her recognizable among all the others. When Aphrodite, Athena, and Hera stand before Paris, it is by comparing and contrasting the bodies of the three goddesses, by registering their differences, that Helen's future seducer can divine the powers and privileges that belong to each one, privileges that will not fail to be granted

---

[30] On this theme, see Giulia Sissa, "Dionysos: Corps divin, corps divisé," in Malamoud and Vernant, *Corps des dieux*, 355.

to him by the one whose favor he will win with his vote. If he chooses Aphrodite, if he hands her the palm, it is because she, the most beautiful one, is also Beauty itself, that Beauty by which every individual in the world, whether animal, human, or divine, is made beautiful and desirable. In its splendor, the goddess's body is the very power of Eros to the extent that Eros is a universal force. Nor is Zeus any more only a king, the king of the gods: he is royalty itself. A monarch who does not derive his power from Zeus does not exist, nor is there a king who does not exercise his functions through him and who does not receive from him, by delegation, the honors and glory reserved for the supreme master. The power of sovereignty finds its anchor in Zeus in the particular figure wherein it is fixed and incarnate. The splendor, glory, and radiant brilliance of a permanent, cosmic, indestructible royalty, which no person can ever overturn, possess a form and a body, even if the former escapes the limitations of form and the latter is beyond a body.

In many ways, the divine super-body evokes and touches on the nonbody. It points to it; it never merges with it. If it were to swing to one side, to turn itself into the absence of body, the denial of body, it would upset the very equilibrium of Greek polytheism in its constant, necessary tension between the darkness in which the visible human body is steeped and the radiant light with which the gods' invisible body shines.

Chapter 2

A "BEAUTIFUL DEATH" AND THE DISFIGURED
CORPSE IN HOMERIC EPIC

He whom the god loves dies young.
—Menander

BENEATH the walls of Troy that have watched him flee in desperation before Achilles, Hektor now stands still. He knows he is about to die. Athena has tricked him; all the gods have abandoned him. Fate (*moira*) has already laid its hand on him. Even though it is no longer in his power to conquer and survive, he must still fulfill the demands that warrior status makes on him and his peers: he must transform his death into eternal glory, change the fate of all creatures subject to demise into a blessing that is his alone and whose luster will be his forever. "No, I do not intend to die without a struggle and without glory [*akleiōs*], or without some great deed whose fame will live on among men to come [*essomenoisi puthesthai*]" (*Il.* 22.304–5; cf. 22.110).

The *Iliad* calls *aneres* (*andres*) those men who are in the fullness of their masculine nature, both male and courageous, who have a particular way of dying in battle, at the acme of their lives. As if it were an initiation, such a death endows the warrior with the set of qualities, honors, and values for which the elite, the *aristoi*, compete throughout their lives. This "beautiful death," this *kalos thanatos*, to use the term employed in Athenian funeral orations,[1] is like a photographic developer that reveals in the person of the fallen warrior the eminent quality of the *anēr agathos*, the man of virtue and

This piece appeared as "La belle mort et le cadavre outragé" in *La mort, les morts dans les sociétés anciennes*, ed. G. Gnioli and J.-P. Vernant (Cambridge and Paris, 1982), 45–76, and was reprinted in *L'individu, la mort, l'amour: Soi-même el l'autre en Grèce ancienne* (Paris, 1989), 41–79. It appears here by the kind permission of the Maison des Sciences de l'Homme, which published *La mort* in conjunction with Cambridge University Press. Translated by Andrew Szegedy-Maszak. Translations of the *Iliad* are from Richmond Lattimore's edition (Chicago, 1951).

[1] The present study owes a great deal to Nicole Loraux, *L'invention d'Athènes: Histoire de l'oraison funèbre dans la "cité classique"* (Paris and The Hague, 1981), trans. A. Sheridan under the title *The Invention of Athens* (Cambridge, Mass., 1986), which analyzes the theme of beautiful death in the Athenian funeral oration. Loraux has published several articles on the same topic: "Marathon ou l'histoire idéologique," *REA* 75 (1983): 13–42; "Socrate, contre-poison de l'oraison funèbre," *AC* 43 (1974): 112–211; "HBH et ANDREIA: Deux versions de la mort du combattant athénien," *Anc. Soc.* 6 (1975): 1–31; "La 'belle mort' spartiate," *Ktèma* 2 (1977): 105–20.

valor.[2] It guarantees unassailable renown to the man who has given his life for his refusal to be dishonored in battle, or to be shamed as a coward. A beautiful death is also a glorious death (*eukleēs thanatos*). For all time to come, it elevates the fallen warrior to a state of glory; and the luster of this celebrity, this *kleos*, that henceforth surrounds his name and person is the ultimate accolade that represents his greatest accomplishment, the winning of *aretē*. Through a beautiful death, excellence no longer has to be continually measured against someone else or to be tested in combat. Rather, excellence is actualized all at once and forever after in the deed that puts an end to the hero's life.

This is the meaning of the fate of Achilles, whose character is both exemplary and ambiguous, embodying not only the demands but also the contradictions of the heroic ideal. If Achilles seems to push the logic of honor to an extreme—to absurdity—it is because he somehow places himself above the standard rules of the game. As he himself explains, since his birth he has been offered two destinies to carry him to where all human existence finds its limit, two destinies that are mutually exclusive (*Il.* 9.410ff.). He can have either the warrior's imperishable glory (*kleos aphthiton*) but a short life, or a long life in his own home without any renown whatsoever. Achilles did not even have to make the choice; he found himself always leaning toward the short life. Dedicated from the outset—one might say by nature[3]—to a beautiful death, he goes through life as if he were already suffused with the aura of the posthumous glory that was always his goal. That is why he finds it impossible, in applying the code of honor, to negotiate, to compromise, to yield to circumstances or power relations; craven settlements are, of course, out of the question, but he cannot make even the necessary adjustments without which the system can no longer function. For Achilles every insult is equally intolerable and unforgivable, no matter where it comes from and however high above him the agent's position on the social scale. Any apology, any honorable offer of compensation (no matter how satisfying to his pride it might seem from its size and public nature) remains empty and ineffective. Like a crime of treason, an insult to Achilles can only be repaid, in his eyes, with the complete and utter humiliation of the guilty party. Such an extreme sense of honor makes Achilles a marginal figure, isolated in the lofty solitude of his wrath. The other Greeks criticize this excess as aberrant, an instance of Error personified, of *Atē* (*Il.* 9.510–12). Agamemnon accuses him of pushing the spirit of competition to the point that he has to be first always, everywhere, and in everything,

---

[2] For Homer's use of *agathos* as an absolute, without any qualification, see *Il.* 21.280 and the comments of W. J. Verdenius, "Tyrtaeus 6–7d: A Commentary," *Mnem.* 22 (1969): 338.

[3] As early as book 1, Achilles declares, "Since, my mother, you bore me to be a man with a short life, therefore Zeus of the loud thunder on Olympus should grant me honor at least"; like an echo, Thetis replies "indeed your lifetime is to be short, of no length. Now it has befallen that your life must be brief and bitter beyond all men's" (*Il.* 1.352–54 and 416–18; see also *Il.* 19.329, 421).

and that as a result he can think of nothing but rivalry, dispute, and combat (*Il.* 1.288, 177). Nestor reproaches him for his conduct in its disregard of the customary order of precedence, in that he goes so far as to contend with a king to whom Zeus has given not only the scepter, power, and command but also the right to the highest honors (*Il.* 1.278). Odysseus, Phoinix, Ajax, and even Patroklos deplore his intractable hardness, his ferocious resentment, and his savage and inhuman heart that is deaf to pity, and as oblivious to the pleas of his friends as it is to the apologies and reparations that ought to satisfy him. Could Achilles then be immune to *aidōs*? *Aidōs* is the feeling of reserve and restraint that functions like a brake in both upward and downward directions to maintain equilibrium in situations in which differences in status or disparities in strength make open, equal competition impossible. It is also the respectful fear that keeps a safe distance between the weakest and the strongest. In making explicit the inferiority of one of the actors, *aidōs* puts him at the discretion of the other, so that, disarmed by this submissiveness, the stronger might take the initiative in establishing friendly relations (*philia*) by according the one who puts himself under the other's protection the share of honor that is due to him. But conversely, *aidōs* is also the renunciation by the stronger of violence and aggression toward the weaker who is at the other's mercy and therefore is no longer a rival. Now it is the reconciliation between the injured party and the one who has agreed to abase himself by an offer of compensation, and thus publicly to acknowledge the honor (*timē*) he had first insulted. Finally, *aidōs* is the relinquishing of vengeance and the restoration of amity between two groups when, after a murder, the blood price representing the *timē* of the victim has been agreed on and paid in full to his kin.[4]

At an assembly of the gods, Apollo too accuses Achilles of having lost all sense of pity, and thereby of disregarding *aidōs* (*Il.* 24.44).

Nonetheless, the weight of such evidence is not primarily psychological in nature. It has less to do with Achilles' character than with the ambiguities of his position, the equivocation of his role within the value system of the epic tradition. Achilles' attitude and behavior contain a paradox that is disturbing so long as one concentrates on individual psychology. Achilles is completely convinced of his superiority in the realm of warfare, and this occupies the highest position on the scale of qualities that make for excellence in his eyes as well as those of his companions in battle. Moreover, there is no Greek, no Trojan, who does not share Achilles' belief and does not recognize him as the undisputed exemplar of martial *aretē* (*Il.* 2.768–69).[5] Although his self-confidence is supported by unanimous agreement among others, it hardly guar-

---

[4] Ajax contrasts Achilles' inflexible spirit with the softer temper of those who accept a blood price (*poinē*) and a settlement (*aidesis*).

[5] At *Il.* 2.768–69, the poet himself presents Achilles' superiority as an objective truth.

antees him safety and security; it is yoked instead to an edgy irritability and a profound obsession with humiliation.

To be sure, Agamemnon's taking Briseis away is an insult that strikes Achilles at his most sensitive point. It strips him of his *geras*, the special portion awarded him from the communal booty. A *geras* is an extraordinary privilege granted under exceptional circumstances; it acknowledges superiority, either in rank or in status (as for Agamemnon) or in valor and daring (as for Achilles). Over and above any material advantage, a *geras* has value as a mark of prestige and a consecration of a social supremacy: everyone gets a share, determined by lot, but the elite and only the elite receive a *geras* in addition. Confiscating Achilles' *geras*, then, somehow denies his preeminence in battle, the very heroic quality that everyone concedes to him. The other soldiers maintain silence—admittedly tinged with disapproval—in the face of the king's misconduct, and it makes them accomplices with him in the crime for which they will have to pay the price. Nonetheless, Achilles' reaction displays a number of troubling characteristics. Agamemnon is not trying to insult him personally, and never, even at the hottest point of the argument, does he denigrate Achilles' outstanding martial prowess. Achilles demands that Agamemnon give up his own prize, Chryseis, for the sake of the common good; in order to rid the Greek camp of the plague, the girl must be returned to her father, who is a priest of Apollo. Agamemnon is willing to do so, on the condition that he receive a *geras* in return, so that he, the king, might not be the only one who has to live without his portion of honor (*Il.* 1.119). If it means that he will have to get the *geras* of one of his companions—be it Ajax, Odysseus, or Achilles—no matter, although he predicts that the other will be furious (*Il.* 1.138–39; cf. 145–46). It is at this point that Achilles explodes, and his wrath reveals the real split that divides the two men. Achilles sees no common ground between the *timē* inherent in kingly status, the kind of *timē* Nestor extols as coming from Zeus (*Il.* 1.278–79), and the kind the warrior gains by his ceaseless toil "in the front rank" where danger is omnipresent. So far as he can see, in this war that belongs primarily to Agamemnon and his brother, Agamemnon constantly leaves it to others to give their lives in the heart of the fray; lagging back (*opisthe menōn*) in the shelter of the camp (*Il.* 9.332; cf. 1.227–29), near the ships, he is not a man to join his noble companions in an ambush, nor does he offer himself as a combatant in a duel to the death. "All that," Achilles tells Agamemnon, "seems like death to you [*tode toi kēr eidetai einai*]" (*Il.* 1.228).[6] For all that he is the kingliest (*basileutatos*) among the lords, he has not crossed the boundary that separates ordinary men from the truly heroic. The latter, by accepting from the beginning the fact that life is short, devote themselves completely and single-mindedly to war, adventure, glory, and death. For the man who adopts Achilles' chival-

---

[6] Diomedes makes the same assessment of Agamemnon at *Il.* 9.30–50.

ric perspective, it is one's own life itself that is at stake in every test of honor
(*Il.* 9.322). Since a reversal means that one has lost once and for all, that one
has lost life itself, success must carry value with it at a level that surpasses,
and is not measurable by, normal distinctions and awards. The logic of heroic
honor is one of all or nothing, and it operates outside of and beyond hierarchies
of rank. If Achilles is not recognized as supreme and in a way unique, he feels
himself reduced to nothing. Without meeting any overt resistance, he declares
himself *aristos Achaiōn*, the best of the Greeks, and he boasts that in the past
he has carried the burden of the war and in the future will be the only defense
against the Trojan onslaught. Therefore he can present himself not only as
dishonored, *atimos*, due to the insult he has suffered (*Il.* 1.171, 356), but
also—if he lets it pass without comment—as the feeblest coward, a less than
nothing (*outidanos*), a homeless and worthless drifter, a kind of nonperson (*Il.*
9.648). Between the perpetual glory that is his destiny and the lowest degree
of contempt there is no intermediate level where Achilles can find a place.
Every affront to his dignity brings him from the heights to the depths, because
what is being challenged through him is a set of values that must be accepted
without reservation or equivocation if it is not to be wholly diminished. To
insult Achilles is to put the coward and the champion in the same category and
to give them, as he says, the same *timē* (*Il.* 9.319). Heroic action is thus
stripped of its function as an absolute criterion, a touchstone that shows what
a man is worth.

It is for this reason that Odysseus, Phoinix, and Ajax fail in the mission
entrusted to them to soften Achilles' resolve and persuade him to give up his
anger. Although they use the same words, Achilles does not speak the same
language as the envoys sent to fetch him. Agamemnon has come to his senses,
and on his behalf the ambassadors offer all that a king can give and more in
such circumstances: first, Briseis herself whom he is ready to give back, just
as she was when she was taken, along with an oath that Agamemnon has not
slept with her; tripods, gold, pitchers, horses, female slaves and concubines;
finally, whichever of Agamemnon's own daughters Achilles might choose as
a wife, along with a lavish dowry and, to go with this marriage that would
make Achilles his son-in-law, the rule over seven cities in his kingdom. Achilles refuses. If he were to accept, he would put himself on the same ground as
his enemy. Such goods are adjuncts to the *timē* of the king and signs both of
his power over others and the privileges attached to his rank. To accept the
king's offer would be an admission that the sheer quantity of his possessions
counterbalances true valor, such as Achilles alone brings to the Achaean army.
In all that they symbolize, the gifts are hateful (*Il.* 9.378). Their very abun-
dance seems to express contempt for the warrior, whose participation in battle
does not put at risk his sheep or oxen, tripods or gold, but his very life, his
fragile *psuchē* (*Il.* 9.322). Agamemnon's treasure, like all the riches the world
covets, consists of things that can always be acquired, exchanged, recovered

if they are lost, or obtained in one way or another. The price the warrior pays to attain virtue is of a completely different order: "A man's life cannot come back again, it cannot be lifted nor captured again by force, once it has crossed the teeth's barrier" (*Il.* 9.408–9). It is his life—his very identity, in its heroic form—that Achilles has put at the service of the army. And it is his life that Agamemnon has insulted in treating the hero the way he did. For Achilles, no wealth, no mark of honor, no social distinction could take precedence over a *psuchē* that nothing in the world can match (*ou gar emoi psuchēs antaxion*); by risking his life fearlessly in all the battles that Agamemnon shuns like death, Achilles has already dedicated himself to glory inspired by action.

After Odysseus speaks, old Phoinix argues that if Achilles accepts the reparations, as is customary and correct, and returns to battle, the Achaeans "will honor [him] like a god"; but if he refuses, they will never give him the same respect (*ouketh' homōs timēs eseai*), even if he comes back later and saves them from the misery of war (*Il.* 9.605). It is a wasted effort. By now Achilles sees a sharp division between two kinds of glory, two kinds of honor. The one is ordinary *timē*: public esteem, ready to extol him, to reward him with a literal king's ransom, if and only if he yields. The other is extraordinary *timē*: the eternal glory that is his destiny if he remains the same as he has always been. For the first time, Achilles openly rejects the Achaeans' praise, which he had once sought more than anything else. He tells Phoinix that he now has as little need of this latter *timē* (*ou ti me tautēs chreō timēs*, *Il.* 9.607–8) as he does of Agamemnon and his offer—they mean as much to him as a splinter of wood (*Il.* 9.378). He is concerned only with the honor in the destiny controlled by Zeus (*Dios aisa*, *Il.* 9.608),[7] the early death (*okumoros*, *Il.* 1.417; 18.95) that his mother had foretold: "Now it has befallen [*aisa*] that your life must be brief and bitter beyond all men's" (*Il.* 1.417–18). Once it has been accepted, however, an early death has its corollary in immortal glory, of which the epic hero sings.

Achilles' refusal highlights the tension between ordinary honor, the societal approval necessary for self-definition, and the much greater demands of heroic honor, in which one still needs to be recognized, but now as set apart on another level, to be famed "among men to come." This tension appears in outline at those points where the two types of honor are so closely linked as to seem almost blended.

This is the case in book 12 when Sarpedon exhorts Glaukos to take the lead among the Lycians in attacking the wall the Greeks have built (*Il.* 12.310–28). Why, he asks, are we honored in Lycia with all the privileges and honors of a king? Why do men treat us as if we were gods? Is it not because we feel obliged always to stand in the Lycians' first line of battle (*Lukioisi meta prōtoisin*) so that all the Lycian warriors can say, "Indeed they are not without

---

[7] *Phroneō de tetimesthai Dios aisēi.*

glory [*aklees*], these kings of our Lycia . . . since they fight in the forefront''
(*Il.* 12.318–21)? Just as Achilles is a son of Thetis, Sarpedon is a son of Zeus;
among the Trojan warriors, in his courage and his prowess in battle, he is like
a lion whose gnawing hunger drives him, heedless of danger, after his prey.
He does not care that the flock is in an enclosed pasture, guarded by herdsmen
armed with pikes and accompanied by dogs. Once he is on the attack, nothing
will turn him away. There are only two possible endings: either he will snatch
his victim, against and despite all odds, or he will be struck by a spear and fall
(*Il.* 12.305–6). The same spirit makes Sarpedon ready to attack the Greeks'
barricade, behind which death awaits him. Without hesitation he leaps over
the parapet and plunges into the fray. When he sees his companions flee before
Patroklos, who is wearing Achilles' armor and is in a murderous fury, he
rebukes them; he calls out his intention to go into single combat with the man
we know is destined to kill him (*Il.* 16.434). Sarpedon meets him in order to
''know'' him, to find out what he is, that is, to use a fight to the death to
determine his ''worth'' as a warrior (*Il.* 16.423).[8] Leaving aside the love Zeus
feels for him and the special treatment accorded by the gods to his corpse,
Sarpedon's attitude makes him resemble Achilles; both of them belong to the
same sphere of heroic existence, and they share a radical definition of honor.

Nonetheless, if we believe Sarpedon's words, there seems to be a direct
correspondence between the status of a king and the excellence of a warrior,
between the *timē* due to the former and the *kleos* sought by the latter. To fight
in the front line, as Achilles and Sarpedon do, underlies and justifies their
royal privileges; it could be said that to be a king, one must behave like a hero,
and to be a hero, one must be born a king. Such an optimistic vision joins
together the diverse factors of social prominence and personal virtue; it also
reflects the ambiguity of Homeric terminology, in which, according to their
context, the same words—*agathos*, *esthlos*, *aretē*, and *timē*—can denote high
birth, wealth, success, martial courage, and fame. There is no clear distinction
among the concepts.[9]

Still, in Sarpedon's own speech we find a trace of the fissure that, in Achilles' case, brutally separates heroic life—with its hopes, its demands, its peculiar ideals—from ordinary life controlled by a social code of honor. First
Sarpedon lists the advantages granted a king, such as comfort, good land,
good wine, renown, and a place of honor, and he says that they are like the
price men pay for the benefits wrought by the king's exceptional valor on the
battlefield. Sarpedon, however, then adds a comment that lays bare the true
nature of heroic activity and thus undercuts the previous statement: ''Suppos-

---

[8] The phrase is *ophra daeiō tis hode krateei*. Hektor displays the same attitude toward Diomedes at *Il.* 8.532 and 535; at *Il.* 3.53, Hektor urges Paris to confront Menelaos ''to learn what sort
of man he is.''

[9] On this point, see the classic studies by A.W.H. Adkins; for example, *Moral Values and
Political Behavior in Ancient Greece* (London, 1972), 12–16.

ing that you and I, escaping this battle, would be able to live on forever, age-less, immortal, so neither would I myself go on fighting in the foremost nor would I urge you into the fighting where men win glory. But now, seeing that the spirits of death stand close about us in their thousands, no man can turn aside nor escape them, let us go on and win glory for ourselves or yield it others" (*Il*.12.322–28).[10] Hence it is neither material advantage, nor primacy of place, nor the tokens of honor that can propel a man to stake his *psuchē* in the pitiless combat where glory is won. If it were only a matter of getting the goods one enjoys during life and loses with its end, there would not be a single warrior, Sarpedon claims, who would not bolt at the moment when, while enjoying life, he would have to risk losing everything along with it. The real meaning of heroic activity lies elsewhere. It has nothing to do with practical calculation or with the need for social prestige. Rather, it is in a way meta-physical. The gods have so arranged it that the human condition is not only mortal but also, like all earthly life after its youthful efflorescence, subject to the debilitating effects of age. Heroic striving has its roots in the will to escape aging and death, however "inevitable" they may be, and leave them both behind. Death is overcome when it is made welcome instead of merely being experienced, and when it makes life a perpetual gamble and endows it with exemplary value so that men will praise it as a model of "imperishable glory." When the hero gives up a long life in favor of an early death, whatever he loses in honors paid to his living person he more than regains a hundredfold with the glory that will suffuse his memory for all time to come. Archaic Greek culture is one in which everyone lives in terms of others, under the eyes and in the esteem of others, where the basis of a personality is confirmed by the extent to which its reputation is known; in such a context, real death lies in amnesia, silence, demeaning obscurity, the absence of fame.[11] By contrast, real existence—for the living or the dead—comes from being recognized, val-ued, and honored. Above all, it comes from being glorified as the central fig-ure in a song of praise, a story that endlessly tells and retells a destiny admired by all. In this sense, the hero, by the fame he has acquired in pledging his life to battle, inscribes his reality as an individual subject on the collective memory of the group; the death that has given his biography its conclusion has also given it permanence. Through the public arena of those exploits in which he was wholly engaged, he continues, beyond the reach of death, to be present in the community of the living. Converted into legend and linked with others like it, his personality forms the skein of a tradition that each generation must learn and make its own in order to enter fully into social and cultural existence.

Heroic honor goes far beyond ordinary esteem, the relative and ephemeral

---

[10] The same theme appears in Callin., frag. 1.12–15 (Edmonds); also Pind. *Ol*. 1.81ff.: "Since we must die, why sit in the shade and uselessly pass a hidden old age, far from all beauty"; also Lys., *Epitaph*. 78.

[11] See Marcel Detienne, *Les maîtres de vérité dans la Grèce archaïque* (Paris, 1967), 20–26.

marks of rank; in its quest for the absolute condition of *kleos aphthiton*, it assumes the existence of a tradition of oral poetry, which serves as a repository of shared culture and as societal memory for the group. In what we have come to call the "Homeric world," heroic honor and epic poetry are inseparable. There is no *kleos* except that which is sung, and—except for the praise of the gods—sung poetry has no purpose other than to recall the great deeds, *klea andrōn*, performed by the heroes of ages past. Epic poetry preserves such deeds in memory by making them more vivid than the audience's small quotidian lives.[12] A short life, a feat of arms, a beautiful death: all these have meaning only to the extent that they are contained and celebrated in a song and thereby confirm the hero as *aoidimos*, worthy of being sung. The literary transformation by epic endows the hero with the status, the fullness of existence, and the permanence that alone can justify the extreme demands of the heroic ideal and the sacrifices it entails. When an honor is required that surpasses honor, it has a "literary" dimension. This is not to say that heroic honor is only a stylistic convention and the hero only a fiction. The glorification of a "beautiful death" in Sparta and Athens during the high classical period shows that the heroic ideal retained its importance and its effect on behavior, even in historical contexts as far removed from the Homeric world as the city-state. Still, in order for heroic honor to stay alive at the heart of a society and put its stamp on the whole system of values, poetry has to be more than a pastime. Poetry must continue to play a role in education and upbringing; it serves to transmit, to teach, and to make manifest within each individual the alloy of knowledge, beliefs, attitudes, and values that make up a culture. Only epic poetry has the importance and power to confer on the hero's quest for deathless glory both institutional solidity and societal approval, without which the quest would be merely a subjective fantasy. We might be surprised to find a yearning for an afterlife that was reduced, as we might think, to "literary" immortality; if so, we would be misunderstanding the differences that separate the archaic Greek individual and society from our own. There is a structural relation between the ancient personality—exteriorized, grafted onto public opinion—and epic poetry, that functions as *paideia* in its glorification of exemplary heroes and their will to live on in "imperishable glory." The modern personality—an interiorized ego, unique, apart—has the same structural relation with its "purely" literary genres, like the novel, the autobiography, or the private diary, which preserve the hope of living on as a special immortal spirit.

Of all the characters depicted in the *Iliad*, Achilles is the only one who is

---

[12] Hes., *Theog.* 100; see Detienne, *Les maîtres*, 21–23. I owe a great deal to the fine book by James Redfield, *Nature and Culture in the Iliad: The Tragedy of Hector* (Chicago, 1975), esp. 30ff.

shown actually performing poetic song.[13] When the envoys sent by Agamemnon arrive at the Myrmidons' camp, Achilles is in his tent. Accompanying himself on the cithara, he is singing for himself and for Patroklos, seated across from him. What does Achilles take pleasure in when he sings under such circumstances? The very subject that the *aoidoi*, with Homer prime among them, sing in poems like the *Iliad*: "He sings of the deeds of heroes" (*Il.* 9.189). Achilles is the model of the heroic warrior; in choosing a short life and deathless glory, he embodies an ideal of honor so elevated that, in its name, he will reject both the gifts of the king and the *timē* of his own companions in arms. He is the one the great epic shows, at this critical moment in his career, singing about the exploits of heroes. What a literary tactic, what an image *en abîme*![14] But the lesson of the episode is clear: Achilles' great deeds are glorified by Homer in the *Iliad*, yet to exist fully in the eyes of the hero who longs to perform them, they must be reflected and preserved in a song that exalts their fame. As a heroic character, Achilles exists to himself only in the mirror of the song that reflects his own image. The song also reflects, in the form of *klea*, the exploits to which he has chosen to sacrifice his life so that he will forever after be the Achilles sung by Homer in the *Iliad* and by all the Greeks to come.

To pass by death is also to escape the process of aging. For the Greeks death and old age go together (Mimn. frag. 2.5–7, Edmonds). Growing old means that one must watch the fabric of life gradually becoming frayed, damaged, torn by the same power of destruction, the *kēr*, that leads to death. *Hēbēs anthos*, says Homer. It has been shown that this formula, taken up and developed by the elegiac and lyric poets, directly inspired the funerary epitaphs that extol the warriors who are taken in "the flower of youth," that is, dying in combat.[15] Just as a flower fades, so do the qualities that make life worthwhile: once vigor, beauty, grace, and agility have shed their glow on a person during his "shining youth" (*aglaos hēbē*), they do not stay fixed and firm but soon wither and then vanish. The flower of age—when one enjoys the full maturity of one's life's strength—is the burgeoning growth of springtime, of which the old man, in the winter of his life, before even descending to his grave, already

[13] See Pierre Vidal-Naquet, "L'*Iliade* sans travesti," preface to the folio translation of the *Iliad* by Paul Mazon (Paris, 1975), 32.

[14] For a similar action in the *Odyssey* with a different meaning, see Françoise Frontisi-Ducroux, "Homère et le temps retrouvé," *Critique* 348 (May 1976): 542. A parallel to Achilles' song about heroic activity is Helen's depiction of it in weaving: *Il.* 3.125 and 6.357–58.

[15] See Loraux, "нвн." She writes: "When it celebrates the *aretē* of a warrior, every verse epitaph tends to use epic formulae, of which *aglaon hēbēn ōlesan* is only one instance among many in the *dēmosion sēma*" (24). Regarding the use of the formula "he [or they] lost their shining youth" to denote death on the battlefield, she notes: "Such continuity between the aristocratic epitaph, praising an individual, and the collective, democratic epitaph of the *dēmosion sēma* deserves close attention, because it suggests the persistence of a specific representation of the dead man as young" (20).

feels himself deprived.[16] That is the meaning of the myth of Tithonos: what good is it to have immortality if one is not protected from aging? More shrewdly, Sarpedon tells Glaukos of his dream of eluding both old age and death, of being *agēraos* as well as *athanatos* (*Il.* 12.323; cf. 8.539). Then and only then could it be said of the warrior's exploit that the game is not worth the effort. Poor Tithonos, daily sinking deeper into senility in the heavenly sanctuary where Eos had to leave him, is no more than a specter of a living man, an animated corpse; his endless aging dooms him to an illusion of existence that death has completely destroyed from within.[17]

To fall on the battlefield saves the warrior from such inexorable decay, such deterioration of all the virtues that comprise masculine *aretē*. Heroic death seizes the fighter when he is at his *akmē*, a fully adult man (*anēr*), completely intact in the integrity of a vital power still untouched by any decrepitude. He will haunt the memory of men to come, in whose eyes his death has secured him in the luster of ideal youth. Thus the *kleos aphthiton* the hero gains through his early death also opens to him the path to eternal youth. Just as Herakles has to endure the pyre on Mount Oeta in order to marry Hebe—and thereby be confirmed as *agēraos* (*Theog.* 955)—it is a "beautiful death" that makes the warrior altogether *athanatos* and *agēraos*. In the imperishable glory conferred on him by the song about his deeds, he becomes immune to aging in the same way that, as much as it is humanly possible, he escapes the destruction of death.

This theme of the warrior's guaranteeing himself perpetual youth at the moment he accepts death in battle can also be found again with various modulations, in the rhetoric of the Athenian funeral oration. But, as Nicole Loraux has observed, its origins must be sought in epic; the Athenians do use it at public funerals to praise those who by their civic spirit have given their lives during the year on behalf of their city. When the theme is so used, it is a projection onto the figure of the hoplite—citizen-soldier, adult, and father of a family—of the heroic image of the warrior of epic who is, above all, a young man. Within Homeric society, the contrast between *kouroi* and *gerontes* is not simply a matter of age, and the *gerontes* are not all "aged" in our sense of the term. Nonetheless, there *is* a sharp distinction between two spheres of activity and competence. Warfare privileges physical strength and valiant ardor, while

---

[16] On the association of youthful military prowess and springtime, see ibid., 9–12; she refers to Pericles' funeral oration (doubtless the *epitaphios* for Samos), wherein the Athenian statesman compares the youth, whom death in battle has stolen from the city, with springtime that has faded from the year. Cf. Arist., *Rhet.* 1.7.1365a31–33 and 3.10.141a1–4.

[17] See *Hom. Hym. Aph.* 1.218–38; also Mimn. frag. 2.5–7 (Edmonds): "For Tithonos Zeus decreed a deathless evil, old age, which is still worse than a horrible death." The phrase "deathless evil" involves a play on words, *kakon aphthiton*, that recalls and contrasts with *kleos aphthiton*. The young warrior who dies gets imperishable glory; the old man, alive forever, gets imperishable misery.

planning requires speaking ability and prudence. Between the bold adventurer (*prēktēr ergōn*) and the eloquent advisor (*muthōn rhētōr*), the difference is principally one of age (*Il.* 9.52–61; 11.786–89). The wisdom of the *gerōn* counterbalances the impetuousness of the young men, designated by the term *hoplōteroi*, which defines youth by its ability to bear arms (*Il.* 3.108–10). If the "deep-voiced speaker" from Pylos, old Nestor, offers copious wise advice, and his experience in combat appears more in the form of comments than in exploits, it is because age is weighing him down and he is no longer a *kouros* (*Il.* 4.321).[18] Advising and speaking (*boulē*, *muthoi*) are the province and privilege of the *gerontes*; the younger men (*neōteroi*) have the task of spear-work and asserting themselves in their own strength (*Il.* 8.157).[19] Hence we find the formula, repeated like a refrain, that punctuates most of Nestor's lengthy orations to his troops. Whether giving them instructions or encouraging them in a struggle in which he will play only a marginal role, he says, "Ah, if only I were young again, if only my strength were what it was [*eith' hōs hēboimi biē de moi empedos eiē*]" (*Il.* 7.157).[20] Nestor regrets the loss of his martial prowess along with his vanished youth. In this context, *Hēbē* is less a precisely defined age group than the time of life when one feels oneself in a state of superiority, when success and acclaim (*kudos*) seem to follow you naturally, seem linked to your undertakings (*erikudēs hēbē*; *Il.* 11.225)—more prosaically, when you are in full possession of your powers: physical power, above all, but also suppleness of the body, flexibility, steadiness in the legs, and swiftness in movement (*Il.* 11.669; 13.512–15; 23.627–28). To possess *hēbē* is to combine all the qualities that make a full-fledged warrior. Idomeneus is a formidable fighter but already graying (*mesaipolios*, 13.361), and when he admits his fear before Aeneas's onslaught, he calls to his companions for help and explains, "He has the flower of youth, which is the greatest *kratos* [*kai d'echei hēbēs anthos, ho te kratos esti megiston*]" (*Il.* 13.484). Valiant as he is, Idomeneus feels the burden of age: "no longer in an outrush could his limbs stay steady beneath him [*ou gar et'empeda guia*] either to dash in after his spear, or to get clear again" (*Il.* 13.512–13). As Emile Benveniste has shown, *kratos* does not merely denote physical strength, like *biē* or *ischus*, but the superiority that enables a warrior to dominate his opponent, to prevail against him and vanquish him in combat. In this sense, the warrior's *aristeia* is to some extent included in *hēbē*, and we can understand more clearly how the heroic point of view conjoins the warrior's death with youth. Just as ordi-

---

[18] He says, "If I was a young man then, old age has taken me now" (*Il.* 4.321).

[19] *Il.* 4.323–25; cf. 3.150; in Troy the *dēmogerontes* sit in council, because "for them age has put an end to warfare, but they are excellent speakers."

[20] Cf. also 11.670; 23.629; and 4.314–15, where Agamemnon tells Nestor, "Aged sir, if only, as the spirit is in your bosom, so might your knees be also and the strength stay steady within you." In the same way, at 8.103, Diomedes says "Your strength is broken, and bitter age is on you."

nary honor is paralleled by heroic honor, ordinary youth—merely a question of age—has a counterpart in heroic youth, which is radiant in combat and finds its fulfillment in death on the battlefield. Here we can quote Nicole Loraux, who has understood and expressed the point superbly:

> Homeric epic gives two very different versions of the death of the *kouros*. This is not surprising: while youth is a pure quality for the hero, it is a prosaic physical fact for those whom the gods have less favored. Although the death of young soldiers is a frequent occurrence in the *Iliad*, it is not always touchingly glorious. . . . In some cases youth is only one characteristic among others, which does not distinguish one death from among the vast and ultimately unimportant number of victims. In other words, youth as a quality does not inform the warrior's last moments, and he dies manfully but without any special glory. For the hero, by contrast, death takes place under the sign of *hēbē*; even if youth had not been specifically attributed to the warrior, he possesses it at the exact moment he loses it; *hēbē* is the last word, for both Patroklos and Hektor, whose "spirit flies to Hades, mourning its fate, leaving behind strength and youth" (*lipous' androtēta kai hēbēn, Il.* 16.857, 22.363). In fact this mention of a youth that is lost and mourned, but also exalted, is denied to all the other combatants; *hēbē* becomes a type of charisma, reserved for the heroic elite—for Achilles' most valiant opponent and for the man who was not just Achilles' friend but his double.[21]

The *hēbē* that Patroklos and Hektor lose along with their lives is one they possessed more fully than other *kouroi*, though the latter might have been younger. It is this same *hēbē* that Achilles guarantees for himself in perpetuity by choosing a short life and an early, heroic death. While the warrior is alive, his youth appears primarily in vigor (*biē*), strength (*kratos*), and endurance (*alkē*); when he has become a weak, lifeless corpse, the glow of his youth persists in the extraordinary beauty of his body. In Homer the word *sōma* means precisely a body from which life has fled, the husk or shell of a once-living being. So long as the body is alive, it is seen as a system of organs and limbs animated by their individual impulses; it is a locus for the meeting, and occasional conflict, of impulses or competing forces. At death, when the body is deserted by these, it acquires its formal unity. After being the subject of and medium for various actions, more or less spontaneous, it has become wholly an object for others. Above all, it is an object of contemplation, a visual spectacle, and therefore a focus for care, mourning, and funeral rites.[22] During the course of a battle, a warrior may have seemed to become a menace, a terror, or comfort, occasioning panic or flight, or inspiring courage and attack. Lying on the battlefield, however, he is exposed as a simple figure with identifiable

---

[21] Loraux, "HBH," 22–23.

[22] On this point, see the remarks of J.-P. Vernant in *Problèmes de la personne*, ed. I. Meyerson (Paris, 1973), 54, and Redfield, *Nature and Culture*, 178ff.

attributes: this is truly Patroklos, and this Hektor, but reduced to their external appearance, to the unique look of their bodies that enables others to recognize them. For the living man, of course, an imposing presence, grace, and beauty have their place as elements of personality, but for the warrior in action, such attributes are eclipsed by those highlighted by battle. What shines from the body of the hero is less the charming glow of youth (*chariestatē hēbē*)[23] than the sheen of the bronze he is wearing, the flash of his sword and breastplate, the glitter of his eyes, the radiance of the ardor that fires him (*Il.* 19.365, 375–77, 381, 398). When Achilles reappears on the battlefield after his long absence, stark terror seizes the Trojans as they see him "shining in his armor" (*Il.* 20.46). Beside the Scaean gates Priam groans aloud, batters his head, pleads with Hektor to return to the shelter of the walls. Priam has just been the first to see Achilles: "He swept along the flat land in full shining, like that star which comes on in the autumn and whose conspicuous brightness far outshines the stars that are numbered in the night's darkening, the star they give the name of Orion's Dog, which is the brightest among the stars and yet is wrought as a sign of evil and brings on fever for unfortunate mortals. Such was the flare of the bronze that girt his chest in his running" (*Il.* 22.25–32). When Hektor himself catches sight of Achilles, on whom the bronze shines "like flaming fire or the rising sun," he too is terrified; he turns and takes flight (*Il.* 22.134–35). The active, terrifying radiance of the live warrior must be differentiated from the remarkable beauty of his corpse, preserved in a youthfulness that age can no longer mar. Hektor's *psuchē* has scarcely left his body, "losing its strength and its youth," before Achilles strips the armor from the torso. The Achaeans rush together in order to see the enemy who, more than any other, had done them harm, and in order to aim more blows at his body. As they approach the hero, now no more than a *sōma*, an empty and inert cadaver, "they marvel at Hektor's size and at his admirable beauty [*hoi kai thēēsanto phuēn kai eidos agēton Hektoros*]" (*Il.* 22.370–71).[24] We might be surprised at this reaction if old Priam had not already illuminated the difference between the pitiable and frightful death of an old man and the beautiful death of a warrior cut down in his prime. "For a young man all is decorous [*pant' epeoiken*] when he is cut down in battle and torn with the sharp bronze,

---

[23] *Il.* 24.348: the subject is Hermes, who has disguised himself as a young prince whose beard has just begun to grow. At 3.44–45, Paris's beauty (*kalon eidos*) is no disguise, for he has neither strength nor courage (cf. 3.39, 55, 392). At 21.108, Achilles tells Lykaon, who is pleading for his life, "I too, as you see, am handsome and tall [*kai egō kalos te megas te*]," but this means that Lykaon's death is imminent. Beautiful as Achilles may be, death hangs over his head too; the day is near when his life will be taken in battle. This is not Achilles in the fury of action, but the hero seeing himself under the sign of death. On Agamemnon's beauty, "kingly" rather than soldierly, cf. 3.169–70.

[24] Cf. *Od.* 24.44: when Achilles has died, his "beautiful body" is washed in warm water; also Eur., *Supp.* 783: the sight of the dead Argive soldiers is beautiful—*kalon theama*—though bitter.

and lies there dead, and though dead still all that shows about him is beautiful [*panta kala*]" (*Il*. 22.71–73).

In Priam's mind, the description of the young warrior, beautiful in his death, hardly supplies a motive for Hektor to go up against Achilles; rather it should force Hektor to take pity on the horrible death that awaits an old man like Priam if, deprived of his son's assistance, he should die on the sword or the spear of his enemies. The repulsive picture painted by the aged king strikingly explains how unnatural and scandalous it is when a warrior's death, a "red" death, befalls an old man; the latter's dignity calls for an end that is tranquil, almost solemn, surrounded by the quiet of his home and family. The blood, the wounds, and the grime on the corpse of a young hero recall his courage and enhance his beauty with masculine strength, but on an old man—gray-headed, gray-bearded, withered—their ugliness becomes almost obscene. Priam envisions himself not merely dead at his own gates, but dismembered and torn by dogs, not just any dogs but his own dogs, raised and fed by him in his palace, who will revert to savagery and make him their prey, and after feasting on his flesh and gnawing his genitals, will stretch out, sated, in the entryway they so recently guarded. "When an old man is dead and down, and the dogs mutilate the gray head and the gray beard and the parts that are secret, this, for all sad mortality, is the sight most pitiful" (*Il*. 22.74–76). Priam is describing a world turned upside down, with all its values reversed, bestiality installed at the center of the domestic hearth, and an old man's dignity turned into an object of derision in its ugliness and shame, with everything human that belonged to his body destroyed. A bloody death is beautiful and glorious when it strikes the hero in the fullness of youth; it raises him above the human condition and saves him from common death by conferring sublime luster on his demise. The same kind of death, for an old man, drops him beneath the level of humanity and changes his end from a shared fate into a horrible monstrosity.

In one of the surviving fragments of his poetry, Tyrtaeus imitates this passage of the *Iliad*, using some of the same formulas.[25] The differences that often appear both in the details and in the overall picture derive from the Spartan context: the hoplite in the phalanx, fighting shoulder to shoulder and shield to shield, is no longer the champion of Homeric epic. His duty is to stand fast without leaving his position, not to distinguish himself in individual combat. To ensure that "dying is a fine thing [*tethnamenai gar kalon*] when one has fallen in the front rank, a man full of heart" (frag. 6.1–2 Prato), it must occur in defense of the fatherland. Only then does the dead man's glory remain forever, and only then is the hero immortal (*athanatos*) even though he has gone

---

[25] In addition to the commentary by Carlo Prato on this fragment (see his edition of Tyrtaeus [Rome, 1968], 93–102), see C. R. Dawson, "*Spoudaiogeloion*: Random Thoughts on Occasional Poems," *YClS* 19 (1966): 50–58; Verdenius, "Tyrtaeus," 337–55.

beneath the earth (frag. 9.31–32 Prato). Thus there is no longer so radical a breach as there was between heroic honor and honor plain and simple; at Sparta there is no incompatibility between long life and martial valor, between glory (as Achilles defines it) and old age. If the soldiers who are able to stand fast in the line also have the good fortune to return home safe and sound, they share for the rest of their lives in the same honor and glory as those who fell. When they grow old, their excellence deserves the respect of the whole city (frag. 9.39ff. Prato).

Sparta thereby uses the prestige of the epic warrior's achievement and of heroic honor as a means of competition and social advancement. From the *agōgē* on, there is something like a codified rule of glory and shame; judging by military accomplishments, the city apportions and assigns praise or blame, respect or contempt, marks of esteem or of abasement, condemning the "tremblers" (*tresantes*) to the humiliating insults of women and to censure and dishonor (*oneidos kai atimiē*) in the community at large (cf. Herod. 7.231).

For Tyrtaeus, moreover, "the man who is older [*palaiōteros*] and more revered [*geraios*]," whose death is contrasted with that of a youth (*neos*), is not the miserable dotard described by Priam to arouse Hektor's pity, but a brave hoplite; this old man courageously fought and died "in the front rank," the place in the phalanx normally occupied by the *neoi*. We could think that his sacrifice only deserves to be extolled even further. On the contrary, if fragment 6 was claiming that it was fine (*kalon*) to die in the first rank, this same death becomes despicable for the older man who falls ahead of the *neoi*. In the "ugliness" decried by the word *aischron* there is a hint of "moral" disapproval: the horror of the scene serves to exhort the *neoi* not to yield their place in the forefront to men older than they. The whole context, however, with its contrast between beautiful and ugly and the "spectacular" quality of the entire description, reveals the persistence of an "aesthetic" vision—in the broadest sense of the term—of heroic death in its close attachment to *hēbē*.

> Indeed it is an ugly thing when an old man, fallen in the front rank, lies before the young men, with his white head and gray beard, having breathed out his brave strength into the dust, clutching his bloody genitals—a horror for the eyes and shameful to see [*aischra ta g'ophthalmois kai nemesēton idein*] in his nakedness. For the young men all is proper [*neoisi de pant'epeoiken*] when they are in the brilliant flowering of their youth, an object of admiration for men [*andrasi men thēētos idein*] and desire for women [*eratos de gunaixi*] in life [*zōos eōn*], and beautiful in death in the first rank [*kalos d'en promachoisi pesōn*]. (Frag. 7.21–30 Prato)

It seems true, then, as Dawson suggests, that there is a double dimension to beauty, just as there is to honor and youth. At the end of his discussion of Tyrtaeus, Dawson concludes, "Sensuous beauty may come in life, but true beauty comes in heroic death."[26] Beauty in heroic death—this is certainly the source of the rule ascribed to Lycurgus, according to which Spartan warriors allow their hair to grow long and flowing, without cutting it, and give it special care on the eve of battle. The hair on a man's head is like the flower of his vitality, the foliage of his age. Hair shows the age of the person whose head it adorns; at the same time, it is a part of the body that has a growth and a life of its own—when cut it grows back, it preserves itself without decaying—so that it can represent the individual. One can offer a clipping of one's hair as if it were a gift of one's self. Just as the old man is identifiable by his white head and beard, *hēbē* too is marked by the first appearance of a downy beard and by an adult's haircut.[27] There is a well known connection between *kouros* and *keirō*, "to cut one's hair"; more generally, the great phases in a person's life, changes in status, are highlighted by the cutting and offering of a lock of hair, or sometimes even by cutting all of it off, as in the case of a new bride at Sparta. In the *Iliad*, the companions of Patroklos, including Achilles himself, cut off their hair over the corpse of their dead friend before consigning him to the pyre. They cover the whole body with their hair, as if they were clothing it for its last journey with their own youthful, manly vitality: "his corpse completely covered with hair that they cut from their heads and then placed on him" (*Il.* 23.135–36).[28]

His companions adorn the dead man with that which most embodies their nature as fierce warriors, while his wife (if he has one) or his mother (as in Hektor's case, for example) offer the precious garments they have woven for him; thus they connect him, even in the hereafter, with that female realm to which he was linked by being a son or a husband. When Xenophon explains the wearing of long hair as a way of making the Spartan soldiers look "taller, nobler, and more terrifying" (*Rep. Lac.* 11.3),[29] he does not contradict the criterion of beauty this custom confers on them; he only emphasizes that it is not a matter of any kind of attractiveness, like Paris's sensuous beauty or feminine loveliness, but of the beauty unique to a warrior. It is this latter kind, no doubt, that was sought by Homer's warriors, those the epic calls "long-haired Achaeans [*karē komoōntes Achaioi*]."[30]

Herodotus offers us a revealing episode (7.208–9). Before testing the resistance of the Spartan squadron guarding Thermopylae, Xerxes sends a Persian horseman to spy on them. On his return, the spy reports that he saw the Spar-

---

[26] Dawson, "*Spoudaiogeloion*," 57.

[27] Cf. Aesch., *Ag.* 78–79: "What is an aged man when his foliage is all withered?"

[28] For Achilles' own hair, cf. 23.144–52; cf. Andromache's laments for her husband Hektor (*Il.* 22.508–14).

[29] Cf. Loraux, "La 'belle mort,' " 105–20.

[30] *Il.* 2.443, 472; 18.359; 3.43. The last passage is particularly telling, for the "long-haired" Achaeans justly laugh at the youthful beauty of Paris, who, far from being a brave warrior, has no courage, strength, or tenacity.

tans exercising in the palaestra and combing out their long hair. The king, astonished, summons the exiled Spartan ruler Demaratos and asks him for an explanation. "It is a Spartan custom," Demaratos says, "that when their men are about to risk their lives, they groom their hair." Victory or death was the law at Sparta, and at Thermopylae the choice was reduced to one of its terms: to die well. On the eve of a battle in which life is at stake, it is one and the same thing to impress the enemy with a "tall, noble, terrifying" appearance and to prepare to die on the battlefield, to leave a beautiful corpse, in its youth, like that of Hektor admired by the Greeks.[31]

If the youth and beauty of the fallen hero's body reflect the shining glory for which he sacrificed his life, the mistreatment of an enemy's corpse takes on a new meaning. Charles Segal and James Redfield have emphasized the importance in the *Iliad* of the theme of the mutilation of the corpse: in the course of the poem it steadily increases in force until it culminates in the deranged fury of the abuse Achilles inflicts on Hektor's corpse. There can be no doubt that the poet is using this motif to convey the ambiguities of heroic warfare. When battles become more heated, chivalrous combat—with its rules, its code, its prohibitions—is transformed into savage struggle, in which the bestiality that lurks in violence comes to the surface in all the participants. It is no longer enough to triumph in a lawful duel, to confirm one's own *aretē* over another's; with the opponent dead, one attacks his corpse, as a predator does its prey. Since the victor can not fulfill the formulaic wish to devour the body raw, he dismembers and consumes through the mediation of dogs and birds. Thus the epic hero is doubly threatened with the loss of his humanity; if the hero dies, his body might be given over to the beasts, not in a beautiful death, but in that nightmarish horror described by Priam; if the hero kills and then mutilates the corpse, he risks a descent into that very savagery Priam ascribed to his dogs. All this is true enough, but we must ask whether the link is not even tighter between the heroic ideal and the mutilation of the corpse: does not the hero's beautiful death, which grants him eternal glory, have as its necessary corollary, its sinister obverse, the disfigurement and debasement of the dead opponent's body, so as to deny him access to the memory of men to come? If, in the heroic point of view, staying alive means little compared with dying well, the same perspective shows that what is most important is not to kill one's enemy but to deprive him of a beautiful death.

Aikia (Homeric *aeikeiē*), the action of *aikizein*, of disgracing or doing outrage to the corpse appears, even on the linguistic level,[32] as the negation of that propriety, *pant'epeoiken*, that Homer and Tyrtaeus attribute to the body

---

[31] Cf. Plut., *Lyc.* 22.1: long hair will make the handsome more noble, and the ugly more terrifying.

[32] Cf. Louis Gernet, *Recherches sur le développement de la pensée juridique et morale en Grèce* (Paris, 1917), 211. The terms contain, with an alpha privative, the root -*weik*, which marks concurrence, conformity, resemblance.

of the *neos* exposed on the field of battle, and the replacement of *panta kala* by *aischron*. *Aikizein* is also *aischunein*, "make ugly," "debase."[33] It involves obliterating from the body of the dead warrior those marks of manly youth and beauty that are manifested there like visible signs of glory. In place of the beautiful death of the hero suffused with *hēbē*, the effort is made to substitute the vision of the frightful doom that haunts old Priam's thoughts: a body stripped of all youth, all beauty, all masculinity (that is the meaning of the strange allusion, in both Tyrtaeus and Homer, to the genitals devoured or held blood-soaked in the hand), and finally of all humanity. Why such relentlessness against what Apollo calls inert clay (*kōphē gaia*, *Il*. 24.54)? Why the desire to ferret out the person from an enemy's corpse whose *psuchē* has already fled and is now only an empty husk? Why, unless the person remains connected to this dead body and to that which its appearance, its *eidos*, represents? For the hero to attain *kleos aphthiton*, it is essential that his name and exploits be known by men to come, that they persist in memory. The first condition is that they be celebrated in a song that will never perish; the second is that his corpse have received its portion of honor (*geras thanontōn*, *Il*. 16.457, 675), that he not have been deprived of the *timē* that is owed to him and that will let him enter into the farthest reaches of death, bringing him to a new state, to the social status of death, all the while remaining a bearer of life's values, of youth, of beauty that the body incarnates and which, on him, have been consecrated by heroic death.

What does it mean to enter into the furthest reaches of death? The fatal blow that strikes the hero liberates his *psuchē*, which flees the limbs, leaving behind its strength and youth. Yet for all that, it has not passed through the gates of death. Death is not a simple demise, a privation of life; it is a transformation of which the corpse is both the instrument and the object, a transmutation of the subject that functions in and through the body. Funerary rites actualize this change of condition; at their conclusion, the individual has left the realm of the living, in the same way as his cremated body has vanished into the hereafter, and as his *psuchē* has reached the shores of Hades, never to return. The individual has disappeared then from the fabric of social relations in which his existence was a strand. In this respect, he is henceforth an absence, a void, but he continues to exist on another plane, in a form of being that is released from the attrition of time and destruction. The hero survives in the permanence of his name and the luster of his renown, both of which remain present not only in the memory of those who knew him when he was alive, but for all men in ages to come. This inscription in societal memory takes two interdependent and parallel forms. The hero is committed to memory, memorized, in the field of epic song which, to celebrate his immortal glory, is placed under the sign of Memory, making itself memory by making him memorable. The hero is

---

[33] Cf. *Il*. 22.75, which can be compared to 22.336; also 18.24, 27; 24.418.

also commemorated in the *mnēma*, the memorial constituted at the end of the funeral rites by the construction of a tomb and the raising of a *sēma*, serving like epic to evoke for men to come (*essomenoisi*) a glory that is now certain not to perish.[34] Its very fixity and stability contrast the grave marker with the fleeting, transitory nature of the values that graced the human body during life. "It remains without moving, changeless [*empedon*], once it has been placed over the tomb of a man or a woman who has died" (*Il.* 17.432–35). *Empedos* means "intact" or "immutable"; if the qualities that comprise a warrior's *aristeia*—ardor (*menos*), might (*biē*), the limbs (*guia*)—had this character of *empedos*,[35] the warrior hero would be immune to old age. He would not have to lose his youth and beauty in a heroic death in order to acquire them definitively in the world beyond. In its own way, by the immutability of its material and shape, and by the continuity of its presence, the *mnēma* conveys the paradox of the values of life, youth, and beauty, which one can ensure for oneself only by losing them, which become eternal possessions only when one ceases to be.

The treatment of the corpse in the funerary ritual derives from a paradox of the same kind. First it is beautified; it is washed with warm water to cleanse it of soil and stain; its wounds are effaced with an unguent; the skin, rubbed with oil, takes on a special sheen; perfumed and adorned with precious materials, the corpse is then laid out on a litter to be viewed and mourned by the dead man's near and dear ones (*Il.* 18.346–53; *Od.* 24.44–46). In the Homeric tradition, the corpse is then burned on a pyre whose flames consume all that is made of flesh and blood, that is, everything both edible and subject to decay and thus attached to that ephemeral kind of existence where life and death are inextricably mingled. All that remains is the "white bones," incorruptible and not entirely burned to ash; these are easy to distinguish from the ashes of the pyre so they may be collected and deposited in a tomb. If we compare sacrificial ritual with funerary practices, we can say that "the fire's part" is reversed: the flames of the funerary pyre consume that which the sacrifice preserves to be consumed by men. The victim's flesh, laden with fat, is the share of "mortal men" who dine on it, since they must eat in order to subsist, obeying the exigencies of a perishable being that must be nourished indefinitely if it is not to be extinguished. The "white bones" of the sacrificed animal, inedible and incorruptible—inedible because incorruptible—are burned on the altar as the share of the immortal gods who receive them in the form of fragrant smoke. In funeral rites, these same white bones remain under the earth as the trace—extended by the burial mound, the *sēma*, the stele—that is left behind

[34] The same formula to describe the *sēma* appears at *Od.* 11.76 and *Il.* 22.305: *kai essomenoisi puthesthai*; at *Od.* 4.584, Menelaos orders the erection of a tomb for Agamemnon, "so that his glory [*kleos*] might remain forever," and at *Il.* 7.91, Hektor believes that the tomb of an enemy he has beaten will remind future generations of his triumph, so that his *kleos* will not die.

[35] For the use of *empedos*: with *menos*, *Il.* 5.254; with *biē*, 4.314; with *guia*, 23.627.

by the person of the deceased; in his absence, it is the form in which he remains, present to the world of the living. The fire of the funerary pyre, by
contrast, consumes and sends into the realm of the invisible, along with the
perishable flesh and blood, a person's entire physical appearance and the attributes that can be seen on the body: stature, beauty, youth, individuality,
glamor, flowing hair. These corporeal aspects incarnate values that are at once
aesthetic, religious, social, and personal, and define the status of a singular
individual in the eyes of the group. These values in turn are all the more precious for being so fragile and newly in bloom, as the life that made them
flower immediately withers them. The visible form of the body, such as is
displayed when it is laid out for viewing at the beginning of the funeral rites,
can only be saved from corruption by disappearing into the invisible. If the
beauty, youth, and masculinity of the corpse are to be definitively his and are
to be attached to the figure of the deceased, they require that the body have
stopped being a living hero.

This finality of funerary practices is most clearly revealed precisely where
they are missing and especially where they are ritually negated in the procedures of outrage visited on the enemy corpse. In its attempt to deprive the
enemy of access to the status of a glorious death his heroic end had earned for
him, his mistreatment, by the nature of the cruelty it inflicts, allows us better
to understand the means that funerary rites normally use to immortalize the
warrior in his beautiful death.

One kind of cruelty consists in defiling the bloody corpse with dust and in
tearing his flesh, so that the enemy will lose his individual appearance, his
clear set of features, his color and glamor; he loses his distinct form along with
his human aspect, so that he becomes unrecognizable. When Achilles begins
to abuse Hektor, he ties the corpse to his chariot to tear off its skin,[36] by letting
it—especially the head and the hair—drag on the ground in the dust: "A cloud
of dust rose where Hektor was dragged, his dark hair was falling about him,
and all that head that was once so handsome [*paros charien*] was tumbled in
the dust" (*Il.* 22.401–3). By dirtying and disfiguring the corpse, instead of
purifying and anointing it, *aikia* seeks to destroy the individuality of a body
that was the source of the charm of youth and life. Achilles wants Hektor to
be like Sarpedon: "No longer could a man, even a knowing one, have made
out the godlike Sarpedon, since he was piled from head to ends of feet under
a mass of weapons, the blood and the dust" (*Il.* 16.637–40). The reduction of
the body to a formless mass, indistinguishable now from the ground on which
it lies, not only eradicates the dead man's unique appearance; such treatment
also eliminates the difference between lifeless matter and a living creature.
Thus the corpse is no longer the visible aspect of the person but the inert clod
of which Apollo spoke. Earth and dust defile the body because their contact

---

[36] *Il.* 24.21 and 23.187; both passages contain the verb *apodruptō* (flay, lacerate).

pollutes it, inasmuch as they belong to a realm that is the opposite of life. During the process of mourning, at the point when the relatives of the dead man bring him closer to life by making one last reflection of life glow on his corpse, they in turn draw closer to the deceased by simulating their own entry into the formless world of death; they inflict on their own bodies a kind of fictive outrage by defiling themselves and tearing their hair, by rolling in the dust, by smearing their faces with ashes. Achilles does the same when he learns of Patroklos's death: "He befouls his charming face [*charien d'ēischune prosōpon*]" (*Il.* 18.24) just as he defiles the fair face of Hektor in the dust.

There is another type of *aikia*: the body is dismembered, hacked up, torn into pieces; the head, arms, hands, and legs are removed, chopped up piece by piece (*melēisti tamein, Il.* 24.409).[37] Ajax, in fury, cuts the head of Imbrios from his delicate neck and hurls it like a ball (*sphairēdon*) to roll in the dust (*Il.* 13.202). Hektor would like to impale Patroklos's head on a stake after having severed it from his neck (*Il.* 18.176–78). Agamemnon kills Hippolochos and then "cuts off his hands and severs his neck with his sword, and rolls him like a piece of wood [*holmon hōs*] through the crowd" (*Il.* 11.146–47). A head like a ball, a torso like a log: in losing its formal unity, the human body is reduced to the condition of a thing along with its disfigurement. In *Pythian* 4, Pindar says, "He comes to cut the branches of a great oak with a sharp-edged axe and defile its astounding beauty [*aischunei de hoi thaēton eidos*]" (4.263–64). It is precisely such beauty that astonishes the Greeks when they look on the dead Hektor, and that is the target of the outrage directed at the corpse, an attack on the integrity of the human body.

The dismemberment of the corpse, whose remains are scattered here and there, culminates in the practice described in the first verses of the *Iliad* and recalled throughout the poem: leaving the body as food for dogs, birds, and fish. This outrage carries horror to its height. The body is torn to pieces and devoured raw instead of being consigned to the fire that, in burning it, restores it to wholeness in the world beyond. The hero whose body is surrendered to the voracity of wild animals is excluded from death while also having fallen from the human condition. He cannot pass through the gates of Hades, for he has not had his "share of fire"; he has no place of burial, no mound or *sēma*, no location for his body that would mark for his society the site where he is to be found; there he would continue his relations with his country, his lineage, his descendants, or even simply with the chance passers-by. Excluded from death, he is equally banished from human memory. Moreover, to hand someone over to wild animals does not mean only to deprive him of the status

---

[37] We will pass over the problems of *maschalismos*, for which one should consult E. Rohde, *Psyche: The Cult of Souls and Belief in Immortality among the Greeks*, 8th ed., trans. W. B. Hillis (New York, 1925; reprint, 1966), vol. 2, app. 2, 582–86; these problems occupy another level of analysis which will be the subject of a future study.

of a dead man by preventing his funeral. It is also to dissolve him into confusion and return him to chaos, utter nonhumanity. In the belly of the beasts that have devoured him, he becomes the flesh and blood of wild animals, and there is no longer the slightest appearance or trace of humanity: he is no longer in any way a person.

There is one last kind of outrage. Free rein is given to the powers of corruption that are at work in the bodies of mortal creatures; the corpse, deprived of burial, is left to decompose and rot on its own, eaten by the worms and the flies that have entered into his open wounds. When Achilles is preparing to re-enter combat, he worries out loud to his mother. What will happen to Patroklos's body while the battle lasts? "I am sadly afraid, during this time, for the warlike son of Menoitios that flies might get into the wounds beaten by bronze in his body and breed worms in them, and these make foul the body, seeing that the life is killed in him, and that all his flesh may be rotted" (*Il.* 19.23–27).[38]

The body abandoned to decomposition is the complete reversal, or inversion, of a beautiful death. At one extreme is the youthful and manly beauty of the warrior whose body inspires amazement, envy, and admiration, even among his enemies; at the other is that which surpasses ugliness, the monstrousness of a being become worse than nothing, of a form that has sunk into the unspeakable. On one side is the imperishable glory that raises the hero above the common fate by making his name and individual appearance endure in human memory. On the other side is an infamy more terrible than the oblivion and silence reserved for the ordinary dead, that indistinct cohort of the deceased normally dispatched to Hades where they merge into the mass of those who, unlike the "glorious heroes," are called the "nameless," the *nōnumnoi*.[39] The mutilated corpse shares neither in the silence that surrounds the ordinary dead nor in the song praising the heroic dead. Neither living, because it has been killed, nor dead, because it has been deprived of funeral rites; as a scrap of matter lost on the edge of existence, it represents that which can neither be celebrated nor forgotten—the horror of the indescribable, absolutely unspeakable, which cuts you off altogether from the living, the dead, and the self.

Achilles, the glorious warrior, the fighter for heroic honor, exerts all his energy in dishonoring the corpse of the Trojan champion, who was his opposite number in the enemy camp and who, by killing Patroklos, killed someone like Achilles' other self. The man of imperishable glory plans to doom his rival to the most extreme kinds of disgrace. He will not succeed. There is much talk in the *Iliad* of dead warriors surrendered to dogs and birds. But

[38] Cf. also *Il.* 22.509 and 24.414–15.

[39] Hes., *WD* 154; Aesch., *Pers.* 1003; cf. J.-P. Vernant, *Mythe et pensée chez les Grecs: Etudes de psychologie historique*, 10th ed. (Paris, 1985), 35, 68–69.

whenever threats of disfigurement are specified and abuse is committed, it involves a warrior whose body is ultimately saved. The horror of the disfigured corpse is evoked for Sarpedon, Patroklos, and Hektor—that is, for the three characters who share with Achilles the quality of a hero. In these three cases, the allusion to disfigurement leads, by a contrastive effect, to an emphasis on the beauty of a heroic death, which, in spite of everything, brings the dead man his tribute of immortal glory. When Sarpedon falls to Patroklos's spear, it is his valor and courage that induce the Achaeans to lay hold of him to abuse his corpse (*Il.* 16.545, 559). In the ensuing fracas, Sarpedon is already unrecognizable, covered as he is from head to foot with blood and dust. Zeus dispatches Apollo to wipe off the black blood, to wash him in the river's running water, to anoint him with ambrosia, to dress him in splendid garments, and to hand him over to Sleep and Death, who are to transfer him to Lycia. There his brothers and parents will bury him in a tomb, under a stele, "for this is the honor due to the dead [*to gar geras esti thanontōn*]" (*Il.* 16.667–75).

To counter Achilles' anxiety about the possibility that Patroklos's body may rot, eaten by worms, Thetis replies: "Even if he lies here for a full year, his flesh will remain always intact [*empedos*] or even better than before [*ē kai areion*]" (*Il.* 19.33). Supporting her words with deeds, the goddess infuses ambrosia and rosy nectar into Patroklos's nostrils, so his flesh may remain intact (*empedos, Il.* 19.38–39). During the whole time Achilles is relentlessly abusing Hektor's corpse, dragging it in the dust, giving it over to the feasting of dogs, Aphrodite drives the animals away from the dead man night and day. "She anoints him with divine oil, fragrant of roses, fearing that Achilles would tear off his skin by dragging him" (*Il.* 23.186–87). For his part, Apollo brings a dark mist from the heavens. "He did not want the heat of the sun to dry the skin too quickly around the muscles and the limbs" (*Il.* 23.190–91; 24.20–21). "Too quickly" means before the body is returned to Priam and undergoes the funeral rites that will send it into the hereafter intact, in the integrity of his beauty, *eumorphos*, as Aeschylus says in the *Agamemnon* about the bodies of the Greeks buried under the walls of Troy.[40] As he is making his way toward Achilles' tent, Priam meets Hermes, disguised as a young horseman. Priam asks him if his son has already been cut to pieces and thrown to the dogs. Hermes replies:

> Aged sir, neither have any dogs eaten him, nor have the birds, but he lies yet beside the ship of Achilles at the shelters, and as he was [*keinos*]; now here is the twelfth dawn he has lain there, nor does his flesh decay nor do worms feed on him. . . . It is true, Achilles drags him at random around his beloved companion's tomb . . . yet he cannot mutilate him [*oude min aischunei*]. You yourself can see

[40] The fallen Greeks rest *eumorphoi* in Trojan soil—so *Ag.* 454, which recalls the *eumorphoi kolossoi* of line 416.

[*thēoio ken autos*] when you go there how fresh with dew [*eerseēeis*] he lies, and
the blood is all washed from him, nor is there any corruption [*oude pothi miaros*].
So it is that the blessed immortals care for your son, though he is nothing but a
dead man; because in their hearts they loved him. (*Il.* 24.411–24)

In all three cases the scenario is about the same. The gods miraculously
save the hero from the shame of abuse that—by disfiguring, denaturing, his
body until it is no longer recognizable as his own, or even as a human body,
or even as a body at all—would reduce him to a state of nonbeing. To preserve
him as he was (*keinos*) when death took him on the battlefield, the gods perform the human rituals of cleansing and beautification but use divine unguents:
these elixirs of immortality preserve ''intact,'' despite all the abuse, that youth
and beauty, which can only fade on the body of a living man, but which death
in battle fixes forever on the hero's form, just as a stele remains erect forever
to mark a tomb.

Epic uses the theme of the disfigurement of the corpse to underscore the
exceptional position and status of heroic honor, of a beautiful death, of imperishable glory: they far surpass ordinary honor, death, and renown. In that agonistic culture, one proves one's worth only against another's, on top of and
to the detriment of a rival. As a result, the heroic qualities imply their opposite, a radical form of dishonor, as far beneath the norm as heroism is above
it: an absolute annihilation, a definitive and total disgrace.

With the constant allusions to bodies devoured by dogs or rotting in the sun,
the story uses the theme of the mutilated corpse to outline the place where the
double inversion of the beautiful death occurs. In the case of the hero, however, this vision of a person reduced to nothing, plunged into horror, is rejected at the very moment it is described. War, hatred, and destructive violence cannot prevail against those who are inspired by the heroic definition of
honor and are pledged to a short life. From the moment a great deed has been
accomplished, its truth cannot tarnish; it becomes the raw material of epic.
How could the body of the hero have been disfigured and his memory eradi-
cated? His fame lives in memory forever, and it inspires the direct vision of
the past that is the privilege of the epic poet. Nothing can spoil a beautiful
death: its aura stems from and continues to shine through the diffusion of epic
language, which speaks of glory and thus makes it real forever after. The
beauty of *kalos thanatos* does not differ from that of the song, which in celebrating such beauty transforms itself into deathless memory in the unbroken
chain of generations.

Chapter 3

INDIA, MESOPOTAMIA, GREECE: THREE IDEOLOGIES OF DEATH

IN ORGANIZING a joint colloquium on funerary ideology with our friends from the Istituto Orientale of Naples, our intention was to proceed together to two sorts of confrontations: first, between archaeological documents and written sources, and second, between different civilizations, especially Greek and those of the East.

These two different kinds of comparative studies could not quite mesh together. Each posed singular problems of method and substance. Above all, a notion of ideology was put into play that, according to the perspective adopted, entailed different implications and required strategies of research that in some respects were quite dissimilar.

The debate between archaeologists and historians of ancient societies in the field of funerary studies is well defined and its subject sufficiently precise. How can this mass of mute documents retrieved from tombs and necropolises be made to speak? What relations are there between this special "language" of *Realia* and that other, ordinary, language that historians, attuned to texts, have to know? To what extent does this dual documentation, once the necessary adjustments have been made, allow us access to society as a whole, with its stratifications, hierarchies, opposing categories of statuses, age-classes, and gender, and also, in the background, its history with its changing course? Bruno d'Agostino and Alain Schnapp undertook to present this array of questions.[1] My remarks will be limited, therefore, to another side of the inquiry. I will emphasize one point only. The objective in the line of research I have just outlined was to assemble, under the rubric of funerary ideology, all the significant elements that, in practices as in discourses pertaining to death, refer to forms of social organization and structures of the group, reflect the gaps, balances, and tensions within a community, and attest to its dynamic nature, the influences it has received, and the changes that have taken place. Through the grid of questions imposed on it, the world of the dead (or at least that which

This text was the introduction to the collective volume *La mort, les morts dans les sociétés anciennes*, ed. G. Gnioli and J.-P. Vernant (Cambridge and Paris, 1982), which contained the papers given in 1977 at a colloquium in Ischia on ancient funerary ideology. It was published as "Inde, Mésopotamie, Grèce: Trois idéologies de la mort," in *L'individu, la mort, l'amour: Soi-même et l'autre en Grèce ancienne*, 103–15. Translated by Froma I. Zeitlin.

[1] "Les morts entre l'objet et l'image," in Gnioli and Vernant, *La mort*, 17–27.

remains to us) emerges as the reflection and the more or less direct, more or less mediated, expression of the society of the living, sometimes even in travestied or fantastic form.

This aspect of our research is fundamental and every contribution is conscious of it to some degree. Nevertheless, when we shift from examining the funerary evidence that permits us to discover, as in a mirror, the profile of a society at a precise moment of its evolution and turn instead to compare the attitudes about death in two particular cultures, two different types of civilization, other problems arise. The concept of funerary ideology finds a much larger field of application and even, as we think, a new dimension. We no longer proceed from the universe of the dead to that of the living in order to find in the first the trace of the second. We depart from the society as a whole, in the sum of its practices, institutions, and beliefs and, using a multileveled analysis, we strive to discern the particular face conferred on death by that society. How does it position itself in relation to death—that is, during its existence in the present, in the image it forms of its past, and in its expectation of the future—in brief, in its traditions, its life, and its survival? What domains, what place did the members of that society assign to death? What is it that is subject to death; what escapes it, in individuals, in diverse groups, or in the whole of the social body? What significance, what role did that society find for it in the system of values whose task it is to assure at the same time not only the proper functioning of the social organization, but its duration, its permanence, and its continuous reproduction?

Every human group thinks of itself and aspires to be an organized whole—an order. It affirms itself as the world of culture: it is the "civilized" one. This is the measure by which the group defines itself in relation to everything that is deemed other than itself: chaos, the shapeless, the wild, and the barbarian. Similarly, each society must confront this radical alterity, this extreme absence of form, this nonbeing par excellence that comprises the phenomenon of death. Society must, in one way or another, integrate death into its mental universe and institutional practices. For a human group to establish a common past, to elaborate a collective memory, and to root the present of all its members in a "yesterday" that has vanished but must still be remembered and shared by all, means first conferring a social status on certain dead personages or on certain aspects of these personages. As a result of an appropriate funerary ritual, this status determines that, in their condition as the dead, they remain inscribed in the heart of present life, intervene here as the dead, and play their part in the mastery of social forces on which depend the equilibrium of the community and the permanence of its order.

Funerary ideology then no longer seems like that echo in which the society of the living would be duplicated. It defines the entire effort that makes use of the social imagination in order to develop an acculturation of death, to assimilate death by civilizing it, and to assure its "management" on the institutional level in keeping with a strategy adapted to the requirements of collective life. One might almost speak of a "politics" of death, which every social group must initiate and continue according to its own rules so it may affirm its own specific character and maintain itself in structure and orientation.

When we compare the great civilizations of the past from this point of view, what strikes us is the variety of responses they gave to these problems of the social integration of death. Each has in some way fabricated a death, sometimes several—to fit its own scale and preference. In this respect, the colloquium at Ischia will not have proved without value. It has opened certain paths of research. Without claiming to follow them all and limiting myself to the three cultural areas involved, I would like to propose here some brief remarks to which a comparison of Indian, Mesopotamian, and Greek facts concerning the status of death seems to lend itself.

From Brahmanic India to ancient Mesopotamia, the face of death changes so profoundly that in an essay on the historical typology of death, it is tempting to put these two social models at either end of the scale. The contrast is not limited to the fact that the ancient Mesopotamians assign to inhumation in their funerary practices the place and role the Indians reserve for incineration. Whether the corpse is buried in the ground or burned on a pyre, in both cases but by different procedures, a funerary scenario is initiated that proceeds on the model of a rite of passage. Death is treated as a change of state, an entry into a world other than that of the living, an access to an elsewhere. But according to the rite's modality, this alterity, this "otherness," is defined as opposite in locality, status, and function to the conditions of human life and society. Among the Mesopotamians, on the one hand, extreme care is expended in safeguarding the integrity of the corpse. Their concern is that the bones—the armature of the body, the imperishable foundation of each being— be preserved intact and subsist in that state in the underground dwelling place where the dead individual resides. For the Indians, on the other hand, their desire is to make the remains of the body disappear completely. They want to eradicate the slightest trace of what the living individual was here below so that, purified of his attachments to terrestrial existence and transmuted now into a sacrificial oblation, he may be reconstituted in a "space without limit." Once they are burned, the flesh and tendons are gathered up and mixed with ashes, together with whatever bits of bones that, even after a double cremation, can still be discerned. Then all is dispersed to vanish in the waters of a river, just as the dead person must disappear into the world beyond.

The attitudes both groups exhibit after the funeral confirm and continue these two opposite trends. The Mesopotamians show the same scrupulous and anxious attention for tombs, those nocturnal and subterranean enclosures reserved for the dead. They must take care that these remain immutably "in place," inviolate, maintained forever just as they are, preserved from pillage and destruction, and sheltered from anything that could alter their contents and trouble the peace of the dead in their new domain. The Indians, for their part, know no burials; they excavate neither tombs nor cenotaphs and erect no funerary monuments. Their dead are assigned no space; they have no location where their presence could be installed. Deprived of all territory, they are effectively nowhere.

These divergences correspond to other, more fundamental, differences. Through and despite the boundary that separates the dead from living, the Mesopotamian funerary "strategy" aims at maintaining a continuity between the subterranean and terrestrial worlds. Both the integrity of the skeleton and the presence in the tomb alongside the dead of objects that belong to him and are signs of his property highlight the tie attaching the dead person to what he was when alive, preserving for him even in the new state of death the marks of his old familial and social status. In the bones, in the tomb where they are deposited, and in the land that covers them, a continuity is maintained with the dead man's lineage and ethnic group, on the one hand, and on the other, with the territory where all his relatives, composed of the same substance as he, have their dwelling, together with their houses, cities, and cultures. Deep down in their graves, the dead thus constitute the roots that, in giving the human group its point of anchorage in the land, assures its stability in space and its continuity in time. When a victor undertakes to destroy an enemy nation or to reduce it to servitude, he must first tear it away from its dead; that is, he must extirpate its roots. The tombs are opened and violated; the bones are crushed, pulverized, and dispersed to the four winds. The moorings of these people are broken; their communities drift aimlessly. Like a cadaver deprived of burial and thrown to the wild beasts, whose ghost, lacking the power to enter the kingdom of the dead, is condemned to wander without end, these communities are sentenced to aimlessness, marginality, and chaos. In the Mesopotamian outlook, a society cut off from its dead no longer has a place on the stage of terrestrial space. With its uprooting, it loses its stability, consistency, and cohesion.

Paradoxically, the Indian politics of death tends, in its essentials, to achieve a break of precisely this kind: to tear the deceased away from the social identity he had when alive, to cut him off from the community of which he was a part, to efface his presence from the earthly space where his group is implanted. Funerary cremation does not only function as a sacrifice. It is the model of the entire sacrificial activity that finds its end and its meaning in this terminal oblation in which one makes a gift of oneself. Everything happens as if the ensemble of ritual practices and the social order itself had no object other than to prepare for this last act, this final passage, where the individual, in order to complete himself, to reach his "perfection" in the sacrificial fire, must disappear in respect to everything he was, in the complete effacement of the personal acts and social ties that constituted him in his particularity.

In rooting themselves in their dead, the Mesopotamians linked the stability of human society to a strict delimitation of territory, to an organization con-trolled by a space occupied by a sedentary population. For them, what was menacing and evil was represented as a figure of wandering, of a formless expanse: realms of nomadism and exile, of desert and of outermost bound-aries. In this way terrestrial and human order was valorized. This was what had to be maintained. The condition of "perfection" for both individual and groups resided in its integrity.

The Mesopotamian ideology of death operates in the framework of a reli-gion of the "intraworldly" type where the essential is the correct administra-tion of existence here below. Life is accepted, recognized, and exalted for itself, not as preparation for a death, which, far from completing the individ-ual, leads him to an impoverished and diminished existence: the shadow of what he was when alive. The positive content of life, that which gives it its worth, the religious values incarnated there, do not come from the subterra-nean world—from the dead, from the darkness. Present among mortal crea-tures in a necessarily limited and degraded form, what is good belongs to the gods on high, to the heavens, and to the light of day.

There is one figure, however, whose status and functions at the summit of the Mesopotamian social edifice place him at the margin of the common run of folk; this is the king. His task is precisely to assure the extension of divine blessings over the whole of the territory he rules. It is through him that the brilliance of the gods on high can illuminate the existence of those other hu-man beings destined to return to the earth from which they came. Thus in the case of the king, it is not sufficient to bestow a surplus of magnificence upon his funeral and his subterranean dwelling place. Because he is the intercessor, the mediator with heaven, his corpse is not laid to rest at the bottom of his tomb, but after his death is kept standing upright in the form of a statue that is erected in the palace or in the temples. An immortal body is made for him in a precious material whose unchanging brilliance reflects the plenitude of life that only the gods possess.

As for the Brahmanic Indian communities, they do not seek to implant their permanence in the earth but find their roots instead in the world beyond. Col-lective life and the social order, both strictly ritualized, have value only to the extent that they aim from the beginning to be transcended, that they are a prelude to another level of existence, to a different domain of reality. Death is not the interruption of life, nor its enfeeblement, its mere shadow. It consti-tutes the horizon without which the course of existence, for both persons and groups, would have no direction, meaning, or value. To integrate the individ-ual into the community, to assign him his exact place, role, and status, is to fix the order of stages that in this world allow him to exit from it step by step, to free himself from it in order to rejoin the absolute.

Indian funerary ideology can only be understood as part of a religion whose orientation is essentially "extraworldly." Under these conditions, the outstanding individual can no longer be a king or any other personage whose function is calibrated to the totality of the social body. This person is one who, having excluded himself from society—its norms and rites—has discovered in his lifetime how to unbind himself from life and attain the "perfection" ordinarily acquired in cremation on the funeral pyre: namely, the person who renounces. Having been "roasted" in the fire of his asceticism, he realizes on this earth and in his person the goal toward which the ritualization of the whole of social life tends and which can only be gained by this route at the endpoint of death. Contrary to the ordinary dead, the cadaver of the renouncer has no need to be burned; it is so already. Consequently, he is buried in the ground, in the seated posture of meditation, with his head erect. A tumulus is built above his grave as a center of pilgrimage. The difference here from the usual funerary practices is very striking. In the distance that opens up between the two, one might be tempted to connect the funeral treatment accorded the Indian renouncer with the practices applied in Mesopotamia to the ordinary dead, who, like him, are buried, and also to the king, whose head, like his own, is placed in a vertical position. In reality, however, these analogies only highlight the contrast between the two strategies of death. The localized tomb of the renouncer provides a root for the community, but this group is not a social one. Neither family, nor ethnic group, nor caste, this collective partakes of a wholly different order that marks a spiritual, not a hereditary, bond. Above all, interment instead of cremation signifies that the renouncer, once delivered from life and brought back to the absolute in the world below, incarnates in the heart of Indian society the whole notion of wandering, that utter solitude—the status radically outside society—in which the Mesopotamians saw a form of misfortune and evil. What Indian society, in its functioning, structures, and practices, relegates to the extreme limits of its horizon as the ultimate goal of its order, is the very thing that, for the Mesopotamians, represents a power of confusion and a force of social chaos.

What place should we assign the Greeks in relation to these two contrasting ideologies of death? If one relies on the evidence of epic to construct a model of heroic death, one that leaves a lasting imprint on Hellenic culture, the Greeks seem close to the Indians in their custom of burning corpses on a pyre. But a fundamental difference immediately leaps to mind. Once the fire is extinguished, the Greeks pick out the remains of the bones, not to scatter them as the Indians do, but to collect them and carefully preserve them in a container. These vestiges of the corpse that the flame has purified of any corruptible element are placed in a grave beneath the earth. On the other hand, through the place occupied from now on by his remains, the dead person, as among the Mesopotamians, is thought to remain closely bound to a specific locale. Moreover, the erection of a tumulus surmounted with a dressed stone or an embedded post emphasizes the desire to inscribe the presence of the dead person even on the surface of the soil and to indicate this fact to the living for

all time. Would we therefore situate the Greeks in the middle, halfway between India and Mesopotamia? Not at all. They worked out a funerary ideology that can be deciphered as their particular social strategy for treating the
dead. This strategy is very much their own and, in comparison with the two
preceding cultures, situates the Greeks not in the middle, but quite clearly
elsewhere.

Several contributions to this colloquium on comparative funeral practices
treat the problems of Greek death in its particularities, in what remains constant and what is transformed from the archaic to the Hellenistic periods. One
piece[2] traces the line of evolution that leads from the "beautiful dead" of epic,
from the corpse of the young warrior lying in glory on the battlefield, to the
abstraction of the civic "beautiful death," where, in the realm of the social
imagination, with every shadow and contradiction removed, is expressed the
ideal representation that the Athenian democracy of the fifth century desired
to make of itself.

I will therefore restrict myself here to selecting a few of the features that
separate the Greeks from the Indians and Mesopotamians and that shed light
on the originality of their position with regard to death. Two elements are
especially important in this respect: the first concerns the role of memory, the
second, the place of the individual, envisaged in the uniqueness of his biography.

Alongside the mass of ordinary dead, burned collectively on the pyre, destined for anonymity and nonremembrance, as among the Indians, Greek epic
portrays the figure of exceptional personages who, in and through their deaths,
obtain what among humans constitutes the consecration of excellence, the
prize of perfection—an imperishable glory. *Menos* (ardor) and the heroic virtue that animates these men destine them in advance to die in combat in the
flower of their youth, and by the same token, remove them from the decrepitude of old age as from that silence in which the name of the common dead
founders, irremediably effaced in oblivion. The heroes endure so as to live
forever in the collective memory as exemplary personages, models whom the
commemoration of poetic song continues to transmit and actualize throughout
successive generations. In the status of the glorious dead that remembrance
confers on them in its two institutional forms—the memory of song, indefinitely repeated, and the memorial of the funerary monument, forever visible
to the eyes—the heroes acquire a social reality and a symbolic efficaciousness
that the society of the living cannot do without. By the grand deeds they accomplished, the glory they obtained in dying, they constitute the "men of
yesteryear." They are the "past" of the group, the background of present life.
They are the roots, but no longer, as in Mesopotamia, of the different familial

[2] Nicole Loraux, "Mourir devant Troie, tomber pour Athènes: De la gloire du héros à l'idée de
la Cité," in Gnioli and Vernant, *La mort*, 27–45.

lines. They are rather the roots of a cultural tradition that cements a community through which it recognizes itself, because it is through the exploits of these dead heroes, as they are continually recalled, that social existence in its "civilized" form takes its meaning and value in the eyes of the living.

In Greece, then, the same strategy for dealing with death both inspires the treatment of the corpse and presides over the development of oral epic. In the first case it is a matter of giving the individual who has lost his life access to a new condition of social existence, to transform his disappearance—his absence—from the universe of the living into a positive and stable state: the status of the dead. In the second instance, this strategy is designed to inscribe the presence of certain of the dead at the center of communal life. By turning that ultimate trial in which the hero loses his life into the criterion of perfection, into the touchstone of excellence, the essential values and social virtues appropriate to this world here below are enhanced. Heroic death sublimates and transforms these qualities and confers on them a brilliance, a permanence, and a resistance to destruction that they do not enjoy in the duration of present existence.

Compared to the common run of men, the hero is a being apart, who can be included in the same category as the renouncer in India and the Mesopotamian king. But he has his own way of being exceptional. If he tries to complete himself—if he is in quest of plenitude—he does not follow the line of renunciation, of flight from the world, by eradicating his acts and cutting himself off from society. Rather, this "plenitude" lies in pushing to its extreme point the logic of human action and life. Through his great deeds, the hero incarnates here below on this earth an ideal of perfection that carries "worldly" values and social practices beyond their mundane reality. The life of the hero is indeed his own and remains so even to the far end of death, because it is in the confrontation with death that his life reveals his authentic essence. The character of the hero, by the exacting rigor of his life story and the uncompromising demands of his *arete*, confers a new dimension on the usual norms of collective life and habits of the group. He inaugurates a form of honor and virtue that outstrips ordinary honor and virtue.

It is also not his status and role in the social body, his function as king, that, as in the case of the Mesopotamian monarch, earn the hero a special death. Rather, it is the series of exploits that have made him what he is and that, even though he is sometimes in overt conflict with the community of his peers and its recognized leaders, give him the uniqueness of a personal destiny.

One of the original features of Greek cities—this "political" humanity—is that, having passed from prince to hero, they used a dead character as a social symbol and communal model, one who is defined no longer by his family ties or his position in the group but rather by his career in life, which is his very own, and by the particular form of existence he himself has chosen and which remains always linked to his name.

Differently used and oriented according to the sociopolitical context, this symbolism of a memorable individual's "beautiful death" underwent transpositions and transformations whose study is no longer a matter for comparative synchronic analysis of different models of civilization, but rather for a historical inquiry that situates funerary ideology in the framework of a society as a whole at any given moment of its development.

What this means is that the two different perspectives adopted in this colloquium, as earlier outlined, are far from being mutually exclusive, but are really complementary. In each case, one must be confronted with the other so they may be combined.

At the end of this preface, I will not feel I have finished without a last observation that displaces and extends the debate further. My remarks, inspired by Laurence Kahn and Nicole Loraux, are intended to emphasize that no human discourse has ever finished speaking of death, this mute object that brings everything to an end. I mean death in its proper sense, which must be distinguished from the dead, who are easier to acclimatize on an ideological terrain.

To take the example of the Greeks, one finds in epic, at the very core of the song that glorifies the heroic "splendid" dead and represents them as the model of completed man, some passages that directly challenge the imagery of death implied in funerary institutions. Despite the coherence and compactness of the edifice that structures the celebration of the dead, a negation suddenly opens a gap in which death is profiled as the opposite of all that has been said of it. Contrasted with the Achilles of the *Iliad*, the hero who chose a brief life to win imperishable glory in the memory of men, is the Achilles of the *Odyssey* who, in the underworld, delivers this last message to Odysseus: the most miserable, the most wretched life in the light of the sun is worth more than this existence that he leads from now on, honored by all, in the kingdom of the shades. In counterpoint to the Muses of the *Iliad*, whom the bard invokes so that through his verses he may revive the great deeds of heroes before his listeners, are those other singers and musicians, those "counter-Muses," who are the Sirens of the Odyssean episode. Their song has the same charm as that of the daughters of Memory and they also dispense a knowledge one cannot forget. But whoever yields to the seduction of their voices, to the temptation of the knowledge they possess, does not enter there to live forever in the splendor of eternal renown. Instead, he reaches a shore "bleached white with bones of men rotted away, and the skin shriveling upon them."

If it is given to the living man to hear in advance the song that will tell of his remembered glory, what he discovers is not a "splendid death" and immortal renown, but the horror of a corpse and its decomposition: a frightful death. Death is a threshold. To speak of the dead, to memorialize them, sing of their exploits, and evoke them in words and in celebration, is the affair of the living. Beyond the threshold, on the other side, a face of terror: the unspeakable.

Chapter 4

PANTA KALA: FROM HOMER TO SIMONIDES

HEKTOR has fallen before the walls of Troy. His corpse lies in the dust. All the Greeks crowd around his inert body, one to plunge his lance into it, another his sword. This scene of cruel violence is accompanied by the poet's comment: "The Achaeans admired the bearing and enviable beauty of Hektor [*hoi kai thēēsanto phuēn kai eidos agēton Hektoros*]" (*Il*. 22.370). An astonishing formula and one that might seem out of place, had not Priam given us the key to it just a little before. In order to dissuade his son from confronting Achilles outside the walls, the old king contrasts two ways of dying in war. And the contrast between the two types of death illuminates the fundamental aspects of the heroic ideal and the hero as the epic presents them. War brings the old man a pitiable, degrading death, which casts him, whatever his rank, into a state of ugliness, *to aischron*, and subjects him to a kind of dreadful ridicule whereby he loses, along with the dignity of his age, his status as a man. On the other hand, Priam declares, for the young man, the *neos*, fallen in the battle fray of Ares, his body torn by the sharp bronze, everything is seemly, *pant'epeioiken*, everything becomes him. In what he displays in death, *panta kala*, everything is beautiful (*Il*. 22.71–73).

Why and in what way is everything beautiful when it comes to the corpse of a young warrior sprawled in the dust, covered with blood and wounds? It is because a warrior's death, a bloody death, when it results from a confrontation willingly undertaken in order to prove one's valor, is like a photographic developer that reveals in the person of the fallen warrior the eminent quality of an *anēr agathos*; it shows on his *sōma*—that identifiable corporeal entity he has become now that he is dead—and this quality shines in its beauty on his body. What is more, as long as one is in the flower of youth, there is no other way to acquire, as one does at the end of an initiation, this set of values and virtues for which the elite of the *aristoi* strive, except to dedicate oneself wholly to war, deeds of valor, and death.

Such is indeed Achilles' point of view. In his view, a rigid boundary separates the authentic hero from the rest of men, independent of any question of status and rank, of social function and preeminence. Agamemnon may well be the most kingly among all the kings. Nevertheless, he has not crossed the

Published originally as "*Panta kala*: D'Homère à Simonide," *ASNSP*, ser. 3, vol. 9 (1979): 1365–74, and reprinted in *L'individu, la mort, l'amour: Soi-même et l'autre en Grèce ancienne* (Paris, 1989), 91–101. Translated by Froma I. Zeitlin.

boundary to the heroic world. As Achilles tells him, the warrior's ordeal, which is the daily bread of the hero, "seems to you like death [*to de toi kēr eidetai einai*]" (*Il.* 1.228). The hero is one who, by fighting in the front ranks, has chosen to live in order to risk his life at each encounter—his mortal life, his *psuchē*—which, by contrast to all the goods of this world, all the ordinary honors and dignities of state that one can always regain, buy back, or exchange, can never be recovered once it has been lost (*Il.* 9.408–9). It is his own self in the totality of his heroic destiny that the warrior engages and puts at stake when he risks his *psuchē* (*Il.* 9.322). Life for him has no other horizon than death in combat. Only this kind of death lets him accede to a state of glory. The fame that is henceforth attached to his name and his person represents the conclusion of honor, its extreme point; it is *aretē* completed and accomplished. In a beautiful death, excellence no longer has to be measured indefinitely against others and keep proving itself in confrontation; it is realized at one stroke and forever in the exploit that puts an end to the life of the hero.

The case of Achilles is exemplary in this regard. The dilemma that marks his destiny from the beginning has a paradigmatic value: either a long life at home, in peace, and the absence of all glory; or a short life, a swift death, and imperishable glory, *kleos aphthiton*. Hektor too knows it well. When he perceives that his own day has come, that the fatal *kēr* has already laid its hand on him, it is then he decides to face it in order to transform his death into an imperishable glory and to turn the lot that is common to all creatures who are subject to death into a benefit that is his own and whose brilliance will belong to him for ever. "No, I don't intend to perish without a fight or without glory [*akleiōs*] or without some exploit which men in the future will come to know through its telling [*essomenoisi puthesthai*]" (*Il.* 22.304–5).

In a culture like that of archaic Greece where each person exists as a function of others, in the gaze and through the eyes of others, the true, the only death is oblivion, silence, and obscure indignity. To exist, whether living or dead, is to be recognized, esteemed, and honored. Above all, it is to be glorified, to be the object of praise, to become *aoidimos*, worthy of a song that recounts a destiny admired by all in an act that is continually renewed and repeated. Through the glory the hero has won in dedicating his life to combat, he inscribes his reality as an individual subject in the collective memory. He expresses himself in a life story that death, by putting an end to it, has made permanent and unchanging.

The structural links between excellence achieved, a brief life, a beautiful death, and imperishable glory can only be understood in the context of an oral poetry that celebrates the *klea andrōn proterōn*. Through the memory of song and in the form of praise, it constitutes the collective past in which a community takes root and through its continuity recognizes the permanence of its values.

In this sense, epic is not only a literary genre. Together with the funeral and following the same lines as the funeral, it is one of the institutions the Greeks developed to give an answer to the problem of death in order to acculturate death and integrate it into social thought and life.

It must therefore be recognized that the heroic "beautiful death" contains a metaphysical or religious dimension. This is particularly evident in the remarks of Sarpedon to Glaukos in book 12 of the *Iliad*. After having explained that all the material privileges and all the honors accorded them by the Lycians are the price they are paid for their exceptional valor, Sarpedon adds an observation that unveils the true extent of the heroic engagement and brushes aside as mere trivialities all the arguments of a utilitarian kind or of the prestige he had at first invoked. "If surviving this war," he says, "would permit us to live indefinitely without knowing either old age or death [*agērō t' athanatō te*], I would certainly not go out to fight in the van nor would I send you to battle where a man wins glory. . . . But since no one can escape death, let us go, and either let us give the glory to another or let another give it to us" (12.322–28). It is therefore not a matter of earthly possessions, the marks of honor in this world—all those advantages enjoyed during one's lifetime but that will be lost when one loses one's life. These are not what incite a warrior to risk his *psuchē* in battle. The true reason for the heroic exploit lies elsewhere; it depends on the human condition, which the gods have willed to be subject to the decrepitude of old age and death. The deed of valor is rooted in the desire to escape both of these conditions. The way to get beyond death is to make it the stakes of a life, which thereby acquires an exemplary value and which men to come will celebrate forever as a model. The way to escape old age is by dying in the flower of one's youth, at the acme of one's virile strength. Through death the hero is now fixed forever in the brilliance of an unchanging youth. In the mirror of the song that reflects his glory, he knows nothing of old age even as he avoids the anonymity of death. Hence amidst all the warriors who die, whatever their age may be, Homer reserves the following formula only for authentic heroes, like Patroklos and Hektor, even though both of them are far from being youthful: "His *psuchē* flew off to Hades, leaving behind its vigor and youth [*androtēta kai hēbēn*]" (*Il.* 16.857; 22.363).

The "youth" (*hēbē*) that, along with their lives, Patroklos and Hektor leave behind them, and which they therefore incarnate more fully than other *kouroi* who are less advanced in age than they are, is the quality with which Achilles, because of his short life, is forever invested. *Hēbē*, this supreme power, this *megiston kratos*, manifests itself in the living active warrior through its vigor, power, speed, fortitude, and élan. Over the corpse of the hero, who lies there without strength and life, the brilliance of youth shines in the exceptional beauty of the now inert body, which, in the immobility of its form, has become a pure object of vision, a spectacle for others.

Let us turn now to the other side, to the hideous face of a warrior's death.

The aged Priam does not only envision himself struck down at the gates of his palace, a combatant no longer to be met on the battlefield, but rather as a prey to be brought to ground. He describes himself devoured by his own dogs, who in an instant turn savage to feed on his flesh and devour his genitals. "Is there any sight more pitiable than when an old man is dead and down, and the dogs mutilate his gray head and gray beard and his private parts?" (*Il.* 22.74–76). What Priam evokes is the reverse of a beautiful death—the dignity of the old man turned into an object of mockery in its ugliness and shame, the destruction of all that is human in a corpse. Bloody death, beautiful and glorious when it strikes in the fullness of youth, raises the hero above the human condition in marking him with the sign of a man of courage (*agathos anēr*). The same death, when an old man undergoes it, reduces him to a subhuman state. In and by the degradation of his corpse, it makes him into a horrible monstrosity.

This final nightmare, which Priam fears, is that which each combatant, when blinded by hatred, dreams of inflicting on his enemy. When a warrior has fallen in battle, the two camps struggle to lay their hands on his body. What do his friends want? In giving him the *geras thanontōn*—that is, in having him pass through the entire funeral ritual from the exhibition of his body, now adorned, washed, anointed with oil, and perfumed, to the cremation of the corpse and the erection of a *sēma* to recall his memory for men to come [*essomenoisi puthesthai*] (the same formula applies to the funerary memorial as to epic song)—the friends of the deceased expect to ensure forever his status as one of the beautiful dead, a glorious hero. And what do his enemies want? In doing outrage to his remains, in delivering him to dogs and birds to be devoured raw, in leaving him to rot without burial, they want to deprive the enemy not of life—that has already happened—but of death. They would bar his access to that beautiful death he has earned by dying fully armed, the best death a warrior can wish for.

To the *panta kala* (everything is beautiful), to the *pant' epeoiken* (everything is seemly) of the young warrior whose virile beauty, heightened by wounds and blood, strikes even his enemies with astonishment and envy—to these is strictly opposed, even in the vocabulary, the body of the one whom maltreatment has reduced to being nothing and no one: neither alive because one has killed him, nor dead since, deprived of his funeral, he has not had his "part of the fire." He is just a bit of refuse lost on the margins of existence, a form that has sunk down into the unnameable: total ugliness, total infamy. We spoke of vocabulary. On the one hand, *pant' epeoiken*, on the other, with an alpha privative, its denial: the Homeric *aeikeiē*, the action of *aekizein*, that is to say, the substitution of *aischron* (ugly) for *kalon* (beautiful). To *aekizein* is to *aischunein*, to make ugly, to abase.

One of the functions during the funeral rite of cremation on the pyre is to preserve the *panta kala*. This is done by sending into the world beyond a corpse still intact in the integrity of its form and its beauty, or as Aeschylus puts it in the *Agamemnon* apropos of the dead Greeks buried on Trojan soil, the *eumorphoi* (those of fair figure). What the fire of the funeral pyre consumes so as to leave nothing but the bones, the *ostea leuka*, are the entrails, tendons, and flesh, everything in the body that will decompose. If a man is to retain in death his beauty, youth, and virility as qualities permanently attached to his person, his remains must cease to exist in the world of the here and now. They must disappear from the eyes of the living (*Il*. 22.53) just as the hero must have ceased to live on this earth.

In the strategy for dealing with death, funerary rites and epic poetry share certain parallels and continuities, but epic goes much further. Through glorious praise, a small minority of the elect (by contrast to those "without names" who are the ordinary dead) are assured the permanence of their names, their renown, and the exploits they accomplished. In this way praise completes and crowns the process that the funeral in its own way had already engaged: to transform an individual who has lost his life, who has ceased to be, into the figure of a character whose presence as one who has died remains forever inscribed in the memory of the group.

Aikia, despoilment, is to the funerary ceremony what blame is to praise. If poetic eulogy, like the funeral, aims to install the beautiful dead man in perpetual glory, its inverse—blame, fault-finding, spiteful derision (*psogos*, *mōmos*, *phthonos*)—seeks to produce the contrary effect: to tarnish his value, make ugly his beauty, and debase the person in just the same way as *aikia* despoils the corpse of the abhorred enemy. Gregory Nagy has well demonstrated that already in Homer, as in the later poetic tradition, the vocabulary of blame assimilates the malicious and the envious to those dogs Priam imagined hurling themselves on his corpse to tear it to pieces.[1] Through insult and invective, one devours the hero (*daptō*, *haptomai*); one feeds and grows fat on him; one gorges oneself and feeds on hateful words. Under the bite (*dakos*) of ill-speaking, as under the teeth of vultures, the *panta kala* of the beautiful dead that praise has established forever is degraded and corrupted: only the *aischron* remains.

II

This positioning of the different elements that constitute the heroic beautiful death and fix its status in epic allows us, I think, to explain certain aspects of Simonides' poem to Scopas that are found at the end of his text: "Everything is beautiful [*panta toi kala*] there where nothing is vile [*aischra*], nothing is mingled." This verse recalls and replies to the *panta kala* of Priam's speech, even though, as many have noted, the poem, in its displacements and trans-

---

[1] *The Best of the Achaeans: Concepts of the Hero in Archaic Greek Poetry* (Baltimore, 1979), 59–97.

positions, also echoes Tyrtaeus (frag. 10; frag. 7 Prato).[2] At the end of the sixth century, praise is no longer concerned with the hero of old; it does not sing of the exploits of men whom death has endowed with another dimension, who belong to the world beyond and no longer have any reality in this world other than that imperishable glory with which the memory of the song invests them. From now on the poet celebrates a living individual to whom he is bound by a personal relationship of *philia*. He glorifies him in a language and in a use of comparisons that refer to heroic characters and legends. The slippage takes place not only between a relative excellence that can always be revoked and that, like everything human, is subject to *sumphora* (chance), and an excellence, as illustrated by the heroic feat, that is wholly fulfilled and realized forever.

Simonides' recall and testing of Pittakos's formula is intimately linked in the text, as Gentili has edited it, to the problem of praise and blame.[3] "It is difficult to become an authentically exemplary man [*andr' agathon alatheōs genesthai*], foursquare [*tetragōnon*] in his arms and legs and in his thought, fashioned without blame, without reproach [*aneu psogou tetugmenon*]." As Jesper Svenbro has shown,[4] to become an *anēr agathos, aneu psogou tetugmenos*, is to gain access to a form of imperishable glory through the eulogy that celebrates one's excellence. This glory is analogous to that which the memory of epic song confers on the hero or to what the funerary memorial accomplishes for certain of those who have died, when it is in the form of a sculpted stele representing a *kouros*, like the twin *kouroi* of Cleobis and Biton erected by the Argives at the beginning of the sixth century, *hōs andrōn aristōn genomenōn* (Herod. 1.31.) Like the monumental figure of the dead man, the poetic eulogy gives stability and permanence to one who is otherwise subject to vicissitude. It fixes individual success, good fortune, or merit into a continuity of existence, which, by contrast to the heroic exploit, seem in this period to be fugitive, inconstant, and ephemeral events in the drift of circumstances.

It is no longer a question of finding in the course of a human life an excellence that is fulfilled, a success that is completed, like those consecrated by means of a beautiful death. Success is managed by the gods and they dispense it as they wish, offering it to some men only because they love them (*phileōsin*). However lucky, powerful, or rich one may be, one can never count on obtaining such a privilege—and even less so, on keeping it. To be *esthlos* or

[2] See, most recently, A.W.H. Adkins, "Callinus 1 and Tyrtaeus 10 as Poetry," *HSCP* 81 (1977): 59–97.

[3] Bruno Gentili, "Studi su Simonide," *Maia* 16 (1964): 297. The fragment in question is 37/52 in *PMG* 282–83.

[4] *La parole et le marbre: Aux origines de la poétique grecque* (Lund, 1976). Reference is made here to the Italian version, completed and revised, trans. P. Rosati, under the title *La parola e il marmo: Alle origini della poetica graeca* (Turin, 1984), 125–45.

agathos anēr permanently and forever is therefore not just difficult, as Pittakos claims. It is impossible. Only divinity possesses this "part of honor," this *geras*. Neither is it the heroic exploit and its immortalizing value that, for a poet like Simonides, will define the *agathos anēr*, whom he must build up like a solid and stable statue by granting him the memory of song. But if along with success, the god gives the *aristeia* of an achievement that is definitively concluded, the poet, for his part, bestows praise (*epainēmi*) on those he loves (*phileō*), and this is what makes them "become" *alatheōs andres agathoi*. That is, he authenticates them in people's memory as though they were exemplary men. For this to happen, it is necessary and sufficient that the one the poet is charged with celebrating has, of his own will, done nothing that is base, low, or ugly (*aischron*); then one can sing of his beauty.

This play of *kalon* and *aischron* recalls with a polemic point the contrast which Tyrtaeus, echoing Homer, had rigorously posed between the one who has "become *anēr agathos* in war," and those whose life is plunged into ugliness. According to Tyrtaeus, the outstretched corpse with the point of a lance in his back is ugly. Ugly too is the bloody and stripped corpse of the old man fallen in the place of the young. By contrast, the death of the young, fallen in the first ranks, is beautiful, as a man of courage (*agathos anēr*) who faces the enemy. For the body of that man, desired by women and admired by men as long as he was alive, everything is decorous, everything becomes beautiful, when he lies on the battlefield. That Simonides refers to this tradition, which is directly rooted in epic, is particularly evident in fragment 531 where he himself alludes to "that burial of brave men [*andrōn agathōn*], whose death is beautiful [*kalos ho potmos*]." But he does so in order to distance himself from the heroic ideal just as he does in the poem to Scopas. To inaugurate his praise, he demands neither the more-than-human perfection of a total success, nor the transfiguration of death into glory, nor the totally irreproachable life of the hero *panamōmos*. He demands a virtue adjusted to the city's standards, that of a man of good sense, *hugiēs anēr*, who is neither wicked nor clumsy and who knows a "justice useful to the city." It is this man, his close friend, whom he will celebrate if the man has done nothing disgraceful willingly (*hekōn*). No blame will mingle in with his praise (*ou min ego mōmasomai*), even if the individual whose merit he boasts of is not totally "irreproachable." A eulogy without envy like this one[5] and the absence of any element of blame or reproach normally define the attitude toward the dead rather than toward the living, because the deceased have become as though "consecrated" by a death that has separated them from the human domain of conflicts and enmities.[6] But this time, it is not because the hero is fulfilled and sacralized by his death

---

[5] Cf. Pind., *Ol*. 11.7, and schol. ad *Nem*. 7.61–63.

[6] Cf. Archil., frag. 83 Lasserre-Bonnard, already expressed in *Od*. 22.412; Demos., *Vs. Boeot.* 11.49, *Vs. Lept*. 104; Isoc., *Yoke* 22, *Antid*. 101; and Plut., *Solon* 21.1.

that blame no longer has a place. The *panta kala* reserved by Homer and Tyrtaeus for the warrior fallen in combat in the flower of his youth is transformed in Simonides into the *panta kala* that applies in all cases where the glorified personage, without being *panamōmos*—a quality that belongs only to the gods—has done nothing *aischron* that can be imputed to him personally. "Everything is beautiful where no villainy is mixed in." Blame need not be mingled with praise in those cases where ugliness is not mingled with his actions. Then *panta kala* and the praise of the poet, the commissioned singer in the city, can be expressed in the language and forms made for memorializing the heroic exploit, for singing of the men of long ago, the warriors fallen in combat: the beautiful dead.

By this readjustment of the system of values, the accord in commemorative poetry between the spoken and the real is not truly broken. The poet can celebrate, praise, and construct his memorial of "imperishable glory" because the *agathos anēr* is no longer defined by the demands of the heroic ideal. The "purity" of the praise is embedded in the purity of an *aretē* that appears glorious and memorable when nothing *aischron* has been mixed in with it.

At the turning point of the sixth and fifth centuries, glorious memorialization, inherited from epic, expresses in the form of the *enkōmion* (the eulogy) those new aspects that excellence and exemplary status have now acquired in the framework of the civic community.

PART TWO

Gender

Chapter 5

FEMININE FIGURES OF DEATH IN GREECE

To SPEAK of death, Greek uses a masculine noun: Thanatos. In figural representations Thanatos appears, together with his brother Hupnos, Sleep, as a man in the prime of life, wearing a helmet and armor.[1] Lifting up the corpse of a hero fallen on the field of battle and bearing it off to a distant place so that it may receive funeral honors, the two divine brothers can be distinguished from ordinary warriors only by the wings they wear on their shoulders. There is nothing terrifying and even less that is monstrous about this figure of Thanatos, whose role is not to kill but to receive the dead, to transport the one who has lost his (or her) life. In visual art and epic representations, this virile Thanatos can even assume the form of the warrior who has been able to find the perfect fulfillment of his life in what the Greeks call ''a beautiful death.'' As a result of his exploits—in and through his heroic death—the warrior fallen on the front line of battle remains forever present in men's lives and memories. Epic continually celebrates his name and sings of his imperishable glory; sixth-century steles present him on his tomb for public viewing, forever standing erect in the flower of his youth, in the brilliance of his virile beauty.

The masculine figure of Thanatos therefore does not seem to incarnate the terrible destructive force that descends on human beings to destroy them, but rather that state other than life, that new condition to which funeral rites offer men access and from which none can escape, since, born of a mortal race, all must one day take leave of the light of the sun to be delivered over to the world of darkness and Night.

In its fearful aspect, as a power of terror expressing the unspeakable and unthinkable—that which is radically ''other''—death is a feminine figure who takes on its horror: the monstrous face of Gorgo, whose unbearable gaze transforms men into stone. And it is another feminine figure, Ker—black, grim, evil, horrible, execrable—who represents death as a maleficent force that

A first version of this text appeared in *Lettre Internationale* 6 (1985): 45–48, under the title ''La douceur amère de la condition humaine.'' A revised and extended version with notes was published as ''Figures féminines de la mort en Grèce'' in *L'individu, la mort, l'amour: Soi-même et l'autre en Grèce ancienne* (Paris, 1989), 131–52. The English translation appeared in *Diacritics* 16 (1986): 54–64. Translated there by Anne Doueihi, now revised and corrected by Froma I. Zeitlin.

[1] For example, red-figured Attic kraters, New York 1972–11–10, Louvre G 163. On this subject see D. von Bothmer, ''The Death of Sarpedon,'' in *The Greek Vase*, ed. S. L. Hyatt (New York, 1981), 63–80.

sweeps down on humans to destroy them, and who, thirsting for their blood, swallows them to engulf them in that night in which, as fate ordains it, they will perish.

Certainly, Thanatos is not "peaceful and ever gentle to mortals," as is his brother, Sleep. According to Hesiod, Thanatos has a "heart of iron, an implacable soul of bronze," but, as the poet quickly makes clear, it is because "he holds forever the man he has taken" (*Theog.* 764–66). No one escapes Thanatos; no one returns from his dwelling place. Even cunning Sisyphos, who twice succeeds in tricking Thanatos, finally has to pass through the dire experience. Thanatos is inexorable, but the picture painted of Ker is altogether different. In the *Iliad*, the "destructive Ker" is depicted in full action on Achilles' shield: "She carries a warrior, still alive in spite of his fresh wounds, or another still unhurt, or one already dead whom she drags by his feet through the carnage, and on her shoulders she wears a robe stained red by men's blood" (*Il.* 18.535ff.). The author of the *Shield*, a poem attributed to Hesiod, describes the same scene, but elaborates the description:

> Their white teeth clattering, the black Keres—grim, terrifying, frightful, dripping with blood—fought over the fallen corpses. Greedy, they all wanted to inhale the dark blood. They would dig their huge claws into the flesh of the first warrior they snatched, either as he lay dead, or as he collapsed from his wounds, and his soul would immediately fall to Hades, into icy Tartaros. Then, when they had their fill of human blood, they would toss the corpse behind them and rush back in their fury to the clash of battle. (248ff.)

We are no longer, as with Thanatos, in the sphere of the "irremediable" lot from which no mortal creature can escape, but which the hero, by the very manner in which he encounters it, makes the occasion for a glorious survival in the memory of men. We are rather in the realm of evil forces, of sinister furies assuaging their bloodthirsty hatred.

Thanatos is male, Gorgo and Ker are female; does the opposition of the sexes correspond to the two faces of death to which I have referred elsewhere?[2] Thanatos is closer to the notion of "the beautiful death" that, as the ideal of the heroic life, guarantees a glorious immortality. Gorgo and Ker are nearer to all the repulsion and horror that can be mobilized by the transformation of a living being into a corpse and of a corpse into carrion. But one can go one step further. Funerary ritual, the status of the dead, the beautiful dead, the figure of Thanatos—these are all various means by which the living make the dead present, more present even, among the living, than are the living themselves. This is a social strategy that attempts to domesticate death, to civilize it—that is, to deny it as such by transforming the dead,—and particularly a

---

[2] "Mort grecque, mort à deux faces," *Le Débat* 12 (1981): 51–59, reprinted in *L'individu, la mort, l'amour*. A translation appeared in *Mortality and Immortality: The Anthropology of Death*, ed. S. C. Humphreys and Helen King (London, 1981), 285–91.

certain few of the dead, into the very past of the city (a past made continuously present to the group through the mechanisms of collective memory). Gorgo and Ker are not the dead as the living remember, commemorate, and celebrate them; rather, they represent the direct confrontation with death itself. They are death proper, that domain beyond-the-threshold, the gaping aperture of the other side that no gaze can penetrate and no discourse can express: they are nothing but the horror of unspeakable Night.

This dichotomy is too harsh, no doubt. The picture needs touching up, or at least some additions, to get the proper shadings. There are feminine figures of death—Sirens, Harpies, Sphinxes, and others—in whom attractiveness, pleasure, and seduction are combined with anguish and frightfulness; there are zones in which Thanatos interacts with Eros and where the warrior's fight to the death shares a hazy boundary with the attraction and sexual union of man and woman.

II

We will have to pursue several paths not only in order to discern those zones in which Thanatos and Eros, Death and Desire, are neighbors, but also in order to locate those among Greek figures of death who borrow from the face of a woman, especially that of a young girl, the power of strange fascination and the disquieting charm of her beauty.[3] The first of these paths takes us back to origins. In the *Theogony*, the birth of Aphrodite immediately precedes a catalogue of Night's children, whose three firstborn are given three names for death: odious Destiny (Moros), black Ker, and Thanatos (190–212).

Almost from the moment of her birth, Aphrodite is framed between Eros and Himeros, Love and Desire, who thereafter never leave her side (*Theog.* 201). From the first day, her lot (*moira*) and her privilege (*timē*) are, together with pleasure's gentle sweetness, the whispers of young girls, *parthenioi oaori* (*oaros, oarismos* means tender babbling, whispering; *oaristus*, a lovers' meeting; *oarizein*, intimate whispering; all these terms are related to *oar*, the feminine bed-companion, the wife with whom one exchanges, among other things, pillow confidences). Yes, the whispers of young girls—but also lies, deceitful talk, *exapatai*, and the union of lovers (*philotēs*).

Let us now look on the other side, at the children of Night—dark Nyx who seems to be completely opposite to shining, golden Aphrodite. The feminine figure of death, Ker, occupies a special place among this sinister brood. Night is the power that first arises, along with Erebos, directly out of Chaos, the primordial gap, when nothing exists in the world but an immense dark abyss, an opening without end and without direction. Chaos, abyss, is related to *chainō, chaskō*: to open up, gape open. In *Iliad* 23.78, the phantom of Patro-

---

[3] Some of these paths have already been indicated by L. Kahn-Lyotard and N. Loraux. See their article "Mort" in *Dictionnaire des mythologies*, ed. Yves Bonnefoy (Paris, 1981).

klos, appearing suddenly to Achilles, refers to the death that destiny has reserved for him in the form of "horrible Ker who opened her mouth to swallow
me." The verb that is used, *amphichainō*, indicates that when Ker opens her
mouth to swallow you, she sends you back to the original abyss; Night and
her progeny are like the trace and the continuation in today's organized cosmos of that obscure primordial indistinction. Whom do we see in this lineage
that, Night, having barely emerged from Chaos, engenders from herself, without union with anyone, as if she had fashioned her progeny out of her own
shadowy material? Next to the dark, negative forces incarnating death, misfortune, privation, and punishment, there appear the beautiful young girls
known as the Hesperides (*Theog.* 215). In the extreme west, at the edge of the
world where each evening the sun is swallowed up in order that it too may
disappear into the night, these virgins guard the golden apples entrusted to
their care. The apple: a fruit that a lover offers his beloved in declaration of
his love, symbol of erotic union, promise of eternal marriage. But the fact that
the young girls are in an inaccessible garden, located beyond the ocean that
marks the frontier of the world and guarded by a ferocious dragon, tells us that
while Zeus and Hera may have been united there,[4] mortals may only reach
it—as they sometimes dream of doing—by passing through death.

More significantly still, among Night's progeny, among the scourges engendered by the ancient goddess, there appears Philotes and Apate, Loving
Tenderness and Deceit—the two beings who belong to Aphrodite as her privilege (*timē*) and her portion (*moira*). But this is not all. Associated with the
sinister squadron of Clashes, Battles, Manslaughters, and Murders—all forms
of violent death—Deceitful Lies (*Pseudees Logoi*) also find their place. These
recall the love-talk of young girls, with their deceitful ruses (*exapatai*)—all
the more so since other passages in Hesiod are explicit on the point: Hermes
places *pseudea th'aimulious te logous*, "lies and deceitful words," in the
breast of the first woman, Pandora, from whom issued "the race of feminine
women" (Hes., *WD* 78). Hesiod also warns his male reader not to let a woman
dupe his senses with deceitful babbling (373, 788). Furthermore, it seems
hardly necessary to point out that when women did not yet exist—before Pandora was created—death did not exist for men either. Mingling with the gods,
living like them in the Golden Age, men even remained young like the gods
throughout their existence, and a kind of gentle sleep took the place of death
for them. Death and woman arose in concert together.

III

That Hesiod's image of woman—her seductiveness, the attraction she exercises over men, her Aphroditean nature—is thus in complicity with the noc-

---

[4] [E.g., Eur., *Hipp.* 742–52. Ed.]

turnal Powers of death may be attributed to what has been called Hesiod's misogyny. However, this would both simplify Hesiod, whose "misogyny" should be put back into its cultural context, and overlook valuable details of a more general import concerning the exchanges that connect Eros and Thanatos and the ways in which each contaminates the other.

Amorous whispers, a tender meeting of a boy and a girl—these we find again in a passage of the *Iliad* (22.122–29) where they have seemed to some to be inexplicable and out of place. The passage in question occurs at the culmination of the narrative. Alone at the walls of Troy, awaiting Achilles who is rushing forward to confront him, Hektor hears his parents beseeching him to return to safety like the other Trojans. If he accepts hand-to-hand combat, they tell him, his death is certain. Hektor questions himself, debating with his heart. For a moment he dreams of an impossible accord that would allow the warring confrontation of the two men to be avoided. He could lay down his shield and spear, take off his helmet and his arms, walk toward Achilles and offer him Helen and all the riches that the Achaeans could wish for. However, if he approached the Greek without his warrior's equipment, *gumnos*— a term which in this military context means "unarmed"—his enemy would kill him without mercy. But the text does not merely say *gumnos*; it adds a comparison that displaces the word's meaning: *gumnos*, "exactly like a woman."

This evocation of a meeting with the enemy in which one of the warriors (Hektor) would feel he was in the position of a quasi-woman in relation to the other (Achilles) gives the Trojan an opportunity to make a remark that has continued to intrigue commentators. "No," Hektor says to himself, "it is not the moment to talk to him gently whispering [*oarizein*] like a young man and a girl, in the way a young man and a young maiden whisper together. Better to bring on the fight with him as soon as possible to end our quarrel." There is certainly an opposition in this passage between the hand-to-hand combat of male warriors under the sign of Thanatos and the amorous encounter of a boy and a girl under the sign of Eros. But to be expressed and in order to make sense, this opposition presupposes a basic analogy between these two ways of "rapprochement," of meeting and getting together.

There are several proofs of this analogy. First, on two occasions the term *oaristus*, "intimate rendezvous" (which is thus less out of place on Hektor's tongue than has been supposed), is used in the *Iliad* to designate the direct confrontation of hand-to-hand close combat of fighters on the front line: *oaristus promachōn* (*Il.* 13.291), and, in a more general sense, "to perish or survive—this is the *polemou oaristus*, the intimate rendezvous of battle" (17.228).

In the second place, the feminine values of *gumnos* emphasized by Hektor are confirmed at the end of the duel in which each of the two adversaries had hoped to touch the other. "Come closer," Achilles had said to Hektor in the course of another encounter, "come closer and die more quickly" (*Il.* 20.429). Once the Trojan hero is dead, Achilles, as is customary, takes off Hektor's armor. There is Hektor, then, stretched out on the ground. He is *gumnos*—disarmed, denuded, as he had for a moment considered doing to himself in order to avoid the trial of combat. The Achaeans crowd around him. Each one strikes a blow at him, saying to his neighbor, "See now, this Hektor is much softer to handle [*malakoteros amphaphaasthai*] than he was when he set fire to our ships" (*Il.* 22.373–74). *Malakos*, soft, limp, refers to the feminine or the effeminate. In the background of murderous hand-to-hand combat, the latent presence of images of carnal union is also indicated by the manner in which the heroic warriors attribute to their weapons of virile combat, the spear and the sword, a desire to satisfy themselves with the enemy's flesh. "My long spear," Hektor says to Ajax, "will devour your white flesh [*chroa leirioenta dapsei*]" (13.830). White as the lily, Ajax's flesh? On vases, as it is well known, male figures are painted brown; it is the women who are white.

An entire series of terms, then, through their convergence, underline the intersection of images of combat to the death with the erotic embrace. *Meignumi*, sexual union, also means to join and meet in battle. When Diomedes "joins with the Trojans" (5.143), it means he meets them hand to hand, he is close upon them, he is with them. In front of Hektor, when he invites his men "not to the dance, but to battle," Ajax says that the Greeks have nothing else to do but to "mix" ardor and arms, to come to grips with the enemy, close up, body to body, *autoschediēi mixai* (15.510).

Similarly, *damazō*, *damnēmi*, mean to subjugate, to tame. One subjugates a woman whom one makes one's own, just as one subjugates the enemy one slays. Before combat, each warrior boasts of soon subjugating his adversary. But in the *Theogony*, it is Eros whom Hesiod celebrates as having the power of subjugating every god and every mortal (122). Eros's mastery, the yoke he imposes, is the sign of a kind of magic, *thelxis*. Eros is a sorcerer. When he takes possession of you, he snatches you away from your ordinary concerns, out of the horizon of your day-to-day life, to open up a new dimension of existence for you. And this transformation from within, which delivers one totally into the god's power, is what the Greeks express in saying that Eros envelops your head and your thoughts like a cloud, that he surrounds you and hides you, *amphikaluptein*.[5] Death too, when it seizes a person to take him or her from the world of light to that of night, hides that one in the hooded mantle of a dark cloud. Death covers the face, made invisible, with a mask of darkness.

In the tribute he pays to Eros, Hesiod defines him using the epithet *lusimelēs*, he who unbinds, who loosens, breaks the limbs (*Theog.* 120, 911). In

[5] For example, Paris says to Helen: "Never before has Eros enveloped my senses to such an extent" (*Il.* 3.442).

the joust of love, desire breaks the knees: at the sight of Penelope, the suitors' knees falter, "are loosened [*luto gounata*] under the charm of love" (*Od.* 18.212)[6] The same applies to the power of death in the warriors' struggle. When a fighter falls and does not rise again, it is said his knees are broken, undone (*Il.* 5.176; 11.579; 15.332; 21.114; 22.335). Why the knees? They are the seat of a vital energy, a virile power related to the humid element. These reserves of force disappear completely at death; the dead are the *kamontes* or *kekmēkotes*, those who are tired, exhausted, empty. But these forces also flow away and are spent in the toil of war with its fatigue, its sweat, its tears of pain and grief, just as they are spent in the toil of love in which a man dries up, losing his freshness and his juices while the woman, all liquidity, flows all the more. Because of the desire that emanates from her, especially from her eyes and moist gaze, the mere presence of a woman is enough to soften and liquefy male powers, to disarm a man and make him weak in the knees. In this difference, which sets it in opposition to masculinity while attracting men to itself with an irresistible force, femininity acts like death. A fragment of Alcman states it precisely: "By the desire that loosens the limbs [*lusimelēs*], she [a woman] has a gaze that is more dissolvant [*takeros*: languishing, liquefying, dissolving] than *Hupnos* or Thanatos."[7] A woman's gaze more liquefying than death: here Thanatos takes on the face of a woman, no longer the repulsive, monstrous face of Gorgo or Ker, but one that is overwhelming because of its beauty. It is attractive and dangerous at the same time because it is the object of an impossible desire, a desire of that which is other.

Alcman's ordeal opens a new path for us. The poet does not call the desire that undoes him *himeros*, he calls it *pothos*. Plato explains the difference between the two terms very clearly. *Himeros* designates the desire for a partner who is present, a desire ready to be satisfied. *Pothos* is the desire for what is absent, a desire that is a suffering because it cannot be fulfilled; it is regret, nostalgia (Plato, *Crat.* 420a–b). *Pothos* is an ambiguous feeling since it implies the passionate élan of one's whole being toward the plenitude of a beloved presence and at the same time the painful shock of absence, the realization of an emptiness, of an unbridgeable distance. As a term, *pothos* also belongs to the vocabulary of mourning. When a man dies, before the funeral ceremony his relatives ritually deprive themselves of food, drink, and sleep. Overcome by *pothos* in relation to the deceased, they remember him continuously, vowing, as Achilles vows to Patroklos, to remember him always—to be haunted by him, one would have to say. By a long effort of evocation they make him present, but only at the moment in which they see him before them in the form of his double, his *eidōlon*. When they speak to his double as if to

[6] Cf. Archil., frag. 212 (Tarditi), Sappho, *Poet. lesb. frag.* 130 (Lobel-Page).
[7] *PMG* (Page) 3 (Pap. Ox. 2387), frag. 3, col. 2.

him in person, this ungraspable presence disappears. The manner in which the dead are present entails in itself an irremediable absence.

A play of absence in presence; the obsession with someone who is absent and who fills your whole horizon, and yet whom you can never grasp because that one belongs to the realm beyond. This is the experience in mourning that a living person has of his or her relation to someone dead, with one who has disappeared into the world beyond. In the same way this is how the lover experiences desire with all its incompleteness in his powerlessness to have his sexual partner always to himself, to make her entirely and forever his own. Funereal *pothos* and erotic *pothos* correspond exactly. The figure of the beloved woman whose image haunts and escapes the lover intersects with that of death.

In the *Persians*, Aeschylus evokes the barbarian women whose husbands, gone to do battle for Xerxes, have fallen in distant lands and will not return. "The beds are filled with the tears of their *pothos* for their spouses; each Persian woman remains abandoned, alone without her partner. She accompanies her husband with the *pothos* she feels for him" (133–39). The same theme is taken up in the *Agamemnon*, but this time it is the amorous *pothos* for Helen that, reigning supreme over Menelaos's heart, populates the palace deserted by his wife with phantoms (*phasmata*) of the beloved, with her apparitions in dreams (*oneirophantoi*) (406). Radiant with charm, haunting and ungraspable, Helen is like a person from the beyond, doubled in this life and on this earth in herself and her phantom, her *eidōlon*. A fatal beauty created by Zeus to destroy human beings, to make them kill one another at the walls of Troy, she, more so than her sister Klytemnestra, deserves the appellation "slayer of men" (749).[8] She who is "most beautiful" also incarnates the horrible Erinys, the savage and murderous Ker. In her, desire and death are joined and intimately mingled.

IV

One of the chapters of Emily Vermeule's fine book on aspects of death in archaic Greece (from which we have borrowed much) is entitled "On the Wings of the Morning: The Pornography of Death."[9] The subtitle is provocative, but entirely justified by the visual and literary documents she has collected on the theme of death as abduction by a divinity. An entire aspect of the Greek social imagination concerning death refers to such winged supernatural Powers as Eros, Hupnos, and Thanatos, who, for the love of a mortal whose beauty has seduced them, make him disappear from here below in order to be united with him, carrying him off into the world beyond. This sudden

[8] Cf. Eur., *Hel.* 52–55, *El.* 1282–84, *Or.* 1639.
[9] *Aspects of Death in Early Greek Art and Poetry* (Berkeley, 1979).

disappearance without a trace (*aphanismos*), this escape into the beyond by a human being who is wrested away from earthly life and transported into the other world, can, according to the circumstances, lead to a better or worse situation, or to one that is both better and worse at the same time. It can be an uncommon promotion that liberates the happy elect from the limitations of mortal existence, installing them on the Isle of the Blessed or arranging a place for them beside the gods on Olympos—as when Zeus abducts Ganymede, or when Eos, the Dawn, takes away Tithonos, and Hemera, Orion. It may be quite simply that the unknown of death, while most often dreaded, is nonetheless hoped for since through it the soul avoids the ills assailing the individual. One may reach the point of longing to share in the fate of Oreithyia and be carried off on the wings of Boreas the North Wind, or Thyella, Tempest, or Harpyia, Hurricane. Penelope, for example, in desperation, wishes for just such an end in the *Odyssey* (20.63–81).

These stories of abduction by some winged demon that so pleased the Greeks have one point in common. This is, to use Vermeule's terms once again, that in their eyes, "love and death were two aspects of the same power, as in the myth of Persephone or Helen of Troy." Vermeule, an archaeologist, has assembled the most expressive images in which one and the same figure represents the two faces of this ambiguous power, as for instance in the scene of *psychostasia* (weighing of souls) found on the Boston Throne, where a young man, his large wings outspread and a smile on his lips, weighs the *eidōla* of two warriors—two naked young men—on a scale in order to decide which of the two who are fighting to the death he must carry off. Who is holding the scales? Is it Eros, or is it Thanatos? The beautiful ephebe, winged and smiling, is both one and the other at the same time.[10]

I will not discuss the dossier of images and texts Vermeule has collected on the winged demonesses with the breast and face of a woman—Harpies, Sphinxes, and Sirens—whom the Greeks, since the archaic age, depicted on tombstones to guard and watch over the dead. Like Dawn, like the winds, Boreas and Zephyros, and like the Tempests (Thyellai), the Harpies are powers that "ravish" in both senses of the word. In the Greek, the word for "ravish" is *harpazein*—that is, to seize and carry off. The Sphinx is called "Ker, ravisher of men," *harpaxandra Kēr*, in Aeschylus's *Seven against Thebes* (777). These female monsters who combine feminine charm with predatory talons or the claws of a wild beast are at times represented holding a dead person the way a mother holds her child, carrying him off, perhaps to a better world. At times they are depicted pursuing a man out of erotic desire or sitting astride him to have intercourse with him; or again attacking him to tear him to shreds and devour him. "The dead," writes Vermeule, "are their victims and lovers at the same time."

[10] Ibid., 159.

Vermeule's demonstration suffices; I would like to add to it, however, only by juxtaposing two episodes of the *Odyssey*. The first relates to the Sirens, the second to Kalypso.

V

It is Kirke who warns Odysseus and teaches him the ruse that, if he wishes to "escape" death and Ker, will save him and his men. The problem is to "escape" the seductive song of the Sirens' divine voices and their flowering meadow (*Od.* 12.158ff.). In the manner of Eros the magician, they charm and bewitch (*thelgousi*) all human beings who approach them; they charm them with their melodious song, but none who listens to them returns to his home. Rather, the Sirens remain fixed in place in their meadow encircled by a heaped-up mass of whitened bones and putrefied corpses with desiccated skins. In order not to hear the Sirens, therefore, the sailors must plug their ears with wax. As for Odysseus, if he wants to hear their song he must choose either to be lost like everyone who is caught by these creatures' spell, or let himself be tied up both hands and feet to the ship's mast.

Up to this point everything about these bird-women seems clear. Their cries, their flowering meadow (*leimōn*, meadow, is one of the words used to designate female genitalia), their charm (*thelxis*) locates them in all their irresistibility unequivocally in the realm of sexual attraction or erotic appeal.[11] At the same time, they are death, and death in its most brutally monstrous aspect: no funeral, no tomb, only the corpse's decomposition in the open air. Pure desire, pure death; without any social adjustment, they are on neither one side nor the other.

But the story becomes more complex. The boat advances. As it passes close by the Sirens, the breeze that impels it onward suddenly dies down. There is no breath of wind. There is no wave. A god has put the sea to sleep. It is the *galēnē*, the flat calm, the serenity of the port, of safety after the storm, or of a land where all life is forever fixed. The crew is deaf and Odysseus bound up. The Sirens watch the boat as it rows by. What do they do? They intone a harmonious song (*entunon aoidēn*), as does a bard before his audience. This song is especially addressed to Odysseus, for whom it is composed. "Come here, come to us, Odysseus, Odysseus, the pride of the Achaeans." *Poluainos, mega kudos Achaiōn*: the formula is the same as the one that the *Iliad* puts into Agamemnon's mouth when he praises Odysseus (*Il.* 6.73).[12] To seduce the *Odyssey*'s navigator, clinging to life as he is tossed from one ordeal

---

[11] On the erotic value of *leimōn*, which can designate the female genitalia, see André Motte, *Prairies et jardins de la Grèce antique* (Brussels, 1973), 50–56, 83–87. On its funereal or macabre value, see 250–79. The flowering meadow where the bewitching Sirens are encamped is strewn with bones and the rotting flesh of human debris (*Od.* 12.45–46).

[12] See the analysis of Piero Pucci, "The Song of the Sirens," *Arethusa* 12 (1979): 121–32.

to another, the Sirens celebrate in his presence that very Odysseus whom the song of the *Iliad* immortalizes: the virile male warrior whose glory is indefinitely repeated from rhapsode to rhapsode and remains imperishable. In the mirror of the Sirens' song Odysseus sees himself not as he is, struggling on the surface of the sea, but as he will be when he is dead, as death will make him, forever magnified in the memory of the living, transmuted from the suffering and misfortune of his actual, miserable existence to the glorious brilliance of his fame and of the story of his exploits. What sparkles in the Siren-women's tempting words is the illusory hope for the listener to find himself living as a mortal under the light of the sun, and at the same time surviving in imperishable glory with the status of a dead hero. It is as if, through the Sirens' seductive bodies, soft voices, and flowering meadow, the boundaries that close off human existence were opened up and one could cross these without also at the same time ceasing to exist.

The Sirens, in effect, promise Odysseus that after having tasted the pleasure of their song, he will leave again, sailing the sea to his home, but wiser through having learned all that they know. And this knowledge whose secret they are able to impart is what the bards sing—what happened at Argos and by the walls of Troy, all that took place long ago on earth—and which, in order to become the object of praise, had first to disappear and slip into invisibility.

When a bard invokes the Muses it is in order to make the noble deeds of the hero of days gone by live again for the people today. The Sirens are the opposite of the Muses. Their song has the same charm as that of the daughters of Memory; they too bestow a knowledge that cannot be forgotten. But whoever succumbs to the attraction of their beauty, the seduction of their voices, the temptation of the knowledge they hold in their custody, does not enter that region to live forever in the splendor of eternal renown. Instead, he reaches a shore whitened with bones and the debris of rotting human flesh. If it is given to a living man to hear in advance the song that will sing his glory and his memory, what he discovers is not a beautiful death and immortal glory, but the horror of the cadaver and of decomposition: a frightful death. Death is a threshold. One cannot pass over it and remain alive. Beyond the threshold, from its other side, the beautiful feminine face that attracts you and beckons to you is a face of terror: the unspeakable. For the man firmly planted in mortal life, the Sirens' charm, the enticement of their bodies, the sweetness of their voices, are related to the Gorgo's horrifying grimace and the heart-chilling stridency of her inhuman howling.

And what of Kalypso? From the first verses of the *Odyssey*, the nymph rises up and occupies the foreground of the scene. The poet begins his narrative with her (1.11–16).[13] In front of the gods assembled on Olympos, Athena

[13] These same lines are repeated in the text at the beginning of book 5, where, as in book 1,

declares Kalypso responsible for the misfortunes besetting her protégé. It is to her that Zeus then immediately sends the messenger Hermes with the command to allow Odysseus to set sail and return home. By its placement at the beginning of the narrative and its frequent repetitions throughout the text,[14] this whole episode—the figure of Kalypso, the goddess's love for a mortal, the long captivity in which she keeps Odysseus close to her,[15]—confers upon the wanderings of the king of Ithaca their real significance and reveals what is actually at stake in the entire Odyssean adventure: whether the hero will or will not return, by way of his homeland, to the world of mortals.[16] "All the other heroes who had saved their necks from death had reached their home. . . . He alone was left still longing to return and longing for his wife because an august nymph held him by force, far away, in the depths of her caverns, Kalypso, the all-divine, who burned to have him as her husband" (1.11–15).

Derived from *kaluptein*, "to hide," Kalypso's name, in all its transparency, reveals the secret of the powers incarnated by the goddess. In the depth of her cave she is not merely "the hidden one"; she is also and above all "the one who hides others." In order to "hide" Odysseus, Kalypso did not, like Thanatos and Eros, have to kidnap and ravish him. In this particular she differs from the divinities whose example she invokes before Hermes to justify her case, and who, in order to satisfy their amorous passion for a mortal, carried that one off with them into the beyond, making him suddenly disappear, still living, from the face of the earth (5.120ff.).[17] Thus Eos, the dawn goddess, "ravished" Tithonos, and Hemera ravished Orion.[18]

---

they serve to introduce the holding of the assembly of the gods and the decision (this time effective, having already been taken but not put into action in book 1) to send Hermes as a messenger to Kalypso in order to transmit to her the command to liberate Odysseus. On the duplication of this episode and its bearing on the poem's narrative chronology, see E. Délébecque, *La construction de l'Odyssée* (Paris, 1980), 12–13.

[14] 1.11–87; 4.555–58; 5.11–300; 7.241–66; 8.450–53; 9.29–30; 12.389, 447–50; 17.140–44; 23.333–38.

[15] As Odysseus himself states in 7.259–61, in response to a question posed by Arete, queen of the Phaeacians, Odysseus remained with Kalypso for seven years. Seven years, out of a total time span of about eight or nine years of wandering from the end of the Trojan War until his return to Ithaca, says a good deal about the position this sojourn occupies in the journey as a whole.

[16] On this point, see Pierre Vidal-Naquet, "Valeurs religieuses et mythiques de la terre et du sacrifice dans l'*Odyssée*," in *Le chasseur noir: Formes de pensée et formes de société dans le monde grec* (Paris, 1981), 39–68 (transl. Andrew Szegedy-Maszak, under the title *The Black Hunter: Forms of Thought and Forms of Society in the Greek World* [Baltimore, 1986], 15–38).

[17] On this "abduction" by a supernatural power, see also *Il.* 8.346–47, *Od.* 20.61, and above all, *Hom. Hym. Aph.* 1.202–38.

[18] In his *Homeric Problems* (68.5), Heraclitus, interpreting the loves of Hemera and Orion allegorically, underlines the connection between Thanatos and Eros. "When a young man of noble family and great beauty dies," he writes, "one euphemistically calls his funeral procession, which takes place at dawn, a 'kidnapping by Hemera,' as if he were not dead at all but had been ravished because he was the object of an erotic passion."

This time, it is shipwrecked Odysseus who himself came to the extreme west, to the end of the world, landing at Kalypso's rocky cave, that "navel of the seas,"[19] embellished with woods, ravishing springs, and soft meadows reminiscent of the erotic and macabre "flowering meadow" encircling the rocky isle where the Sirens sing to charm and destroy those who hear them.[20]

The island on which the nymph and the man cohabit, cut off from everything and everyone, in the solitude of their erotic encounter—their isolation together—is situated in a sort of marginal space, a place apart, distant from the gods and distant from mortals (*Od.* 5.136, 209; 7.257; 8.453; 23.336). It is another world that is neither the world of the ever-youthful Immortals, even though Kalypso is a goddess,[21] nor that of humans subject to old age and death, even though Odysseus is a mortal, nor is it that of the dead beneath the Earth in Hades. It is a sort of nowhere-land into which Odysseus has disappeared, swallowed up without leaving a trace, and where he lives a life as though in parentheses.

Like the Sirens, Kalypso, who also sings with a beautiful voice, charms Odysseus by constantly singing litanies of amorous tenderness, *aei de malakoisi kai amulioisi logoisi thelgei*. *Thelgei*: she enchants, she bewitches him to make him forget Ithaca, *hopōs Ithakēs epilēsetai* (1.56–57; cf. 5.61).

For Odysseus, to forget Ithaca means to cut the ties that still connect him to his life and to those who are close to him, to those who, for their part, are attached to his memory, whether they hope against all odds for the return of a

---

[19] Located where the sun sets, at the extreme limit of the world, the island is nevertheless called *omphalos thalassēs*, navel of the world (1.50), and is also designated as *nēsos ogugiē*, Ogygian island (1.85), a qualification Hesiod applies to the waters of the Styx, the infernal river flowing *beneath* the earth, across the black night, at the bottom of Tartaros (*Theog.* 806). It is in the same subterranean place where Hesiod, contrary to the tradition (which places Atlas at the extreme west), situates this father of Kalypso "supporting the vast sky with his head and arms, without losing strength" (*Theog.* 748). When Homer speaks of the "navel of the sea" in relation to the island where Kalypso resides, it is so he may immediately evoke the goddess's father, that Atlas of wrongful mind who "knows the profound abysses of the entire sea," and who, at the same time, "holds the high columns that now separate the sky and earth" (*Od.* 1.50–54). The mythic geography of the Greeks places Atlas, in his role as deeply rooted cosmic pillar reaching through the earth up to the sky, sometimes at the far west, sometimes at the very bottom, and sometimes at the navel of the world. These are all ways of saying that he is not *in* this world that men know. Kalypso's island, situated in the far west, Ogygian like the Styx, at the navel of the sea, also has no location in human space. It is a figure of "elsewhere."

[20] *Od.* 5.72 refers to Kalypso's "soft meadows [*leimones malakoi*]," and at 12.158, to the Sirens' "flowering meadow [*leimōn anthemoeis*]."

[21] The nymph is several times called *thea* or *theos*, "goddess": 1.14 and 51; 5.78; 7.255; and especially 5.79, where the couple Kalypso-Hermes are referred to as two gods, *theoi*; 5.138, where, before giving in, she admits that no god can oppose Zeus's will; and 5.192–94, where the couple Kalypso-Odysseus is that of a god and a man, *theos* and *anēr*. This divine status is confirmed by the fact that, even though they have their meals together, Kalypso eats nectar and ambrosia like the gods, while Odysseus eats bread and wine like a human mortal (5.93, 165, 196–200).

living Odysseus, or whether they are preparing to construct the funerary *mnēma* (memorial) for him if he is dead. But as long as he remains a recluse, hidden on Kalypso's island, Odysseus's condition is that of neither the living nor the dead. Although he still has his life, he is already and in advance withdrawn from human memory. To repeat the words of Telemachos (1.234), he has become, by the will of the gods, invisible, *aïstos*, among all men. He has disappeared, ''invisible and unknown,'' *aïstos*, *apustos*, outside the range of what human eyes and ears can reach, ''hidden in darkness and silence.'' If he had at least died normally beneath the walls of Troy or in the arms of his comrades in misfortune, ''he would have had his tomb, and what great glory, *mega kleos*, he would have left for the future and for his son,'' but the Harpies took him away. The living have nothing more to do with a man who is nowhere; deprived of remembrance, he has no fame; concealed in the invisible, vanished, effaced, he has disappeared without glory (*akleiōs*) (1.241). For the hero whose ideal is to leave behind him a *kleos aphthiton*, an imperishable glory, can there be anything worse than to disappear like this, *akleiōs*, without glory?[22]

What is it, then, that Kalypso's seduction offers Odysseus in order to make him ''forget'' Ithaca? First, certainly, it is to avoid the ordeals of the return, the sufferings of the journey, all those difficulties that she, being a goddess, knows in advance will assail him before he finally finds his native land again (5.205ff.). But these are only trifles. The nymph offers him much more. She promises, if he agrees to stay with her, to make him immortal and to keep old age and death away from him forever. Like a god, he will live in her immortal company, in the permanent brilliance of youth. Never to die, never to know the decrepitude of growing old—this is what is at stake in the love the goddess would share with him (5.136, 209; 7.257; 8.453; 23.336). But in Kalypso's bed there is a price to pay for this escape outside the boundaries that limit the human condition. To share divine immortality in the arms of the nymph would be, for Odysseus, to renounce his career as an epic hero. By no longer figuring as a model of endurance in the text of an *Odyssey* that sings his trials, he will have to accept his effacement from the memory of men to come, being dispossessed of his posthumous celebrity, sinking into the obscurity of forgetfulness, even if he is eternally alive. Ultimately, he will have to accept an immortality as anonymous as the death of those humans who have been unable to assume a heroic destiny and who form the indistinct mass of those ''without name,'' *nōnumoi*, in Hades (Hes., *WD* 154),[23] swallowed up in the night of a silence where they will remain ''hidden'' forever.

[22] Cf. ''A 'Beautiful Death' and the Disfigured Corpse in Homeric Epic,'' above, chap. 2.

[23] In the context of archaic Greek culture where the category of the person is quite different from today's ''self,'' only the posthumous glory of death can be said to be ''personal.'' The immortality of an ''invisible and unknown'' person is situated outside that which constitutes for the Greeks the individuality of a subject, that is to say, essentially, his renown. Cf. ibid.

The episode of Kalypso locates for the first time in our literature what one might call the heroic refusal of immortality. For the Greeks of the archaic age, this form of eternal survival that Odysseus would share with Kalypso would not truly be "his," since no one in the world would ever know of it, nor would they remember, in order to celebrate it, the name of the hero of Ithaca. For the Homeric Greeks, as opposed to ourselves, the important thing is not the absence of death—a hope that seems to them absurd for mortals. It is rather the permanence among the living in their commemorative tradition of a glory acquired in life—at the price of life—during the course of an existence in which life and death are indissociable.

On the shore of this island where only a word would be enough to make him immortal, Odysseus, sitting on a rock, facing the sea, laments and weeps all day long. He melts, he dissolves in tears. His *aiōn*, his vital juices flow unceasingly, *kateibeto aiōn*, in the *pothos*, the regret for his mortal life (1.55; 5.82–83, 151–53, 160–61), just as at the other end of the world, at the other pole of the married pair, Penelope, on her side, consumes her *aiōn*, weeping out of sorrow for the vanished Odysseus (19.204–9, 262–65). She weeps for someone living who is perhaps dead. He, on his isle of immortality, cut off from life as if he were dead, weeps for his living existence as a creature destined to die.

For all the nostalgia he feels in regard to the evanescent and ephemeral world to which he belongs, our hero no longer enjoys the charms of the nymph. Odysseus's vitality spends itself in tears "because the nymph no longer pleases him [*epei ouketi hēndane numphē*]" (5.153). If he goes to sleep with her at night, it is because he must. He joins her in bed—he who does not want her, she who wants him.[24]

Odysseus thus rejects the immortality that is a feminine favor. In cutting him off from what life means to him, it leads him finally to think of death as desirable. No longer *eros*, no longer *himeros*, no longer love or desire for the girdled nymph; he desires only to die, *thaneein himeiretai* (1.59).

Nostos, the return; *gunē*, Penelope, the wife; Ithaca, his homeland; his son; his old father; his faithful companions—and then *thanein*, to die. In his distaste for Kalypso, in his refusal of a nondeath that is also a nonlife, these others are the objects toward which his amorous impulse, his nostalgic desire, his *pothos*, are directed: toward his life, his precarious and mortal life, his trials, his wanderings resumed again and again without cease, toward the destiny of a hero of endurance that he must assume in order to become himself—Odysseus—that Odysseus of Ithaca. His is the name the text of the *Odyssey* still sings today, his the returns it narrates, his the imperishable glory it celebrates. The poet would have had nothing to tell—and we nothing to hear—if

---

[24] He unites with her by necessity, *anankē*, against his will, because she wants him (5.154, 155).

Odysseus had remained far from his own people, immortal, "hidden" by Kalypso.[25]

To the feminine figure who incarnates that which is beyond death, in her double dimension of erotic seduction and temptation to immortality, the Greeks preferred the simple human life—under the light of the sun, the bittersweetness of the mortal condition.

---

[25] "It is a maxim among men that when an exploit has been accomplished it must not remain hidden [*kalupsai*] in silence. What it requires is the divine melody of praising verses" (Pind., *Nem.* 9.13–17).

Chapter 6

DEATH IN THE EYES: GORGO, FIGURE OF THE *OTHER*

WHY STUDY Gorgo? The reason is that for a historian, and a historian of religion in particular, the problem of alterity or "otherness" in ancient Greece cannot be limited to the representation the Greeks made of others, of all those whom, for the purposes of reflection, they ranked under different headings in the category of difference, and whose representations always appear deformed because these figures—barbarian, slave, stranger, youth, and woman—are always constructed with reference to the same model: the adult male citizen. We must also investigate what could be called extreme alterity and ask about the ways in which the ancients attempted to give a form in their religious universe to this experience of an absolute other. The issue is no longer one of a human being who is different from a Greek, but what, by comparison to a human being, is revealed as radical difference: instead of an other person, the other of the person.

Such, we think, were the sense and function of this strange sacred Power that operates through the mask, that has no other form than the mask, and that is presented entirely as a mask: Gorgo.

In certain qualities she is close to Artemis.[1] In the sanctuary of Artemis Orthia in Sparta, among the votive masks dedicated to the goddess (the young had to wear likenesses of these in the course of the *agōgē* in order to execute their mimetic dances), there are many that reproduce the monstrous and terrifying face of Gorgo.

But the otherness that the young of both sexes explore under the patronage of Artemis seems to be situated entirely on a kind of horizontal plane where

---

The French text originally appeared as *La mort dans les yeux: Figures de l'Autre en Grèce ancienne* (Paris, 1985), and its translation is published here with the kind permission of Hachette. In the original, the subject of Gorgo was preceded by an analysis of the roles and functions of the goddess Artemis. Because, strictly speaking, the title referred to Gorgo and because a number of other pieces on Artemis are included in the present volume, it seemed practical to separate the two parts, retaining the original title for this text about Gorgo, and shifting the general survey of Artemis, now called "The Figure and Functions of Artemis in Myth and Cult," to head those other essays, each of which treats specific aspects of Artemis in greater detail. A portion of the essay on Gorgo was given as a lecture in English at Princeton University in 1980 under the title "Face to Face with Terror: Gorgo," translated by the late Thomas Curley. The entire text was revised and completed by Froma I. Zeitlin.

[1] Both have affinities with the *Potnia therōn*, the great feminine divinity, mistress of the wild beasts and of wild nature, who preceded them in the Creto-Mycenaean world and whose legacy each inherits in her own way by profoundly transforming it in the context of civic religion.

the question is one of time or space. This is the kind of alterity that marks the first moments of human life, which is punctuated by various stages and passages until the time when a man and a woman become fully themselves. This same alterity rules over the frontiers of civic territory, uncultivated lands, far from the city and civilized life, on the margins of the wild. The wildness Artemis seems to share with Gorgo, however, is manifested by her in a different way in that Artemis emphasizes the wild and gives it a place only in order better to relegate it to the periphery.

In determining that the young, in their differences from the group, may experience different forms of alterity on the boundaries, Artemis sees to it that they embark correctly on their learning of the model to which, one day, they will have to conform. From the margins where she rules, she prepares the return to the center. The nurture of the young she practices in a zone of the wild aims at their satisfactory integration into the heart of civic space.

The alterity Gorgo incarnates is of a very different type. Like that of Dionysos, it operates according to a vertical axis. This alterity no longer concerns the early part of life nor those regions far removed from the civilized horizon. Rather, it is one that, at any moment and in any place, wrenches humans away from their lives and themselves, whether with Gorgo, to cast them down into the confusion and horror of chaos, or with Dionysos and his worshippers, to raise them up high, in a fusion with the divine and the beatitude of a golden age refound.[2]

THE MASK OF GORGO

Plastic representations of Gorgo—both the *gorgoneion* (the mask alone) and the full feminine figure with a gorgon face—appear not only on a series of vases, but from the archaic period on, they can be seen on the façades of temples or as *acroteria* and antefixes. We find them as emblems on shields or decorating household utensils, hanging in artisans' workshops, attached to kilns, set up in private residences, and also, finally, stamped on coins. This representation first appears early in the seventh century B.C.E., and by the end of the second quarter of the same century, the canonical types of the model are already codified in their essential features. Leaving aside the variants in Corinthian, Attic, and Laconian imagery, we can, on a first analysis, identify two fundamental characteristics in the portrayal of Gorgo.

First, frontality. In contrast to the figurative conventions determining Greek pictorial space in the archaic period, the Gorgon is always, without exception, represented in full face. Whether mask or full figure, the Gorgon's face is at all times turned frontally toward the spectator who gazes back at her.

---

[2] Cf. Françoise Frontisi-Ducroux and J.-P. Vernant, "Figures du masque en Grèce ancienne," *Journal de Psychologie* 1–2 (1983): 68.

Second, monstrousness: whatever kinds of distortion are involved, the figure systematically plays on the confusion of human and bestial elements, juxtaposed and mingled in a variety of ways. The enlarged rounded head recalls
the face of a lion. The eyes are staring; the gaze is fixed and piercing. The hair
resembles an animal's mane or bristles with snakes. The ears are overly large,
deformed, at times like those of a cow. Horns sometimes grow from the skull.
The gaping, grinning mouth extends so far that it cuts across the breadth of
the face, revealing rows of teeth, fangs, or wild-boar tusks. The tongue thrusts
forward and protrudes outside the mouth. The chin is hairy or bearded, and
the skin is sometimes furrowed with deep wrinkles. The visage looks more
like a grimace than a face. In disrupting the features that make up a human
face, it produces an effect of disconcerting strangeness that expresses a form
of the monstrous that oscillates between two extremes: the horror of the terrifying and the hilarity of the grotesque. Despite the evident contrasts between
the horror of Gorgo and those Satyrs and Silenoi, who, on a scale of monstrosity, tend more toward the grotesque, there are still significant collusions between them. These two types also have noticeable affinities with the stark and
crude representation of the sexual organs—both masculine and feminine—a
representation that, just like the monstrous face whose equivalent it is in certain respects, also has the power to provoke both sacred fear and liberating
laughter.

To clarify the play between the face of Gorgo and the image of the female
sexual organ—as between the *phallos* and the figures of Satyrs and Silenoi,
whose humorous monstrosity is also disturbing—a word should be said about
the strange figure of Baubo, a personage with two aspects: a nocturnal specter,
a kind of ogress, related, like Gorgo, Mormo, or Empusa, to infernal Hekate,[3]
but also like an old woman whose cheerful jokes and vulgar gestures provoke
Demeter's laughter and thus induce the goddess mourning for her daughter to
break her stubborn fast. The correlation between the relevant texts[4] and the
statuettes of Priene, which represent a female reduced to a face that is also a
lower belly,[5] gives an unequivocal meaning to Baubo's gesture of lifting her
dress to exhibit her intimate parts. What Baubo actually displays to Demeter

---

[3] Cf. Orph., *Fr.* 53 (Kern); Orph., p. 289.3.2 (Abel). A first version of this part of the text
appeared in a shorter and somewhat different form in *Pour Léon Poliakov: Le racisme, mythes et
sciences*, ed. M. Olender (Brussels, 1981), 141–55.

[4] Clem. Alex., *Protrep.* 2.21 = Orph., *Fr.* no. 52 (Kern); Arnob., *Adv. nat.* 5.25, p. 196, 3
Reiff = Orph., *Fr.* 52 (Kern).

[5] For these statuettes, see J. Raeder, *Priene: Funde aus einer griechischen Stadt* (Berlin, 1983),
especially figures 23a, b, c. On the entire collection of evidence pertaining to Baubo, see Maurice
Olender, "Aspects de Baubo: Textes et contextes antiques," *RHR* 1 (1985): 3–55, and see the
English translation in abridged form in *Before Sexuality: The Construction of Erotic Experience
in the Ancient Greek World*, ed. David Halperin, John J. Winkler, and Froma I. Zeitlin (Princeton,
1990), 83–113. See also the remarks of Froma I. Zeitlin in "Cultic Models of the Female: Rites
of Dionysus and Demeter," *Arethusa* 15 (1982): 26–34.

is her genitals made up as a face, a face in the form of genitals; one might even say, the genitals made into a mask. By its grimace, this genital face becomes a burst of laughter, corresponding to the goddess's laugh, just as the terror of the one who looks at Gorgo's face corresponds to the grimace of horror that cuts across it. The *phallos*, one of whose names is *baubōn*,[6] emphasizes the relationship with Baubo and acquires a symmetrical function at the opposite pole of the monstrous. Normally, the *phallos* adds to the humor and accentuates the grotesque quality of those amusing monsters who are the Satyrs, but in initiations it produces an effect of sacred dread, of terrified fascination, which is expressed by the gestures of certain feminine individuals, who shrink away from its unveiling.

Moreover, there are two mythic versions of Demeter's laughter during the time she is searching for her daughter, and in each, the protagonist, in order to produce a liberating shock as an antidote to grief, resorts to indecency in different ways. According to the first version, Iambe, *graia Iambē*, the old Iambe, as Apollodorus says (1.5.1),[7] mocks Demeter and interrupts her mourning with the obscene jokes, the *aischrologia*, used at the Thesmophoria or at the *gephurismos* of the Eleusinian procession.[8] Iambe can be considered as the feminine of Iambos, the iamb, with its musical element of satyric song and its poetry of invective and derision. The liberating effect of an unbridled sexuality, close to the monstrous by virtue of its anomic character, operates in and through language: insulting witticisms, obscene insults, and scatological jokes—everything the Greeks understood in the expression *skoptein* or *paraskoptein polla*. In the second version, Baubo replaces Iambe and puts the same procedures on the visual level; she substitutes spectacle for words, she displays the object rather than naming it. When she crudely exhibits her genitals with a kind of obscene wiggle, Baubo makes the merry face of a young boy peep out, that of the child Iacchos, whose name evokes the mystic cry of the initiates (*iachō, iachē*) but who also is related to the *choiros*, the piglet (Athen. 3.98d), and likewise, of course, to the feminine genitals.[9]

Frontality and monstrosity: these are the two features of Gorgo's iconography that suggest questions about her origins. Antecedents have been sought in the Near Eastern, the Creto-Mycenean, and the Sumero-Accadian worlds.[10] Some scholars have suggested parallels with the figure of the Egyptian Bes

---

[6] Cf. Herod., *Mim.* 6.19.

[7] Cf. the three Graiai who are the sisters of the Gorgon.

[8] *Aischrologia*: to speak of vulgar and shameful things. On the *gephurismos*, cf. Hesych., s.v. *gephuris, gephuristai*; on the ritual exchange of insult and abuse among women at the Thesmophoria, cf. H. W. Parke, *Festivals of the Athenians* (London, 1977), 86–87.

[9] Cf. in particular, Aristoph., *Ach.* 764–817.

[10] Bernard Goldman, "The Asiatic Ancestry of the Greek Gorgon," *Berytus* 14 (1961): 1–23; Spyro Marinatos, "Gorgones kai gorgoneia," *Arch Eph* (1927–28): 7–41; and Ernest Will, "La décollation de Méduse," *Rev. Arch.* 27 (1947): 60–76.

and especially with that of the demon Humbaba as he is represented in Assyrian art.[11] Despite their value, these studies miss what I consider the essential fact: the specific form of a figure that, whatever borrowings or transpositions may have taken place, still stands out as a new creation that is very different from the antecedents invoked to explain it. The originality of this image cannot be grasped without considering how it is related in Greek archaic life to ritual practices and mythic themes, and above all, to a supernatural Power, which emerges and asserts itself just when the symbolic model that represents it is constructed and fixed in the particular form of the Gorgon's mask.

For this reason, Jane Harrison's efforts at interpretation seem finally unsuccessful. Relying on several figurative analogies among Harpies, Erinyes, and Gorgons, she tried to connect them all to the same "primitive" religious base and make them different types of "Keres"—evil spirits, phantoms, pollutions.[12] But it is not methodologically recommended to combine five different figures in the same vague category without concern for the clear and distinct differences that give each its appropriate significance and particular place in the system of divine Powers. The Erinyes have neither wings nor masks; the Harpies have wings but no masks. The Gorgons may be winged, but they are the only ones represented with the face of a mask (cf. Aesch., *Eum.* 48–51). The affinities between Gorgo and the Mistress of the Animals, the Potnia, as Theodora Karagiorga strongly emphasizes,[13] are more promising. There are shared contacts between the two types, and their iconographical representations reveal resemblances or, at least, parallels with each other. These should be taken into account. In certain of her aspects, Gorgo appears as the dark face, the sinister reverse of the Great Goddess whose legacy Artemis, in particular, will later inherit. But even here, the fact that there are also differences and discrepancies between the two models ought to warn us against a pure and simple assimilation. It still remains crucial to understand why and how the Greeks developed a symbolic figure that, in its combination of frontality and monstrosity in a single form, can be clearly distinguished from all the others so as to be instantly perceived for what it is: the face of Gorgo.

Let us take an example to illustrate these rather abstract ideas. On the François vase (ca. 570 B.C.E.), all the gods are represented in stock form. All are shown in profile with the exception of three figures: the Gorgon, represented on the internal side of the two handles; Dionysos, carrying an amphora on his shoulders; and Calliope, one of the Muses. In the cases of Gorgo and Dionysos, whose faces are treated like masks, frontality is not surprising; in a way, it is self-evident. For Calliope, this same frontality would be a problem were

---

[11] Clark Hopkins, "Assyrian Elements in the Perseus-Gorgon Story," *AJA* (1934): 341–53, and "The Sunny Side of the Greek Gorgon," *Berytus* 14 (1961): 25–35.

[12] *Prolegomena to the Study of Greek Religion* (1903; reprint, New York, 1957), chap. 5, "The Demonology of Ghosts and Sprites and Bogeys," 163–256.

[13] *Gorgeie Kephale* (Athens, 1970).

this Muse not represented in the procession of the gods as playing the syrinx—
that rustic flute called the pipe (or flute) of Pan. I will later argue, expanding
on the pertinent observations of Paul Laporte,[14] that to blow into the flute is
for many reasons equivalent to becoming the head of the Gorgon. On the vase,
however, the images of the Mistress of the Animals on the outside correspond
to the Gorgons painted on the inside of the handles. This design simultaneously associates and opposes the two types of Powers with each other. The
contrast can be seen on several planes. First and foremost, the Gorgons are
shown full face, the Mistresses in profile, like all the other gods or heroes on
the vase. In addition, the Gorgons are running, their knees bent, while the
Mistresses are immobile, standing erect in a hieratic pose. The Gorgons have
short *chitōns*, the Mistresses long tunics that cover them down to their feet.
The bristling hairstyle of the first contrasts with that of the second, which is
drawn back on the shoulders with a band, in the more typical way. The mask
of the Gorgon's face, as depicted in images, has a value, therefore, that fits in
with a whole series of other indications, which unambiguously marks its difference from the model of the Potnia, the Mistress of Wild Beasts.

If this were an iconographical study, the task would be to explore this network of signs and draw up an inclusive list of the image's significant elements
and the interactions of these in various similar series—grouped by their place
of origin, the nature of the objects, and their representational themes. Not
being an archaeologist, I can only point out the place occupied by certain
animals (snakes, lizards, birds, wild animals, even hippocampi) in the imagery of the Gorgo, especially the horse. In figural representations, the horse
(or horses, when two are placed symmetrically) is associated with the Gorgon,
sometimes as a part of herself, her extension or emanation, sometimes as the
little one she nurses and protects, sometimes as the progeny to which she gives
birth, or the mount on which she rides, and sometimes, finally, in connection
with the myth of Perseus, as the horse Pegasos, who at the moment of her
death leaps forth from her slashed neck. In contrast to the myth, therefore, the
imagistic associations between the Gorgon and the horse provide a surplus,
even an overflow, of meaning.

A Face of Terror

But let us turn now to the texts and the indications they give about the myths
and ritual elements that belong to the Gorgon so we may illuminate her character, her modes of action, her areas of intervention, and the forms of revelation assigned to this Power become a mask.

With Homer the stage is already set on which Gorgo will make her appearance and play her various roles. In the *Iliad*, the scene is martial (5.738ff.;

---

[14] "The Passing of the Gorgon," *Bucknell Review* 17 (1969): 57–71.

8.348; 11.36–37). Gorgo figures on Athena's aegis depicted on Agamemnon's shield. On the opposing side, when Hektor, bringing death into the fray, tosses his hair in all directions, "his eyes have the look of the Gorgon." In this context of merciless confrontation, Gorgo is a Power of Terror, associated with "Fear, Rout, and Pursuit which chills the heart." But this terror, whose presence she incarnates and which in some way she mobilizes, is not "normal"; it does not result from the particular situation of danger an individual may confront. It is pure fright—Terror—as a dimension of the supernatural. This fear is not secondary, nor is it motivated, like the kind aroused by an awareness of some danger. It is primary. Gorgo instantly and on her own inspires fear because she appears on the battlefield as a prodigy (*teras*), a monster (*pelōr*), in the form of a head (*kephalē*), terrible and frightening both to see and hear (*deinē te smerdnē te*), possessed of a face with terrifying eyes (*blosurōpis*) that cast a fearful glance (*deinon derkomenē*).

In the *Iliad*, the Gorgon mask and eye operate in a strictly defined context; they appear as an integral part of the equipment, the mimicry, and even the grimacing expression itself of the warrior (man or god) who is possessed by *menos*, battle fury. The face and eyes somehow concentrate the power of death that radiates from the body of the warrior, who is clad in armor and ready to manifest the extraordinary battle strength, the valor (*alkē*) residing in him. Gorgo's flashing gaze acts in conjunction with the dazzling gleam of bronze that rises up to the sky from helmet and armor, spreading panic. By its gape the monster's distended mouth evokes the fearful war cry that Achilles raises three times before the battle as he shines resplendent in the flame that Athena causes to flash forth from his head. "One might say it was like the piercing sound of the trumpet," and it is precisely this "brazen voice" in Achilles' throat that is enough to send shock waves of terror through the enemy lines (*Il*. 18.214–21).

It is not essential to accept Thalia Howe's etymology connecting *Gorgō*, *gorgos*, and *gorgoumai* to the Sanskrit *garg*,[15] in order to appreciate the aural connotations of the Gorgon mask. Howe states: "It is clear that some terrible noise was the originating force behind the Gorgon: a guttural animal-like howl that issued with a great wind from the the throat and required a hugely distended mouth." Our observations will be more limited and more precise. We know through Pindar (*Pyth*. 12.6ff.) that a piercing groan (*eriklagtan goon*) issues from the swift jaws of the Gorgons pursuing Perseus, and that these cries escape both from their maiden mouths and from the horrible heads of snakes associated with them. This inhuman, shrill cry (*klazō, klangē*) is the same one uttered by the dead in Hades (*klangē nekuōn, Od*. 11.605). We shall

---

[15] "The Origin and Function of the Gorgon Head," *AJA* 58 (1954): 209–21. Under the name Thalia Feldman, the author developed and extended her analysis in "Gorgo and the Origins of Fear," *Arion* 4 (1965): 484–94.

have occasion to return to the implications of these auditory features. But to underline the connections, on both visual and aural levels, between the mask of Gorgo and the facial mimicry of the berserk warrior, we will press one significant detail. Among the elements that, in addition to the terrifying cry, the gleam of bronze, and the flames leaping from his head and eyes, invest the warrior with the power to cause fear, there is one expression that Aristarchus already noticed: the gnashing or grinding of the teeth (*odontōn kanachē*). Françoise Bader has clarified the meaning of this audible "rictus" by connecting it through parallels in Irish legend with the image of the Indo-European warrior as reconstructed by Georges Dumézil.[16] Ps. Hesiod, speaking in his poem the *Shield* about the "heads of terrible snakes" that cast fear (*phobeeskon*) over the tribes of men, takes up the Homeric expression: "the gnashing of their teeth echoed" [*odontōn kanachē pelen*]" (164). At line 235, referring this time to the snakes worn by the Gorgons, hot on the heels of Perseus, the poet says that these monsters "thrust forth their tongues, gnashed their teeth in fury [*menei d'echarasson odontas*], and cast wild looks." When Achilles, blazing in his armor, his eyes shining with a ray of fire, grimaces, gnashes his teeth, and hurls an inhuman battle cry in the manner of aegis-bearing Athena (Pind., *Ol.* 6.37), the enraged hero, possessed by *menos*, displays a face in a Gorgon's mask.

Blazing brilliance of arms, unbearable radiation from head and eyes, violent war cry, gaping grin, and gnashing of teeth: one can add to this list yet another feature linking the monstrous face of Gorgo to the warrior possessed by *menos* (murderous fury), namely, the terrifying effects of hair. When we come to mark the horse's place in the bestiary closely associated with Gorgo and indicate Medusa's equine affinities, we will point out what the adjective *gorgos* means when used of the horse. For the moment, let us note that it is the same term Xenophon uses to characterize the quality ascribed to young Spartan warriors by virtue of their long hair. That the young men do not cut their hair after leaving the *ephebeia* has nothing to do with stylish appearance or personal choice. It is the mark of a strict obligation for a whole-age class, and it consecrates their status: "Lycurgus enjoined on those who left the *ephebeia* to wear their hair long with the idea that they would thus appear taller, more noble, and more terrible [*gorgoterous*]" (*Rep. Lac.* 11.3). Plutarch confirms and clarifies Xenophon:

In time of war, too, they relaxed the severity of the young men's discipline, and permitted them to beautify their hair and ornament their arms and clothing, rejoicing to see them, like horses, prance and neigh for the contest. Therefore they wore their hair long as soon as they ceased to be youths, and particularly in times of danger they took pains to have it glossy and well-combed, remembering a certain

[16] "Rhapsodies homériques et irlandaises," in *Recherches sur les religions de l'antiquité classique*, ed. Raymond Bloch, Hautes études du monde gréco-romain, 10 (1980), 61–74.

saying of Lycurgus, that a fine head of hair made the handsome more comely still, and the ugly more terrible. (*Lyc.* 22) [trans. B. Perrin]

A gloss tells us that the name given to this procedure for glazing long hair is *xanthizesthai*, that is, a term used "among the Lacedaimonians" meaning "to attend to one's hair."[17] *Xanthos* means "blond" in the sense of "gilded," suggesting the idea of a brilliance that describes both gold and fire. *Xanthos* is different from *chlōros* (yellow-green), which connotes paleness, even weakness. (Fear, *deos*, is called *chlōron*.) Xanthos is also the name of a horse, an immortal warrior horse. One of the horses of Achilles, sprung from Zephyr and Podarge, is called Xanthos. Xanthos is also the name of the horse of Castor, who of the two Dioscouroi represents the young man and the knight. Among the Macedonians, the term designates the festival of purification for the cavalry, the *Xanthika*, in the course of which sacrifice was made to the god Xanthos.[18] There is a connection between the wild manes of war horses and the coppery blond color of the hair that the young warrior, once having left the *ephebeia*, wears like a flowing mane.

In the *Life of Lysander*, Plutarch mentions, but rejects, another interpretation also found in Herodotus.[19] This explanation connects the Lacedaimonian custom of keeping the hair long with a battle over the territory of Thyrea when there was a clash between two elite corps of three hundred combatants, who represented the flower of warrior youth for the two contending cities, Argos and Sparta. The Argives were finally vanquished. "From this moment on," says Herodotus, "the Argives shaved their heads while beforehand, custom had obliged them to have long hair. . . . The Lacedaimonians, who until this battle had kept their hair short, promulgated the opposite rule and now take pride in wearing long hair" (1.82). Plutarch protests this explanation that ascribes the Spartan custom to the victors' desire to distinguish themselves from the vanquished: "It is not true that the Spartans, seeing the Argives cut their hair as a sign of mourning after the serious defeat they had undergone, let their own hair grow to emphasize their victory and to do the opposite of their enemies. . . . It is rather an institution of Lycurgus who said that long hair enhances beauty and makes ugliness more terrifying" (Plut., *Lys.* 1.2).

Nevertheless, if we retain not so much the "historical" basis of Herodotus's story that it claims to give to the Spartan regulation, but rather the relation of opposition established between shaved hair, the shame of defeat, and mourning, on the one hand, and on the other, long hair, victory, and celebration, we can see that the two explanations of the custom are not contradictory. Heightened by long, flowing hair, the manly beauty of the warrior contains a "terrifying" aspect whose effect on the battlefield is, in the active meaning of the

[17] I. Bekker, *Anecdota Graeca* (Berlin, 1814), 284.
[18] Hesych., s.v. *Xanthika*. Suda, s.v. *enagizōn*.
[19] Herod. 1.82; cf. Plat., *Phaed.* 89c.

word, a "sign" of victory, just as shorn hair, along with other manifestations of mourning, is one of the ritual means used during the funeral to link the survivors to the dead. With their faces disfigured and made ugly, the living are connected to that world of dim and feeble phantoms to which the dead, whose disappearance one mourns, must descend.

The contrast between long and short hair clarifies perhaps another Lacedaimonian custom. At Sparta the tradition was kept of marriage by abduction of one's future wife. "The young woman, thus carried off, was put in the hands of a woman called *numpheutria*, who shaved her head, and decked her out in the dress and shoes of a man" (Plut., *Lyc.* 15.5). That this is a rite of passage, replete with disguise and inversion of sexual status, no one will deny. But that is not the whole of it, nor even perhaps the essential, if we consider that the young boy, having become a complete man when he leaves the *ephebeia*—as the girl becomes a complete woman on entering into marriage—keeps his hair long precisely as a sign of his full virility. In the hoplite formation, this same virility preserves the memory and, as it were, the trace of the "fury" that in heroic times had to inhabit the soul of the young warrior in order for him to bring terror into the enemy camp. In shaving the head of the young bride, everything that could be still considered masculine and martial—and wild— in her femininity is extirpated in her new matrimonial state. The face of Gorgo must not be introduced into the husband's house under the mask of the bride.

Hesychius notes that at Sparta, the name of *pōlos* was given to the young person, whether boy or girl, both of them equally noncivilized and not yet integrated into the community. *Pōlos* is the young horse, the colt or filly. In *Lysistrata*, Aristophanes evokes the *korai*, the young virgins of Sparta: "Like fillies, the girls bound with quick steps all along the river Eurotas, raising up the dust; and their hair is tossed like those of the bacchants who brandish the thyrsus and frolic about" (1308ff.).

The wild quality of the male warrior is expressed by his long hair, which flows like a horse's mane. The wild quality of the girl shows up in her loose hair, which makes her like a frisky and unconstrained filly. In the case of the young married woman, the ritual of the shaved head plays with these two contrasting symbols, which are reinforced in their opposition, since if the wife must be marked off from the *parthenos* on entering into the conjugal state, she must by the same ploy be clearly distinguished from her husband.

In cutting the hair of new brides, the idea is not only to domesticate these untamed fillies, but also to exorcise the disturbing wild quality that Athena and Artemis, the two virgins excluded from marriage, retain, each in her own way: Athena the warrior with the face of Gorgo she wears on her breast, Artemis the *kourotrophos*, the wild one, with the Gorgon side of her character and with the masks used in initiatory rites for the young over which she presides.

With the *Odyssey*, the setting is changed. The scene has shifted from a martial to an infernal locale. The underground haunts and the realm of Night are not, however, a world of silence. In book 11 (632ff.), Odysseus recounts his arrival in the land of Hades. The assembled crowd of the dead raises a prodigious clamor (*ēchē thespesiē*). "Green fear gripped me," explains the hero, "lest from the depths of Hades noble Persephone send me the gorgonean head of the terrifying monster" [*gorgeiēn kephalēn deinoio pelōrou*]" (633–35). Odysseus immediately turns away. Gorgo is at home in the land of the dead and she forbids every living man entrance into that domain. Her role is symmetrical with that of Kerberos: she prevents the living from entering the realm of the dead, while Kerberos prevents the dead from returning to the land of the living (Hes., *Theog.* 770–73). Like Homer, Aristophanes locates the Gorgons in Hades next to Kerberos, Styx, and Echidna (*Frogs* 477). Apollodorus relates how all the *psuchai* fled before Herakles as he descended to the underworld, all except Meleager and the gorgon Medusa (ps. Apollod. 2.5). From the very depths of Hades where she lives, Gorgo's head, like a vigilant watchman, surveys the borders of Persephone's realm. Her mask expresses and maintains the radical otherness, the alterity of the world of the dead, which no living person may approach. In order to cross the threshold, one would have had to confront the face of terror and, beneath its gaze, to have been transformed oneself into the image of Gorgo, into that which, in fact, the dead already are: heads, empty heads, robbed of their strength and *menos*, the *nekuōn amenēna karēna* of the Homeric formula (*Od.* 10.521, 536; 11.29, 49).[20]

The face of the living human being, in the particularity of its features, is one of the components that make up the individual. But in death, this head to which one is reduced, this head that from now on is weak and without vigor, comparable to a man's shadow or his reflection in a mirror, is submerged in darkness. It is a head clothed in night, the equivalent in Hades of those faces that, in the light of day, certain heroes such as Perseus cover with the helmet of Hades to make themselves imperceptible to the eyes of the living. The *Aidos kuneē*, the dog-skin cap, which serves as the head-covering for Hades of the underworld, "contains the gloomy shadows of Night," as Hesiod puts it in the *Shield* (226). It envelops the whole head as if in a dark cloud; it masks it, and just as with someone who is dead, it makes the wearer invisible to all eyes.

The affinities of Gorgo with the underworld turn the inquiry in two directions. In the first place, they suggest we make a detour to Etruscan data and insert a parenthesis for Altheim's thesis, taken up and modified especially by Agnello Baldi and J. H. Croon.[21] Recalling the derivation of the Latin *persona*

---

[20] Cf. R. B. Onians, *The Origins of European Thought*, 2d ed. (Cambridge, 1954), 98ff.

[21] Franz Altheim, "Persona," *ARW* 27 (1929): 35–52; Agnello Baldi, "Perseus e Phersu,"

(mask, role, person) that comes from the Etruscan Phersu, Altheim proposed an equivalence both between this Etruscan Phersu and Greek Perseus and between Phersipnai and Persephone. Phersu figures on two frescoes from the so-called tomb of the Augurs at Tarquinia (ca. 530 B.C.E.). On one of the lateral walls of the mortuary chamber two personages confront each other. One wears a dark mask that hides his face and a white beard that seems to be false. An inscription names him Phersu, which would therefore mean masked man, mask-bearer. This masked figure holds onto a long cord, which is wound around his adversary's arms and legs. One end of this leash is attached to the collar of a dog who bites the left leg of the second wrestler, whose head is enveloped in a white cloth and who grasps a club in his right hand. Blood flows from his wounds. The same group of two figures is represented on the facing wall. The masked man no longer has a leash or a dog. He is in full flight, pursued by his adversary, toward whom he turns his head and stretches out his right arm with raised hand. It is difficult to interpret these two scenes, and no explanation seems fully satisfying. Altheim suggests a ritual struggle to the death in a funerary game in honor of the dead man. The term Phersu would designate the Bearer of the mask who officiates at the ceremony. For J. H. Croon, the mask constitutes a mode of representing the spirit of the dead in funeral games. During a ritual dance, the Bearer of the mask mimes and actualizes the Power of Beyond-the-Grave, just as Persephone, through the mask of Gorgo she controls, herself presides over the lower world. Onians, however, interprets these scenes differently:[22] the fighter, armed with the club and attacked by the dog, would be Herakles in his descent to the underworld; Phersu must then be interpreted as Hades, who is finally vanquished and put to flight. For Agnello Baldi, Phersu, Perseus, and Hades are one and the same divinity. Whatever he may be, on the Etruscan mural paintings of Orvieto and Corneto, Hades is depicted with a cap of wolfskin or dogskin, which recalls both the *kuneē* which Perseus uses and the mask of Phersu.

The second direction offers us more secure terrain. It lets us follow Hesiod to the ends of the world where the *Theogony* places the Gorgons and associates them with the whole lineage of their monstrous relatives. The Gorgons belong to the offspring of Phorkys and Keto, whose names evoke both a monstrous hugeness and the cavernous depths at the bottommost points of land and sea. In fact, in addition to their common feature of monstrousness, all the children of this couple live "far from gods and men," in subterranean regions beyond Okeanos, on the border of Night, there to play the role of watchmen, even bogeys, who bar the way to forbidden places.

Aevum: Rassegna di scienze storiche, linguistiche, e filologiche 35 (1961): 131–35; J. H. Croon, "The Mask of the Underworld Daemon: Some Remarks on the Perseus-Gorgon Story," *JHS* 75 (1955): 9ff.

    [22] Onians, *Origins*, 429 n. 1.

Born from the union of Pontos and Gaia, Phorkys and Keto first produce the Graiai, maidens old from birth, who combine within themselves the young and the old, the freshness of beauty and a wrinkled skin like the rough film that forms on the surface of chilled milk and which in fact bears their name: *graus*, wrinkled skin.[23] The first of the Hesiodic Graiai is named Pemphredo; *Pemphrēdōn* is a species of voracious wasp that burrows holes underground.[24] The second is called Enyo, which brings to mind the mistress of battles and the violent war cry (*alalē*) raised in honor of Enyalios.[25]

Sisters of the Graiai, the three Gorgons, whose group combines mortal and immortal qualities,[26] live beyond the boundaries of the world in the direction of Night, in the land of those nymphs, the Hesperides, maidens "with shrill voices" (*liguphōnoi*). The mortal Gorgon, whose name is Medusa, coupled with Poseidon in a soft meadow of spring flowers, like the one in which Hades ravished the young Kore in order to transform her into Persephone. When Perseus cut off Medusa's head, Chrysaor sprang forth from her gaping neck and so did the horse, Pegasos, who flew off into the heavens.

Chrysaor begot three-headed Geryon, he who makes his voice heard (*gēruō*), who lets a *gēruma* burst forth like the *hupertonon gēruma*, the very shrill sound that the piercing Etruscan trumpet produces (Aesch., *Eum.* 569). Geryon is associated with one of the offspring of the third brood of Phorkys and Keto, the horrible Echidna, half maiden, half serpent, who lives in the secret depths of the earth, far from gods and men. Among other monsters, this Echidna in turn gives birth to two roaring, growling, and barking dogs, Orthos, dog of Geryon, and the corresponding Kerberos, dog of Hades, the beast with fifty heads, "with a voice of bronze," who guards the echoing halls (*domoi ēchēentes*) of his master and of the dread Persephone.

In these same infernal places, this realm of shadow and terror, drips the water of Styx, the great oath of the gods. This primordial water (*hudōr ōgugion*) brings to those gods guilty of perjury the equivalent of the death they can never undergo: a temporary *kōma* that enshrouds them, depriving them of breath and voice for one great year just as death enshrouds the head of men with eternal night. In this sense, Styx represents for the gods what Gorgo does for human beings—an object of terror and fright. Just as Styx is *stugerē athanatoisi*, horror for the immortals (Hes., *Theog.* 775), so too the Gorgons, on whom no human may look without immediately perishing, are *brotostugeis*, horror for mortals (Aesch., *Prom. vinct.* 799). Styx is also the screech owl,

[23] Arist., *de gen. anim.* 743b6; cf. Athen. 585c.

[24] Arist., *Hist. anim.* 623b10 and 629a22.

[25] Xen., *Anab.* 1.8.18, 5.2.4; Heliod., *Aethiop.* 4.17.4–5.

[26] The two sisters of Medusa are immortal. Perseus kills Medusa. But the head of the monster, once cut off, keeps all its deadly power: it changes to stone those who gaze at it, and continues to do so forever as did the living head of Medusa.

the sinister double of the owl, the ill-omened bird characterized by its large head, evil eye, and nocturnal cry.[27]

In the netherworld regions of Hades, Darkness, and Fear, monstrous sights and sounds combine to express the "alterity" of those powers as alien to the realm of the celestial gods as they are to the world of humans. They constitute an entirely separate jurisdiction of beings with whom, as Aeschylus says of the Erinyes—the *graiai palaiai paides*, the ancient maidens—neither god nor man nor beast will consort (*Eum.* 68).

Disquieting noises are so much a part of the universe to which the Gorgons belong that in the verses of the *Shield* that describe how they run, Hesiod adds auditory details to the purely visual indications that until now were used to portray the decoration on Herakles's shield: "Beneath their feet the shield clattered with a great strident and resounding noise [*iacheske sakos megalōi orumagdōi oxea kai ligeōs*]" (232–33). The only other references to noise in the text, as we have seen, have to do with the clacking jaws of snakes that terrorize humans or of those that coil around the Gorgons's waists.

Snakes take pride of place among the monstrous offspring of Phorkys and Keto. The shrill sounds that issue from the Gorgons's throats or are produced by the vibration of their jaws are also those of the snakes that gnash and clack their teeth in concert. Along with the snake, the dog and the horse complete the trio of animals whose shape and voice enter most particularly into the composition of the "monstrous." If the "brazen voice" of Kerberos (*chalkeophōnos*) resounds in the halls of Hades, so too we hear the Erinyes, when Aeschylus compares them to Gorgons, producing a strident growling and groaning (*oigmos, mugmos oxus*). They groan (*muzō*) just as the extended moans of tortured men "groan" in the underworld (*Eum.* 117, 189). They "make sounds like a dog" (*Eum.* 131) and the term used, *klangainō*, recalls the *klangē* of the dead in the *Odyssey* as well as the shrill complaint (*eriklagtēs*) of the Gorgons and their snakes.[28]

The horse too, by its behavior and the sounds it makes, at times betrays the disquieting presence of a Power of the Underworld manifesting itself in animal form. The horse is skittish; it tends to bolt abruptly as a result of a sudden fright like that provoked by the demonic power of Taraxippos, the Terror of horses (*to tōn hippōn deima*; Paus. 6.20.15), and it can become wild and frenzied enough to devour human flesh. It also bristles, drools, and perspires with a white foam. Added to these qualities are its neighing, the din of its hooves hammering the earth, the dull gnashing of its teeth (*brugmos*), and finally, the sinister sound of the bit between its jaws that induces terror by "making murder resound" (Aesch., *Supp.* 123, 208). In equestrian vocabulary, *gorgos* takes on a quasi-technical meaning. For the horse, *gorgoumai* is to paw the

---

[27] Hesych., s.v. *stux*; Ant. Lib., *Met.* 21.5; Ov., *Fast.* 6.33.
[28] *Od.* 11.605; Pind., *Pyth.* 12.38.

ground. Xenophon notes in the *Equestrian Art* that the nervous and impetuous horse is terrible to behold (*gorgos idein*), that its widely flared nostrils make it *gorgoteros*, and that when horses are mustered as a troop, with their pounding, neighing, and snorting amplified by their numbers, this is the time when they appear most spirited and fiery (*gorgōtatoi*, *Eq.* 10.17; cf. 1.10, 14; 11.12).

The Flute and the Mask: The Dance of Hades

Certain musical instruments, when used orgiastically to provoke delirium, play on this scale of infernal sounds. The effect of Terror these produce in their hearers is all the more intense when the musicians and their instruments are not seen and the source of the sounds is concealed. These sounds seem to rise up directly out of the invisible, to come up from the beyond like the disguised voice of a ghostly Power, an echo come from afar and mysteriously resounding here on earth. A fragment from Aeschylus's *Edonians*, quoted by Strabo (10.3.16), is significant in this regard: "One, holding in his hands the pipe, the labor of the lathe, blows forth his fingered tune, even the sound that wakes to frenzy. Another, with brass-bound cymbals, raises a clang . . . the twang shrills; and unseen, unknown, bull-voiced mimes in answer bellow fearfully, while the timbrel's echo, like that of subterranean thunder, rolls along inspiring a mighty terror."

But among all the musical instruments, the flute, because of its sounds, melody, and the manner in which it is played, is the one to which the Gorgon's mask is most closely related. The art of the flute—the instrument itself, the way it is used, and the melody one extracts from it—was "invented" by Athena to "simulate" the shrill sounds she had heard escaping from the mouths of the Gorgons and their snakes. In order to imitate them, she made the song of the flute "which combines all sounds [*pamphōnon melos*]" (Pind., *Pyth.* 12.18ff.). But the risk in playing the role of the shrieking Gorgon is actually to become one—all the more so as this *mimēsis* is not mere imitation but an authentic "mime," a way of getting inside the skin of the character one imitates, of donning his or her mask. The story is told that Athena, wholly absorbed in blowing into the flute, did not heed the warning of the satyr, Marsyas, who, when he saw her with distended mouth, puffed-out cheeks, and a face wholly distorted by the effort of getting a sound from the flute, said to her: "These ways do not become you. Take up your weapons, put down the flute, and compose your features." But it was only when she looked at herself in the waters of a river and saw that what the mirror reflected was not the beautiful face of a goddess but the hideous rictus of a Gorgon that she threw away the flute once and for all, crying "be damned, shameful object, outrage to my body; I will not surrender myself to this ignominy." Frightened "by the deformity that offends the sight," she gave up the instrument that her intelligence was able to invent. Nevertheless, the flute was not altogether lost for everyone. Marsyas seized it; the flute became the pride and joy of the satyr, "the brute who claps his hands," a monster whose ugly face harmonizes with the melody and playing of the instrument.[29] Marsyas's glory is also his misfortune. Athena discovered that by playing the flute she had descended to the level of monstrosity. Her face was demeaned to become a semblance of a Gorgon's mask. Marsyas, however, thinks that by playing the flute he can raise himself to the level of the god, Apollo. He claims victory over the god in a musical contest. But in the hands of Apollo, the lyre produces a melody in harmony with human song and its accompanying words. On the other hand, in the huge mouth of the satyr, even when it is covered with a piece of leather, the *phorbeia*, and a halter to soften the violence of his breathing and mask the distortion of his lips, the *aulos* or *syrinx*, the double flute or the flute of Pan, leaves no room for human song or voice. At the end of the contest, Apollo is declared the winner; he flays Marsyas alive, hanging his skin in a cave at the springs of the Meander[30]—just as Athena, according to certain versions, wears over her shoulders as an aegis, not the head but the flayed skin of Gorgo.[31]

What do these stories about the affinities between the flute and the mask of terror teach us?[32] First, of course, that the sounds of the flute are alien to articulate discourse, poetic song, and human speech. Second, that the flutist's distorted face, deformed to look like a Gorgon's, is that of a person possessed by madness and disfigured by anger and who, as Plutarch observes, ought, like Athena, to look at himself in the mirror in order to calm himself and recover his normal human state (*De tranq. an.*, 456a–b). Aristotle's remarks go even further. If Athena rejected the flute, he observes, it was not only because this instrument deforms the face, but also because the flute contributes nothing to the improvement of intelligence (*Pol.* 1341bff.). The goddess is opposed to the kind of instruction that prevents the use of speech. And, above all, flute music has the least ethical and the most orgiastic character. It produces its effects not through a mode of instruction (*mathēsis*) but by purification (*katharsis*), "for everything that belongs to the Bacchic trance and to all impulses of this sort depends, from the instrumental point of view, on the flute" (*Pol.* 1342a3; 1342b5). Thus the flute is the instrument par excellence of trance, orgiastic celebrations, delirium, and of rituals and dances of posses-

---

[29] Arist., *Pol.* 1341bff.; ps.Apollod. 1.4.2; Athen. 14.616e–f; Plut., *Mor.* 456bff.

[30] Herod. 7.26; Xen., *Anab.* 1.2.

[31] Eur., *Ion* 995–96; ps.Apollod. 1.6.1, Diod. Sic. 3.69.

[32] In addition to the two versions of the laughter of the Mother, distracted from her mourning by Iambe and Baubo, Euripides adds a new one that is different and instructive. This time, it is the Mother's act of taking up the flute that, along with the noise of cymbals and tambourine, takes the place of the obscene joking and exhibition of genitals. "Then Kypris, the most beautiful of goddesses, for the first time made echo the bronze with the infernal voice and seized the tambourine of taut leather. And the goddess mother began to laugh; charmed by the sounds, she took into her hands the low-sounding flute." *Hel.* 1338ff.

sion. Citing mothers, whose children have difficulty sleeping, and who, in order to calm them, rock them and sing them lullabies instead of leaving them alone in silence, Plato declares: "It is as if, in the full sense of the words, they play the flute in front of their children [*kataulousi tōn paidiōn*] as before frenzied bacchants [*ekphronōn bakcheiōn*], who are cured by the use of the movements of both dance and music" (*Laws* 7.790d). To play the bacchant or corybant is to hear or to think one hears flutes. Corresponding to Plato's remark, "those who play the corybant think they hear flutes" (*Crito* 54d), is Iamblichus's assertion: "Certain ecstatics hear flutes, cymbals, drums or some melody and are thus in a state of enthusiasm [*enthousiōsin*]. . . . Flutes both excite or heal passions of frenzy; some melodies cause a trance [*anabakcheuesthai*], others put an end to it [*apopauesthai tēs bakcheias*]" (*De myster.* 3.9).

There are several ways, however, of being a bacchant, and in states of possession, it is not always the same divinities who take hold of their worshippers, put the bit and bridle on them, and ride them into the cavalcade of madness. In contrast to the bacchant of Dionysos, whom the imagery associates with figures of Maenads along with their exuberant escort of Satyrs and Silenoi, we must distinguish what Euripides calls a "bacchant of Hades" (*Haïdou bakchos*, *Her. fur.* 1119) who is compelled by the rabies of a frenzied madness, *Lussa*, to dance while playing a tune of terror (*Phobos*) on the flute. What is this sinister power of enragement that finds its rhythm in the flute, "the music of madness"? The tragic poet supplies the answer: "It is the Gorgon, daughter of Night, and her vipers with their hundred clamorous [*iachēmasin*] heads; it is Lyssa of the petrifying gaze" (884). In this dance, which transforms Herakles into Terror itself—both the internal terror that possesses and torments him and the external terror he stirs up around him—"neither the tambourines nor the friendly thyrsus of Bromios appears. She [Terror] wants blood, not the bacchic libation of the juice of the vine" (891–95; cf. Eur., *Or.* 316–20). During the attack of frenzy in the course of which Fright, like a supernatural power, takes possession of Herakles, the music of the flute and the hero's face both take on the hideous appearance of Gorgo's mask: "Horrible, horrible is the music of this flute [*daion tode daion melos epauleitai*]," sings the chorus. As for Herakles, at the onslaught of the trance, "already he tosses his head and silently, with terrifying looks, rolls his twisted eyeballs [*gorgōpas koras*]" (*Her. fur.* 868). A little later, "the face distorted, he rolled his eyes where there appeared a network of blood-red veins and foam trickled on his thick beard. . . . He rolled the wild eyes of a Gorgon [*agriōpon omma Gorgonos*]" (931, 990).

In addition to the evidence from tragedy, whose import for our understanding of possession phenomena Jeanmaire has already observed,[33] several other similar texts can be added. According to Xenophon, those who are possessed

[33] *Dionysos: Histoire du culte de Bacchus* (Paris, 1951; reprint, 1970).

by certain divinities "have a more gorgonlike gaze, a more frightening voice, and more violent gestures" (*Symp.* 1.10). In Plato's *Laws*, Clinias questions the Athenian stranger about the nature of the sickness that both keeps children awake during the night and agitates those bacchants hearing the flute. The Athenian stranger replies: "Each sickness consists in being afraid [*deimainein*] and these fears [*deimata*] arise from a weakness in the soul. When one opposes an external impulse to such perturbations, the motion coming from outside masters the internal motion of fear and frenzy, and in mastering it, brings calm and tranquillity. . . . Every soul which from its youth is haunted by such fears will become more and more the prey of panic frights" (7.790e–791b). In the Hippocratic *Sacred Disease*, the author enumerates a series of divinities to whom people refer the perturbations that trouble them. "To those who are subject to fear [*deimata*], terrors [*phoboi*], and deliriums [*paranoiai*] at night, who leap from their beds or rush outside the house, they say that attacks of Hekate are responsible and assaults of heroes [i.e., the dead]" (4.31ff.). Like Gorgo, whom in certain respects she resembles closely enough to be sometimes invoked by her name (Hipp., *Ref. her.* 4.35), Hekate, who "sends ghosts" (Eur., *Hel.* 569) and whom the Orphic Hymn celebrates as "she who plays the bacchant with the souls of the dead," appears here as the Power of Terror, risen from the other world to take possession of humans during the night in the form of a dread that casts them outside themselves.

According to Plato, fears of this kind in the adult have their origin in childhood. Citing the childish anxiety that the wind, especially a strong one, will blow on the soul to disperse it on its exit from the body, he says in the *Phaedo* that perhaps "within us there is, as it were, a child whom these sorts of things frighten. Try to persuade the child not to have the same fear of death as it does of *mormulukeia*, hobgoblins" (77e). The Socrates of this dialogue then observes that getting rid of such fears requires an accomplished charmer and a daily incantation until the child is pacified by these spells.

Since these texts attribute our irrational fears to holdovers from childhood,[34] it pays to reexamine the dossier assembled by Rohde[35] and to look in the sphere of popular superstition and the child's world for the expressions of this same Power of Fear—fear as a category of the supernatural—that Gorgo's mask seems to embody, be it in a martial or an infernal context. Lamia, Empousa, Gello, and above all, Mormo translate into the world of childhood what Gorgo represents for adults. The *mormulukeion*, the bogeyman, corresponds to the *gorgoneion*.

For the child, Mormo is a mask, a head. As we see in Callimachus's *Hymn to Artemis* (50ff.), this can be Hermes's face, daubed with ashes, that, in order

---

[34] Cf. also Plut., *Mor.* 1105b.

[35] *Psyche: The Cult of Souls and Belief in Immortality among the Greeks*, 8th ed., trans. W. B. Hillis (New York, 1925; reprint, 1966), vol. 2, app. 5, 588–89.

to frighten children by imitating Mormo, has been transformed into a strange visage, a face enveloped in darkness and with no recognizable features. By this otherness, this alterity, it resembles the monstrous face of the Cyclops with his gorgonlike eye and the din that accompanies him, reverberated, amplified, and displaced by a formidable echo. In Theocritus (*Id*. 15.20), Mormo no longer resembles the Cyclops's face but rather that of a horse. To scare her child and keep him quiet, the mother cries out: "Mormo, horsey bites [*daknei hippos*]." These terrifying monsters in the shape of masked heads, looking like the Cyclops or a horse, are thought to seize and steal children, devour them, and give them over to death. These figures are in proximity to death; they belong to its domain, even when they wander in the midst of the living. They are a variety of revenants, phantoms, Doppelgänger, *eidōla*, and *phasmata*, like those sent by Hekate and called *Hekataia* (schol. ad Ap. Rh. 3.8–1). When a man is possessed by *Lussa* and imitates the Gorgon in his gestures, facial expressions, and cries, he becomes a kind of death-dancer himself, a bacchant of Hades. The terror that shakes him and compels him to dance to the horrible melody of the flute rises directly out of the lower world: it is the power of a dead man, an avenging demon pursuing him for expiation or vengeance, an *alastōr*, a criminal defilement (*miasma*), that weighs on him personally or that he has inherited from his ancestors. The author of the *Sacred Disease* observes that magi, exorcists, beggar priests, and other charlatans claim to heal those afflictions he has just mentioned through "purifications" and "incantations," and he remarks that they treat such invalids "as the carriers of *miasma*, as *alastoras*, those stained with blood, and as *pepharmakeumenous*, expiatory victims" (4.37–39). Euripides saw matters no differently when in his *Orestes* he portrayed the young man in a delirious state after the murder of Klytemnestra. The chorus addresses Orestes to propose as the cause "some *alastōr*, which allows your mother's blood to enter the house, the blood which arouses your madness [*ho s'anabaccheuei*]"—more precisely, "that which agitates you like a bacchant" (337–38). Louis Gernet has pointed to the ambivalence of such terms as *alastōr*, *miastōr*, and *aliteiros*, which apply both to the phantom of the victim of violent death who vengefully pursues his murderer and to the criminal who is the object of that pursuit. The same demonic power of terror engulfs them both and binds them to each other. The reason is that the culprit himself is troubled, agitated, and terrorized because the dead person cannot rest in peace and "returns" to trouble, agitate, and terrorize the one whose mind he haunts and who in turn becomes this fury, this rage, this Fright of which he is both cause and victim.[36]

[36] Louis Gernet, *Recherches sur le développement de la pensée juridique et morale en Grèce* (Paris, 1917), 146, 320. On this reciprocity of terror and trouble—*phobos, deima, tarassō*—in the victim's ghost and in the murderer stained with his blood, see Plato, *Laws* 9.865d–e. It is said that the man who has died a violent death "is no sooner dead than he is irritated against the one who killed him and himself, full of terror and fear [*phobou kai deimatos*] because of the violence

The Goddess-Heads

Until now we have only referred to mythic stories and iconographic representations that treat the monstrous face of Gorgo. Medusa is not the object of any cult that would serve either to honor her or to ward her off. But in Greek religion there exist fearful Powers, related to Gorgo in the sense that they appear only in the form of heads. These goddess-heads, the Praxidikai, have the ritual task of executing vengeance and guaranteeing oaths. According to Hesychius, Praxidike is a *daimōn* who finishes things off, bringing matters, both words and deeds, to their appointed term. This is the reason why her images are heads, and the same goes for the sacrifices made to her. Photius and the Suda (s.v.) confirm the fact that only the head of this goddess is set up.[37]

The chthonic or netherworld aspects of Praxidike are emphasized in an Orphic Hymn.[38] Assimilated to Persephone, Praxidike is hailed as "queen of those beneath the earth," *katachthoniōn basileia*. She is also called "mother of the Eumenides," those figures whose "frightening faces," *phobera prosōpa*, according to Aeschylus (*Eum.* 989–90), express clearly enough the role they play in the city—to incarnate Fright and the terrible (*Phobos* and *to deinon*). At line 19 of the Hymn, it is said that she supplies the fruits of the earth (providing, of course, that this earth, free from all defilement, is not smitten with sterility by the goddess).

What happens in her cult? Pausanias recounts how after the destruction of Troy, Menelaos, on his return home safe and sound, had built on the very site where Paris and Helen first consummated their adulterous union an *agalma* of Thetis (out of gratitude for his safe return) and of Praxidike, to thank her for the punishment of the guilty (3.22.2). At Haliarte in Boeotia, near Mount Tilphossion and the spring Tilphousa, there is an open-air sanctuary of the Praxidikai used for oath taking, but not for oaths sworn lightly (*ouk epidromon ton horkon*, Paus. 9.33.3). The meaning of this stipulation is clear in light of the sanctuary of the Eumenides, founded by Orestes at Keryneia, that does not give access to all and sundry, nor *ex epidromēs*. The reason given is that anyone who enters stained with blood or burdened with some impurity immediately loses his mind under the sway of terror (*autika . . . deimasin ektos tōn phrenōn ginesthai*, Paus. 7.25.7). At the sanctuaries of both the Praxidikai and the Eumenides, whoever was imprudent enough to risk swearing an oath lightly, without having made sure of his perfect religious purity, immediately found himself suffering an acute crisis of fear, like the one that struck Orestes

---

done to him, cannot look at his murderer . . . without being seized with fear [*deimainei*] and disturbed himself [*tarattomenos autos*], the victim disturbs [*tarattei*] his murderer as much as he can, using his memory of him as an aid in order to disquiet him in his soul and acts."

[37] On the head as the element necessary for completeness, cf. Plato, *Gorg.* 505d, *Tim.* 69a.

[38] Orph., *Hym.* 29.5–6 (Quandt).

precisely in the place called *Maniai* (Madnesses), a name, that, according to Pausanias, designates the Eumenides (8.34.1).

There is another sanctuary in Arcadia where the most serious oaths on the most important matters are sworn, that of Eleusinian Demeter at Pheneus (Paus. 8.15.1–3). There one swears by the *petrōma*, the rock. Constructed of two interlocking stone blocks (they conceal writings concerning the mysteries that are taken out every other year and read to the initiates), the *petrōma* has a sphere on top in which is contained the mask of Demeter Kidaria. During the Great Rites this mask is worn by the priest, who with his rod strikes those who dwell underground, *tous hupochthonious paiei* (that population of the dead of whom Praxidike is called queen). The epithet given to this masked Demeter, who is associated with the underworld and is a guarantor of solemn oaths, comes from the word *kidaris*, which has two meanings: first, that of a cap or mask (Hesychius s.v.), and second, an Arcadian dance Athenaeus compares to the *alētēr*, the "wandering dance" of the Sicyonians (14.631d).

The Praxidikai, goddess-heads, and Demeter Kidaria, the goddess of the mask, guarantee the inviolability of an oath that is meant to inspire men with the same sacred terror as that aroused in the netherworld by the water of Styx, the primordial water (*ōgugion hudōr*) on which the gods swear. *Ogugios* is an adjective formed from the name of Ogugos, a primordial mythic being, the doublet of Okeanos, who, according to certain traditions, seems to have been the first king of the gods. The first flood is supposed to have taken place in his time, before the one associated with Deucalion, and the surface of the earth was submerged by the eruption of a mixture of subterranean and celestial waters. Ogugos is best known in Boeotia (Paus. 9.6; 9.33.5) where he is specifically associated with the Praxidikai.[39] According to Photius (s.v.), the daughters of Ogugos are Alalkomene, Thelxinoe, and Aulis, "who were later called Praxidikai." Panyassis, according to Stephanos of Byzantium (s.v. *tremilē*), speaks of an Ogygian nymph called Praxidike.

The Boeotian Praxidikai are not only associated with the Stygian waters and with Ogugos. They are related to a spring, rising from underground, whose name is Tilphousa and whose waters, again like those of Styx, are fatal for all human beings. Tiresias, whose tomb is nearby, died for having drunk of it. Corresponding to the deadly spring of Tilphousa is the spring of Ares, which is at the origin of the foundation of Thebes and feeds the river Dirke. The serpent (*drakōn*) who guarded this spring to prevent any access to it and who is sometimes said to have been the progeny of Ares and Ge, seems in fact, as the scholia to Sophocles's *Antigone* (126) claims, to have been the offspring of Ares and the Erinys Tilphossa. Another tradition, preserved by Callimachus (frag. 652 Pfeiffer), represents matters differently. Having coupled in the form of a mare with Poseidon, the Erinys Tilphossa (or Telphousa) gives birth to

---

[39] See Francis Vian, *Les origines de Thèbes* (Paris, 1963), 230ff.

the horse, Areion, just as Medusa, coupling with the same god, gives birth, along with Chrysaor, to Pegasos, the horse, whose name recalls a spring (*pēgē*) or, according to Hesiod, the flowing waters (*pēgai*) of Okeanos, the boundary of the world.

Several observations should be made at this point:

(1) From the regions where he was born, beyond Okeanos and in the direction of Night, Pegasos flies skyward, to dwell there with Zeus. But because his function is to transport (*pherōn*) thunder and lightning, he hovers between the aether where he resides and the chthonic realm (*chthōn*) to which he belongs (Hes., *Theog.* 284–86).

(2) Styx is that daughter of Okeanos whose waters flow at the deepest point below the earth in the abode of Night, where murmur the springs (*pēgai*) of the Earth, Tartaros, the Sea, and the Heavens, whose waters are still conjoined and mingled with one another (*Theog.* 736–38; 807–9). This is a frightful chaotic region (*chasma mega*) "which the gods abhor [*ta te stugeousi theoi*]" (739). The primordial waters of Styx represent this original chasm not only because of the *kōma* in which they shroud perjured gods or the death they bring to mortals, but by their strange location. Already in Hesiod, Styx, situated underground in black night, in the shadowy land of the house of Hades, inhabits at the same time a dwelling "surrounded by towering rocks with silver columns raised heavenward on all sides" (775–79). The "primordial" meaning of Styx establishes it at the lowest and highest points as if it contained both extremes, just as the Graiai combine the young and the old, and the Gorgons, the mortal and immortal. The same is true for the Arcadian Styx described by Herodotus (6.74) and Pausanias (8.18.4). The waters of Styx, waters of the nether depths, bring death to every living being; no receptacle, no material, not even gold (except, to be sure, "the horn of a horse's hoof") has the power to contain them, and they trickle down from a lofty, rocky cliff, so towering that Pausanias says he knows of "no others that rise to such a height." Thus the waters of the underworld flow from on high, as if from the heavens.

(3) In J. H. Croon's work mentioned earlier,[40] the author observes that representations of the *gorgoneion* can be found in most of the places where hot springs exist. Thus of the twenty-nine ancient cities whose coins bear the figure of Gorgo, there are at least eleven where we know of a spring in the vicinity. This is true, in particular, of Seriphos, a rocky island, a place about which Croon insists that, apart from the hot spring where festivals take place every year even to this day, no reason can be found to account for the central role it plays in the legend of Perseus and Medusa.

(4) The spring Tilphousa with its deadly waters, associated with the Praxidikai and the Erinys Tilphossa (or Telphousa) of Boeotia, who in the form of a mare gave birth by Poseidon to the horse Areion, has its double in Arcadia

---

[40] Croon, "Mask," 11ff.

in the personage of a Demeter Erinys, who is located at Thelpousa on the banks of the Ladon and whose waters rise from several springs in the area (Paus. 8.25). This Demeter couples in the form of a mare with Poseidon, himself turned into a horse, and gives birth to the stallion, Areion, and to a girl with a secret name that suggests she is a doublet of Kore, the maiden who is shared between the darkness of the underworld and life in the light of the sun. The Demeter of Thelpousa has two aspects and two names. Her "furious" side is matched by a "calm" one. When she has appeased her anger and bathed in the waters of the Ladon, she is Demeter Lousia, "the bathed one," "the cleansed."

The same polarity between a power of madness that causes delirium and an assuaging power that produces calm and a return to a state of normality is evident in another Arcadian form of the raging, equiform Demeter. At Phigalia there is a cave consecrated to Demeter Melaina, "the black one" (Paus. 8.42.1–7). The Phigalians agree with the people of Thelpousa about the union of Demeter. According to them, however, the fruit of this union was not the horse, Areion, but she whom they call Despoina, the Mistress. Like the Erinys, Melaina oscillates between a state of frenzy and one of calm. Her name, the Black One, recalls those divinities that appeared to Orestes at Maniai under two guises: black, as long as he was insane and a prey to panic; white, as soon as he cut off a finger in atonement for his criminal defilement and recovered his sanity at a place called Akē (i.e., Remedies) (Paus. 8.34.2–4). Demeter Melaina, in her maddened state, was portrayed seated on a rock. Her body was that of a woman but she had the head and hair of a horse. Figures of snakes and other wild beasts rose up from this horse's mask, in a manner similar to Gorgo.

The Despoina, daughter of Demeter the mare and Poseidon Hippios, had her temple at Lycosura where she was worshipped by the local people above any other divinity. Excavations have restored fragments of her cult statue, particularly her drapery, on which are seen eleven female figures with animal heads (notably horse heads) who play various musical instruments while they dance. Small terra-cotta statues have also been found, and these too are of draped women with animal heads. One last detail concerning the sanctuary of the Despoina: toward the exit from the temple a mirror was hung on the wall. If one looked in it, one did not see oneself. The mirror did not reflect human faces. Like a window opening onto the beyond, all it reflected clearly on its surface were the statues of the gods and the throne where the Mistress sat in state with the procession of masks on her drapery.[41]

(5) The polar extremes of these goddesses, who can sometimes inflict the confusion of madness and at other times bring a cure, are matched by the polarity of the springs and waters sometimes associated with them. Above

---

[41] See "In the Mirror of Medusa," below, chap. 7.

Nonacris, in the neighborhood of Arcadian Styx, there is a cave where the daughters of Proitos went to hide when they were struck by madness and were wandering in a trance. Melampos came there with his secret rites and purifications to lead them in the direction of Cleitor, to a place called Lousoi, which recalls the Demeter Lousia. There they were calmed and cured in the sanctuary of Artemis Hemerasia, the Assuager (or one who tames; Paus. 8.18.7–8). Just previously Pausanias had noted (17.6) that a traveler who sets out westward from Pheneus, comes to a fork in the road: the path to the right leads to Cleitor and Lousoi; that to the left, toward Nonacris and Styx. Further on in the text he is more precise. The guide points out that in the land of the Cynaethaeans, which borders that of the Pheneates, there is found a cold water spring called Alussos, because it is a remedy for *lussa* (rabid madness) and because to drink from it cures rabies. Pausanias concludes, "In the waters named Styx which are near Pheneus, the Arcadians possess something which has proved a bane for men, while the spring among the Cynaethaeans is a blessing to make up for the evil of the other" (8.19.2–4).[42]

DEATH IN THE EYES

If we were to analyze the myth of Perseus—which tells how, with the aid of the gods, a hero dares to confront the lethal regard of Medusa, how, by cutting off her head, he comes to conquer the face of terror and escape the pursuit of the two remaining Gorgons—we would be obliged, for purposes of comparison, to take up the different versions of the story: from Hesiod and Pherecydes to Nonnos and Ovid. To keep to the essentials, we will only indicate some important points, starting with the presence in myth of the traditional heroic pattern—the exposure of the newborn hero and the trial imposed on him in his adolescence that takes place during a festival banquet in a context of boasts and challenges.

Let us briefly summarize the outline of the story: Akrisios, king of Argos, has a daughter, Danae. If she gives birth to a boy, the oracle announces, the grandson will kill his grandfather. Akrisios immediately immures Danae in a subterranean chamber with walls of bronze. But Zeus comes to visit the girl in the form of a shower of gold. After the birth of their offspring, named Perseus, the cries of the infant attract Akrisios's attention. To escape his predicted fate, the king places Danae and the child in a wooden chest, which he throws into the sea. The waves propel the chest safely to the island of Seriphos where Diktys, a fisherman, brings it back in his nets, shelters Danae, and raises Perseus until his adolescence. Seriphos is ruled by the tyrant Polydektes who covets Danae, but Perseus keeps watch over his mother. Polydektes sum-

---

[42] On *lussa*, see Bruce Lincoln, "Homeric *Lussa*, Wolfish Rage," *Indogermanische Forschungen* 80 (1975): 98–105.

mons the youth of the country to a festive banquet (*eranos*) where all, to put up a good show, vie with each other in parading their generosity. When his turn comes, Perseus, to outdo everyone else, boasts he will offer his host, not the horse he demands, but the head of the Gorgon. Polydektes takes him at his word. Perseus has no choice but to fulfill his promise.

Supernatural birth, expulsion from the human world, abandonment of the infant in the space of that other world symbolized by the immensity of the sea, survival and return among men after going through the ordeal whose normal outcome ought to have been death: Perseus's biography from the very outset, even before the career of his exploits begins, contains all the ingredients needed to give the young man his properly "heroic" dimension.

But the story continues. With Athena and Hermes as guides, Perseus sets out on the journey. To kill Medusa, he must obtain from the Nymphs the instruments of victory over the monster with the fatal gaze; in particular, the helmet of Hades, the *kuneē*, and the winged sandals. And to find the Nymphs, he must first constrain the Graiai to reveal the route that leads to them. Sisters of the Gorgons, the Graiai are also dreadful figures, although they have only one single tooth and one single eye among the three of them. Always on the alert, there is always one who, when the other two sleep, keeps the eye open and the tooth ready at hand. Perseus confronts them and defeats them as in a parlor game of "pass the slipper." He snatches the eye and the tooth at the precise moment when, passing from hand to hand, they are out of service for any of the sisters.

One theme is central to this chain of episodes: the eye, the gaze, the reciprocity of seeing and being seen. This theme appears already in the sequence of the three Graiai with their single tooth and eye, which they pass back and forth so the trio will never be caught by surprise without any defense—without a tooth for eating and an eye for looking (the single tooth is that of devouring monsters and of toothless hags; the single eye that of beings with an ever-vigilant gaze, but whom a bold maneuver can blind).[43] The theme is found again in the *kuneē*, the magical instrument of invisibility concealing from all eyes the presence of the one whose head it covers, and also in the detail that Perseus turned his eyes away at the moment of Medusa's death. He does this when he cuts the monster's throat, and later too, when he brandishes her head to turn his enemies into stone and prudently looks in the opposite direction. The theme finds its full development in those versions, attested from the fifth century on, that insist on the indispensable recourse to the mirror and its reflection that enables the young man to see Gorgo without having to cross

---

[43] To recover their eye and tooth, the old Graiai have to give over the secret of the Nymphs. These young rustic divinities give to Perseus the helmet that makes him invisible, the magic sandals that let him pass from one place to another, and the *kibisis*, the pouch in which he can bury the head of Medusa to hide it from view. To this equipment, Hermes adds the *harpē*, the machete in the form of a sickle used by Kronos to castrate Ouranos.

glances with her petrifying gaze. We should also note the role and meaning of the magical objects, which, more than mere instruments, are talismans that seem to be the true agents of the exploit. There is the cap of invisibility, which gives the living hero the mask of a dead man and thus puts him under the protection of the Powers of Death; the *harpē* and *kibisis*, the sickle and pouch, implements for headhunting;[44] and the winged sandals, which give Perseus a privilege like that of the Gorgons by allowing him to telescope all spatial directions, to reach both the heavens and the underworld, to pass from the shores of Okeanos to the land of the Hyperboreans. Finally, it is worth recalling several significant details: the hostility of Perseus to Dionysos, his satyrs and maenads, whom the hero, at the end of his journey, combats and pursues when they arrive in Argos, as if their frenzied band contained a gorgonlike element in its madness; the play of beauty and ugliness in the person of Medusa;[45] the emphasis on the theme of the mirror and its reflection in a late author like Ovid,[46] and its treatment in iconographic representations. In the images that illustrate the episode of the hero decapitating the Gorgon, Perseus, sometimes viewed full face, looks straight ahead, fixing his eyes on those of the spectator, with Medusa standing at his side. At times he turns his head to look the opposite way; at other times he looks at the face of the monster reflected in a mirror, on the polished surface of a shield, or on the surface of a pool of water.[47]

[44] [As the instrument used for both the beheading of Medusa and the castration of Ouranos, the *harpē* is another important indication of the correspondences between the upper and lower parts of the body, especially between the head (neck and mouth) and the sexual organs, that we have already seen in the dual aspects of Baubo. (For the female, see further Giulia Sissa, *Le corps virginal* [Paris, 1987], 76–93.) Both Ouranos and Medusa give birth from the place (or effects) of severing—Ouranos from his blood and semen, Medusa from her neck. If Medusa's decapitation can be construed as the ''castration'' of her genitalized head, the neck, in particular, is associated with female sexuality, in that, after defloration, the bride's neck is thought to thicken and her voice grow deeper (see the evidence in Ann Hanson and David Armstrong, ''The Virgin's Voice and Neck: Aeschylus' *Agamemnon* 245 and Other Texts,'' (*BICS* 33 1986: 97–100). The *harpē* is primarily an agricultural implement, used to cut off the ''heads'' of grain, but here too, the same correspondence is valid. A field of standing corn is also imaged as an expanse of bristling swords and warriors (cf. the birth of the Sown Men), and the *stachus*, or head of wheat, also represents the ''virginal'' young of both sexes (*Anth. Pal.* 9.362.24–27, and see ''Artemis and Rites of Sacrifice, Initiation, and Marriage,'' below, chap. 12), who may be ''harvested'' in war, death, or defloration.] Ed.

[45] On the tradition that makes Medusa a ravishing young girl, desirous of rivaling the most beautiful goddesses, cf. ps. Apollod. 2.4.3; Ov., *Met.* 4.795ff.

[46] Perseus could only look at the hideous face of Medusa and her petrifying eye in its weakened reflection. The theme is taken up and redoubled by Ovid in the episode of the deliverance of Andromeda, saved by the hero en route while returning home. In his stupidity the marine monster who attacks Perseus throws himself, not on the young man, but on the young man's shadow; with his claws he vainly tears at the reflection that the hero projects on the smooth surface of the sea.

[47] For further discussion, see ''In the Mirror of Medusa,'' below, chap. 7.

Some provisional conclusions to close this inquiry. In contrast to human figures and human faces, the mask of Gorgo, as an isolated head, contains elements in its composition that are marked with strange and unusual features. The usual conventions and typical classifications are syncopated and intermixed. Masculine and feminine, young and old, beautiful and ugly, human and animal, celestial and infernal, upper and lower (Gorgo gives birth through the neck like weasels are supposed to do, who, in producing their young from their mouths, invert buccal and vaginal orifices), inside and outside (the tongue, instead of remaining hidden within the mouth, protrudes outside like a masculine organ—displaced, exhibited, and threatening): in short, all the categories in this face overlap in confusion and interfere with one another. Thus this figure establishes itself right away in a realm of the supernatural that somehow calls into question the rigorous distinctions among gods, men, and beasts, as well as those between different cosmic elements and levels. A disquieting mixture takes place, analogous to the one Dionysos achieves through joy and liberation toward a communion with a golden age. But with Gorgo, the disorder is produced through horror and fear in the confusion of primordial Night.

The telescoping of what is normally kept separate, the stylized deformation of features, and the face breaking into a grimace convey what we have been calling the category of the monstrous, which, in its ambivalence, hovers between the terrifying and the grotesque, oscillating from one pole to the other.

This is the context in which to examine the frontality of Gorgo. The monstrousness of which we speak is characterized by the fact that it can only be approached frontally, in a direct confrontation with the Power that demands that, in order to see it, one enter into the field of its fascination and risk losing oneself in it. To see the Gorgon is to look her in the eyes and, in the exchange of gazes, to cease to be oneself, a living being, and to become, like her, a Power of death. To stare at Gorgo is to lose one's sight in her eyes and to be transformed into stone, an unseeing, opaque object.

In this face-to-face encounter with frontality, man puts himself in a position of symmetry with respect to the god, always remaining centered on his own axis. This reciprocity implies both duality (man and god face each other) and inseparability, even identification. Fascination means that man can no longer detach his gaze and turn his face away from this Power; it means that his eye is lost in the eye of this Power, which looks at him as he looks at it, and that he himself is thrust into the world over which this Power presides.

In Gorgo's face a kind of doubling process is at work. Through the effect of fascination, the onlooker is wrenched away from himself, robbed of his own gaze, invested as if invaded by that of the figure facing him, who seizes and possesses him through the terror its eye and its features inspire. Possession: to wear a mask means to cease being oneself and for the duration of the masquerade to embody the Power from the beyond who has seized on you and whose face, gestures, and voice you mimic. The act of doubling the face with a mask, superimposing the latter on the former so as to make it unrecognizable, presupposes a self-alienation, a takeover by the god who puts bridle and reins on you, sits astride you, and drags you along in his gallop. As a result, man and god share a contiguity, an exchange of status that can even turn into confusion and identification. But in this very closeness, a violent separation from the self is also initiated, a projection into radical alterity, a distancing of the furthest degree, and an utter disorientation in the midst of intimacy and contact.

The face of Gorgo is a mask, but instead of wearing it to mime the god, this figure reproduces the effect of a mask by merely looking you in the eye. It is as if the mask had parted from your face, had become separated from you, only to be fixed facing you, like your shadow or reflection, without the possibility of your detaching yourself from it. It is your gaze that is captured in the mask. The face of Gorgo is the Other, your double. It is the Strange, responding to your face like an image in the mirror (where the Greeks could only see themselves frontally and in the form of a disembodied head), but at the same time, it is an image that is both less and more than yourself. It is a simple reflection and yet also a reality from the world beyond, an image that captures you because instead of merely returning to you the appearance of your own face and refracting your gaze, it represents in its grimace the terrifying horror of a radical otherness with which you yourself will be identified as you are turned to stone.[48]

To look Gorgo in the eye is to find yourself face-to-face with the beyond in its dimension of terror, to exchange looks with the eye that continually fastens on you in what might be described as the negation of looking, and to receive a light whose blinding brilliance is that of the night. When you stare at Gorgo, she turns you into a mirror where, by transforming you into stone, she gazes at her own terrible face and recognizes herself in the double, the phantom you become the moment you meet her eye. To express this reciprocity, this strangely unequal symmetry of man and god, in other terms, what the mask of Gorgo lets you see, when you are bewitched by it, is yourself, yourself in the world beyond, the head clothed in night, the masked face of the invisible that, in the eye of Gorgo, is revealed as the truth about your own face. This grimace is also that which shows on the surface of your own visage as a mask that is put there, when to the tune of the flute you deliriously dance the bacchanal of Hades.

---

[48] [Although women are, even more than men, subject to possession, madness, and bewitchment, the petrifying effect of the Gorgon seems reserved only for men, in a tête-à-tête between a male and the deadly gaze of the female. I know of no case in which Medusa engages with a female figure, although, for other reasons, she can, like Niobe, be turned into stone through excessive grief. Ed.]

PART THREE

Image

Chapter 7

IN THE MIRROR OF MEDUSA

AT LYCOSURA in Arcadia the most honored divinity bore the name of Despoina ("Mistress"). She was represented seated in her temple, enthroned in majesty alongside her mother, Demeter. On either side of the two goddesses and framing their double thrones stood Artemis and a Titan, Anytos. Toward the exit from the sanctuary, there was a mirror set in the wall on the right. Let us listen to what Pausanias says: whoever looks at it, our witness reports, either only sees himself as an obscure reflection, faint and indistinct (*amudros*), or sees nothing at all. On the other hand, the figures of the gods and the throne that supports them show up clearly in the mirror; one can gaze at them there distinctly (*enargōs*) (8.37.7).

In the sacred place where it is affixed,[1] the mirror inverts its natural properties and shifts from its normal role to another and exactly opposite function. Instead of reflecting appearances and returning the image of visible objects placed before it, the mirror opens a breach in the backdrop of "phenomena," displays the invisible, reveals the divine, and lets it be seen in the brilliance of a mysterious epiphany.

An extreme case, no doubt. Yet more clearly than other evidence we have about Greek practices of catoptromancy,[2] it emphasizes the ambiguous status of the image that is reflected in the polish of the metal. The image seems to oscillate between two contrary poles: at times just a sham, an empty shadow, an illusion devoid of reality; at other times, the appearance of a power from the world beyond, a manifestation of an "other" reality that shows up on its smooth surface as in the transparency of spring waters. Remote, foreign to the world of here and now, and ungraspable, this "other" reality is also one that is fuller and stronger than what the world offers to the eyes of mortal creatures.

Originally published in *Lo Specchio e il Doppio: Dallo stagno di Narciso allo schermo televiso* (Milan, 1987) as "Dans l'oeil du miroir: Méduse," and reprinted as "Au miroir de Méduse" in *L'individu, la mort, l'amour: Soi-même et l'autre en Grèce ancienne* (Paris, 1989), 117–29. Translated by Froma I. Zeitlin.

[1] The cult of the Despoina must have included masquerades: on the sculpted drapery worn by the image, part of which has been preserved, human characters with animal heads—ram, pig, ass, donkey—were represented in a frieze, dancing and playing to music; others, votive figurines, were found in the *megaron* where the mysteries were celebrated: figures molded in terracotta, upright, immobile, dressed in a himation with a head of a ram or an ox instead of a human face. Could there have been in the cult as in the myth a proximity of the mask and the mirror?

[2] Cf. A. Delatte, *La catoptromancie grecque et ses dérivés* (Liège and Paris, 1932).

In the daily life of the ancient world, the mirror is above all a women's thing. It evokes the radiance of their beauty, the brightness of their seduction, the charm of their look, their dressed hair and delicate complexions. Women use it to see themselves, to recognize themselves in self-contemplation. To gaze at yourself is to project your own face before you, opposite your own, doubled into a figure you observe as one does an other, yet knowing it is yourself. There is no other way to apprehend oneself in the singularity of one's physiognomy except in this face-to-face through the mirror where one sees oneself in the act of being seen, where one looks at oneself regarding oneself. The face is called *prosōpon* in Greek; it is what one presents of oneself to the gaze of others, an individualized countenance appearing before the eyes of anyone who meets one directly, and it is something like the stamp of one's identity.[3] In seeing your face in the mirror, you know yourself as others know you: face-to-face, in an exchange of glances. Access to the self is gained through an external projection of that self, through being objectified, as if one were an other, in the form of a visage looked at straight in the eyes and whose exposed features gleam in the light of day.

Nevertheless, on the mirror of the temple, the face of the living is murky or effaced. The worshipper who looks at himself when he leaves sees himself not as he is, but as he will be when he has left the light of the sun to enter the land of the dead: a dim shadow, blurred, indistinct, a head shrouded in night, a specter henceforth without a face, without a gaze. *Amudros* is a doublet of *amauros*, the term that in the *Odyssey* describes a nocturnal phantom, and in Sappho, the tribe of the dead.[4] A half-open door into Hades, the mirror recalls to the worshipper who passes before it that his clearly defined face of a living being is doomed to disappear into the kingdom of Night, when the moment comes, and to vanish, engulfed in the invisible. An invisibility by default, one could say, through the lack of light, which never penetrates into the infernal dwellings, hermetically shut off from the rays of the sun. But there is another invisibility that is founded, not on deficiency, but on excess. The brilliance of divine splendor is too intense to be met by the human gaze; its radiance blinds or destroys those who wished to contemplate the divinities face-to-face, to see them *enargeis* as they are in the full light of day.[5] The gods too, in order to show themselves to mortals without the risk of destroying them, clothe them-

---

[3] Cf. Arist., *De part. anim.* 3.2.662b19: "In man the part included between the head and the neck is called *prosōpon*, a name owed, as it seems, to its function. For because man is the only animal who stands upright, he is also the only one who looks you in the face and who speaks to you face to face." On the values of the term *prosōpon*, in its double meaning of face and mask, consult the exhaustive inquiry of Françoise Frontisi-Ducroux, *Prosōpon: Valeurs grecques du masque et du visage*, thesis for the Doctorat d'État, 2 vols. (1988).

[4] *Od.* 4.824 and 835; Sappho 71 (ed. Edmonds, *Lyra Graeca*, vol. 1 [London, 1922]) = 68 Bergk.

[5] Cf. *Il.* 20.131; *Od.* 16.131; *Hom. Hym. Dem.* 111.

selves in appearances that disguise divinity as much as they reveal it. In the same way, the idols, which represent the powers of the world beyond to the eyes of their worshippers, incarnate the divine presence in the temple where they are offered residence without, however, being identified with that presence: the idol is godly, it is not the god. Still, if in the mirror of Lycosura, divine idols appear in their full clarity (*enargōs*), it is because a sort of transmutation is worked on its surface. In being reflected there, the images, fashioned by human hands in the "likeness" of the gods, gleam with an authentic—and unbearable—brilliance of the divine. Instead of being weakened by being doubled in reflection, the image is actually intensified, reinforced, and transformed; it becomes a divine epiphany. Made present as at the conclusion of an initiation, it is the divinity itself who looks you in the eyes at just the moment when you are about to take your leave of the temple.

We have lingered somewhat over the bizarre happening reported by Pausanias in his account of his visit to the Despoina's sanctuary because the anecdote marks in a striking way the particular place ancient culture assigned to the mirror. In the field defined by the ambiguous relations of the visible and the invisible, life and death, the image and the real, beauty and horror, and seduction and repulsion, this homely object occupies a position of strategic importance. To the extent that it seems able to join two normally contrasted terms, the mirror, more than any other device, lends itself to problematizing the entire realm of seeing and of being seen: the eye, first of all, with the shaft of light emanating from it in the act of seeing, just like that other eye, the glowing pupil that is the sun, the star that both sees everything and makes everything visible when it beats down with its rays and is the source of life; second, the real being with its double, its reflection, and its painted or sculpted image; then again, individual identity, the return back on oneself and the projection in the other, as well as erotic fascination; and finally, the fusion in the face of the beloved in whom one searches for oneself and loses oneself, as with a mirror, in beauty and death.

Three myths that, for the most part, inspired ceramicists, painters, and sculptors in their works of art, used the mirror as a device to dramatize these various themes, and to invoke, each in its own way, some aspect of their many implications: Perseus and the Gorgon Medusa, Dionysos and the Titans, and Narkissos.

We will limit ourselves here to the oldest, which is also the most richly attested in the ancient tradition, both literary and representational. We will refer here only to the relevant essentials of the legend of Perseus decapitating Medusa, the central core that has a direct bearing on this inquiry.[6] The whole story in its various sequences is actually constructed around the theme "see—be seen"—an indissociable pairing for the Greeks. It is the same light—emit-

---

[6] See also "Death in the Eyes: Gorgo, Figure of the *Other*," above chap. 6.

ted by the eye, bathing objects with its luminosity, and returned as in an echo by the mirror—that causes the eye to see and things to become visible. Gorgo and her two sisters carry death in their eyes. Their look kills. To see them, even for an instant, is to leave forever the clarity of the sun, to lose life along with sight: to be changed into stone, a blind object, as opaque to the luminous rays as those funerary steles erected over the graves of those who have descended forever into the obscurity of death. If the sight of these monsters is unbearable, it is because by the mixture in their faces of human, bestial, and mineral elements,[7] they embody the figure of chaos, the return to the formless and indistinct, and the confusion of primordial Night: the face itself of death, of that death which has no visage.[8] The Gorgons incarnate Dread and Terror as a dimension of the supernatural. They would instigate Panic, desperate Flight, and Rout, which seem to hover about their heads, if they were not first rooting you to the spot in frozen terror. Impossible to speak of, look on, or even think about, these monsters nevertheless have an imperious presence. If they appear, you will find them always in front of you, fixing you in the eye face-to-face. One glance in their direction and already their gaze reaches and strikes you. Like the image of yourself reflected by the mirror that always sends back your own gaze, the head of the Gorgo—contrary to the artistic conventions of archaic art where characters are always painted in profile—is always represented frontally. The glimmer of its staring eyes beams down on its spectators, sending them its fascinating frontal gaze. Whoever sees the head of Medusa is changed in the mirror of its pupils, as in the mirror of Lycosura, into a face of horror: the phantomlike figure of a being who, in passing through the mirror and leaping over the boundary that separates light from darkness, has immediately sunk down into formlessness and is now a nothing, a nonperson.

II

How will Perseus succeed in decapitating Medusa and appropriating her head? The story, as it proceeds, will put other, complementary questions into place. How is one to see something when the sight of it cannot be endured, see it without glancing at it and without falling under its glance? To exorcise, if not her death-dealing gaze, then at least the terror she inspires, how is one to master that by representing her, by figuring the traits of a monster whose horror thwarts every attempt at figuration? In other words, how is it possible to make seen—to visualize—the face it is impossible to see and the eye that is

---

[7] Cf. ibid.

[8] With a head shrouded in darkness, the dead are without a face. Françoise Frontisi-Ducroux rightly observes that the Gorgo is not called a *prosōpon*, "face," but *kephalē*, "head." And still this head is only represented as a face. When the invisible, in the form of Night, of total obscurity, appears to us, it is a face-to-face meeting with that which is not a face.

forbidden to the gaze in order to appropriate them and turn them against one's enemies?

Three episodes, three tests, three stages in the journey that leads Perseus to a successful confrontation with the horrible face of death. First, the Graiai: these aged maidens, these ancestral dames, born wrinkled and with white hair, sisters of the Gorgons, are possessors of a secret. They know the route that leads to the hidden Nymphs, invisible in a place where no one can find them. Only the Nymphs can furnish those talismans that can turn this impossible exploit into a reality—kill the Medusa, the one Gorgon of the three who is not entirely immortal, then detach from her dead body the head whose eyes and face still retain their lethal power, and finally, carry it off to bring it back into the world of men, escaping the pursuit and terrifying glances of the two furious survivors. Medusa has death in her eyes; the one who will be able to put the head of Medusa in his pouch and hide it there will be declared a master of Terror, *mēstōr phoboio*, lord over death.[9]

The Graiai form a disturbing trio: youthful old witches, they have only one tooth among them and only one eye, which they pass from hand to hand to be used by each in turn. Somewhat reassuring, then, at first glance. But one must not be too confident. Is the single tooth that of an old toothless woman or of a young ogress eating human flesh? One eye for three—this looks a little better. In reality, however, this eye, continually passed from one face to another, is always kept in service, always on the lookout; forever open and alert, it never sleeps. Just as one tooth, if it is a good one, is sufficient for devouring, only one eye is needed to see, providing it can never close. The single eye of the Graiai corresponds in symmetrical and inverse form to the hundred eyes of Argus whom only Hermes, the good voyeur (*Euskopos*), can take by surprise and kill. A hundred eyes for a single body means that Argus looks at all sides at the same time and never ceases to see. When fifty eyes slumber, the other fifty are awake. The result is similar with a single eye for three bodies. One of the three Graiai will always have the eye. To conquer these ladies of the eye and harsh tooth, Perseus, led by Athena and Hermes—the subtle and wily gods who protect him—will have to guess the weak point, leap to the occasion, and aim just right. As in a game of "pass the slipper," the hero finds the precise instant, the brief and mysterious interval where, in transit from one Graia's hand to another's, the eye has no place, not yet or no longer in anyone's use. It is at this moment that Perseus jumps up and puts his hand on the eye, and the Graiai are rendered blind and harmless. They ask for mercy. In return for the eye, they pass on the secret of where the Nymphs reside.

Perseus then goes to hunt down the Nymphs. Huddled together defenseless

---

[9] This is the name given to Perseus by Hesiod in the *Catalogue of Women*, frag. 129.15 Merkelbach-West; cf. on this point, along with others on which we agree, Ezio Pellizer, "Voir le visage de Méduse," *MÉTIS* 2 (1987): 45–60.

in their hiding place, they do not need much pleading to offer the young man
the three means of magic defense against the visual ray of death. They give
him first the *kuneē*, the helmet of Hades, the head-covering that, ''containing
the shadows of Night'' (Hes., *Shield* 227), makes anyone who covers his head
with it as invisible as the god of the Underworld and the hordes of the dead
who populate his empire. To foil the gaze that dispatches the onlooker to the
king of shades, Perseus is masked in night, indiscernible, and though alive,
he assumes a dead man's countenance.

The Nymphs then give him winged sandals like those of Hermes. Thus in
addition to the trait of invisibility, he acquires the faculty of ubiquity, the
power to pass instantly by means of flight from one place to another, to travel
the whole extent of the world from the subterranean dwellings on those frontiers of Night where the Gorgons live to the boundaries of Earth and Heaven.
The helmet, the sandals, no face that can be spotted by the eye that tries to see
you, no fixed place either where the gaze can reach you with its aim.

The third gift is the *kibisis*, the hollow pouch, the deep hunter's bag where
one can bury the head of Medusa, once it is cut off. Enclosed in the darkness
of its hiding place, the head cannot exercise its sinister power until it has been
withdrawn and brandished about. As long as it is kept concealed, the head
with the eye of death can neither see nor be seen. Like a veil cast over a mirror,
the face-to-face meeting with the Gorgon can be interrupted at will. To these
three gifts the gods add a fourth: the instrument of beheading, the curved
sickle, the blade of close combat, of ambush, the weapon of those who cut off
heads—the *harpē*.[10] Thus equipped, Perseus is now properly outfitted to embark on the ultimate phase of his drama. He is come into the presence of the
three Gorgons. The moment has come for action.

In the most complete and consistent version, that of Apollodorus
(2.4.2), the tale of the final action—decapitation—lists a whole series of
seemingly indispensable precautions, even though any one of these would
have probably sufficed to assure the success of the enterprise. In any case,
since he is invisible and can fly through the air, does not Perseus already hold
all the trumps for taking Medusa by surprise and cutting off her head? Still,
he must be sure that the monster's gaze is not going to meet his eye and pierce
the mask of invisibility the hero is wearing at the moment when he spies the
head that has to be severed from its neck. The Gorgons must be approached
under very specific conditions—when they are sleeping and the fire of their
gaze is extinguished under their drowsy eyelids. But timing itself is not
enough. Medusa is always just on the verge of awakening. Like Zeus, whose
gaze strikes like a thunderbolt, she only sleeps with one eye. Care must be
taken then not to repeat the misadventure that befell the monster Typhoeus
(Epimenides 11 frag. B8 DK). Seeing the king of the gods asleep, he thought

---

[10] [Or genitals, as in the case of Ouranos and Kronos. Ed.]

he could take advantage of the moment to snatch his scepter and with it, the sovereignty of the heavens. But Typhoeus had hardly taken a first step when the eye of Zeus struck him and reduced him to ashes.[11] Other strategies must therefore be invented to counter the perils of the eye—the face-to-face ordeal with its exchange of looks and the inevitable reciprocity of seeing and being seen.

First solution: it is Athena who guides the hand of the hero, leads his right arm, and directs his act; Perseus with his eyes averted can see nothing. Second solution, which is added in the text to the first: Perseus acts from one side and looks from the other; to cut Medusa's throat without seeing her, he turns his head and eyes in the opposite direction. Third solution, which synthesizes the first two: Perseus performs by gazing not at the face or eyes of Medusa, but at the reflection presented on the polished surface of the bronze shield, which Athena uses like a mirror to capture the image of the monster. Because the ray is deviated when reflected, the mirror allows him to see Medusa without looking at her. He thus turns away from her as in the second solution, and in keeping his eyes elsewhere, as in the first, Athena's mirror lets him see Medusa from behind, without viewing the monster face-to-face—not in the mortal reality of her person but in an image. Medusa is an exact copy. It is as if the image were she, but also as though she were absent in the presence of her reflection.

Let us pause for a moment at this point when the eye of Gorgo—this mirror transforming the living into the dead—is deprived of its deadly power in and through the mirror where it is reflected. Before the fourth century B.C.E., the motif of reflection (first on the shield of Athena, later also in the waters of a spring, or on a mirror properly speaking) was absent from Perseus's exploit.[12] Now it is introduced on vases and in texts to explain the victory of the hero over Medusa. This then is a new element, something ''modern'' to the extent that it clearly contrasts the image and the real, the reflection and the thing reflected. The motif thus seems connected to the efforts of contemporary painters to give the illusion of perspective, to philosophers' reflections about *mimēsis* (imitation), and also to the beginning of experiments that, from Euclid to Ptolemy, will lead to a science of optics. Still, we must bear it well in mind that this ''modernity'' is not our own. In the context of a culture that cannot separate the seen and the visible, that merges them into the idea of a visual luminous ray—the sight that ''knows color'' in being colored, knows ''white because it becomes white, black because it becomes black,'' as the

---

[11] Cf. Marcel Detienne and Jean-Pierre Vernant, *Les ruses de l'intelligence: La mētis des Grecs*, 2d ed. (Paris, 1978), 116.

[12] The motif appears in texts at the end of the fifth century B.C.E. (Eur., *Andr.*) and on vase paintings (southern Italian) at the beginning of the fourth.

great Ptolemy writes in the second century before our era[13]—in such a context, neither the image nor its reflection nor the mirror can have the status we recognize in these today.

In his treatise *De insomniis*, Aristotle indicates that mirrors tarnish when women use them to look at themselves during their menstrual periods (459b26). This tarnish forms like a bloody cloud on the surface; the stain is difficult to remove when the mirror is new. By just regarding themselves in newly polished metal, the women project their reflections there. Although it is a simple, look-alike image of themselves, it nevertheless impregnates the surface with a crimson haze. Something in the complexion of women, when their menses are flowing, reaches the mirror through reflected rays, is impressed there, and remains even after they have turned away from it. The mirror's image, declares Proclus in his commentary on Plato's *Republic* (290, 1–25 Festugière) acts "sympathetically" to retain the qualities of the bodies from which they came.

Would the reverse case, however, be true? Would the monster's image on the shield, which Athena turns toward Medusa's face to be reflected there, have entirely lost the noxious properties of the model? The answer given by the myth suggests that matters are not so simple as they seemed at first. True, the face-to-face, the shock of gazes, and the reciprocity of seeing and being seen have been avoided, to Perseus's greatest advantage, through the tactic of the mirror. In this sense, it is true that the image of Medusa is something other than Medusa. Yet is this to say that the image is nothing but an illusion, a subjective impression in the consciousness of the spectator? The myth claims exactly the opposite. The image of Gorgo, as presented in reflection on the shield, has a real efficaciousness, an active power that emanates from it in the rays it sends back with an impact like that of its model. It is just that through the intervention of the mirror or the use of some other mode of represented image, this power of radiation is controlled, used for certain ends, and directed according to the disparate religious, military, and aesthetic strategies required. In the "sympathy" they share, there is no absolute break between the image and the real, but rather affinities and means of passing from one to the other.

Athena knows what she is doing when she offers her shield so that the image of Gorgo can be inscribed at its center. She is adorning her defensive weapon with a traditional blazon, an *episēmē*, which the goddess's shield must have in order to fulfill its function: the Gorgoneion that, as its double, corresponds to the true head of Medusa that Athena has worn as the aegis on her breast ever since Perseus gave it to her as a gift. In this sense the detail added in the fourth century to the mythic episode of Medusa's decapitation acquires the value of an aetiological story, which justifies a posteriori the custom that is

---

[13] *Optics* 2.24. Cited by Gérard Simon, "Derrière le miroir," *Le temps de la réflexion* 2 (1981): 309.

attested from the earliest period of representing Gorgo on warriors' shields in
order to heighten their prestige, provoke terror in the foe, and consign them in
advance to flight and death. Exhibited as an image, Medusa's face makes the
warrior a "master of Terror."[14] The Gorgoneion, however, is not only represented on shields. Its figure, multiplied over and over—on pediments of temples, on their roofs as *akroteria* and antefixes, in private homes, on fabrics,
gems, seals, coins, the feet of mirrors, the belly of vases, and the base of
cups—succeeds in visualizing the blinding black sun of death, and in this way
succeeds in neutralizing its horror through the most conventional, even banal,
images by mobilizing and exploiting the terrifying effects that emanate from
this powerful sign. The image of this face that may not be seen[15] is a *teras*, a
prodigy that can equally be described as "terrible to look upon" and "marvelous to behold."[16] As a prodigy, the *eikōn*, the image-reflection of Medusa,
is also close to the *eidōlon* or the double (the image of a dream sent by the
gods, a specter of the dead or the appearance of a phantom).[17] By establishing
a bridge between our world and the one beyond and by making visible the
invisible, the image of Gorgo combines the features of a disturbing and maleficent supernatural presence and a deceptive counterfeit, an illusionist artifice whose aim is to captivate the eyes. Depending on the case, Gorgo's image
can lean toward either the horrible or the grotesque. It may appear terrifying
or ridiculous, repulsive or attractive. Sometimes the charming traits of a feminine countenance are substituted for the traditional mask of the monster who
grimaces in a hideous smile. From the late fifth century, at the moment itself
when the motif of the mirror arises, the turning point begins that will lead to
representing Medusa as a young woman of marvelous beauty. In certain versions of the myth recounted by Apollodorus, Pausanias, and Ovid,[18] it is the
excess of this beauty and its radiance that constitutes the dynamic element of
the drama, whether because it unleashes the jealousy of Athena and impels the
goddess to slaughter her rival, or because it leads Perseus, dazzled by the

[14] See Pellizer, "Voir le visage," 53, on the links that join the exploit of Perseus to the theme
of the shield as a defensive weapon casting terror into the enemy camp. Abas, great-grandfather
of Perseus, is reputed to have invented the shield. Other traditions attribute this invention to the
following generation during a war that pits the twins, Akrisios and Proitos, against each other,
grandfather and great-uncle respectively of Perseus (unless one accepts that Danae was united
with Proitos and not with Zeus).

[15] "How could [Perseus] have seen [the Gorgons]? They cannot be looked at [*atheatoi*]," Lucian has a Nereid say in his *Dial. mar.* 14 (= 323), and see the commentary of Frontisi-Ducroux,
Prosōpon, vol. 1, p. 163.

[16] Aesch., *Eum.* 34: *deina d'ophthalmois drakein*; Hes., *Shield* 224: *theama idesthai*.

[17] On the *eidōlon*, cf. Jean-Pierre Vernant, *Mythe et pensée chez les Grecs: Etudes de psychologie historique*, 10th ed. (Paris, 1985), 326–38, 339–51 ("From the 'Presentification' of the
Invisible to the Imitation of Appearance," below, chap. 8); *Annuaire du Collège de France:
Résumé des cours et travaux* (1975–76): 372–75; (1976–77): 423–41; (1977–78): 451–65. See
also "Psuche: Simulacrum of the Body or Image of the Divine?" below, chap. 10.

[18] Ps. Apollod. 2.4.3; Paus. 2.21.5; Ov., *Met.* 4.754ff.; cf. Lucian, *Imag.* 1–3.

perfection of Medusa's face, to cut off her head after having killed her so he will never have to separate himself from this resplendent visage.

III

At Lycosura a double movement takes place through the medium of the mirror: the faces of humans darken and are obliterated as though swallowed up in the miserable darkness of Night; those of the gods shine with all the brilliance of an incomparable splendor. Superimposed on the mask of Medusa, as though in a two-sided mirror, the strange beauty of the feminine countenance, brilliant with seduction, and the horrible fascination of death, meet and cross.

Chapter 8

FROM THE "PRESENTIFICATION" OF THE INVISIBLE TO THE IMITATION OF APPEARANCE

THE GREEK EXAMPLE

IF ANYONE wants to consider, not only the forms that images have assumed at a given moment in a given country, but also, perhaps more profoundly, the functions of the image as such and the social and cognitive status of imagery in the context of a particular civilization, then the Greek case is certainly a very special example.

First, for historical reasons. During the so-called Dark Ages, that is, broadly speaking, from the twelfth to the eighth centuries before our era, Greece, which as you know has no knowledge of writing, also has no knowledge of imagery in the proper sense of the term, nor does it use systems of figural representation. The same word, *graphein*, it should be noted, is used for writing, drawing, and painting.

The establishment, under the influence of Eastern models, of what can be called a repertory of figures, a palette of images, and the elaboration of a language of art in pottery, sculpture, and relief, comes about toward the eighth century, as though it is starting afresh from a blank tablet. In this as in other areas, we are witness to a kind of birth, or at least a renaissance, which authorizes us to speak of the advent of figuration in Greece.

When the Greeks rediscover imagery, the form it takes amounts to a divestiture so absolute in comparison to the preceding period that, as Pierre Demargne observes, it can be regarded as a "creation *ex nihilo*."[1]

That is not all. In surveying the extensive, diffuse, and uncertain semantics in Greek pertaining to statuary, Benveniste claimed that the Greeks did not have any specific word to designate the statue in our sense of the term. As he states: "The people who fixed the most refined canons and models of plastic art for the Western world had to borrow from others the notion itself of figural representation."[2]

This piece, "De la présentification de l'invisible à l'imitation de l'apparence," appeared first in *Image et signification*, Rencontres de l'Ecole du Louvre (Paris, 1983), 25–37, was reprinted in *Mythe et pensée chez les Grecs: Etudes de psychologie historique*, 10th ed. (Paris, 1985), 339–51, and appears here (with notes added) by the kind permission of Editions la Découverte. Translated by Froma I. Zeitlin. Thanks to Andrew Ford for felicitous counsel.

[1] *Naissance de l'art grecque* (Paris, 1964), 317.

[2] E. Benveniste, "Le sens du mot *kolossos* et les noms grecs de la statue," *RPh.* (1932): 118–35.

Let us take yet another step. Simply to analyze the terms used by the Greeks throughout their history to indicate "statue" shows that what Benveniste called "the notion of figural representation" is not a simple immediate fact that could in some way be defined once and for all. The notion of figural representation does not just come from itself. Neither univocal nor permanent, it is what might be called a historical category; a construct elaborated, not without difficulty, through very different routes in different civilizations.

There are about fifteen expressions in Greek to mean "divine idol" in the many forms it can take: an aniconic form as, for example, a brute stone (*baï-tulos*), beams (*dokana*), a pillar (*kiōn*), and a stele (*herma*): a theriomorphic or monstrous kind like the Gorgon, Sphinx, and Harpies. And there is the anthropomorphic figure in the great diversity of its types. These range from the small wooden archaic idol, poorly fashioned, with arms and legs welded to the body, like the *bretas*, the *xoanon*, and the *palladion*, to the archaic Kouroi and Korai, and finally includes the great cult statue, which is given a variety of names: it can be called *hedos* or *agalma* as well as *eikōn* and *mim-ēma*, the last, however, not used in this precise sense before the fifth century. Now, of all these terms, excluding the last two, there is no single one that has any relation whatsoever to the idea of resemblance or imitation, of figural representation in the strict sense.

In addition, it is not enough to say that late Greek archaism had to create a language of plastic forms for itself from scratch, without also adding that it developed these forms in a quite original way so that, starting from idols that functioned as symbolic actualizations of different models of the divine, it finally arrived at the image, properly speaking: that is, the image conceived as an imitative artifice reproducing in the form of a counterfeit the external appearance of real things.

At the pivotal point of the fifth and fourth centuries, the theory of *mimēsis*, sketched out by Xenophon, and elaborated in a fully systematic way by Plato, marks the moment when in Greek culture the turn is completed that leads from the "presentification," the making present, of the invisible to the imitation of appearance.[3] It is at this time that the category of figural representation emerges in its specific features and, at the same time, becomes attached to *mimēsis*—the great human fact of imitation, which gives it a solid foundation.

The symbol that actualizes, that makes present in this world below a power from the world beyond (a fundamentally invisible being) is now transformed into an image that is the product of an expert imitation, which, as a result of skillful technique and illusionist procedures, enters into the general category of the "fictitious"—that which we call art. From now on, the image derives from figurative illusionism all the more, because it does not belong to the domain of religious realities.

---

[3] See "The Birth of Images," below, chap. 9.

The Archaic Idol: The Xoanon

Another question, therefore, arises. As long as the image is not yet clearly attached to the peculiarly human faculty of creating works through imitation, works that have no reality other than their semblance, whose entire essence is a "faux-semblant," what then is the status of the image? How does it function? What is its relation to that very thing it represents or evokes?

I will confine myself essentially in this essay to the issue of statuary and its role in the representation of the gods, allotting only brief remarks to the figuration of the dead on painted or carved steles, in relief, and in free-standing sculpture.

Figure of the gods, figure of the dead. In each case, the problem is the same: by means of localization in an exact form and a well-determined place, how is it possible to give visual presence to those powers that come from the invisible and do not belong to the space here below on earth? The task is to make the invisible visible, to assign a place in our world to entities from the other world. In the representational enterprise, it can be said that at the outset, this paradoxical aspiration exists in order to inscribe absence in presence, to insert the other, the elsewhere, into our familiar universe. Whatever the avatars of the image may have been, this impossible quest is one that perhaps continues to remain valid to a large degree—that of evoking absence in presence, revealing the elsewhere in what is given to view.

Let us begin with the gods.

First, a general remark. Besides the storytelling that occurs in myth and the organized progression of acts in ritual, every religious system includes a third facet—the phenomenon of representation. Yet for the mind of the spectator who regards it, a figure in a religious context is not simply intended to evoke the sacred power to which it refers, which in certain cases it "represents," as in the case of an anthropomorphic statue, and which in other cases it evokes symbolically. Its larger ambition is quite different.

However the sacred power is represented, the aim is to establish a true communication, an authentic contact, with it. The ambition is to make this power present *hic et nunc*, to make it available to human beings in the ritually required forms. But in its attempt to construct a bridge, as it were, that will reach toward the divine, the idol must also at the same time and in the same figure mark its distance from that domain in relation to the human world. It has to stress the incommensurability between the sacred power and everything that reveals it to the eyes of mortals in what can only be an inadequate and incomplete way. In the context of religious thought, every form of figuration must introduce an inevitable tension: the idea is to establish real contact with the world beyond, to actualize it, to make it present, and thereby to participate intimately in the divine; yet by the same move, it must also emphasize what is inaccessible and mysterious in divinity, its alien quality, its otherness.

To illustrate this far too general concept, I will take the example of a certain type of divine idol in the Greek world.

On numerous occasions Pausanias indicates the presence in some sanctuary or another of a form of idol he calls by the name *xoanon*. This word, of Indo-European origin (by contrast to *bretas*, which has a similar meaning), is connected to *xeō*, to scrape or abrade, a word that belongs to the vocabulary of woodworking. The *xoanon*, as he describes it, is an idol of wood, more or less roughed out in a so-called pillar shape,[4] and of primitive workmanship.

For Pausanias, *xoana* are defined by three characteristics. As idols belonging to the most remote past, everything about them has an air of the archaic: their appearance, the cult whose object they are, and the legends about them.

This "primitive" quality of *xoana* produces a marked effect of "strangeness" in the spectator, which Pausanias stresses by referring to these figures with terms like *atopos* and *xenos* (strange) as a way of indicating their distance from ordinary cultic images.

Primitivity and strangeness. To these Pausanias adds a third feature, which is very directly connected to the other two. Because there is something disconcerting about them, something that is nonimaged in the usual sense of the term, *xoana* contain an aspect of the divine, *theion ti*, some supernatural quality (2.4.5; 10.19.3).

These archaic idols, which often play a fundamental role in the cultic worship of a god and concern that god very directly—even if they do not represent the deity in the canonical figural form—are not, in my opinion, images. Neither in their origins nor their functions have they crossed the threshold beyond which one is entitled to speak of images, *stricto sensu*.

Their origin. The most famous ones are not considered to have been made by the hand of a mortal artisan. Whether a god made them and offered them as a gift to one of his favorites, whether they fell from heaven or were carried in to shore by the waves of the sea, they are not human works.

Their form. To the degree that there is a form—since a simple piece of wood can take the place of an idol—their form counts less sometimes, on the plane of symbolic value, than the material of which they are made: a certain type of tree or even a particular tree the god has selected and with which he or she has a special communion. Additionally, the figure is most often clad in garments that cover and conceal it from top to toe.

Their functions. The idol is not made to be seen. To look at it is to go mad. It is also often shut up in a chest, guarded in a dwelling forbidden to the public. Nevertheless, without being visible as an image is expected to be, the idol is still not invisible in the way a god is whom one cannot gaze at face-to-face.

---

[4] [For a fuller discussion of *xoana* and the multiple forms they may take outside of Pausanias's descriptions, see A. A. Donohue, *Xoana and the Origins of Greek Sculpture* (Atlanta, 1988). Ed.]

The idol is caught in the game of hiding and revealing. Sometimes hidden, sometimes uncovered, the *xoanon* oscillates between the two extremes of "being kept secret" and "being shown to the public." The "sighting" of the image takes place each time in relation to a preliminary "hidden," which gives it its true significance by treating it as a privilege reserved for particular persons, at particular moments, under particular conditions. To see the idol presupposes a specific religious quality and yet also consecrates its eminent dignity. The sight of it, like that of the mysteries, acquires the value of an initiation. In other words, the contemplation of the divine idol seems like an "unveiling" of a mysterious and fearful reality. Instead of being the primary datum that it would be a question of imitating with an image, the visible becomes qualified as a revelation, both precious and precarious, of an invisible realm that constitutes the true and fundamental reality.

FIGURE AND RITUAL ACTION

The idol, however, is not simply brought into the game of hide and display. It is inseparable from the ritual operations that are worked on it. It is dressed and undressed, ritually bathed, and taken out for washing in a river or in the sea. The idol is offered fabrics or veils. It is taken outside and brought back within, where it is sometimes fastened with symbolic bonds, woollen yarn, or golden chains. This is because the idol is represented as mobile. Even if the *xoanon* has no feet or its legs are sealed together, it is always believed to be on the point of escaping, of deserting one place to go off elsewhere, to haunt another dwelling into which it will import the privileges and powers attached to its possession.

When a *xoanon* is involved, the plastic representation can never be wholly separated from ritual action. The idol is made *in order* to be shown and hidden, led forth and fixed in place, dressed and undressed, and given a bath. The figure has need of the rite if it is to represent divine power and action. Still incapable in its immobile and fixed form of expressing any movement other than being turned and led about, it nevertheless conveys the god's action by symbolic gestures of animation and simulation.

In addition, the *xoanon* always makes its appearance at the center of a cycle of festivals that are organized around it and that form a coherent symbolic system with it in which all the elements—plastic sign and ritual actions—combine and correspond with one another. The problem of the *xoanon*'s efficacy outside this system is one that does not arise. It is through the succession of ceremonies of which it is the object that the idol manifests the power of the god. The idol represents divine action by miming it for the duration of the rite far more than it does in its capacity as a figure that locates this action in space.

Embedded within the ritual, the idol in its plastic form has not reached full autonomy. Yet this does not mean either that its status is comparable to that of a post, stake, pillar, or herm. To shackle a *xoanon* with a more or less symbolic bond does not have the same value as planting a post or stake in the ground. The idea of binding the idol implies a mobile image whose escape is arrested by fettering its legs with woollen yarn or a vegetal withy or, in a more precise symbolism, with golden chains. The rite does not fix the image in the soil with the idea of demarcating a center of religious force in that space. It aims at assuring a social group of the permanent preservation of a symbol that has talismanic value. The idol is not especially attached to a point in the earth and it does not localize a divine power. On the contrary, wherever it may be, it confers on its possessor the privilege and, as it were, the exclusivity of certain powers. It marks a "personal" closeness with the divinity, which can be transmitted through inheritance and can circulate in royal families or religious *genē* (clans). This idea of appropriating the idol, a complement of its mobility, is conveyed by the fact that it lodges, at least in the beginning, in the secret recesses of a human house—the dwelling of the king, chief, or priest. In any case, it is a private, privileged residence, not a public site. In the era of the city, when the temple—impersonal and collective—comes to shelter the divine image, the memory of the bond that joined the most ancient *xoana* to a particular house and lineage will still remain very vivid. Athena's *xoanon* sits in Erechtheus's residence at Athens, while in Thebes the *thalamos* of Semele in the palace of Kadmos keeps watch over the image of Dionysos. In the full classical period, the custom is preserved of lodging certain images of a mysterious character in private dwellings rather than in a temple. The priest offers hospitality to the statue in his own house for the duration of his sacerdotal function. Custody of the image consecrates the personal bond that from now on unites him with the divinity. The idol thus comes to function as a sign of investiture. It matters little, in this respect, whether it has some kind of human form or not. The boundary is still rather fluid between the *xoanon* and certain symbolic objects that also bestow a particular religious quality on their possessors.

FIGURES AND SYMBOLIC OBJECTS

The function of this type of *sacra* consists in certifying and transmitting the powers the divinity accords as a privilege to its elect rather than in making a divine "form" known to the public. The symbol does not represent the god, abstractly conceived in and for itself. It does not attempt to instruct anyone about its nature. It expresses divine power insofar as it is handled and used by certain individuals as an instrument of social prestige, a means of getting a hold on and of acting on others.

The scepter of Agamemnon represents these two allied features of a divine symbol and an object of investiture. Charged with efficacious power, it imposes silence on the assembly, gives decision the value of execution, and acknowledges the king to be the offspring of Zeus. Held in the hands and transmitted by heredity, it objectifies in some way the potency of sovereignty. It is a divine object, like the *xoanon*, having been fabricated by Hephaistos, given by Zeus to Hermes, and passed successively to Peleus, Atreus, Thyestes, and Agamemnon. Just like the *xoanon*, the scepter can function just as well as an "idol" of the god. At Chaeronaea, it becomes the object of the principal cult by representing Zeus. But it preserves its ancient values as a talisman whose power must be appropriated and its privileges transmitted. Each year, a new priest takes charge of the divine symbol and carries it into his house to make daily sacrifices to it. The scepter's role at Chaeronaea is taken by a crown for the priest of Zeus Panamaros, a trident among the Eteoboutades, and a shield in the royal family of Argos (or, just as well, a *xoanon*). At Argos, specifically in the ceremony of the Bath of Pallas, the *xoanon* of Athena was not taken out by itself alone; it was accompanied by the shield of Diomedes, which was also "carried" in the procession. In a social context in which divine powers and the symbols that express them do not yet have a fully public character, but still remain the property of privileged families, there is a reciprocal relation between the idol and the symbolic object that assumes the same function.

Two stories, whose parallels highlight this analogy between *xoanon* and *sacra*, help us grasp the turning point of social history which passes from private cult to public cult, and transforms the idol, an object of investiture, a more or less secret familial talisman, into an impersonal image of a divinity made to be seen.

The first is told to us by Herodotus (7.153.7–16). At Gela, in a period of unrest, the city becomes divided against itself. One group of inhabitants secedes and establishes itself on high ground from which it threatens the rest of the community. A man named Telines decides therefore to confront the rebels without any arms other than certain *sacra* he keeps in his possession. Relying on their supernatural power, he goes before the mutineers, calms their revolt, and leads them back to Gela in a renewal of concord and social order. He asked only one compensation in return for his exploit: henceforth his descendants will, like hierophants, provide the priests of the Goddesses, probably Demeter and Kore. The *sacra* he used are precisely those of the cult of these goddesses. Would not this then be the inaugural moment when the cult became public and was adopted as the official cult of the city? Herodotus, it is true, indicates that he does not know how Telines could have obtained these *sacra*, whether he had received them from someone or had procured them himself. But the scholiast to Pindar's second Pythian ode makes clear that this cult had been brought as a family cult from Triopion by the ancestors of Telines when Gela was founded and that only much later had it been instituted as a public one (*Pyth.* 2.30).

The same themes: popular revolt, pacification of sedition, not with violence but with *sacra*, talismans with both political and religious value, belonging to certain families, that by some sort of compromise became objects of public cult in the new social order of the city: all these can be found in the second tale that directly concerns the *xoanon* of Athena at Argos. The custom of carrying the shield of Diomedes, Callimachus tells us, is a very ancient rite instituted by Eumedes, the "favorite" priest of the goddess (*Lav. Pal.* 35–42). Here are the conditions: the population is in revolt, but Eumedes escapes death by the same procedure Telines had used. In his flight he carries off the sacred image, the *palladion*, and no doubt the shield too, that object of royal investiture. He sets these on a rocky escarpment for his protection. Callimachus does not relate the sequel. One can imagine it. Eumedes institutes the rite that henceforth will benefit the entire city and all its citizens with the "favor" that Athena had previously reserved for her "protégé."

In the public cult, however, the value of ancient private *sacra* is also transformed at the same time as it is maintained. Since it ceases to incarnate the privilege of a family or of a closed group, the idol will have lost its more or less secret talismanic value in order to acquire the significance and structure of an image. In this sense, the appearance of the temple and the institution of a public cult not only mark a turning point in social history that is the age of the City but also imply the advent of a new form of representation of the gods, a decisive mutation in the nature of the divine symbol.

THE IMAGE, THE TEMPLE, AND PUBLICITY

More than a place of cult where the worshippers meet, the Greek temple is a residence. The god inhabits it, but it is a residence that has nothing markedly private about it. Instead of being enclosed like the human *oikos*, in a familial interior, the divine house is oriented toward the exterior, turned toward the public gaze. In the palace, a fresco decorated the inside of a room. In the temple, however, the sculpted frieze, projected on the facade, is shown to the spectator who looks at it from the outside. The god resides in the inmost part of the building. But this god is one who from now on belongs to the entire City. The City built the god a house, separated from the human dwelling place, but at the same time it left the acropolis to the divinity and established itself instead in the lower town. Because the god too is public, the inside of the temple is no less impersonal than its exterior. In no longer being a sign of privilege for the one whose house it inhabits, the god reveals his or her presence in a directly visible way to the eyes of all: under the gaze of the City, the god becomes form and spectacle.

The advent of the great cult statue can only be understood in the frame of reference of the temple with its two aspects, as a house reserved for the god and as a fully socialized space. Constructed by the City, the temple is consecrated to the god as his or her residence. The temple is called *naos* (residence) and *hedos* (seat of divinity). And the word *hedos* also means the great divine statue. It is through this image that the divinity comes to live in its house. Thus there is complete reciprocity between the temple and the statue. The temple is made to lodge the statue of the god and the statue is created to exteriorize the presence of the god as a spectacle in the intimacy of his or her dwelling place.

Like the temple, the image has the quality of being fully public. We could characterize this statue by saying that henceforth all its *esse* consists in a *percipi*, all its "being" in a "being perceived." It has no reality other than its appearance, no ritual function other than to be seen. Lodged in the temple in which the god is made to reside, it is no longer taken out and used. Expressive just in its form, it has no further need to be dressed or carried in a procession or bathed. The statue is no longer required to operate in the world as an efficacious force; rather its task is to act on the eyes of the spectators, to translate for them in a visible way the invisible presence of the god and communicate some lesson about divinity. The statue is "representation" in a really new sense. Liberated from ritual and placed under the impersonal gaze of the City, the divine symbol is transformed into an "image" of the god.

THE FIGURE OF THE BODY

This disengagement of the image, properly speaking, takes place through a discovery of the human body and a progressive conquest of its form. Yet we must still specify the import of these assertions. What is meant is evidently not a question of the human body as an organic and physiological reality on which the self relies for its support. If religious symbolism is directed toward the human body and reproduces its appearance, it is because it sees there the expression of certain aspects of the divine. The problem should therefore be posed in the following way: in the case of the *xoanon*, the human aspect is not yet felt to be essential, nor is the form of the body well executed. When monumental statuary turns to translate divinity into a form visible to all, why will it systematically and exclusively give the god the appearance of the human body? And what are the meaning and significance for religious thought of this valorization of the human figure, which appears at this time as the only one appropriate for representing the divine?

Jean Cuisenier has recalled here the interpretation proposed by Hegel to explain this anthropomorphism of divine images in classical Greek religion.[5] Yet what is the exact import of the term "anthropomorphism?" Does it mean that for the Greeks the gods were conceived of and represented in the image of human beings? To me it seems the opposite—that the human body became perceptible to Greek eyes when it was in the flower of its youth, when it was like an image or a reflection of the divine.

[5] "Tradition de l'image en Europe," in *Image et Signification*, 13.

Athletic exercises must have greatly helped to valorize the human body. Nakedness is already an important fact. The first masculine statues in Greece are naked like the athlete in the field or palaestra. But the essential issue resides in the dual nature of the Games, both spectacle and religious festival—national spectacle, one might say, which joins and opposes the diverse cities in a great public competition. Each city is engaged in a struggle in which the victor represents his community more than he does himself. Religious festival too: the contests are sacred ceremonies. In civic religion and in this Panhellenic religion the Games helped shape and in which they take pride of place, the memory of those ritual functions that the *agōn* might well have once had is doubtless lost and gone. But the contest retains its value as an ordeal. Victory *consecrates* the victor in the full sense of the word. It suffuses his person with sacred prestige. In the form of ritual scenario that is the contest, the triumph of the athlete, as seen in Pindar, evokes and extends the exploit accomplished by the hero and the gods; it raises man to the level of the divine. And those physical qualities—youth, force, swiftness, agility, skill, and beauty—that the victor must display in the course of the *agōn*, and which, in the eyes of the public, his naked body incarnates, are still eminently religious values.

But the contests do not put only physical qualities to the test. Other aspects of the body, which the Games present in a religious light to the gaze of the spectators, are also affirmed. When at Delos, says the Homeric Hymn to Apollo, the Ionians participated in boxing, in dance, and in song, when they celebrated the Games, "any chance arrival would think them to be immortals and exempt forever from old age, for he would see the grace in all of them" (149–55). Grace, *charis*: all of a sudden, there shines through the beauty of the human body, like a reflection in a mirror, a value that belongs to the divine which is at the very opposite extreme from a monstrous sacredness. Fashioned in marble, bronze, or gold, the image of the human body must in turn make *charis* into something that can be seen: brightness, luminous brilliance, and the radiance of an unchanging youthfulness.

The horrible grimace of Gorgo symbolizes the powers of terror, chaos, and death. On the opposite side, but in as conventional a manner as the rictus of the mask, the smile on the human figure signfies *charis*—the brightness that divinity bestows in this world below on the body of a human being, when that person, in the flower of his or her youth, reflects the nature of those called the "Fortunate Ones," of one such as Aphrodite, who is called the "Smiling One."

At Lesbos, a public contest consecrated this religious value of corporeal beauty. During a festival called Kallisteia, a beauty contest, the seven most beautiful girls were chosen and grouped into a chorus resembling that of the Seven Muses, goddesses to whom the same city rendered a cult.[6] The Olympic

---

[6] Schol. ad *Il.* 7.118.

victor also, Philip of Croton, the most beautiful Greek of his time, as Herodotus tells us (5.47), was heroized after his death by the inhabitants of Segesta because of his beauty just as other athletes were honored for their strength or stature.

What we call physical qualities can then appear to Greek religious consciousness as "values" that transcend the human, as "powers" of divine origin. In human existence they have only a precarious and inconstant reality, marked with the sign of evanescence. Only the gods possess these qualities in their plenitude as permanent assets inseparable from their nature.

The size, smile, and beauty of corporeal forms of the Kouros and the Kore, along with the movement their bodies suggest, express these powers of life—a life always present, always vivid. The image of the gods fixed by the anthropomorphic statue is that of the "Immortals," the Happy Ones, the "ever young," those who in the purity of their existence are utterly alien to decline, corruption, and death.

THE FIGURE OF THE DECEASED

A second problem immediately follows. If the archaic statue uses the human figure to convey this set of "values" that in their plenitude only belong to divinity and appear like a fragile reflection when they gleam on the body of mortals, we can then understand how the same image, the votive Kouros, can sometimes represent the god himself and sometimes a human person who, by virtue of his victory in the Games or through some other consecration, is revealed as "equal to the gods." But how does it happen that, when erected over a tomb or sculpted on a stele, this very same Kouros can also have a funerary function and be capable of representing a dead person? I have treated this point at length in various articles and studies devoted to the relation between the archaic funerary figure and "beautiful death," *kalos thanatos*. This is the kind of demise that guarantees an imperishable glory for the young warrior fallen on the battlefield in the flower of his age by maintaining in the memory of successive generations the perpetual recollection of what he was: his name, exploits, career in life, and the heroic end that established him forever in his status as the "beautiful dead," the excellent man, *agathos anēr*, fully and definitively complete.[7] A few words then will suffice to recall the essential points needed for our conclusions.

Until the end of the seventh century, Attica maintained a type of stele very close to that which Homeric epic describes: a stone, more or less squared off, that marks the place of the tomb. This stone already assumes a memorial function. In its upright position, fixed, permanent, and immutable, it evokes the

---

[7] [E.g., "*Panta kala*: From Homer to Simonides," above, chap. 4, "A 'Beautiful Death' and the Disfigured Corpse in Homeric Epic," above, chap. 2, and "India, Mesopotamia, Greece: Three Ideologies of Death," above, chap. 3. Ed.]

dead person whose ashes repose underground by emphasizing that, despite his death—his absence—he remains and will remain always present in the memory of men. It is in the course of the sixth century, in a context both civic and aristocratic, that different types of representational steles and the series of funerary Kouroi develop. Death is no longer evoked by the brute stone that has no inscription, but by the visible beauty of a corporeal form that the stone fixes forever with a name, as death fixed it on the corpse of the young heroic warrior whom all admire, because in him, even or especially when he is dead, as Homer and Tyrtaeus say, "everything is fitting, everything is beautiful," *panta kala*.

The figures on the stele or the funerary Kouros are erected on the tomb "in place" of what the living person was, did, and merited. "In place of, *anti*, signifies that the figure is substituted for a person as his or her "equivalent," that, in a certain sense, it does the same thing the living person used to do (as in the inscription on the late fifth-century stele of Ampharete: "This is the dear child of my daughter whom I hold here, the one I held on my knees when we were alive and looked upon the light of the sun; and still I hold him now that we are both dead"),[8] and thus possesses the same beauty and the same value. Yet it implies simultaneously the inverse: a new mode of being, different than the old one, namely, the status of a dead person that the deceased has acquired by disappearing forever from the light of the sun. "I am set up here in Parian marble, in place of a woman, *anti gunaikos*; in memory of Bitte, but for her mother, tears of mourning," proclaims a funerary inscription of Amorgos in the middle of the fifth century.[9] "Instead of a woman": but the formula with its variants makes clear that the person, whose substitute takes her place, is not envisaged in anything other than the qualities she once had. It is "in place of her youth and beauty" that the spouse of the young Dionysia comes to adorn her funerary monument,[10] "in place of her noble character" that the husband of Aspasia builds a *mnēma* for this exemplary woman (*esthlē*),[11] "in place of his virtue and wisdom" that his father, Kleoboulos, erected a *sēma* for the dead Xenophantos.[12] In the figural representation of the dead person, the beauty of the deceased is perpetuated by the beauty of the image as its equivalent. "Your mother has set upon this marble tomb a young virgin who has your height and your beauty, Theris," we read in a funerary epigram of the *Palatine Anthology* (7.649). A stele at Athens that crowns the tomb of a young man recommends that the passerby weep that so beautiful a boy had died, *hōs kalos ōn ethane*. It is on the monument that this youthful beauty, preserved by death before it could fade, can continue to be seen throughout the succession

---

[8] Werner Peek, *Griechische Grabgedichte* (Berlin, 1960), no. 96.

[9] Ibid., no. 54.

[10] Ibid., no. 92.

[11] Ibid., no. 78.

[12] Ibid., no. 34.

of ages. On a *korē* of the middle of the sixth century, the work of Phaidimos, one can read: "He [the father] raised me here, the *sēma* of his daughter Phile, beautiful to look upon,"[13] and on an inscription of Thasos, at the end of the sixth: "Beautiful is the *mnēma* that her father built for the deceased Leorete, for we will never see her alive again."[14]

For the image to acquire the psychological significance of a copy that imitates a model and gives the spectator an illusion of reality, the human figure must have ceased to incarnate religious values; in its appearance, it must have become in and for itself the model to be reproduced. The whole development of sculptural technique orients the image in this direction. But as a result, the new form of plastic language challenges the ancient system of representation. By bringing out the body's properly human dimension, sculpture initiated a crisis for the divine image. The progressive advances in the making of statues must have also aroused a distrustful reaction, as evidenced by the work of Plato: nostalgia for ancient divine symbols, attachment to the most traditional forms of representing the gods, and reservations about all kinds of figuration of the divine. Once it ceases to incarnate the invisible, the beyond, and the divine, the image cannot be constituted as an imitation of appearance without having also aroused anxiety and criticism.

As for the status and destiny of the image in the West, it must be recalled again that by the third century of our era, Plotinus marks the start of another turning point. The image, instead of being defined as an imitation of appearance, will be interpreted philosophically and theologically and, at the same time, will be treated in its artistic form as an expression of essence. Once again and for a long time to come the image will be given the task of representing the invisible.

[13] Ibid., no. 52.
[14] Ibid., no. 40.

Chapter 9

THE BIRTH OF IMAGES

To WHAT EXTENT did the ancient Greeks recognize an order of reality corresponding to what we call image, imagination, and the world of the imaginary? No inquiry of this kind has yet been conducted in a systematic way, but the task is all the more urgent because, at first glance, it might well seem to have no subject. How could the Greeks, masters of the art of "figuration" in drawing, painting, and sculpture, not have had the images in their minds, as we do, that they represented in their works? And for anyone who might be tempted to doubt the value of such psychological "evidence," appeal could be made to the learned testimony of Quintilian, writer in Rome of the first century of our era: "What the Greek call *phantasiai*, we call *visiones*, imaginative visions through which the images of absent things are represented in the soul in such a way that we seem to discern them with our eyes and to have them present before us" (*Instit.* 6.2.29).

Moreover, starting with the fourth century before our era, had not a philosopher like Plato already collected the most diverse types of imagery into one and the same group so as to present a unified general theory? And did he not rank them all together in the framework of the same category of phenomena, those that, whatever their differences, all come under the heading of *mimēsis*, of imitation? In the *Sophist*, the young Theaetetus is asked to specify what an image is, and he replies with a series of examples drawn from the most varied domains. But he is countered by the Eleatic Stranger with the Socratic demand for a definition, both particular and general, that would reveal the common essence of everything that is called an image. What he expects from Theaetetus is a formulation of "what there is in common between all those things which you say are many and upon which, nevertheless, you bestow the single name of image [*eidōlon*], a name you extend to all of these as if they were just one thing" (240a3–5).

IMAGE AND IMITATION

For Plato, everything in human life that is classified as *eidōpoiikē*, of the activity that fabricates an image—everything, just to start with, that has to do

This piece was originally published under the title "Image et apparence dans la théorie platonicienne de la 'Mimêsis,' " in *Journal de Psychologie* 2 (1975), and reprinted as "Naissance d'images" in *Religions, histoires, raisons* (Paris, 1979), 105–37. Translated by Froma I. Zeitlin.

with the plastic arts, poetry, tragedy, music, and dance—all belongs to the domain of *mimētikē*. The formulas in both the *Republic* and the *Sophist* correspond. In the first (*Rep.* 599a7), Plato calls *mimēsis* a "demiurgy of images [*eidōlon dēmiourgia*]," and in the second (*Soph.* 265b1), he says: "*Mimēsis* is something like a fabrication [*poiēsis*], a fabrication of images, to be sure, and not of realities." The maker of an image (*eidōlou poiētēs*), the fabricator of images (*eidōlou dēmiourgos*), is one who is called a *mimētēs*, an imitator.[1] Plato is not content with following the path that Xenophon, with less rigor and without concerning himself with theoretical matters, had opened up in the *Memorabilia*. In the third chapter of this work, Xenophon had already brought about a certain shift of meaning in the vocabulary of imitation. He took *mimos* (mime as both a genre and an actor), *mimeisthai* (to mimic), *mimēma* (product of the action of mimicking), and *mimētēs* (the one who mimics) and employed this set of terms—whose use is not attested before the fifth century and which in all likelihood belonged to the literary genre of the mime with its very specific values of mimicking, aping, and pretending—in order to designate the work of painters and sculptors.[2] Plato takes yet another step: he gives *mimeisthai* a more precise, even somewhat technical value at the same time that he enlarges the field of application by making "imitate" into the common and characteristic feature of all figurative or representational activities.[3] In this way, he seems to have modified the orientation of this semantic grouping and to have upset the balance among the three terms implied in the act of *mimeisthai*—that is, the model, the imitator, and the spectator—to the advantage of the first two (model and imitator), which, from now on, are established as the operative pair in the mimetic relationship. In the fifth century, *mimos* and *mimeisthai* had placed less emphasis on the relation of the imitator to what he imitates than on the one between the imitator-simulator and the spectator who observes him. In acts of simulating and feigning, the idea was not to produce a work that exactly copied the model but to exhibit a style of behavior that would fool others, a way of making oneself look like some person or another,

[1] Cf. *Rep.* 599d3 and 601b11, and also *Soph.* 266a–d; 267a–b; 268d; *Pol.* 306d1–3; *Laws* 668a6: "All of music is representative and imitative [*eikastikē, mimētikē*]"; 668b10: "All creations that are related to music are imitation and representation [*mimēsis, apeikasia*]."

[2] Xen., *Mem.* 3.10.1–8. On the use of the vocabulary of *mimeisthai*, its origin and evolution, cf. Hermann Koller, "Die Mimesis in der Antike: Nachahmung, Darstellung, Ausdruck" (Diss., Bern, 1954); G. F. Else, "Imitation in the Fifth Century, " *CP* 53 (1958): 73–90; G. Sörbom, *Mimesis and Art: Studies in the Origin and Early Development of an Aesthetic Vocabulary* (Uppsala, 1966).

[3] *Rep.* 373b5–8: "The crowd of imitators [*mimētai*], whether those who apply themselves to figures and colors, or those who cultivate music, that is, poets and their retinue of rhapsodes, actors, choral dancers, and theatrical directors." Cf. *Phdr.* 248e: "the poet or any other of those who work with *mimēsis*"; *Soph.* 299d3–5: "painting or any other part of mimeticism"; *Tim.* 19d5–6, where the race of poets (*poētikon genos*) is identified with the tribe of imitators (*to mimētikon ethnos*).

by adopting his (or her) traits. Rather than a representation, the act of *mimeisthai* was a performance, a demonstration. By privileging the relationship of mimic-spectator, the vocabulary of *mimeisthai*, as used in the fifth century, operates between two poles. In the first place, there is deception: in the mimic—and through him—the spectator perceives not the person in question as he really is, but the one the mimic is trying to copy. A second factor is identification: *mimēsis* implies that, by adopting the other's ways, the simulator becomes just like the one he is intending to mimic. In Plato, except where *mimeisthai* is used in an ordinary sense, the accent, on the contrary, is emphatically put on the relationship between the image and the thing of which it is the image, on the relationship of resemblance that joins and yet distinguishes the two. This explicit formulation of the bond of "semblance" that every kind of imitation must activate brings to the fore the problem of the copy and the model and what they are, as much in themselves as in relation to one another. The question then overtly posed is that of the nature of "resembling," of the essence of "semblance."

From this perspective, the mimetic activity of artists who fashion images is analogous to other phenomena, which, this time, are not products of a human operation but of a divine art—natural phenomena, for example, like reflections in water, figures in mirrors, shadows, and visions in dreams.[4] These *eidōla*, these images, are related to the true objects by resemblance and by comparative unreality, just as are the creations of human art. The painter's work is thus comparable to that universe of reflections a mirror produces when it is turned from all sides by the hand that wields it:

> If you want to take a mirror and show it from all sides, in an instant you will make the sun and the stars of the sky appear, in an instant the earth, in an instant yourself and other animals and implements and plants and all the objects of which we have just now spoken.
> —Yes, he says, visible objects [*phainomena*] but without any true reality. . . .
> —And doesn't the painter too in some way make a bed?
> —Yes, a visible bed [*phainomenēn*], he too. (*Rep.* 596d–e)

The Image as Semblance

Thus a field of imagery is clearly delineated that, alongside others, encompasses all the "representational" productions, constituting what today we call works of art. At the same time, by virtue of its definition, it also confers on the image as such an ontological status of its own. If it is understood as the outcome of imitation, the image consists of a pure "semblance"; it has no other reality than this similitude in relation to what it is not, to that other, real thing whose illusory replica it is, both its double and its phantom. It is worth

[4] *Rep.* 510a; 516a4–6; *Soph.* 239b5–7; 266b9–14.

quoting here that part of the exchange in the *Sophist* concerning the actual definition of the image:

Theaetetus: What would we say an image is, o stranger, but a second such object [*heteron toiouton*] made in the likeness of the true one?

Stranger: Do you mean by your "second such object" a true object? What do you mean by this "such"?

Theaetetus: Not a true one, by any means, but only one which resembles it.

Stranger: But by the true, do you mean that which really is?

Theaetetus: Exactly.

Stranger: And by the not-true, do you mean the opposite of the true?

Theaetetus: Of course!

Stranger: That which is like, then, you say does not really exist if you say it is not true.

Theaetetus: But it does exist in a way.

Stranger: But not truly, you mean.

Theaetetus: No, except that it is really a likeness. (240a–b)

FROM APPARITION TO APPEARANCE

This is an important text. It clearly marks the terrain on which Plato stands when he approaches the problem of the image: a narrow ground that follows a path like a thin ridge between two slopes. On one side lies the archaic image, as attested in the uses of *eidōlon* in Homer, conforming to a conception of the image the Greeks had already gone beyond; on the other side is the path that leads to a psychological exploration of the image and in which the Greeks, as yet, are not involved.

The *eidōlon* is defined by Plato as a "second like object," the replica or duplication of the first—its twin in some way. From this point of view, the image belongs to the category of the Same; by its similitude it is the same as its model. At its extreme, if the resemblance becomes identity, it will no longer be an image-portrait facing the true Cratylus but two Cratyluses instead of only one (*Crat.* 432c4–6). But for the image to be the real thing, it must not only be content to reproduce "his form and color"; it should also know how to render what is inside Cratylus—his voice, life, soul, and thought (432b6–10). Such is precisely the case of the archaic *eidōlon* in the three forms it takes: a dream image (*onar*), an apparition sent by a god (*phasma*), and a phantom of a deceased (*psuchē*). The *eidōlon* of Antikleia, Odysseus' mother, and that of Patroklos, Achilles' friend, are not only "wholly similar" and "entirely like" these two beings. In their voices, words, gestures, and thoughts, these *eidōla* incarnate an actual presence that stands before the particular hero, who addresses them and converses heart to heart with one or the other, as though speaking to a real mother or friend. When, however, on seeing them before their eyes, the desire seizes Achilles or Odysseus to embrace their loved ones and press them close, all they can grasp is empty and insubstantial air.[5] The *eidōlon* manifests both a real presence and an irremediable absence at the same time. It is this inclusion of a "being elsewhere" in the midst of a "being here" that constitutes the archaic *eidōlon*, less as an image in the sense in which we understand it today than as a double. This double is not, in fact, a representation of the subject through and through; it is a real apparition that actually introduces here, in this same world in which we live and have eyes to see, a being, which in its temporary form of the same, shows itself to be fundamentally an other because it belongs to the other world. For archaic thought, the dialectic of presence and absence, same and other, is played out in the otherworldly dimension that the *eidōlon*, by being a double, contains, in the miracle of something invisible that can be glimpsed for just an instant. This same dialectic is found again in Plato. However, once transposed into a philosophical vocabulary, it not only changes its register and assumes a new significance, but the terms as well are also in some sense reversed. The image, a "second like object," being defined in some respects as the Same, also refers to the Other. It is not confused with the model because, having been denounced as the nontrue, the not-real, it no longer, as in the case of the archaic *eidōlon*, bears the mark of absence, of elsewhere, and of the invisible, but rather the stigma of a really unreal nonbeing (*ouk on ouk ontōs estin ontōs*, *Soph.* 240b11). Instead of expressing the irruption of the supernatural into human life, of the invisible into the visible, the play of Same and Other comes to circumscribe the space of the fictive and illusory between the two poles of being and nonbeing, between the true and the false. The "apparition," along with the religious values that invest it, gives way to a "seeming," to an appearance, a pure "visible" where the question is not one of making a psychological analysis but of determining its status from the point of view of its reality, of defining its essence from an ontological perspective.

SEEMING

A being of semblance, the image belongs to the order of appearance, to *phainein*: it "makes itself seen," like an appearance of what it is not. The image is therefore as much a "faux-semblant" as it is a "semblance." It only dis-

---

[5] Antikleia: *Od.* 11.153–222; Patroklos: *Il.* 23.65–108.

plays the external aspect, the concrete form, of the thing it imitates, that which the different senses perceive at one moment or another or view from this angle or that. It might seem, as some have supposed, that there is a conflict between the discussion in the *Sophist* and that in the *Republic*. The *Sophist* maintains a distinction between two forms of mimeticism or the fabrication of images (*eidōlopoiïkē*); the first produces icon-copies (*eikones*) that resemble their models by reproducing their actual proportions; the second, on the contrary, produces simulacra-phantasms (*phantasmata*) by sacrificing the exact proportions and substituting those that will create an illusion in the eyes of the spectators (235e6–236c6). But contrary to what has sometimes been maintained,[6] this distinction does not compromise the general and unambiguous affirmation of the *Republic*:

> What is the painter's aim relative to each object? Is it to represent something as it is, or that which seems as it seems [*to phainomenon, hōs phainetai*]? Is it the imitation of appearance or of reality?
>
> —Of appearance, he says.
>
> —The art of imitation [*hē mimētikē*] is therefore very far from the true and, if the painter is capable of executing everything, it is because he only touches a small part of each thing and this part is only the image [*eidōlon*]. (*Rep.* 598 b–c)[7]

The painter's bed, whether it is a faithful copy (*eikōn*) "that borrows from the model the exact relations of length, width, and depth, and assumes in addition each part of the appropriate colors,"[8] or whether it is a simulacrum (*phantasma*) intended to produce an effect of trompe-l'oeil,[9] the painter's bed is always in both cases an imitation of a visible bed produced by the artisan; it is not an imitation of either the idea or essence of the bed (*eidos*).

The opposition Plato establishes at *Sophist* 235d–e between two types of *eidōla* cannot have any fundamental import: it does not at all prevent the phi-

---

[6] For discussion of this thesis and a list of its supporters, see Sörbom, *Mimesis and Art*, 133–38, and Eric Havelock, *Preface to Plato* (Oxford, 1963), 33–34. J. J. Pollitt, *The Ancient View of Greek Art: Criticism, History, and Terminology* (New Haven, 1974), 46–49, discusses the texts invoked by those who claim there was a mimeticism of Forms that Plato would have admitted as both possible and desirable in the domain of art. Henry Joly also accepts this point of view in *Le renversement platonicien: Logos, episteme, polis* (Paris, 1974), 42, 50, 148ff. Cf. also Gilles Deleuze, *Logique du sens* (Paris, 1969), app. 1, and *Simulacre et philosophie antique* (Paris, 1969), 347–61.

[7] Cf. 601b7: "The creator of the image, the imitator, we say, understands nothing of reality; he only knows appearance; isn't that so?"

[8] *Soph.* 235d8–e2. On the values of the term *summetria* (translated by "exact relation") and its use in the ancient vocabulary of art, cf. Pollitt, *Ancient View of Greek Art*, 9–71, 256–58.

[9] "If they reproduce these beautiful forms with their true proportions, the upper parts will seem to us too small and the lower parts too large, because we see the latter close up and the former from far away" (*Soph.* 235e–236a). The relations of the Platonic conception of *mimēsis* and the history of the plastic arts in Greece is an important question that cannot be addressed in this essay. Cf. P.-M. Schuhl, *Platon et l'art de son temps* (Paris, 1952).

losopher from proposing a little later in the same dialogue (240a–b) the general
"negative" definition of the *eidōlon* we have already noted. At 264c–d, *eikōn*,
eidōlon, and *phantasma* are again associated with each other as aspects of not-
being and falseness. Finally, in 266c, it is the art of the painter in general,
without distinction, that is presented as producing a waking dream for those
whose eyes are open. On this point, Sörbom is right to recall that in the *Cratylus*, Socrates contrasts one kind of *mimēsis* with another. The first is that of
painting, which, through the colors nature places at its disposition, imitates
the colors already found in natural objects (434a); the other *mimēsis* is the one
we have the right to demand from names, and this *mimēsis* would no longer
have as its object the sensible properties of things, but rather their essence,
their *ousia* (423d–e; 431d2). There is no better way to declare that painting,
as such, does not aim at essence. The whole passage is meant to make us
understand that the relationship of words—and more generally of discourse—
to the things that are named can only be of the same order as the relation of
semblance between the image and its model. Moreover, we note the exact
parallels between the expressions of the *Cratylus* used to characterize a pictorial imitation that can have nothing to do with essence, and those in the passage of the *Sophist* (235d–e) that some have interpreted as favoring the possibility of a mimeticism of Forms. The *Cratylus* speaks of appropriate colors
and forms (*prosēkonta*), the *Sophist* of appropriate proportions and colors
(*prosēkonta*).[10] There is thus no contradiction between the distinction in the
Sophist concerning the two forms of *eidōla* and the general conclusion reached
in the *Republic*: "Painting and mimeticism in its entirety [*holōs hē mimētikē*]
accomplish their task far removed from truth." This formula corresponds to
the demand for a general definition of mimeticism announced at the beginning
of book 10: "Could you tell me what is imitation in general? [*mimēsis holōs
. . . ho ti pot' estin?*]" (595c7).

DEMIURGY AND IMITATION

Plato's position is therefore perfectly clear; it establishes an opposition between demiurgic activity, on the one hand, and mimetic activity, on the other.
The carpenter is really a "demiurge" of a bed to the extent that, even if he
himself does not know the essence of the bed and has no correct opinion about
it, he produces, on the advice of the user who has this knowledge, a real bed
that corresponds to the end product appropriate to this kind of object. The
painter, on the contrary, is neither a workman nor a producer (*dēmiourgos*,
poiētēs) of any bed (*Rep.* 597d10). Whether he produces a copy or simulacrum, in both cases he remains an imitator (*mimētēs*) of what the artisans produce (597e). What he imitates is not the essence of the bed as the artisan does

---

[10] The same expression is in the *Laws*: 668e2.

when he constructs some particular bed, a bed that, because one can sleep on it, resembles the unique Model, the only truly real bed, even if it is not actually *that* bed.[11] Far removed from the real and the true by three degrees, the painter's *mimēsis* relates to the multiple and different artefacts, not so as to represent them as they are in their functional completeness, that is, in respect to the services they are to give the user, but as they appear, in their visible external aspect (*Rep.* 597e2–598a3). As an expression of different kinds of appearance, the image belongs entirely on the side of "phenomena," of the sensible world with its inconsistencies, contradictions, and relativities. Plato will say of *phantasia* and *eikasia* that they are like a somnolent form of thought, a waking dream. "Will we not affirm that the art of the mason creates a real house, and that of the painter another house, a kind of dream [*onar*] presented by the work of a man's hand to eyes that are open?"[12]

Picked up by Aristotle, for whom all human *technē*—not only artistic creation—is an "imitation of nature" (*mimēsis tēs phuseōs*), the Platonic concept of *mimēsis*, more or less reinterpreted, will, from the Renaissance on, exercise its well-known influence on the development and orientation of Western art. On the other hand, the opposition Plato so sharply establishes between the intellect, at work in *dianoia*, and *phantasia*, immersed in the flux of the sensible, seems to continue in certain modern psychological theories that attach the image to sensation and which have stimulated research, like that of the Würzburg school, on the existence of an imageless "pure" thought.

But these continuities should not mislead us. The problem of the image in Plato belongs to a very different cultural context than our own and its analyses are situated on a wholly other level than that of the psychological study of mental images. The different kinds of *mimēmata* that Plato calls *eidōla*, *eikones*, and *phantasmata* are not apprehended in their aspect as facts of consciousness. They are seen rather as objective products of certain types of art.

SPOKEN IMAGES

In contrast to demiurgic arts, which produce realities, these "imitative" arts are not at all limited to those that, like painting and sculpture, are applied to a material to give it the form of an image meant for the eyes of spectators. All

[11] *Rep.* 596b6: the workman "fixes his eyes on the idea . . . in order to make his work"; 597 a 4: "If he does not make the essence of the bed, he does not make the real bed, but something which resembles the real bed without being it." Cf. also *Rep.* 601dff.: the user knows the essence, the fabricator has a correct opinion of it, the imitator has neither knowledge nor a correct opinion of it.

[12] *Soph.* 266c8–9. Cf. *Rep.* 476c5–8: "Isn't dreaming, whether in sleep or in waking, just this: to take what is similar to something not to be a likeness but to be the thing itself which it resembles?"; 534c5–7: "The man who does not know the good in himself, but only some *eidōlon* of the good, through opinion and not through knowledge—his life is only a dream and a slumber."

of sophistic is included, like painting, in *eidōlopoiïkē*, in *mimētikē*.[13] The sophist is a *mimētēs*, like the painter; more precisely, he, like the poet, is a *mimētēs* in words. His discourse does not express the real any more than the painter draws a true bed or the tragic poet really lives the dramatic action imitated on the stage. The sophist too produces imitations of realities, illusory semblances, *eidōla legomena*, of spoken images. As the Stranger in the *Sophist* says: "The word too contains a technique which can be used to pour enchanting words into the ears of the young who are still a long way from perceiving the realities of truth, by exhibiting to them spoken images of all things so as to make it seem that what they hear is true and that the speaker knows more than anyone else."[14]

The idea that the word of the poet in its relation to what it expresses is also analogous to the figuration of the painter in its relation to the model represented—that is, to an artifice producing a "look-alike image"—had already been stated by Simonides at the turning point of the sixth century: "The word is the image [*eikōn*] of actions." Plutarch qualifies this point as follows: "Simonides calls a picture silent poetry and poetry a speaking picture [*zōgraphian lalousan*], for the actions the painter makes visible in the course of producing them are related by words and are described once they are produced."[15] But for Simonides, this assimilation does not only serve to emphasize the artificial and learned character of the combinatory work the poet achieves with his words, but is intended to give the product of his poetic song the same value of permanence and monumentality, the same "reality," as the works of the sculptor and painter.[16] For Plato, the issue is, on the contrary, to connect the verbal technique of the poet to the inconsistent illusionism of the plastic image.

An illusionist of speech, an imagist in words, the sophist can venture to hold forth on everything without really knowing anything, just as the painter can represent everything through line and color, and the poet can sing of everything in his verses—wars, storms, kings, warriors, navigators, or shoemakers. Whatever the subject represented to the eyes or ears, it is always just a matter of simple resemblance: a game of phantomlike illusions.

As Plato sees it, there is a common bond between claims to a universal competence, the production of counterfeits and phantasmagoria, and the value

---

[13] Cf. *Soph.* 235a: "To return to the sophist, is it now clear that here is a magician [*tis tōn goētōn*], an imitator of realities [*mimētēs tōn ontōn*]?" Cf. also 235b–c; 236c; 239c–d; 240d; 241b6; 264c–e; 265a; 267e; 268c–d. At the end of the dialogue, the art of the sophist is defined as belonging to the mimetic order (*mimētikon*) and, as a producer of images (*phantastikos*), it goes back into *eidōlopoiïkē*.

[14] *Soph.* 234c–d; and, in 234e1–2, the expression *ta en tois logois phantasmata*, "the simulacra included in words."

[15] Simon. frag. 190b Bergk; Plut., *De glor. Athen.* 346f; *Quaest. conviv.*, 748a.

[16] Cf. Marcel Detienne, *Les maîtres de vérité dans la Grèce archaïque* (Paris, 1967), 105–19, and Jesper Svenbro, *La parole et le marbre* (Lund, 1976), 141–42.

assigned to simple entertainment, to gratuitous and entirely nonserious play. "The man who claims to be capable of producing everything by a single art, we know he will only make imitations. . . . Emboldened by his painterly technique he will, exhibiting his drawings from afar to the most innocent among the young folk, give them the illusion that everything he wants to make he is quite capable of completing in fact" (*Soph*. 234b5–10). If someone therefore claims to know a man acquainted with the whole range of crafts and more competent in every art than each of the specialists, "we must tell him that he is naive and that he has doubtless fallen in with a charlatan [*goëtês*] and an imitator [*mimêtês*] who has deceived him and that, if he took him for a universal genius, it is because he is incapable of distinguishing between science, ignorance, and imitation [*mimêsis*]" (*Rep*. 598d2–6). Poets like Homer can well pose as knowing everything in all fields; in fact, pure imitators, "they only create phantoms [*phantasmata*], not real things" (*Rep*. 599a2–3). One must therefore beware of taking all this imagery seriously and of trusting in the knowledge of those who produce it:

> When a man says he knows all things and can teach everything in a short time . . . shouldn't one think it only a joke [*paidia*]?
> —Absolutely.
> —Now, do you know any form of play which is more artistic or more charming than that of imitation?" (*Soph*. 234 a–b)

Considered by themselves, outside any criterion of truth and morality, "all these imitations produced by painting and music have no other aim than our pleasure and it is fair to assemble them under a single name—that of amusement [*paignion*]" (*Pol*. 288c).

PHANTASIA

If the speeches, modes of reasoning, and the eristics of the sophists constitute *eidôla* for Plato, images that in their "appearance" are passed off on the listener as authentic realities, we will not be surprised that in his work the term *phantasia*, derived from *phainein* (appear), does not in any way signify the imagination as a faculty, the power of constructing or using mental images, nor does it even mean those *visiones* of which Quintilian spoke. *Phantasia* is that state of thought where spontaneous assent is given to the appearance of things in the form in which they are viewed, as when we uncritically yield to the spectacle of a stick placed in water that seems to us to be bent. "And the same objects appear bent or straight depending on whether one looks at them in or out of water, concave or convex according to another visual illusion produced by its colors. . . . It is to this disposition [*pathêma*] of our nature that shadow painting [*skiagraphia*], the art of the charlatan [*thaumatopoia*] and all other inventions of the same type are addressed so that they are en-

dowed with the glamor of magic [*goēteia*]'' (*Rep.* 602c10–d5). To this disposition (*pathēma*) or affection (*pathos*) of our nature are referred then both
the "illusions" of sense and the illusionism of the image on which every type
of imitator relies to fool the spectator and have him believe the moon is made
of green cheese. Contiguous with sensation and opinion, from which it is not
clearly distinguished, *phantasia* is defined by its inclusion in ''appearance and
seeming, without really being [*to phainesthai touto kai to dokein, einai de mē*]''
(*Soph.* 236e). Some texts emphasize these affinities. When opinion (*doxa*) is
presented ''through the intermediary of sensation, can such an affection [*pathos*] be correctly named by any other name than *phantasia*?'' ''This affection
that we designate with the word *phainetai* [it seems to me] is a mixture of
sensation and opinion'' (*Soph.* 264a4–6; 264b).

> Is ''appearance'' [*to phainetai*] something to be felt [*aisthanesthai*]?
> —Yes indeed.
> —*Phantasia* [seeming] and *aisthesis* [sensation] are therefore identical.''
> (*Theaet.* 152b–c)

A man who perceives objects from afar without seeing them clearly will ask
the question: ''What can it be which appears to me [*phantazomenon*] behind
this rock, standing upright under a tree?—Isn't this what someone might ask
himself if he saw such objects appearing to his view [*phantasthenta*]?'' (*Phi-
leb.* 38c–d).

THE MIMETIC IN THE ORAL TRADITION

The Platonic interpretation of the image and the theory of *mimēsis* on which it
rests mark a stage in what might be called the elaboration of the category of
the image in Western thought. But, to be understood correctly, these ideas
must be situated in their context, restored to that history of archaic Greek
culture of which Plato is both the destroyer and the heir. In this culture, as
recent studies have shown, which kept its fundamentally oral character until
around the end of the fifth century,[17] the image does not occupy the same
place, take on the same role, or assume either the same forms or the same
meanings as in our modern civilizations. It is sketched out there, but it functions differently both on the level of the individual's private experience and in
the general process of communication within the group as well as in the operations of thought. When Plato completes the rupture with the system of traditional Greek *paideia* in which the aggregate of knowledge (the encyclopedia
of collective knowledge, as Havelock puts it) was transmitted orally from gen-

---

[17] I think here especially of Havelock, *Preface to Plato*, to whose work I am directly indebted
in the pages that follow. On the question of knowing how advanced Athenian literacy (both writing and reading) was in the fifth and fourth centuries, cf. F. D. Harvey, ''Literacy in the Athenian
Democracy,'' *REG* 79 (1966): 585–635.

eration to generation through the recitation and aural reception of poetic songs which were formulaic in style, rhythmically scanned, and sometimes accompanied by dances—this is an entire mode of acquiring knowledge that Plato rejects insofar as it rests on a "mimetic" effect of affective communication that involves the author, the performer (reciter or actor), and the audience of listeners who identify themselves in some fashion with the actions, ways of being, and characters represented in the stories or on the stage. At this level Plato, who, as we have said, wholly altered the orientation of the semantic field of *mimeisthai*, remains faithful to the concept of *mimēsis*, which is attested in the fifth century and which finds its most arresting expression in a passage of the *Thesmophoriazousae* of Aristophanes. It is Agathon, the tragic poet, who speaks: "To match the dramas he must compose, the poet must have the ways of being [*tous tropous*] that match his dramas. Thus, if he composes feminine dramas [*gunaikeia*], he must in his own person [*sōma*] participate in these ways. . . . If he composes manly dramas [*andreia*], this basic quality must be present in his person [*en tōi sōmati*]. The qualities we do not possess must be gotten by *mimēsis*" (149–56).[18] Since one composes dramatic actions "in conformity with one's nature" (167), the poet must himself assume the ways of being (*tropoi*), the character (*ēthos*) of the personages who participate in these actions. He must "imitate" them in order to represent them in his verses. There are two consequences of this idea. In the first place, Plato allows no difference between the practice of literary composition of the poet and the practice of the actor playing these compositions on the stage: in both cases it is a matter of the same *mimēsis*. Secondly, the best poet (for Plato, the worst one) is the one who has the talent for representing all the characters with their various traits and thus appears like a monster who is likely to assume all forms, a magician of metamorphoses—a Proteus. As a result, greater emphasis is laid on the affinities of poetry, as a species of the mimetic, with the polymorphic and gaudy world of becoming and with the inferior part of the soul that is always unstable and in flux and is the seat in us of the desires and passions.

Just as poet and actor are assimilated through imitation to the characters and actions they represent, a similar mimetic effect takes place in the soul of the spectators. On this point again Plato remains faithful to a very ancient tradition, echoed in Xenophon, which implies that the impression produced by a painted or sculpted image depends on *what* it represents—nobility or servility, dignity or baseness, prudence or immoderation, courage or cowardice—not in the *way* in which it represents it (*Mem.* 3.10.5). For Xenophon, the effect the image has on the spectator seems to correspond to the higher or lower moral

---

[18] Aristophanes' text should be compared with the Suda's information about Sophron, the Syracusan author of mimes, a contemporary of Euripides: "He wrote masculine mimes and feminine mimes [*mimous andreious kai mimous gunaikeious*]." Might we consider Plato's remarks in *Rep.* 451c1–3 and *Laws* 669c4 as allusions to these two traditional forms of mime?

quality of the model rather than to the greater or lesser virtuosity of the artist. In an analogous perspective, poetic imitation, according to Plato, sets up such an intimate complicity between the characters represented and their listeners that it makes the emotions represented in the former pass into the soul of the latter: in this way, having as if "nourished and fortified" our passions with the spectacle of misfortunes depicted in others, we become incapable of mastering them in ourselves (*Rep.* 606b6–8). All education is thus confronted with the problem of the mimetic arts and their effects on the spectator. The image is not reality, of course, but the fear is that "one will derive reality from *mimēsis* [*ek tēs mimēseōs tou einai*]." This is because "imitations, begun in childhood and continued in life, turn into character and nature for the body, voice, and thought" (*Rep.* 395c8–d3). Without playing phantoms oneself, it would be enough to see them imitated by another in order to become one in turn.

Through the critique of mimeticism and its effects, it is the content of the instruction transmitted in this way and by this route that is radically disqualified in the eyes of the philosopher by its assimilation to those other phantom forms of *eidōla* that are their counterfeits, the deceptive illusions produced by sculptors and painters.[19]

For Plato, the modes of expression traditionally used in oral communication, whose rhythmic organization and formulaic and musical aspects must comply with the demands of memorization, all have certain features in common, which have them reproduce only the surface, the exterior, the momentary, the particular, and what is merely circumstantial in things, beings, and actions. These features include a narrative texture, an articulation into successive episodes, and a syntactical structure that expresses, not general truths, but localized events. To these we may add procedures of personalization and direct visualization of the acts recounted as well as a dramatic, concrete, and emotional language full of images. All the different forms of the oral message—the poetic narrative (especially when it is in the direct style, when the poet enters in some way into the skin of each of his characters), the tragic dialogue, the grand discourse of the rhetorician, and the eristic of the sophists—have the capacity to fascinate the audience, bewitch it, and charm it (*thelgein*) by the magic of the word. Such is the degree of this fascination that the audience almost physically participates in the rhythmic, verbal, vocal, and instrumental models used for communication, and has the illusion of itself living out what is said. The listeners themselves are invaded by suffering, fear, and pity and it is as though they were transported into the narrative, were included in the oral unfolding of the discourse. But these spells of art (*goē-*

---

[19] *Rep.* 605a7–b1: one is justified in putting the poet on the same line as the painter "for he resembles him in that he makes base works [*phaula*] in respect to truth, and he is like him too because of the appeal he has to the base part of the soul and not to the best part."

teia), to use the term that Plato applies to painting, poetry, and sophistic after Gorgias had used it to glorify the power of rhetorical art,[20] can only put up a stage set around the listeners. They can only construct a facade of illusory images (cf. *Rep.* 365b–c), as inconstant, multiple, and fugitive as the flux of sensible becoming and fleeting emotions in whose encirclement this type of discourse is necessarily contained.

IMITATION AND SENSIBLE BECOMING

Through a colorful medley of words, beings, and particular situations this type of message is constructed in order to represent actions as they appear here and now, to express the desires and passions of the soul, slanted in such a way as to make them manifest to the eyes of someone else—in short, they are confined to the pure realm of visible things (*ta horata*) and of events in the process of becoming (*ta genomena*). Such a message does not have at its disposal either the vocabulary, the conceptual equipment, or the syntax that, like a scientific demonstration or an argued dialogue, would allow it to formulate an authentic reality that is both unified and permanent. This kind of communication can speak of what appears to us here and now, but not of being as it is, always identical to itself. Instead of articulating the true and the real, it creates a semblance, an appearance, through a colorful glitter of words and rhythms that produce an effect of fascination and a vertigo of the mind.

At this level of analysis, there is a fully homologous relation between the painter's modes of expression with their medley of colors, those of the poet or rhetor with their medley of words and rhythms,[21] and the gaudy patterns and multiple forms of a sensible becoming that belongs to ever-changing appearances. The object of the figurative mimeticism of the painter or the representational one of the poet and orator is precisely that which manifests itself to the eyes and ears in a broad variety of forms that display endlessly multiple and contradictory facets. The imitator in words who is the tragedian "will not hesitate to imitate everything in a serious way. . . . he will imitate even what we have just spoken about, the noise of thunder, winds, hail, axles, blocks, trumpets, flutes, and pipes, or any instrument, and additionally, the voices of dogs, sheep, and birds. His entire elocution will only be an imitation of voices and gestures" (*Rep.* 397a3–b2). In truth, it is really "the sound and fury" of the world that come to be reflected in the mirror of the mimetic work of the

---

[20] Gorg., *Enc. Hel.* 10 in DK, 82b11. For Plato, in addition to the references already given, cf. *Soph.* 235a1, 241b6–7; *Menex.* 235a2; *Rep.* 413c1–4, 584a9–10; *Symp.* 203d8.

[21] *Rep.* 601a4–b5: "By means of words and phrases, the poet dresses each art with the colors appropriate to him. . . . If we strip the poet's works of poetic coloring and if he recites these now reduced to themselves, you know, I think, what sort of a showing they make." The "colors" of poetry that account for the way it exercises its charm (*kēlēsis*) are measure, rhythm, and harmony (601b1–3); cf. *Laws* 800d1–4.

poet, matching the demands of a literary genre that has need "of all the harmonies and rhythms to obtain its appropriate expression, since it contains variations of all sorts" (397c3–6). "Skilled at taking all forms and imitating all things" (398a1–3), the poet-imitator whom Plato drives out of the city, after having praised him as one would "a sacred, marvelous, and ravishing" being, is exactly the prototype of the double and multiple man (*diplous*, *pollaplous*) who is at the opposite extreme from the "simple" citizen the *Republic* hopes to create (397e1–2). In fact, mimeticism—of the painter and the poet—maintains an "association, contact, and friendship" (603b2; 603c1) with that part of the soul that, in the image of becoming, is itself inconstancy, variety, and colorful mixture. Imitative practice is alien to wisdom and truth; it cannot attach itself to these nor be inspired spontaneously by them. "Base, and coupling with that which is base in us, mimeticism engenders baseness [*phaulē . . . phaulōi xungignomenē phaula gennāi hē mimetikē*]" (603b5).[22] This is because

> what surrenders to a multiple and varied imitation [*pollēn kai poikilēn*] is the fretful [*aganaktētikon*] part of the soul; the intelligent and temperate disposition, on the contrary, since it always remains approximately the same, is not easy to imitate. . . . And is it not obvious that the poet-imitator is not naturally turned towards this rational principle of the soul nor, if he wants to win the votes of the crowd, is he the right one to satisfy it through his art [*sophia*], but rather he is made for the passionate and varied type [*to aganaktētikon te kai poikilon ēthos*], because it is easy to imitate. (604e–605b)

If the poet in his verses speaks of the gods, his oral mimetic practice will represent them with all the passions, weaknesses, and even crimes that are proper to that part of the human soul to which his art belongs. Even more, although the divine being is in itself wholly simple and incapable of change, he will represent it on the model of sensible appearances, of this "becoming," which it is his habit to depict. He will show the divinity continually taking on various shapes, assuming diverse forms, and modifying its appearance into a host of different figures; or again, the poet will dress up the divinity in the image of that which he himself is as a *mimētēs*. He will make the god into a magician, a deceiver, and an illusionist manufacturer of counterfeits, of unreal phantoms.[23] Far from prompting us to break with appearances and tear ourselves away from shadows and reflections, the art of the poet, even when he gets to evoke simple and permanent being, projects it on a multiple and variegated screen of seeming, once he translates it into his language of imitation.

In the same way, the group of terms, all articulated in order to configure

---

[22] Coupling and engendering assume their fully sexual meanings in the "intercourse" (*prosomilein*) that mimetic activity maintains with the choleric element of the soul.

[23] *Rep.* 380d–381b; 381c7–382a; 382e10–13.

Plato's notion of the image, together emphasize the constant slippages the philosopher sees operating between the image *stricto sensu* and sensible appearances in general, between an imaged vision and all the forms of knowledge that have not succeeded in becoming detached from the universe of seeming. In addition to *phainein*, *phainomena*, and *phantasmata*, which clarify and define the meaning of *phantasia*, the term *eikōn*, which has a technical sense in the fourth century and designates the representational image in its materiality (e.g., a statue), is, in Plato, associated with *eikasia*. *Eikasia* occupies the lowest rung on the ladder in the hierarchy of forms of knowledge, which the *Republic* classifies in its simile of a line divided into four segments.[24] *Eikasia* is less a way of knowing than a form of guesswork, with all the riskiness the term implies. Incapable of apprehending the object itself, of knowing it through a direct grasp of it (*eidenai*), *eikasia* must rely on everything that seems likely to have some "semblance" with the object so as to be able to imagine it in the best way it can. Understood thus in its broad sense, the image not only comes to be integrated into the domain of *doxa* in respect of that which makes it the opposite of *epistēmē*, but it also seems to be introduced into the heart itself of *doxa*, whose boundaries and whose field of application it reveals at one and the same time. Of *doxa* it can be said that, unlike science, it is just "opinion," as uncertain and fluctuating as the objects on which it has bearing. But the connection of *doxa* with the universe of the image is far more intimate and direct. *Doxa* comes from *dokein*, which signifies "to seem, to appear."[25] The field of *doxa* is that of appearances, of those semblances best expressed by the image.

THE DEVALUATION OF THE IMAGE

Plato finally pitches the entire realm of the sensible over to the side of the image. Presented as a discouraging play of shadows and reflections, the image veers off to drift away into some distant "elsewhere," and thus misses out on the entire undertaking of true knowledge. By so doing, Plato comes to preju-

---

[24] *Rep.* 511e: four dispositions (*pathēmata*) of the mind correspond to the four sections of the line according to a descending hierarchy: *noēsis*, *dianoia*, *pistis*, *eikasia*. In 533e3–534a5, the comparison is taken up again and developed further. Cf. Victor Goldschmidt, "La ligne de la République," in *Questions platoniciennes* (Paris, 1970), 203–19. The author has well observed the relations between *eikasia*, techniques of imitation, and the domain of images and reflections.

[25] Cf., for example, *Soph.* 236e–237a, with the wordplay among the terms *phainein*, *dokein*, *doxazein*: "To appear and to seem [*to phainesthai kai to dokein*] without being, to say something without, however, saying what is true, these are matters that are full of perplexity. . . . What formula is there to say or think [*legein ē doxazein*] that the false is real?" Cf. also *Rep.* 476d6; 477e3; 478a10. In the *Phaedrus*, the art of rhetoric is presented as a pursuit of *eikos* (the likely), a formulation of *eikota* (likelihoods), and a holiday taken from truth. And *eikos* itself is defined as *to tōi plēthei dokoun*, the opinion of the masses (literally: what is "seeming" to the masses), 272 e–273b; cf. also 260a1–3.

dice the traditional vocabulary of imagery, to reject the functions archaic thought had recognized in the image as a process of consciousness and a way of acceding to being that started off from its visible manifestations. In the texts of the sixth and fifth century, neither *eikazein* and *eikasia* nor *dokein* and *doxa* nor *phainein* and *phainomena* had yet taken on the essentially negative connotation attributed to them in the philosophical system where, by the same move, Plato founds the first general theory of imitation and simultaneously cuts the image off from the real and from knowledge.

André Rivier, in two related studies,[26] warns us against an anachronistic, because pejorative, interpretation of the set of terms grouped, on the one hand, around *eiskō*, *eikizō*, *eoika*, *eikos*, and *eikōn*, and on the other, around *dokeō*, *dokos*, and *doxa*. He has demonstrated that this vocabulary in its old usages and its deployment in philosophers, such as Xenophanes and Heraclitus, and historians, such as Herodotus and Thucydides, remains alien to what Rivier calls "the problematic of being and seeming." Although central to the thought of the fourth century, this problematic only emerged slowly in the philosophical consciousness of the fifth century under the stimulus of the inquiries of the Eleatic school.[27] This vocabulary, it is true, refers to mediate forms of knowledge. These are contrasted in this respect to the direct grasp of the object, as sight has us do, when it is applied to what we see before us, but even so, they are not wholly stripped of all positive value. Far from being disqualified as illusion, error, false appearance, and gratuitous conjecture, *eikasia*, *dokos*, and *doxa* designate valid intellectual acts. In the case of *eikasia*, use is made of resemblances, comparisons, and analogies, while the case of *dokos* and *doxa* also involves indices and reasonably based similitudes as a way of reaching objects that are not "evident," but remain hidden and invisible, whether in the past or the future, whether in the depth or the background of things. Basically, the question is always one of the same type of procedure, legitimate if it is correctly pursued, a way of grasping *adēla* (what is not shown) through *phainomena* (appearances) with adequate probability. *Adēla* and *phainomena* do not constitute two exclusive domains, defined by their opposition, but are two forms or two levels of reality that interpenetrate in the same universe, coexisting alongside each other, "being composed of or combining with one another in the unity of *phusis*."[28] In this context, *phainomena* could also not be deprived of value. They do not constitute a world of appearances, of counterfeits; they are "the things themselves with which one has dealings,"[29] the material of *historia*, the facts by which intellectual inquiry is guided and which it can use as signposts. This is the status of *phainomena* that

---

[26] *Un emploi archaïque de l'analogie chez Héraclite et chez Thucydide* (Lausanne, 1952); "Remarques sur les fragments 34 et 35 de Xénophane," *RPh.* 82 (1956): 37–61.

[27] Rivier, "Remarques," 59.

[28] Ibid., 59.

[29] Ibid., 59 n. 1.

still can be found in Democritus's formula, which Anaxagoras reports with approval: *Opsis tōn adēlōn ta phainomena* (59b21a DK): phenomena are the vision, the visible aspect, of things that are not revealed to view.

BEING AND SEEMING

We cannot, in the context of this study, undertake an analysis of this mode of archaic thought (which could be called either ''phenomenal'' or ''pre-phe-nomenal'') by retracing its history or specifying the place reserved for the image and the functions it assumes there.[30] We would like only to emphasize the extent of the transition from a positive to a negative pole that takes place between the sixth and fifth centuries in the vocabulary of image, semblance, and seeming, and which finds its endpoint in the first general theory of imita-tion and the image that was worked out by Plato.

By more sharply opposing ''seeming'' to ''being'' and by cutting one off from the other rather than maintaining their association in various kinds of equilibrium, as had previously been done, Plato gives the image its own form of existence and bestows on it a particular phenomenal status. Defined as sem-blance, the image possesses a distinctive character that is all the more marked, since from now on, appearance is no longer considered as an aspect, a mode, a level of reality, a kind of dimension of the real, but rather as a specific category confronted with ''being'' in an ambiguous relation of the ''faux-sem-blant.'' This specificity implies, as its counterpart, the expulsion of the image from the realm of the authentically real, its relegation to the field of the fictive and illusory, and its disqualification from the point of view of knowledge.

In the Athenian fourth century, through the work of Plato, the image is presented as an exterior semblance to the extent that a world of pure appear-ance has been marked out, which has cut its ties with the world of ''being'' and, in this exclusion from the real, has discovered the basis for a paradoxical status, intermediary between nonbeing and being. Assimilated to semblance, to seeming, the image is not a pure nothing but yet it is not something. In a certain sense, this equivocal promotion of seeming inaugurates the psycholog-ical career of the image. Should not an analysis of ''seeming'' make some reference to the subject whose eyes are the ones that see ''appearance''? And can the image function as an imitation of appearance if there is no spectator to look at it? The path seems thus to emerge that will end up by endowing the image with the status of a purely interior existence, by making it into a mode of subjectivity, since it has no other being than that which an individual con-sciousness can confer on it.

Nevertheless, this is not the road that Plato takes when he starts out in quest of what the image is. As soon as he enters the game, after some brief replies

---

[30] I hope to take this matter up in another study.

that are a prelude to the general definition of the *eidōlon*, he avoids it as a path where, if one were to lose one's way, it would be impossible to flush out the sophist, to convince him that he cannot produce anything but "faux-semblants" (*Soph*. 239cff). The sophist asks for the definition of what is called an image from the one who accuses him of being a maker of images. And it is not sufficient, as Theaetetus naively believes, to show him reflections in mirrors or effigies that are painted or sculpted. The sophist will laugh at these examples, made, he will say, for men who see; he will claim, for his part, that he knows neither a mirror nor anything like it, that he has no eyes at all, and has no knowledge of vision (239e5–240a). The sophist must be vanquished on his own territory; he must be tracked down in all his detours and feints by giving him a definition of the image that would be valid even for the blind, because it would be as independent of the fact of vision as of the subject who sees. The stakes for Plato are decisive. The question is to find out whether one can present a definition of the image that is not itself at the level of the image, one founded merely on the simple attestation of the senses. If the image is reduced to the appearance it assumes in the eyes of the spectator when he looks at it, you will confront two types of sophists who, through contrary arguments, will still make fun of you. The first will claim that the image, thus defined, has no more being for him than the fact that he has eyes or sight; the second will profess that there is no other being except the image and will affirm that whatever appears in such and such a way to each person is for that person his only reality, his unique truth. The problem then, when sight and spectator have been excluded from the game at the start, is to articulate what an image is, not in its seeming but in its being, to speak not of the seeming of appearance but of the essence of seeming, the being of semblance, and by this tactic, to avoid the "psychology" of the image. The aim would be to designate the place that semblance occupies in the hierarchy of different types of reality that make up the universe. Only in this situation can the image cease to oscillate between nonbeing and being, identified sometimes with one, sometimes with the other. It is fixed between nonbeing and being without being confused with either of the two, placed in a mediate position that it shares with *doxa*, and that sets up the possibility for error, for false judgment, for attribution of being to that which *is* not, and also for the confusion of the image with that whose image it is.[31] In other words, it would be useless to define the image as sem-

---

[31] Cf. *Rep*. 478 to the end of book 5, particularly in 478d5–10: "Haven't we earlier said that, if we found something of the sort that is and is not, such a thing would lie between that which purely and absolutely is and that which absolutely is not, and that the faculty correlated with it would be neither science nor nescience, but that which should appear to hold a place correspondingly between nescience and science? —Right. —And now there has turned up between these two the thing we call opinion" [trans. Shorey]. *Soph*. 264d3–6: "But now since the existence of false speech and false opinion has been proved, it is possible for imitations of realities to exist and for an art of deception to arise from this condition of mind" [trans. Fowler]. 260c: "For to think or

blance or appearance if this definition could not, at the same time, imply an explicit reference, on the one hand, to Being, as distinct from seeming and anterior to it, and on the other, to Not-Being as the foundation of a possible confusion between appearance and reality.

GOOD AND BAD IMITATION

In this way it becomes possible to reverse the perspective that lies at the heart of *mimesis*, in a strategy not unlike the generalization of the theme of the "image" to cover the entire gamut of sensible becoming. If Being is prior, is it not entitled to take up imitation in some way by the other end, from the side of the Model, and to envisage it from the point of view, not of that which it seems to be, but that which it resembles? The image indeed belongs to the order of seeming, but for Plato, there is no point to seeming without being, no point to an image without a reality, an imitation without a model to imitate. This is how the image can be recognized for what it is. As a mere semblance, cannot the image then function like a springboard as a way of turning back toward the Model? No doubt it can do just this, but without it ever being a question of any spontaneous movement or of something that is immanent in *mimēsis*. This maneuver presumes a rupture, a change of level, a true conversion: the Model is, as such, something *other* than the image, of an *other* nature. It contains nothing of "seeming" that can be reproduced by similarity in appearance, and therefore derives from an entirely different order of knowledge. Painters and "musicians" imitate the same by means of the same; with colors, forms, sounds, and movements they represent that which, in the figured object, is also colors, forms, sounds, and movements. Since they are attached to the order of seeming in things, they endeavor to restore this appearance. Here resides the danger of imitation, its deceitfulness, its "other" side, in a blind pursuit of similitude. As long as it goes from same to same, *mimēsis* can only efface the rupture between image and model, the fictive and the real. Seen from afar or shown to children, the image of the bed, colored by the painter, will give the effect of a true bed because true beds, according to the position of the spectators, also have different appearances. But the Idea of a bed cannot be imitated in this way. Its relationship with the carpenter's bed is not the same as the resemblance of the carpenter's bed to the image of the painter, not only because the Idea is not visible, but above all, because its noetic structure, being unique and permanent, is not relative to the one who looks at it, to the spectator's "point of view." On the contrary, in order to look toward the idea, to contemplate it, one must first have turned away from the multiple perspectives of seeming. One must have already organized one's

---

say what is not—that is, I suppose, falsehood arising in mind or in words. —So it is. —But if falsehood exists, deceit exists. —Yes. —And if deceit exists, all things must be henceforth full of images and likenesses and fancies [*eidōlōn, eikonōn, phantasias*]" [trans. Fowler].

intellectual procedure or, in the case of the artisan, one's demiurgic practice, no longer according to one's own position with respect to oneself, but with reference to that "in itself" which constitutes the fixed point where, at least in thought, one must come oneself to be situated.

Perhaps one might say that the illusionist *mimēsis* of those whom Plato calls "imitators" consists in a simulation of appearances for the purposes of duping someone else. Philosophical *mimēsis*, however, consists in an inward assimilation of oneself to what is other and radically alien to seeming, with the aim of undergoing a change within oneself.[32] The play of same and other is inverted, when one passes from a *mimēsis* of seeming to an assimilation to being. In the first case, the image relies for its resemblance to the model on what in the model never remains like itself; in the second, imitation includes the recognition of the otherness of the model and poses it as other even in its desire for semblance, precisely because the model is that which always remains the same as itself.

The two kinds of mimeticism therefore stand together only to the extent that they are opposed to each other, that they are inscribed on either side of the break between being and appearance. There is no continuity on the route that leads from the bad to the good, but rather a bifurcation at the crossroads where two paths meet. It is only on returning, after one has contemplated the sun of Being and has come back to the cave and its shadows, that one can recover an illusionist mimeticism, but this time, by purging it, by making it as simple and as uniform as possible so it can be made to serve other ends than its own and be subordinated from the outside to the requirements of the Forms.[33]

FINAL REMARKS

How do these analyses enable the psychologist-historian to reply to the question posed at the beginning of this essay concerning the forms of the image and imagination among the Greeks? The work of Plato has seemed to mark the moment when the world of appearances is incarnated, when, faced with the real and in relation to the real, it is posed as its "semblance." We might have expected that, by giving seeming its specificity and consistency, this turning point would have opened the way for the psychological career of the image. But it does not, in fact, do so directly, for at least two reasons. For one thing, the distance between sensation and image is not yet marked in the Platonic perspective. Only in Aristotle is it sketched out in a passage of the *De*

---

[32] Corresponding to this *mimēsis*-assimilation is the use of the verb *homoioun* or *exomoioun*; cf., for example, *Rep.* 613b1; make oneself like a god (*homoiousthai theōi*) as much as is possible for a man; *Tim.* 90d5–8: that someone who contemplates is made like the object contemplated (*exomoiōsai*).

[33] On this point it is sufficient to refer to the fine study of Victor Goldschmidt, "Le problème de la tragédie," *REG* 61 (1949): 19, reprinted in *Questions platoniciennes*, chap. 8, 103–40.

anima, and even there, the hesitations only emphasize the difficulties of making clear distinctions, in the framework of ancient thought, among sensation, image, and opinion.[34] On the other hand, and more profoundly, it does not open a path for the psychological career of the image because, by its connection to *mimēsis*, the image can only always reproduce an already given appearance that is exterior to itself. Imitation constitutes the image in its being, and makes it a semblance; at the same time, it is that which bounds it and excludes it from the field of invention, from innovation, and from creative fabrication. Defined as illusory, the fictive does not yet appear as a human artifice in the full sense of these terms. In the areas where it applies, the Platonic conception of *mimēsis* emphasizes the same absence of a category of the agent, the same lack of a notion of a creative human power, that have been observed in other sectors of Greek culture.[35]

It is not until the end of the second century of our era that we can find the idea of imagination. Speaking of artists like Phidias and Praxiteles, Flavius Philostratus declares that what presided over their most beautiful works was a *phantasia*, an imagination. This imagination is no longer dependent on *mimēsis* but is opposite and superior to it by reason of its *sophia*: "For *mimēsis* can only represent in an image what it has seen, but *phantasia*, in addition, what it has not seen."[36] When the artist rises up to the heavens to bring back images of the gods, he neither imitates nor copies: he imagines. Dissociated now from *mimēsis*, *phantasia* thus seems to have acquired the same power of contemplating the invisible and of passing beyond appearance by acceding to the superior world of Forms that Plato had previously reserved for philosophy.

[34] In the chapter "Les images" in *Nouveau traité de psychologie*, ed. G. Dumas (Paris, 1930), I. Meyerson emphasizes the fact that the differences between sensation and perception, on the one hand, and image, on the other, are those of nature, not of degree, and he rightly observes that Aristotle's analyses are situated at the very origins of psychological study of the image as such (544, 594). After having established that the imagination is not identical either to sensation or to intellection or to opinion, Aristotle defines the imagination in the following way: "A movement produced by sensation in action," *De anima* 3.3.427b14ff., and a little further on he writes: "Images are in some sense sensations, except that they are without material" (432a9).

[35] Cf. J.-P. Vernant, *Mythe et pensée chez les Grecs: Etudes de psychologie historique*, 10th ed. (Paris, 1985), 213–15, 223, 246; Vernant and P. Vidal-Naquet, *Mythe et tragédie en Grèce ancienne* (Paris, 1973), 43–74; Vernant, "Catégories de l'agent et de l'action en Grèce ancienne," in *Langue, discours, société: Pour Emile Benveniste*, ed. J. Kristeva, J.-C. Milner, and N. Ruwet (Paris, 1975), 105–13 (reprinted in *Religions, histoires, raisons*, 85–95); Imre Thoth, "Die nicht-euklidische Geometrie in der Phänomenologie des Geistes," in *Philosophie als Beziehungswissenschaft: Festschrift für Julius Schaaf*, ed. W. F. Niebel and D. Leisegang (Frankfurt am Main, 1974), vol. 20, 3–91, esp. 36 and 84.

[36] Phil., *Vit. Ap. Tyan.* 6.19. "It is the imagination that produced these works, which is a wiser demiurge than *mimēsis*; for *mimēsis* will only fabricate what it has seen, but imagination also what it has not seen, because it will conceive it, in referring itself to reality; and often it is terror that baffles *mimēsis*, while nothing can stop the imagination, for it proceeds undismayed to the goal which it has itself conceived."

Chapter 10

PSUCHE: SIMULACRUM OF THE BODY OR IMAGE OF THE DIVINE?

"HOMER," writes James Redfield, "has no knowledge of the soul."[1] That is, of course, if we take the soul in our sense of the term, for in many passages, Homer mentions the *psuchē* to mean that which leaves the person at the hour of his death to descend into Hades. A living man is never said to possess a *psuchē*, except in those rare cases where, in a temporary loss of consciousness, his *psuchē* momentarily deserts him as though he were dead. Men, therefore, do not have a *psuchē*; once they are dead, they become *psuchai*, flitting shades who lead an impoverished existence in the darkness of the underworld. "The *psuchē*," Redfield justly observes, "is not a soul but a phantom."[2]

Like a phantom, the Homeric *psuchē* belongs to other phenomena that enter, as it does, into the category of what the Greeks in the archaic period call *eidōla*, a word that should be translated not as "images" but rather as "doubles." There are in Homer, in fact, three kinds of supernatural apparitions that are denoted by the term *eidōlon*.

First, the phantom, *phasma*, created by a god in the semblance of a living person such as the one Apollo fabricates "like to Aeneas himself and in his armor [*autōi t'Aineiai ikelon*]" (*Il.* 5.449–53). Aeneas himself is sheltered in the citadel where Apollo has deposited him to remove him from the fray. It is a simulacrum now that the Greeks and Trojans confront in battle, a figure that both sides are convinced is the hero in person.[3] Next, there is the dream, the oneiric image (*oneiros*), considered to be a sleep apparition of a ghostly double that is sent by the gods in the image of a real being. Hence it is a dream figure, "wholly like to Nestor [*Nestori diōi . . . anchista eōikei*]" that comes as a messenger from Zeus to the sleeping Agamemnon to exhort him to summon the Achaean warriors to arms (*Il.* 2.56–58), or it is an *eidōlon* fabricated by Athena with the characteristics of a woman, Iphthime, daughter of Ikarios, whom the goddess dispatches to stand beside Penelope while she is fast

Translated by Froma I. Zeitlin.

[1] "Le sentiment homérique du Moi," *Le Genre Humain* 12 (1985): 96.

[2] Ibid., 97.

[3] The same use of *eidōlon* for the phantom or simulacrum of Iphimede (Iphigenia), Hes. frag. 23a17; of Hera, Hes. frag. 160 = schol. ad Apoll. Rh. 4.58; of Helen, Hes. frag. 358 = schol. ad Lycoph. 822.

asleep.[4] Finally and above all, the *psuchai* of the dead are called *eidōla ka-montōn*, phantoms of the dead.[5] The *psuchē* is addressed in the same way as the person[6] and has exactly the same appearance except that it lacks a real existence, which, by its resemblance to the being whose appearance it has,[7] makes the *psuchē* comparable to a shadow or a dream,[8] to a wisp of smoke.[9]

Phasma, a ghostly simulacrum, *oneiros*, a dream, and *psuchē*, the soul: these may seem to us to be disparate phenomena but, as "apparitions," they all contain a dimension of the world beyond. Their unity comes from the fact that in the cultural context of archaic Greece, they are all perceived by the mind in the same way and all bear an analogous meaning. It is also correct to understand them all as a true psychological category—the category of the double—that presumes a different mental organization than our own. A double is a wholly different thing from an image. It is not a ":natural" object, but it is also not a product of the imagination: neither an imitation of a real object, nor an illusion of the mind, nor a creation of thought. The double is a reality external to the subject and is inscribed in the visible world. Yet even in its conformity with what it simulates, its unusual character ensures its substantial difference from familiar objects and the ordinary setting of daily life. The double plays on two contrasting levels at the same time: at the moment when it shows itself to be present, it also reveals itself as not being of this world but rather as belonging to an inaccessible elsewhere.

Such, for example, is the case of the *eidōlon* of Patroklos that Achilles sees standing before him just as he is falling asleep at the end of a long night of lamentation, during which time Achilles, in his solitary wakefulness, his soul overcome by *pothos* (the nostalgic regret for one who is absent), had kept recalling to mind the memory of his friend. The *eidōlon* stands above the head of Achilles while he lies stretched out there as though it were produced in a dream, but in reality, it is the *psuchē* of Patroklos. What Achilles sees facing him is Patroklos himself: his dimensions, his eyes, his voice, his body, and

[4] *Od.* 4.796–97, 824, 835: the *eidōlon* of a dream has the corporeal aspect of a woman: *demas d'eikto gunaiki*.

[5] *Il.* 23.72, 104; *Od.* 11.83, 476, 602; 24.14.

[6] *Il.* 23.65ff.; *Od.* 11.152ff. and 475ff.; Bacchyl. 5.68.

[7] This complete "similitude" of the *eidōlon* to that of which it is the double is always expressed by words that belong to the vocabulary of *eoika* (it seems, it is fitting) with the verbs *eiskō*, *eikazō* (assimilate) and the adjectives *eikastos*, *eikelos* (comparable, similar). The term *eidōlon*, image, in use from the fifth century B.C.E., is also attached to this group. Thus there is no initial opposition between *eidōlon* (idol) and *eikōn* (image). In the archaic period, the *eidōlon*, as double, assumes the values of a "simulacrum"; it is perceived both as a "supernatural" apparition and as an appearance that conforms to that of which it is the phantom. On this point I disagree with the hypothesis of Suzanne Saïd in "Deux noms de l'image en grec ancien: Idole et icône," *Compte-rendu de l'Académie des Inscriptions et Belles Lettres* (1987): 309–30.

[8] *Od.* 11.207: *skiē eikelon ē kai oneiros*; 222: *eut'oneiros*.

[9] *Il.* 23.100: *eute kapnos*.

his clothing.[10] Nevertheless, when the hero wants to take hold of this figure, the *eidōlon* proves ungraspable: it is a thin vapor that disappears beneath the earth with a tiny, batlike cry (*Il.* 23.100–101; cf. *Od.* 24.7ff.).[11] The *eidōlon*, therefore, has something in it that produces an effect of trickery, deception, and delusion, *apatē*: yes, Achilles' friend is present, but he is also a breath, a wisp of smoke, a shadow, or the flight of a bird.

To understand this play of absence and presence to which the *psuchē* lends itself, a brief word must be said about funerary practices as they appear in Homeric epic. Their finality is revealed all the more clearly through the contrasting situation in which these rites are lacking, when a dead person is deprived of burial, and above all, when these practices are ritually denied as they are in those procedures of despoiling the corpse of an enemy. *Aikia* (outrage) consists in disfiguring—dehumanizing—the body of the adversary, in destroying in him all the values incarnated there, values that are also social, religious, aesthetic, and personal. The body is made filthy with dust and earth so that the person's individual features are lost and become unrecognizable: he is given as food to the dogs, birds, and fish so that, scattered, dismembered, and dissipated, he loses the unity of his form, his structural integrity. He is left to rot, to decompose in the sun so that he can no longer assume those values of beauty in the world beyond, the beauty of youth and vitality that the human body must reflect here below. Finally, instead of being fixed in his tomb, he is reduced to becoming the flesh and blood of wild animals in the bellies of those beasts who have devoured him, so that he loses all trace of his human character. The idea is thus to deprive the enemy of the human status of a dead person, to refuse him this change of state, this ambiguous promotion that the funeral normally brings about. Having disappeared from the world of the living, detached from the fabric of social relations into which he was bound up as a strand, when he was still present, death is now an absence, a void. But the person continues to exist on another level in the form of a being who escapes destruction, first by the permanence of his name and by the glory of his renown, which, celebrated in epic, remain present not only in the memory of those who knew him in life but for all "those to come"; second, by the building of different forms of *mnēma* (memorial), which assured the deceased, if not an ambrosial body—a privilege that only belongs to the gods, precisely

---

[10] *Il.* 23.65. "And here is the *psuchē* of the unhappy Patroklos who comes to him, totally like the hero in his stature, his beautiful eyes, his voice, and his body clothed with the same garments: *pant' autōi megethos te kai ommata kal' eikuia kai phōnan.*" The *psuchē* of Patroklos, Achilles says, "resembled him mightily [*eikto de theskelon autōi*]," *Il.* 23.107.

[11] The same scenario appears in the case of Odysseus, faced with the *psuchē* of his mother Antikleia, who has come up from the house of Hades to drink a little of the blood from the victim sacrificed by her son and thereby recover the knowledge that death had made her lose. The dialogue between mother and son is conducted like one between two real and living persons. Odysseus, while he is speaking, also has one desire: to clasp his mother's *psuchē* in his arms. Three times she escapes from his hands, flitting away like a shadow or dream (*Od.* 11.205–7).

because they have no blood and their flesh is not corruptible—at least an equivocal substitute for what the body represents during life in its function as the armature of individuality and a guarantee of the permanence of the social subject. *Mnēma*, *sēma*, and stele have convergent functions in this respect: in different forms and on different levels, they convey the paradoxical inscription of absence in presence. At the end of funerary rites, the human body, by the fact that it has definitively entered into the domain of death, assumes in the eyes of the living the form of a reality with two aspects, each of which refers back to the other and implies its counterpart: one, a visible aspect, localized here below, hard and permanent like the stone erected over the tomb; the other, an aspect of the world beyond, ubiquitous, ungraspable, and fugitive like the *psuchē* exiled into the realm of elsewhere. The *psuchē* is like a body; as shown on works of art, on vases, it is represented like a miniature body, a *corpusculum*; it is the double of the living body, a replica that can be taken for the body itself that has the same appearance, clothing, gestures, and voice. But this absolute likeness is also a total insubstantiality. The *psuchē* is a nothing, an empty thing, an ungraspable evanescence, a shade: it is like an airy and winged being, a bird in flight.

The stone is just the opposite: compact, massive, and enduringly present in the spot in which it is fixed in the earth. But this material substance no longer resembles the form of the living body in its previous appearance; rather, it replicates the form of a radical otherness from its actual being, just like one of the dead. The marker attests to the strangeness of the deceased's status in the world beyond, of his exile into an other realm where all the realities here on earth are inverted. The stone is as cold, hard, dull, opaque, rough, crude, and fixed as the young and living body is warm in the heat of the sun, supple, brilliant, luminous in its gaze, soft to the touch, and nimble and mobile in its movements. Funerary stele and *psuchē* thus together convey the new social status of the dead person in two complementary ways: his existence in the world beyond, which reveals itself to humanity on earth in the form of an absence.

For the *psuchē*, the obvious fact of appearance, down to the exactitude of the most concrete details and the complete similarity to the figure of the living person, are like the investiture of an emptiness, a veil of illusion cast over a nonbeing: the *psuchē* is not this body as seen in itself but rather its ghostly image, its double, an *eidōlon* just like those dreams, visions, illusions, and *phasmata*.

As for the stele, its materiality is very much the opposite of the insubstantial shade, the winged dream, and the ungraspable vision. The being the stele evokes as its substitute is given in the brute form of a stone, like the absence of someone who has vanished, spirited off elsewhere, winged like a vision, an apparition, and a *psuchē* of the dead.

II

A very different conception of the soul, opposite to this Homeric *psuchē*, is elaborated in the milieu of the philosophical-religious sects like the Pythagoreans and Orphics, and seems to be linked to spiritual exercises designed to escape from time, from successive reincarnations, and from death through acts of purifying and liberating the little particle of the divine everyone carries within himself. A fragment of Pindar[12] already attests to this change. Although the *psuchē* is still defined in the Homeric way like an *eidōlon*, it is no longer the simulacrum of the dead person after death. Now that it is present within the living person, it can no longer take the form of a ghostly double of a vanished body. In its continuous duration, it is now the double of a vital being: *aiōnos eidōlon*.[13] This double, which is of divine origin and escapes the destruction that is the fate of mortal bodies, slumbers when the limbs are active. It awakens when the body is asleep and shows itself in the form of dreams, thus revealing to us the lot that awaits us in the other world after our death.

But it is with Plato that the inversion of the values attributed to the body and soul is finally completed. Instead of the individual being intimately bound to a living body and a *psuchē* presented like the *eidōlon* of the body that is no longer here, its phantom or double, it is now the immortal *psuchē* that constitutes one's real being in the interior recesses of each and every individual during the period of one's life.[14] The living body therefore changes its status: it now becomes a simple appearance, an illusory, insubstantial, fugitive, and transitory image of what we ourselves truly and always are. In the ghostly world of appearances, the body is "that which is made to look like the semblance of the soul."[15] No longer are there *psuchai* that are *eidōla*, phantoms of those whose bodies have been reduced to ashes on the funerary pyre; rather, it is "the bodies of the deceased (their corpses) which are the *eidōla* of those who are dead."[16] We have thus passed from the soul, ghostly double of the body, to the body as a ghostly reflection of the soul. And this reversal of the relation between body and soul explains why Plato, the first theoretician of the

---

[12] Pind. frag. 2, *Thren.*, ed. Puech = frag. 131.62 Bergk-Schroeder.

[13] On the "vital" values of *aiōn* and its relation to *psuchē*, cf. *Il.* 16.453 and 19.27.

[14] "In this life itself, what constitutes our self in each of us is nothing other than the soul." *Laws* 12.959a7–8; cf. also *Alc.* 1.130c; *Phd.* 115c–d; *Rep.* 5.469d.

[15] "For each of us the body is only the image of resemblance which accompanies the soul [*to de sōma indallomenon hēmōn hekastois hepesthai*]" (*Laws* 959b1).

[16] "It is correct to say that the corpses of those who are dead are the *eidōla* of the deceased [*teleutēsantōn legesthai kalōs eidōla einai ta tōn sōmata*]" (*Laws* 959b2–3). Cf. also *Phd.* 81 d 1–4: the soul on earth, still attached to the body, "roams among tombs and graves, so it is said, around which some shadowy phantoms of souls [*psuchōn skioeidē phantasmata*] have actually been seen, such wraiths [*eidōla*] as souls of that kind afford, souls that have been released in no pure conditon, but while partaking in the seen; and that is just why they are seen" [trans. Gallop (Oxford, 1975)].

image as an imitative artifice and a fiction, uses a term to designate mimetic activity in general that is the most charged with archaic values, the least "modern" of those available at this time in the vocabulary of the image.[17] From the philosopher's perspective, it is a question of disqualifying the image, of demoting it in comparison to true realities. The image is indeed an *eidōlon* in the sense that it derives from a kind of magic; like the Homeric *psuchē*, it bewitches minds by assuming the exact appearance of that of which it is the simulacrum; it passes itself off for something it is not. It is nothing but semblance, and the pure similitude that defines its nature as an image marks it with the sign of a total unreality. The image thus keeps its character of a ghostly double. What replaces an apparition of an otherworldly being and an irruption of the "elsewhere" in front of our eyes are now the chicaneries of appearance, the illusionism of resemblance, that continues as long as one lives with one's body confined in the realm of mere seeming.

To pass from seeming to being requires reminiscence, *anamnēsis*, to find again the memory of that to which the soul is related and whose presence in the body, its immersion in the flux of the sensible, had made us forget. In the *Phaedo*, before explaining his theory of *anamnēsis*, Plato defines philosophy in a way that conforms to what he calls an ancient tradition, naming it a *meletē thanatou*. By this he means a discipline or a practice for death which consists in purifying the soul through a process of concentration that, starting from all the points of the body where it has been dispersed, gathers the soul back to itself so that, reassembled and unified, it can unbind itself from the body and escape from it (*Phd.* 67c3ff., 80e2ff.). Purification, concentration, separation of the soul: all these are terms that also mean recollection, *anamnēsis*, and that define the asceticism of the philosopher whose aim is to make his soul as emancipated in this life as it will be after death.

From Plato's perspective, of course, this practice of and for death is actually a discipline of immortality. When the soul detaches itself from a body to which Plato applies the same images of flux and flow as to becoming, it emerges from the river of time to gain a permanent and unchanging existence, as close to the gods as mortals can get. The *psuchē*, which in each of us is "ourself," has a "daimonic" character: it is a particle of the divine in human beings.

In this sense, we might say that in this terrestrial world where nothing is permanent, where everything is destined to disappear, the *psuchē* constitutes in each human creature the reflection projected therein by the unchanging and immortal Being. It is the fainter or more distinct trace of that Being, its darkened image—in short, its double or phantom, the *eidōlon* of the divine for which the philosopher, like Achilles haunted with sorrow for Patroklos, continues to yearn.

---

[17] See "The Birth of Images," above, chap. 9.

III

The human body, visible and perishable, is the simulacrum of an immaterial and immortal soul; the human soul in turn is the simulacrum of the divine, of Being as being, of the One. What in Plato, however, was only suggested or sketched finds its explicit formulation in Plotinus in the third century of our era.

For Plotinus, the One, or God, eternally immobile in its complete perfection, produces "images" by a radiation comparable to the light that emanates from the sun. Insofar as these images express the One, they are inferior to it. Dependent on it, engendered from it, these images draw their existence from the link they must preserve with their source and model (*Enn.* 5.1.6.25ff.). The One produces as its first image *nous*, or intelligence.[18] On the next level, the soul arises as the *eidōlon nou*, the reflection of intelligence, an image that is already obscured, a simulacrum of this *nous* from which it cannot be separated.[19] Like the *eidōlon* of that which has engendered it, the soul is inferior to the *nous*. It revolves around intelligence; it is the light that radiates from *nous*, its trace of the world beyond. On the one hand, the soul remains merged with intelligence, is filled with it, and takes pleasure from it; the *psuchē* takes part in it and itself has the power to think. But on the other hand, it is in contact with what follows, or rather, the *psuchē* also engenders beings that are necessarily inferior to it (*Enn.* 5.1.7.36–47).

What does it mean, asks Plotinus, to descend into Hades (*Enn.* 6.4.16.37ff.)? If Hades designates the world below, the inferior place, does the expression mean that our soul, our *psuchē*, is found in the same place as our bodies? But what if the body no longer exists?

Since the soul is not separable from its *eidōlon* (from this body whose reflection or simulacrum it is), how could it not be in the same place where its body-reflection (*eidōlon*) can be found? Yet, even so, a turning of the soul toward Intelligence and the One is always possible. "If philosophy were to free us entirely, only the *eidōlon* [the body-reflection of the soul] would descend into the lower regions. The soul would live purely in the intelligible world without being separated in any way from it" (*Enn.* 6.4.16.41–43). To be a philosopher would therefore mean to turn oneself away from the body-simulacrum of the soul to return to that of which the soul is also the simulacrum and from which it remains separated as long as it is content to reflect it instead of being identified with it. The idea is that the soul would lose itself there to find itself again, no longer as an image, a double, similar to the exterior model, but as a single and authentic being in the full coincidence of the self with the self through an assimilation to the god who is the All.

---

[18] "We declare that the *nous* is an image [*eikōn*] of the One." *Enn.* 5.1.6.33 and 7.1.

[19] *Enn.* 5.1.6.46; 7.39; *eidōlon nou*; 5.3.8.9–13: the *psuchē* is a simulacrum (*eidōlon*), an image (*eikōn*).

PART FOUR

Divinity

Chapter 11

THE FIGURE AND FUNCTIONS OF ARTEMIS IN MYTH
AND CULT

WHY ARTEMIS? Certainly she is a seductive figure whose youthfulness combines many charms with many dangers. But the interest she has inspired in me
and the questions I have asked myself about her have their origin in a much
more extensive inquiry conducted over the last few years on various ways of
configuring the divine.[1] How did the Greeks represent their gods, and what
are the symbolic links, the relations that, in the eyes of a worshipper, associate
a divinity with some type of idol whose task it is to evoke, to "make present"
that god before him? It was in this context that I encountered the problem of
Greek gods with masks—that is, those who are represented by a simple mask
or whose cults contain masks, either votive offerings or objects carried by the
celebrants. Essentially, three Powers of the world beyond are involved: Gorgo
(the Gorgon Medusa), Dionysos, and Artemis. What traits do these Powers
share, despite their differences, that might relate them to that zone of the supernatural expressed by the function of the mask? The hypothesis is that, according to the modalities appropriate to each, all have a connection with what,
for want of better terms, I will call "alterity" or "otherness." These Powers
are all involved in the experience the Greeks constructed of the Other, in the
forms they gave it.

   Alterity is too vague a concept and too broad but, given the fact that the
Greeks knew and used it, I do not think the term is at all anachronistic. Plato
opposes the category of the Same to that of the Other in general, *to heteron*.[2]
Of course, it will not do to speak of alterity as such without each time distinguishing and defining the precise types of alterity involved: that which is other

---

The French text originally appeared as the first section of *La mort dans les yeux: Figures de
l'Autre en Grèce ancienne* (Paris, 1985), and its translation is published here with the kind permission of Hachette. Because, strictly speaking, the title referred to Gorgo and because a number
of other pieces on Artemis are included in this present volume, it seemed practical to separate the
two parts, retaining the original title for Gorgo, and putting this general discussion of Artemis as
the preliminary introduction to the essays that follow, which take up various aspects of Artemis
in greater detail. Translated by Froma I. Zeitlin with supplementary notes added from the relevant
reports in the *Annuaire du Collège de France: Résumé des cours et travaux* that are published
each year.

   [1] Cf. *Annuaire du Collège de France* (1975–76 through 1983–84).

   [2] *Tim.* 35a3ff.; *Theaet.* 185c9; *Soph.* 254e3; 255b3; 256d12–e1. In the *Parmenides*, the Other
is opposed to the One, as to Being: 143c2ff.

in relation to the living creature, the human being (*anthrōpos*), the civilized person, the male adult (*anēr*), the Greek, and the citizen.

From this point of view one might say that the monstrous mask of Gorgo conveys an extreme alterity, the terrifying horror of that which is absolutely other, unspeakable, unthinkable—pure chaos. For a human being, this is the confrontation with death—the death that the eye of Gorgo imposes on those who meet her gaze, transforming every single thing that lives, moves, and sees the light of the sun into a fixed stone, frozen, blind, and shrouded in darkness. With Dionysos, the music changes. At the heart itself of life on this earth, alterity is a sudden intrusion of that which alienates us from daily existence, from the normal course of things, from ourselves: disguise, masquerade, drunkenness, play, theater, and finally, trance and ecstatic delirium. Dionysos teaches or compels us to become other than what we ordinarily are, to experience in this life here below the sensation of escape toward a disconcerting strangeness.

And Artemis? Let us look at her: not the whole of Artemis in the details of her sanctuaries and her various forms,[3] but in her essentials—in what gives this divine Power her specificity and suggests a unity and coherence in her multiple functions.

ARTEMIS, OR THE FRONTIERS OF THE OTHER

Daughter of Zeus and Leto, sister of Apollo, holder like him of the bow and the lyre,[4] Artemis has two sides. She is the Huntress, the one who runs in the woods, the Wild One, the Archer, who shoots wild animals with her weapons and whose arrows, when used among humans, sometimes strike women unexpectedly to bring them sudden death.[5] She is also the Maiden, the pure Parthenos, dedicated to eternal virginity, the one who leads, in joyous dance, music, and beautiful song, that gracious chorus of adolescent girls she makes her companions—the Nymphs and Graces.

Where does Artemis come from? This question has been much discussed. For some her name is purely Greek. Others see in her a stranger whose origin is sometimes Nordic, or sometimes, on the contrary, Eastern—either Lydian or Aegean. In many respects her imagery in the archaic period recalls the figure of that great Asiatic or Cretan goddess who has been named "Mistress

---

[3] Cf. Lily Kahil, "Artemis," *LIMC*, where one will find all the necessary details.

[4] Cf. Georges Dumézil, *Apollon sonore et autres essais* (Paris, 1982), 13–108. In the case of the goddess, the epithet that designates her as *chrusēlakatos*, with the golden arrow, contains an ambiguity that evokes the double aspect of a Power—both huntress (murderous) and virginal (feminine). *Chrusēlakatos* also means "with golden shuttle." Cf. *Il.* 20.70 and *Od.* 4.122 for each of these meanings.

[5] Because she strikes abruptly, without anyone expecting her, and because she kills with one blow, Artemis is endowed with a "sweet arrow," and the death she sends is a "tender death." Cf. *Od.* 5.123; 11.172–73; 18.202; 20.60 and 80.

of the Animals'' or ''Lady of the Beasts,'' *Potnia therōn*, precisely the title
one passage of the *Iliad* attributes to her (*Il.* 21.470). In any case, one thing
apppears almost certain: the name of Artemis seems to be included on the
Linear B tablets of Achaean Pylos. This means she would have been present
in the Greek pantheon from the twelfth century B.C.E. on, and if she is sometimes described as *xenē*, stranger, by the ancients themselves, this term does
not refer to any non-Greek origin, but rather, as in the case of Dionysos, to
the ''strangeness'' of the goddess, her distance from the other gods by reason
of that alterity or otherness she bears.[6] If the question of origins still remains
insoluble today, one can, however, trace those characteristics that, beginning
with the eighth century, give Artemis her own physiognomy and make her an
original divine personage, who is typically Greek in that she occupies a place
in the pantheon and fulfills roles and functions that belong only to her.

How has Artemis traditionally been viewed? With two sets of traits. First,
she is the goddess of the untamed world on all levels: wild beasts, noncultivated plants and lands, and the young insofar as they are not yet integrated
into society, not yet civilized. Second, she is considered a goddess of fertility,
who makes everything grow—plants, animals, and humans.

What should we make of this standard opinion? Let us look first at her place
and at those sites that are hers, and then at her role and functions.

Her Place

''Let all the mountains be mine,'' declares Artemis in Callimachus's hymn to
her (18), and she makes it clear that only rarely does she descend into the city,
only if there is some specific need of her. But in addition to the mountains and
woods, she haunts all the other places the Greeks call *agros*, noncultivated
lands that mark the boundaries of the territory, those *eschatiai* that lie beyond
the fields. She is *agrotera* (rustic), but she is also *limnatis*, associated with
swamps and lagoons. She has her place on the shores of the sea, in the coastal
zone where the lines between earth and water are not clearly defined. She also
can be found in the interior regions where an overflowing river or stagnant
waters create a space that is neither entirely dry nor yet altogether aquatic and
where all culture seems precarious and perilous. What is the common denom-
inator among these different places that belong to the goddess and where her
temples are built? We should not think of a totally wild space representing a
radical alterity with respect to the town and the humanized terrain of the city.
What really counts is the presence of boundaries, border zones, and frontiers
where the Other is manifested in the regular contacts that are made with it,

---

[6] Cf. Vernant, *Annuaire du Collège de France* (1982–83): 443–57, translated in this volume as
''Artemis and Rites of Sacrifice, Initiation, and Marriage,'' below, chap. 12.

where the wild and the cultivated exist side by side—in opposition, of course, but where they may also interpenetrate one with another.

Her Functions

First of all, the hunt.

On the frontier of two worlds, marking their limits and guaranteeing their proper articulation by her presence, Artemis presides over the hunt. In pursuing wild animals to kill them, the hunter enters the domain of the wild. He enters there but he must not go in too far. Many myths relate quite precisely what threatens the hunter if he crosses certain limits: danger of turning wild or bestial. Nevertheless, for the young man, the hunt constitutes an essential element of his education, of the *paideia* that integrates him into the city.[7] On the edge of the wild and of the civilized, Artemis introduces the adolescent into the world of ferocious wild beasts. But the hunt is conducted in a group and with discipline; it is a controlled art, regulated with strict imperatives, obligations, and taboos. It is only if these social and religious norms are transgressed that the hunter, falling outside the human domain, becomes savage like the animals he confronts. In jealously making sure that these norms are respected, Artemis sacralizes the intangibility of a frontier whose extreme fragility is emphasized by the hunt to the extent that it may challenge that frontier at any moment.

Artemis, then, is not wildness. She sees to it that the boundaries between the wild and the civilized are permeable in some way, since the hunt allows passage from one state to the other. At the same time, however, these boundaries remain perfectly distinct, for if they were not, men would become savage, as once happened, for example, as Polybius tells us, in the case of the Arcadians of Cynaetha in the third century. As a result of having neglected the rites and usages supervised by the goddess, they regressed to a precivilized stage. Abandoning their towns and cities to live on their own, they displayed the same kind of ferocity in massacring one another that impels wild animals to devour each other (4.20–22).

REARING OF THE YOUNG

Artemis is the Kourotrophos par excellence. She takes all the little ones in charge, both animal and human, whether male or female. Her function is to nurture them, to make them grow and mature until they become fully adult. With human offspring, she leads them to the threshold of adolescence. Abandoning to her their lives as children, they must, with her consent and assistance, cross this threshold in order to accede to a fully socialized status through rituals of initiation over which she presides—the young girl entering

[7] Cf. Xen., *Cyn.* 1.18.

into the state of wife and mother, the ephebe into that of citizen-soldier. Matron, hoplite: these are the states that constitute the model of what a woman and a man must become in order to arrive, along with the others, at a social identity. During the time when they are growing up, before they have taken that step, the young, like the goddess, occupy a liminal position that is uncertain and equivocal, where the boundaries separating boys from girls, the young from the adults, and beasts from men are not yet clearly fixed. They fluctuate and slide from one state to another; the girls take on the roles and behavior of boys; the young play the role of adults, claiming that status as if they were already mature and full-grown; and human creatures are assimilated to wild animals.

One single example: Atalanta, the most Artemisian of all *parthenoi*, the virgin who wants to remain in the sphere of Artemis all her life without ever crossing to the other side of that boundary, which makes the girl into what she is supposed to become, a wife and matron like all the other women.[8] After her birth, Atalanta is nourished in the woods by a she-bear who nurses her with milk from her teats and licks her just as she does her own cubs so as to "shape her in the ways of a bear."[9] The little girl grows so quickly that in a few years she has the size, strength, and speed of an adult. Not only is her beauty boyish, as is all of her behavior, but she is so masculine that she terrifies all who meet her.[10] Having become *teleia* or *hōraia*, that is, having reached the age when a woman is mature and is supposed to prove fertile, she refuses the *telos* of marriage, the fulfillment of her femininity. This is the goal toward which Artemis must lead the girl to abandon her there; the girl in turn escapes from the goddess at the appointed time and becomes a woman. In dedicating herself completely to Artemis, in wishing, like Artemis, to be a young virgin forever, Atalanta reduces the whole of femininity to its preliminary stage. She refuses to recognize and cross the boundary that separates the alterity of the young from adult identity. This is why everything with Atalanta gets so confused. The child, the *pais*, is no longer distinguished from the mature woman. The girl, instead of being separated from the boy, tends toward hypermasculinity. The human creature turns into a bear. When marriage is finally imposed on Atalanta, it is transformed at first into a race, a savage pursuit in which the girl, who is to be betrothed, tracks and kills her suitor as in the hunt. Then

---

[8] On Atalanta, Theog. 1287–94; ps. Apollod. 3.9.2; Ael., *Var. hist.* 13; Ov., *Met.* 10.560–680, 8.318–445. For the interpretation of this figure and her legend, cf. Marcel Detienne, *Dionysos mis à mort* (Paris, 1977), 80–88; trans. M. and L. Muellner, under the title *Dionysus Slain* (Baltimore, 1979), 26–34.

[9] Lycoph., *Alex.* 137 and the scholia ad loc.

[10] "Atalanta, when still a young child, was of a greater height than is usual for women . . . she had a male physiognomy, a terrible look. . . . She had nothing of her sex. . . . She combined two qualities, equally astonishing: an incomparable beauty and an air that inspired terror. . . . One would not ever meet her without feeling a chill of terror" (Ael., *Var. hist.* 13.1.1).

when Aphrodite intervenes to madden the girl with love, marriage is transformed into a bestial union where the husband and wife are eventually changed
into lions.[11]

But this is precisely the point. The world of Artemis is not that of Atalanta.
It is not closed in on itself, shut up in its own alterity. It opens out onto adulthood. The role of Artemis is to enable the young to leave her when the moment
comes. While accompanying them to the other side, into the territory of the
Same, she institutes the rites by which she dismisses them.

At Brauron in Attica, on the banks of the river, the little girls of Athens, as
a preparation for marriage, had to be secluded in the sanctuary of Artemis at
some time between their fifth and tenth years in order to become little bears,
"to imitate the bear." What kind of bear is this? A wild bear but one that has
left the woods to become progressively tamed in the sanctuary of the goddess,
to get used to being around human beings and to become familiar with them.
Unlike Atalanta, the little girls who, under Artemis's rule, undergo the course
of the bear are not made wild. Like the bear, they too are domesticated little
by little so that at the end of this ordeal that keeps them far from their homes,
they in turn may be able "to cohabit in marriage with a man."[12]

In accompanying the young all along their route from embryo to maturity,
in instituting the rites of passage that consecrate their leaving the margins and
entering into civic space, Artemis is not the incarnation of a total wildness; the
Kourotrophos acts rather to establish a definite line of demarcation between
boys and girls, young and adults, beasts and men. As a result, it becomes

[11] [Atalanta is also closely related to two other *parthenoi* whose myths of animal metamorphosis link up with her story to form a set. "Each adventure only takes on its full meaning when
confronted with those of the two others that are both similar and different. . . . At the age when
Kallisto ought still to remain a *parthenos*, she is joined to Zeus against her will. Artemis, discovering Kallisto is pregnant, punishes her by changing her into a bear (in certain versions the metamorphosis takes place at the moment of giving birth). In her animal form, the girl still retains
human feelings until Zeus makes her into the constellation of the Bear in the heavens. Through
the story of her misfortunes, all the categories of human, bestial, and divine are called into question. In the Arcadian legends, Kallisto contributes to the fixing of these boundaries as a result of
the son she had borne from Zeus, but insofar as she herself crossed these limits, she attests to their
precariousness. Polyphonte, as *parthenos*, does not only have ursine feelings like Atalanta; she
really joins in sexual union with a bear. She becomes a bear sexually both because she did not
keep herself pure and because she did not renounce a wildness that was external to marriage. She
gives birth to twins, Savage and Mountain Man, giants and eaters of human flesh, who scorn gods
as much as they do men. She is metamorphosed into a bird of ill omen, a kind of owl, the Stux,
in whom is expressed a complete reversal of values. In these three cases and in different forms,
limits are posed and transgressed—those that separate the young from the adult, the *parthenos*
from the matron, the girl from the boy, the wild from the tamed, the animal from the human, and
the human from the divine. But none of these myths implies any identification of Artemis with
the bear or with any other animal." *Annuaire du Collège de France* (1980–81): 398–99.]

[12] Suda, s.v. *arktos ē Braurōniois*. For the ensemble of texts relating to the *arkteia* at Brauron,
cf. William Sale, "The Temple Legends of the Arkteia," *RhM* 118 (1975): 265ff., and Claudia
Montepaone, "L'*arkteia* à Brauron," *Studi storico-religiosi* 3 (1979): 343ff.

possible to articulate both the chastity required of the young girl and the marriage that completes the woman in her adult state, the impulses of sexuality and the social order, the savage life and the civilized life.[13]

From the margins over which she rules, Artemis takes charge of the education of the young and thus assures their integration into the civic community. Making them pass from the "other" to the "same," she presides over this change of state, this leap, by which the young cease being young in order to become adults, but this time without entailing any confusion in status between youth and adulthood or any effacement of the boundaries between them.[14]

---

[13] ["This complex interplay in which rupture and continuity are associated finds its expression in the vocabulary. The *numphai*, the *parthenoi*, are those virgins who accompany the goddess, who attend her in the hunt as well as in the choruses, and who, as a result—boyish hunt, feminine chorus—straddle both sides, as though, at this age, the frontier between the sexes still remained somewhat fluid. But *numphē* is also the young married woman, the wife; and the term *parthenos* is sometimes used to define the young spouse who is not yet the mother of a family. Thus, when sexual initiation takes place by the regular routes of social integration, in and through marriage, there is not only a break, a change of status for the girl, but also continuity, regular progression, a process of taming conducted by Artemis in wild surroundings that in some way finds its fulfillment and its end in the context of the family and the city." *Annuaire du Collège de France* (1980–81): 401–2.]

[14] ["What then is the relation between chaste Artemis, the rude enemy of marriage, and sexuality? She prepares the little girls by making them ripen, rendering them nubile. She leads them to the threshold of marriage where sexual union is accomplished in its most 'cultivated' form. Nevertheless, even in this case, as we have seen in Callimachus, the girls' souls are 'terrified' by the song of Hymenaios, as by a bogey (*tēn kourēn mormussetai*, *Hym. Art.* 70; *ēthea kouraōn mormussetai*, *Hym. Del.* 296–97). For the *parthenos*, the first day of marriage can constitute what the *Palatine Anthology* calls the 'common terror of virgins' (9.245). In this respect, the sexual act is represented, even in marriage, as violence and brutality that takes place during a struggle that is reminiscent of the hunt and war, as a wound that will cause blood to flow. Like a bogey that puts fear into the virginal heart, it inscribes a form of savagery within the conjugal institution itself. This savagery, however, has nothing to do with Artemis; she refuses it by her rejection of marriage.

"We speak of sexuality in marriage. But when sexuality is not tamed, when it is not civilized by marriage, then its quality of masculine violence, of a hunt in which the companions of Artemis become prey, and its aspects of abduction and rape, all serve to accentuate this savage quality.

"On the horizon of the *parthenoi* dedicated to Artemis, we perceive in both myths and in rites, the specter or at least the threat of rape and seizure: that is, of a conduct that, instead of integrating femininity into culture by a ceremony that clearly fixes the boundaries between the Artemisian girl and the married woman, makes it the occasion of an ensavagement of the two sexes. The *numphē* loses her virginity but does not succeed in crossing the line that makes her a woman in the full social sense of the term.

"Until now we have envisaged a sexuality that the girl undergoes, which is imposed on her by the male. In the state of the *numphē* and *parthenos*, however, there is also a sexuality that is experienced from within. This is the kind that seizes the daughters of Proitos and makes them run, indecently clad, through the mountains, like fillies maddened by desire. Artemis Hemerasia must calm them by retaming them so they can be wed in the proper way.

"One of the functions of Artemis is to permit and prepare the integration of sexuality into

CHILDBIRTH

As a virgin goddess who rejects every erotic contact, Artemis nevertheless, under the title of Lochia, is the mistress of childbirth. This is because giving birth constitutes both the end of the girls' gradual maturation for which the goddess is responsible and the beginning, for the newborn, of the career in life that also belongs to her. Another reason is that childbirth introduces an animal element into the social institution of marriage. First, while the union of the conjugal couple relies on a social contract, the act of procreation produces an offspring similar to a little animal, a creature still alien to every rule of culture. Second, the bond that joins the child to the mother is viewed as "natural" and not, like the one that connects it to the father, social. Finally, giving birth—the production of human offspring the way beasts produce their own—displays to Greek eyes, with its screams, its agony, and its delirium, the wild and animal side of femaleness precisely at the moment when, by giving the city a future citizen, the wife is reproducing the city itself and therefore seems most integrated into the world of culture.[15]

---

culture. There are different forms of sexuality that can be more or less assimilated into the civilized, as the case may be. As *hagnē parthenos*, Artemis's function is to deny sexuality in such a way that it can only emerge in the conjugal context. But, by its very radicalism, this temporary rejection also runs the risk of giving sexuality over to all forms of deviance.

"By default, at first: the *parthenoi*, having arrived at maturity, refuse the fulfillment of marriage. They become hunters, boys, and perpetually young. Next, by excess: whether passively, subjected to abduction and rape, or actively, when they are possessed by sexual frenzy. The Nymphs of Artemis sometimes refuse all contact with men, sometimes unite furtively with shepherds, satyrs, and Pan; they attract mortals by seducing them and then make them vanish.

"But too much or too little, whether sexuality is a terror or an unbridled desire, whether one persists in a definitive refusal or offers oneself to all comers, whether as prey or as hunter, Artemis does not intervene to personify a complete wildness but—in a situation where sexuality is not yet in place, where it is located in an empty space or in an overflow—her function is to allow for an exact demarcation between boys and girls, young and adults, and to see to it that chastity and marriage, sexuality and the social order, savage life and civilized life are correctly articulated." *Annuaire du Collège de France* (1980–81): 402–3.]

[15] ["It is not so much marriage that integrates the *parthenos* into the cultivated life, that domesticates her by putting the wild filly under the yoke, but rather childbirth. As long as she does not have a child, the young wife has not entirely broken with the status of *parthenos*. What definitively cuts the links to the girl's virginal world is less perhaps the penetration of the feminine body in the first sexual contact than, inversely, the issuing forth of the offspring, as it makes its way out of the maternal womb. Although this tearing of the entrails attests to the savage and animal side of femininity through the cries, pains, and frenzy that accompany it, it brings the woman to a full and entire socialization. In a certain way, as Nicole Loraux has shown, this violent and brutal combat, this form of cruel struggle that the woman undergoes in giving birth, not only brings the woman to a socialized state but raises her to the same level as a man. If she dies when giving a future combatant to the city in the child she leaves behind, she is masculinized to the point of becoming equal to a warrior fallen on the battlefield for his country. But if in the case of the *parthenos*, the boundary between the sexes was not yet decisive, the *gunē gametē* who emerges from childbirth, even though she acquires a kind of male dignity, is still fixed in a sexual

WAR

Artemis plays her part finally in the conduct of war, although she is not a warrior goddess.[16] Her interventions in this domain are not of a bellicose kind. Artemis is not a combatant; she is there to guide and to save, both Hegemone and Soteira. She is invoked as a savior in critical situations, when a conflict threatens the city's continued existence, at a time when it is threatened with total destruction. Artemis is mobilized when too much violence is used during a military engagement, when warfare abandons the civilized codes through which the rules of martial struggle are maintained and moves brutally into the realm of savagery.[17]

In these extreme cases, the goddess does not have recourse to either physical or military force in order to bring deliverance. Rather, she acts by means of a supernatural manifestation that muddles the normal arena of combat in order to destroy the aggressors and give the advantage to those under her protection. The former she blinds, leading them astray on the roads or troubling their minds with confusion and panic. To the others she offers a kind of hyperlucidity by guiding them miraculously through the dark or by illuminating their minds with a sudden inspiration. In the first case, she effaces and confuses the boundaries, whether in nature or in the mind, while in the second, just when the boundaries are obscured, she allows her favorites to discern their outlines.

BATTLE

Before unleashing an attack, it is customary, as a preliminary of battle, to sacrifice a goat to the goddess on the front lines of the army where the enemy is in view. Here again it is the savagery lurking in the background of war that the presence of Artemis, on the threshold of battle, both recalls and aims to avoid. The goat one sacrifices to her shares the ambiguous status of the goddess in her pivotal position, for it is the least tame of all domestic animals. The sacrifice of the goat evokes in advance the blood that must necessarily be shed in the brutality of combat, but at the same time, it turns the threat back on the enemy. Once the army is drawn up in battle order, the sacrifice averts the danger of a fall into confused panic or into the horror of a murderous frenzy. At the point where the camps intersect and at the time when the critical moment has arrived—in this liminal situation—the *sphagē*, the bloody sacrifice of the animal, involves more than the boundary that separates life from death, peace from warrior combat. It tests the limits established between the

---

role that does not interfere at all with that of a man. See Nicole Loraux, 'Le lit, la guerre,' *L'Homme* 21 (1981): 36–67.'' *Annuaire du Collège de France* (1980–81), 404.]

[16] See ''Artemis and Preliminary Sacrifice in Combat,'' below, chap. 14.

[17] Cf. Pierre Ellinger, ''Le gypse et la boue: I. Sur les mythes de la guerre d'anéantissement,'' *QUCC* 29 (1978): 7–55; ''Les ruses de guerre d'Artémis,'' in *Recherches sur les cultes grecs et l'Occident* 2, Cahiers du centre Jean Bérard, 9 (Naples, 1984), 51–67.

civilized order, where each combatant has his place and is expected to play the role he has been taught in the gymnasium from childhood on, and a domain of chaos, given over to the kind of pure violence found among the wild beasts who know neither rule nor justice (Hes., *WD* 276–80).

The hunt, the care of the young, childbirth, war, and battle—Artemis always operates as a divinity of the margins with the twofold power of managing the necessary passages between savagery and civilization and of strictly maintaining the boundaries at the very moment they have been crossed.

ON THE MARGINS OF THE MONSTROUS

Artemis is, with Dionysos, one of the Greek divinities whom the Greeks in their imaginings situate far from Greece, as a god come from outside, from foreign lands. Such is the case of Taurian Artemis whose idol Athens and Sparta both claimed to possess after it was brought back by Orestes from the land of the Scythians. Foreign, barbarian, savage, and bloody, Taurian Artemis belongs to a people located at the antipodes of Greece. The Taurians of Scythia do not know the laws of hospitality. They incarnate the *axenon*, the *amikton*, the inhospitable, and the refusal to mingle with others.[18] But what role does this barbarian Artemis play, the one who thirsts for human blood— for Greek blood—when she is welcomed by the Greeks and integrated into their cult? Then she becomes goddess of civilized humanity, of those who, unlike the barbarian and the savage, can find a place for someone who is not one of their own, for a *xenos*. From the moment foreign Artemis becomes Greek, her alterity shifts to the other side and her function is reversed. She no longer embodies, as in Scythia, the impossibility, attributed to the savage, of being neighbors with the civilized. On the contrary, she demonstrates the capacity implied by "culture" of integrating what is foreign to itself, of assimilating the other without, however, becoming savage.

The Other as a component of the Same, as the condition of one's own identity: this is the reason why the Mistress of the Margins also appears as a civic goddess and city founder in the sanctuaries where she has the young cross the boundary to adulthood, where she leads them from the limits to the center, from difference to similitude. For all those who were different at the beginning, those who were opponents or even enemies, she institutes a common life in the framework of a unified group of now identical beings. The examples of this function are numerous and clear—from Artemis of Tyndaris to the Triklaria of Patras and the Orthia of Sparta.[19]

---

[18] Cf. Eur., *Iph. Taur.* 402 and 1388.

[19] On Artemis of Tyndaris, cf. Françoise Frontisi-Ducroux, "Artémis bucolique," *RHR* 198 (1981): 46ff., and "L'homme, le cerf, et le berger: Chemins grecs de la civilité," *Le temps de la réflexion* 4 (1983): 58ff.; on Artemis Triklaria at Patras, cf. "Artemis and Rites of Sacrifice,

One word on this last case. For the Greeks Orthia represented the barbarian, the Scythian Artemis. She took charge of the entire process of initiation of young boys from start to finish. What does the legend of the foundation of her sanctuary tell us about her role? (Paus. 3.16.9–11). Her altar was the focus, around which were grouped the different components of archaic Sparta—the four *ōbai*, the tribes implanted each on its own terrain, in its own village, all of whom at the beginning were strangers to one another. Their purpose is to proceed together to the first sacrifice. The affair starts off badly; in the course of the sacrificial ceremony, the groups begin to quarrel. They kill one another and it is the blood of future citizens, not yet assembled into a single community, that drenches the altar of the goddess, as later the blood of the young will do when, in the ordeal of the whip, they submit to rituals of initiation. The institution of a cult with its regular procedures not only allows for the integration each year of a new class of young to be assimilated to adults. By the same action, it also realizes the harmonious integration of diverse, even hostile, elements, the fusion into a unified and homogeneous ensemble of all the participants, who will henceforth define themselves as the ones in comparison with the others, as the *Isoi*, the *Homoioi*, the Equals, the Similar Ones. Through the intermediary of this foreign Artemis, the bearer of alterity, the Greek city, by adopting her as its own, starts from and with the Other so as to constitute what it perceives as its Same.

At the end of this survey, which has ranged far and wide over Greece, let us pose the question: why study Artemis? For the pleasure it gives, of course, if not to understand her fully, then at least to attempt to understand her: to try to understand those others who are the ancient Greeks and also ourselves. Not that the Greeks are our model or that their way of doing and seeing things can be transposed to ours, however tempting this may be, considering how timely this problem of the Other is for us and how many facets it contains. Rather, because the distance makes us see more clearly that if every human group, every society, every culture thinks and lives what it imagines to be *the* civilization whose identity must be maintained and permanence assured in the face of irruptions from the outside and pressures from within, each group is also confronted with the problem of alterity in the variety of its forms. From death, the absolute Other, to those changes that, in the flux of generations, are continually produced in the social body, the community also makes a place for the necessary contacts and exchanges with the "stranger," which no Greek city can do without. The Greeks in their religion expressed this problem by granting it all its dimensions, including the philosophical one that Plato will later develop: the Same is not conceived as and cannot be defined except in relation to the Other, to the multiplicity of others. If the Same remains en-

Initiations, and Marriage," below, chap. 12. On Artemis Orthia, see "Between Shame and Glory: The Initiation of the Young Warrior at Sparta," below, chap. 13.

closed on itself, thought is not possible—and let us add, neither is civilization. In making the goddess of the margins into a power of integration and assimilation, as when they take Dionysos, who incarnates the figure of the Other in the Greek pantheon, and install him at the center of the social system, right out front in the theater,[20] the Greeks pass on an important lesson. They invite us not to become polytheists, to believe in Artemis and Dionysos, but to construe the idea of civilization as giving each his or her place. They invite us to an attitude of mind that not only has moral and political value, but that is properly intellectual and is called tolerance.

[20] Cf. J.-P. Vernant, "Le Dionysos masqué des Bacchantes d'Euripides," *L'Homme* 93 (1985): 31–58, now in J.-P. Vernant and P. Vidal-Naquet, *Mythe et tragédie en Grèce ancienne*, vol. 2 (Paris, 1986), 237–70, trans. Janet Lloyd under the title "The Masked Dionysus of Euripides' *Bacchae*," in *Myth and Tragedy in Ancient Greece*, (New York, 1988), 381–412.

Chapter 12

ARTEMIS AND RITES OF SACRIFICE, INITIATION, AND MARRIAGE

1. Xoanon and Strangeness

AT BRAURON and at the Limnaion of Sparta, as in other places that claimed the same privilege, the idol of Artemis was reputed to be the ancient *xoanon* that, according to legend, Orestes, when afflicted with wandering and madness, was supposed to have taken away from the Taurid where this fetish had fallen from heaven, in order to bring it back to Greece along with his sister Iphigenia. In Euripides (*Iph. Taur.* 85–91, 1448–61), it is at Halai Araphenides that Orestes set up this effigy of Artemis Tauropolos, while Iphigenia remained at Brauron as the goddess's temple guardian, to be buried there after her death. But Pausanias (1.23.7; 1.33.1), discussing the Athenians' claim to possess this relic, notes that the ancient *xoanon* was preserved at Brauron. Plutarch follows the same tradition: the Pelasgians, who had "abducted" the women from Brauron while they were celebrating Artemis, had, along with their captives, carried off the *xoanon* of Taurian Artemis. This triple infraction of the rules—of war, gender relations, and religious obligations—unleashed the long series of disturbances that from then on the abductors would suffer: in their contacts with strangers when they tried to settle among them, in their internal relations with their own wives and children, and in their relations with the gods. Condemned to marginal status and wandering from one place of exile to another, achieving neither full integration with others nor a real unity among themselves, they still carried the old *xoanon* with them. This they never abandoned in the course of their journeys, although the panic it caused made them lose their way, until the day when the idol became the object of a fixed cult and presided over the definitive emplacement of the human group through the founding of a united city.

According to Pausanias (3.16.9–17), the authenticity of the barbarian *xoanon* is probably in favor of Spartan Orthia. Among other indications, the one he finds most reliable for supporting his opinion refers to the very conditions that prompted the founding of the cult. First, as soon as the two "find-

This text was published in the *Annuaire du Collège de France*, representing the year's work in 1982–83, and is translated by Froma I. Zeitlin, with the omission of the last paragraph pertaining to Artemis Orthia and the Spartan *agōgē* that was later treated fully in the essay "Entre la honte et la gloire: L'identité du jeune Spartiate." See "Between Shame and Glory: The Identity of the Young Spartan Warrior," below, chap. 13.

ers'' of the idol of Orthia (Astrabakos and Alopekos of the Agides line) set eyes on the idol, they immediately lose their minds and, like Orestes, are driven astray by madness. Then, when the different elements of the Lacedaimonian social body (the Limniates, the Cynosurians, the people of Mesoa and Pitane) meet to sacrifice together to Orthia, they begin to quarrel to such an extent that, in the mayhem, they reach the point of drenching the goddess's altar with their blood. Many lost their lives during this combat. A sudden epidemic finished off the rest of them. Madness, murder, sedition (*stasis*), plague: with such results, how could one fail to recognize the authentic *xoanon* that came from the land of the Scythians?

In the case of our Artemis, the responsibility rests on those features that, in a general way even though to different degrees, belong to the type of archaic idol, made of wood, roughly carved, with legs and arms welded to the body, that the Greeks call a *xoanon*. The *xoanon* does not simply constitute the most ancient, most primitive form of the cultic figure. It contains an aspect of strangeness that Pausanias expresses by the terms *atopos* and *xenos*, and that emphasizes the disturbing, dangerous, disconcerting, even exceptional and ''barbarian'' nature of the Power whose manifestation it is. A third related characteristic can be added to these two: there is something divine in the *xoanon*, some supernatural quality (Paus. 2.4.5; 10.19.3). To lay one's hands on a *xoanon*, to appropriate it for oneself, whether individually or as a group, is both a jealously guarded privilege and a very great hazard. This is because it is not a man-made work, an image fashioned by the expert hand of an artisan. Constructed by the gods, fallen from heaven, or brought in by the tides, the idol conceals a sacred power that cannot be handled without special care.[1]

To find the *xoanon*, to look at it, is often, as in the case of the *xoanon* of Taurian Artemis, to be condemned to wandering, both materially and mentally. One no longer has a place in which to settle, a group into which to integrate oneself; at the same time, it means to lose one's reason, to go mad. If the simple sight of the idol suffices to provoke madness, if it cuts the spectator off from his community by casting him outside himself, it is because in certain respects the *xoanon* is closely akin to the mask. The mask, as I have said with regard to Gorgo, conveys the alterity, the ''otherness'' of a kind of supernatural power that can only be met face-to-face: approaching it entails a resolve both to confront it and, at the same time, to fall under the fascination of its glance at the risk of being wrenched away from oneself and projected into an elsewhere. In the case of the *xoanon*, as in that of the mask, to see the face of the god is to find oneself invaded by a power of strangeness, possessed by a madness that, if it does not destroy you, transforms you from inside out.

In the Greek Artemis, the barbarian *xoanon* conveys the presence of a

---

[1] [On the *xoanon*, see ''From the 'Presentification' of the Invisible to the Imitation of Appearance,'' above, chap. 8. Ed.]

strangeness that manifests itself through deviance and aberrancy: the wandering of a vagabond outside the city and that of a madness outside good sense (*paraphrōn*). This contact with the Other corresponds to one of the goddess's functions. Herself situated on the margins, on the frontier between the wild and the civilized, she is the patron of the young on the borders. In their alterity, their difference from adults, she takes charge of them in order to prepare them, under her protection and with her consent, to cross the threshold that will integrate them into the community. This transition, which depends on their relinquishing to Artemis what is her due, will make them the "same" as the adults from whom, until now, they have been kept apart. Passage from the "other" to the "same" implies a discipline in which one learns to become as similar or more similar to the "same" as those who are the "same" (*homoioi*), but it also entails aberrant, deviant, even deranged forms of behavior that mark one's "otherness." Yet once they have become ritualized, these actions are no longer viewed as signs of an individual madness; they now constitute a collective exercise that gives both alterity and conformity a regular shape. Each is now clearly defined, easy to recognize, and perfectly distinct, even though the lines are drawn during the phase of passage that, if it does not altogether assimilate the two modes, must in part bring them closer together.

The example of Artemis Triklaria at Patras will allow us to illustrate these remarks in a very concrete way. In this sanctuary, the peoples of Aroe, Athenia, and Mesatis originally met together near a river called then Ameilichos, the Unyielding. A *parthenos* was priestess there until her marriage. The cult contained a communal *pannychis* (nocturnal ceremony) that was celebrated each year for the goddess and Dionysos. That night a certain number of *paides*, boys and girls, used to go down to bathe in the river. Pausanias (7.19.1–5) relates the *aition* that justifies the association of the two divinities and gives the reason for the ritual.

During her sacerdotal term, Komaitho, priestess of Artemis, falls in love with Melanippos, who returns her love twice over. Her parents refuse to give their daughter in marriage to this young man. The two young people go away and in the sanctuary of the goddess, they boldly give in to their passion. Even more, they continue afterward to use the *hieron* (sanctuary) as if it were a *thalamos* (nuptial chamber). By blurring the boundaries, their misconduct not only effaces the distinction between *parthenos* (virgin) and *gunē* (woman), between *neos* (youth) and *anēr* (man), but makes the priestess of Artemis a creature of Aphrodite and her temple a bower of love. The disturbance immediately produces its results: the earth no longer bears fruit, *karpon oudena*; humans die in great numbers. The oracle is consulted and reveals the fault of the two guilty parties, who are sacrificed on the altar of Artemis. And each year the flower of the local youth—the most beautiful girl, the most beautiful young man—will have to be sacrificed to the goddess. For life to be perpetuated, for the group to reproduce itself normally, or, in other words, for the new generation of adolescents to be able to occupy its place in the world of adults through an integration that does not upset its stability, this cohort of young people, in the exemplary form of the most beautiful *parthenos* and the most beautiful *neos*, must be offered as first fruits to Artemis to whom they belong and from whom they cannot be separated without the goddess's consent. A price must be paid if the youth are to cease being what they are and become what Artemis prepares them for when she has them grow up. To become an adult means that the young must renounce themselves, forsake the goddess, and "die" to the state of *parthenos* and *neos* that belongs to Artemis. Doing away with the two most beautiful adolescents, who represent the entire cohort of youths of that year, is the tithe the city must pay, the first fruits it must give the divinity in order for the young generation, like the new harvest, to be ready for consummation. The first fruits, just gathered, the first grain, still green, are not touched by the cultivator. He consecrates them to the goddess so as to desacralize the rest, to cut the ties that keep them still in this phase of "push forth," "grow," and "ripen," over which the Kourotrophos, in her role of nurse and teacher, maintains control. Once the first fruits are surrendered, the food becomes good to eat and the *parthenoi* good to marry.

In some sense, all fruit, to be edible, must first be "emancipated" from the goddess's domain, which implies that it must first be "abandoned" to her in symbolic form by a delegation of the tithe. And every *parthenos*, to be "consumable" and put at the city's disposition, must have been, by some procedure, emancipated from dependence on the goddess. By delegation or by a wholly other form of symbolic substitute, the *parthenos* must be "offered" to Artemis, sacrificed or immolated, at least metaphorically, on her altar.

The function of the ritual is to translate the fact that the young belong to Artemis, marking their complete *devotio* to the one who has "nourished" them at the very moment when they have ripened and have been brought into perfect accord with the adult model. This is the moment when the young leave the goddess as they leave their time of growth so they may be integrated into the group of those whose maturity now destines them, if they are girls, to marriage and childbirth, and to war and political life, if they are boys.

Let us look at the story Pausanias tells about how this shift from "real" sacrifice to prematrimonial ritual operates (7.19.5–9). It is said, he writes, that human sacrifices to Artemis Triklaria ended in the following way. A Delphic oracle had announced that the sacrifice would come to an end when a foreign king, *xenos*, arrived in the land, bringing a foreign divinity, *xenikon agomenos daimona*. A double strangeness, a double alterity: both the king and the god. Now, after the capture of Troy, when the spoils are divided, Eurypylos receives a *larnax* as his portion. In this box is an *agalma* of Dionysos. Hephaistos made it and Zeus gave it to Dardanos. Eurypylos opens the box and discovers the image. At the first sight of it he goes mad, *ekphrōn*. Seized by delirium, by *mania*, he only recovers his lucidity at rare intervals. Instead of returning to Thessaly, he goes to Cirrha, then to Delphi, where he asks the god about his malady. The oracle tells him that when in the course of his wanderings he meets a people who are offering a *thusian xenēn*, a strange sacrifice, there is the spot where he must set up the *larnax* and take up residence. Eurypylos returns to the sea again, disembarks at Aroe, and meets a *parthenos* and a *neos* along the way, who are being led to the altar of Artemis Triklaria. Just when he grasps that here is the predicted *thusia xenē*, the inhabitants of the country recognize in him the *xenos* king, the bearer of a *daimōn xenos*.

This encounter between a strangeness internal to Patras (human sacrifice, barbarity) and a double external strangeness (a king without a city, out of his mind; an unknown god whose idol is hidden in a casket because just the sight of it, like that of the *xoanon* of Taurian Artemis, is sufficient to drive one mad)—this encounter, through its accumulated oddities, will finally cancel them all: first, by healing Eurypylos and giving him a fixed residence, and then by instituting a ritual that, by joining Dionysos and Artemis in the same cult, makes the "foreign god" into the Aisymnetes of Patras, and transforms the bloodstained and monstrous sacrifice to Artemis into a peaceful and beneficent festival of the city. The new rite will produce the same effect as did the former immolation on the altar: to integrate the strangeness of the youth into the familiar order of adults, to assimilate their otherness to the communal norm. But from now on, it will produce these results in conformity with Greek ideas about the gods and about sacrifices that, in their rules of piety, are in accordance with forms of civilized life. The city will absorb what is not itself, its other—or at least one of the forms of its other—without having itself to become other. It does so, even in assimilating the other to the self (foreign gods, barbarian rites, youth gone wild) by maintaining the boundary between a type of alterity conceived as barbarism or savagery and a condition presented from the outset as defining culture, sociability, Greekness, and the adult norm.

This ritual consisted of a *pannychis* in honor of the two divinities who, in civic religion, represent poles of otherness. On that night, the priest of Dionysos took out the *larnax* of the god and exposed it outside: a nocturnal fete, instead of a celebration in full daylight, and a festival at which the idol, invisible and kept hidden in fear of madness, was now revealed. Such is the *geras*, the "exceptional" privilege bestowed on this night when the passage will take place from youth to adult status, from the strange and the alien to the normal and communal. But it is a time when, as a price to be paid for integration, the danger of turning wild is merely going to be acted out and mimed and, through this ploy, be averted in favor of a civilized procedure.

Alterity survives, transposed, in the atmosphere of the festival, at night, in the presence of the secret idol, in the nocturnal footraces of boys and girls that seem to take place by the light of burning torches. Under the direction of nine male citizens and nine matrons chosen by the city, a certain number of local children of both sexes are garlanded just like the *parthenos* and *pais*, who formerly were led to the altar of Artemis to be sacrificed there. Their garlands are made of young stalks of wheat; *stachus* is the term used, a word that means both the grain which has just matured and the young human offspring, the *agamos stachus*, the virginal grain, harvested too soon, as an anonymous epigram of the *Palatine Anthology* tells us (9.362.24–27). This garland of grain assimilates the new generation of young people to the vegetal first fruits that Artemis demands as a preliminary offering so the harvest may become ready for consumption. Instead of being steered, like their predecessors of legend, to the altar of Artemis, the newly "ripe" boys and girls go down instead to the river whose name was "reversed" when the ritual was civilized (the Ameilichos is now called Meilichos, the Gentle). The young people bathe there together, and in the waters of the river they symbolically find the nuptial union that Komaitho and Melanippos, without a preliminary lustration, had consummated in the sanctuary of the goddess as if it were a wedding chamber (*thalamos*). But before this time, the young of the two sexes had deposited garlands of grain near Artemis, which, in allusion to the first victims, dedicates them forever to the goddess in their youthful status. It is as if, through these garlands given up to the goddess, they are both the young who are "sacrificed" to her and the ones, now ripe, who are liberated from her charge. Instead of grain given to Artemis, they put garlands of ivy around their foreheads and, thus arrayed, they go to the temple of Dionysos Aisymnetes, the god who, a stranger like them, was integrated into the civic cult with the title of Master and Arbiter. The nocturnal ritual, the controlled and regulated orgiastic behavior of this *daimōn xenos* who henceforth was adapted to Greek culture, guaranteed the young their own integration into the civic community by contriving a change of status through which the young ceased to be young in order to become adults, yet without entailing any confusion in status between youth and adult or any effacement of the boundaries between them. At Patras, ever since the city accepted and made him its patron, Dionysos, figure of the Other, has played his part in civilizing the "strange" sacrifice that Artemis demanded before opening the way to the young which leads them from the margins where she rules to the fully socialized space of the citizen.

Elsewhere, however, there is no need for Dionysos. It is Artemis who personally assumes all the responsibility for the qualities of otherness and savagery with which the rite first needs to play and then absorb. Whether at Brauron or Halai in Attica, the cults of Artemis Orthia in Sparta, the Nemorensis of Aricia, the Facelitis (Artemis of the faggots) of Tyndaris—in the background of the ritual we find each time, through the *xoanon* brought back by Orestes, the outline of the disturbing figure of a foreign and barbarian goddess, who has come from the Taurid in the land of the Scythians. Françoise Frontisi-Ducroux's remark with reference to the Italian and Sicilian traditions of this same Artemis is fully pertinent here. She observes that at Tyndaris, the goddess's function is "mixing"—first, in the sphere of literary art by the creation of a bucolic genre defined as "mixed" because it associates the gross rusticity of shepherds with the polished refinement of city folk, and second, in the civic sphere, because "the social group's prosperity and survival seems to be linked here to contact and mixture" of different elements (sailors and shepherds on one side, Greeks and Sicilians on the other).[2] Frontisi-Ducroux notes that this mixture takes place under the authority of a goddess who has come not only from far away, but from a place that incarnates the inhospitable (*axenon*) and refusal of mixture (*amikton*).[3] Greek and Latin traditions are unanimous on this point. The Taurians sacrifice all *xenoi* to their goddess, all the strangers they find on their territory, shipwrecked folk or travelers, including those Greeks they captured by an attack on the high seas.[4] On this plane, the Scythian is presented as the contrary of the Greek. He is not content with refusing to recognize the rules of hospitality, that is, the duty to receive another and to establish a two-sided relation with the stranger that both associates him and keeps him at a distance. When he slaughters the Hellene, the paradigm of civilized man, on the altars of his goddess, the Scythian also singles him out as the sacrificial victim of choice. Foreign, barbarian, sanguinary, Taurian Artemis comes from a country that is conceived as the antipodes of Greece and of culture. The Greek is not only a foreigner who is sacrificed there because these people refuse mixture, because they are inhospitable and hostile to an outsider, but he is the one who is pursued on the open sea, as one tracks a beast because, more than any other's, his blood pleases the goddess. But if, by his refusal of *xenia*, the Scythian is thus represented as the barbarian absolute, the other of the Greek, what can one expect from his goddess? What can she bring when she is welcomed, integrated, and naturalized as a Greek? What does she become when her power is recognized by the civilized man, that is, by the one who avoids the savage and the barbaric precisely to the extent that he finds a place for one who is not him, the *xenos*? When Taurian Artemis, to whom every Greek must be sacrificed, herself becomes Greek, there is a shift in her "alterity" and she changes her meaning and function. She no longer conveys, as in the Scythian land, the radical impossibility that characterizes the savage of ever living alongside the civilized and relating to it. On the contrary, in Greece she embodies culture's distinctive capacity for integrating what is foreign to it and for assimilating the other without the risk of itself turning savage.

On this point, we should reread the debate in the *Life of Apollonius of Tyana* (6.20) that, according to Philostratus, took up the subject of flagellation at the altar of Orthia and pitted the philosopher, admirer of Sparta, against Thespe-

---

[2] "Artémis bucolique," *RHR* 198 (1981): 46.

[3] Cf. Eur., *Iph. Taur.* 402, 1388.

[4] Herod. 4.103; ps. Apollod. 4.26–27; Diod. Sic. 4.44.7; Lucian, *Dial. deor.* 3.23; Ov., *Trist.*, *Ex ponto* 2.2.58; Pomp. Mel. 1.1.11; Clem. Alex., *Protrep.* 111.

sion, its critic. For the latter, to treat the elite of young citizens, the future magistrates, like slaves, by whipping them, is to turn Greek values the wrong way around. No, says Apollonius, it is a question only of respecting a god's demand: Scythian Artemis wants to be honored in this way. How could the Greek gods, retorts Thespesion, admit the use of the whip in the education of free men? Apollonius must then explain that, in welcoming Taurian Artemis, the Greeks accepted the goddess along with her powers, but modified the cruelty of the ritual to make it a civilized ordeal of endurance, "for it is not fitting that any of the Greeks adopt barbarian ways." Thespesion does not admit defeat, however, and his arguments, sophistic as they are, show how, even in the third century of our era, the consciousness of Artemis's "strangeness" was maintained, and show the problems involved in her cult regarding the equivocal relations between savage and uncultivated, barbarian and Greek. Thespesion upholds, one by one, three orders of propositions. (1) If it is savagery for the Scythians to sacrifice a few occasional strangers to their goddess, what can be said of the Lacedaimonian custom of banishing all outsiders (*xenēlasia*)? To answer this charge, Apollonius has to distinguish between a ban on residence affecting all strangers at Sparta to protect the purity of their institutions, and *amixia*, the refusal of mixture, particular to the Scythians and not to the people of Lacedaimon. (2) Is not the acceptance of a divinity who has come from Taurus and the Scythians an exemplary sign of men adopting foreign customs (*xena nomizontōn*)? (3) Even from the perspective of so-called civilized values, the practice of Scythian sacrifice is superior to the Lacedaimonians' substitute rite, "fit only for slaves," which is inspired by it but diminished in value under the pretext of its acculturation. The "barbarian" would then not always be on the side to which the Greek had tried to relegate it!

2. HUMAN SACRIFICE

Artemis's strangeness culminates in her demand for human blood. We have therefore examined the modulations of this theme, first in Attica, where it is associated with the legend of Iphigenia, a virgin sacrificed to the goddess who claims as her property "the most beautiful product of the year" (Eur., *Iph. Taur.* 20–21). At Halai, some drops of blood from a man's neck stain the altar and serve as a ransom for the girl's survival (1458ff.). Second, in Laconia: at Sparta, Lycurgus replaces ancient human sacrifice by sprinkling the altar during the flagellation of the young men (Paus. 3.16.10–17). Finally, in Italy; at Aricia or Nemi, at the end of a duel to the death, the priesthood is accorded to the fugitive slave who had escaped his master and who, cut off from all social bonds, outside the law, outside society—in short, a nonperson—succeeds in slaughtering the priest who had previously held the post (Strabo 5.3.12; Paus. 2.27.4).

Without lingering too long over what we had treated elsewhere (that is, the vast documentation of prenuptial rites and the import of a death before the wedding that affects the young, both boys and girls, associated with Apollo and Artemis), we recalled the homologous relation between marriage and death that the ancients strongly emphasized (Artemid., *Oneir*. 2.49, 65). Our next question therefore was to consider the various ways in which, under the sign of Artemis, prematrimonial rituals dramatize, like a play, the death of the young by both evoking and avoiding their sacrifice on the altar. This human sacrifice proves as necessary as it is impossible; necessary, because the young, as such, belong to Artemis, and impossible, because this slaughter, more than a sacrifice, would constitute a monstrous impiety.

Every virgin, attaining the state of matrimony, must die first for Artemis. She must vanish in her status of *parthenos* through and for Artemis, but at the same time, made ripe and adult, she escapes the goddess and is freed from her. Dedication and liberation, death and salvation, destruction and fulfillment: the rite adjusts its mimetic procedures between these opposite poles, bringing them into concert by moving from one to the other without renouncing either. It is in this sense, we think, that the use of "substitutional" practices should be first interpreted.

At Mounychia and Brauron, in the context of the *arkteia* where the little girls had to "imitate" the bear, a very curious and significant story is told to explain the sacrifice of a goat to Artemis. Its hero, who passes into proverb, was a certain Baros or Embaros, presented sometimes as the founder of the sanctuary at Mounychia. We will keep to the major points of this story, which exists in several versions, all of which essentially agree with one another. Everything begins with a she-bear. She is not yet in her proper place. Sometimes she appears in the middle of the Piraeus in an urban space where she does not belong; sometimes she turns up to lodge in the sanctuary of Artemis. She causes damage; the Athenians—or young people—kill her. Plague: sickness or famine. The oracle anounces that the sickness will end if a father, renewing Agamemnon's gesture, offers his daughter to Artemis as a sacrifice in return for the bear that was killed. This is when Baros-Embaros enters the scene. He promises to give (*dōsein*) his daughter to the goddess, on the condition that he and his descendants obtain the priesthood for life. The offer is accepted. He takes his daughter, dresses her appropriately (*diakosmēsas*), and hides her in the *adyton* of the sanctuary. Then he takes a goat, dresses (*kosmēsas*) it in feminine clothing, calls her his daughter, and sacrifices her "as if she were his daughter." All this is conducted in the greatest secrecy, without anyone's knowledge. The plague ceases. The god, when consulted, proclaims that henceforth one must continue to sacrifice in the same way as did Baros-Embaros. The father then reveals his trick. From that day on, "the *korai* have nothing more to fear from acting the bear before marriage, *hōsper aphosioumenai ta tēs thērias*, as if, with this expiation, they had averted [the stigma of] any bestial element.''[5] This is a formula that should also be compared with the scholia to Theocritus 2.66; those who are on the point of marriage are the basket-bearers, the *kanēphoroi* for Artemis, *epi aphosiōsei tēs parthenias*, in expiation of their virginity, so that the goddess does not take vengeance on them. Another scholiast is more specific: ''The rite is like a defensive measure taken before Artemis in regard to their virginity, so that the goddess not become angry with those who are just on the point of losing it.''

Let us summarize: at the beginning, a ''displaced'' bear. Made to haunt the woods and mountains, she is found in the masculine space of the streets of the Piraeus or in the sacred space of Artemis's sanctuary. When she is struck down by men, her murder must be expiated. The father is required to offer the goddess the life of a young girl who is still ''Artemisian'' like the bear. Baros-Embaros invents and institutes the procedure that resolves the problem. A goat takes the place of the girl, who takes the place of the bear whom the boys took away from Artemis by killing her. Hidden in the *adyton*, the little girl ''mimes'' the bear that had been secluded in the sanctuary. Disguised under her dress, the goat ''mimes'' the girl slaughtered at the altar. Through this play of sliding substitutions, this sequence of simulated equivalences, everything is accomplished without anything really being executed. At the end of the story, the girl can ''play the bear'' without fear, just as, at the end of the mimetic rite that keeps her temporarily enclosed in the most secret part of the temple, she is freed to go back to the city to meet up again with the boys, the killers of the bear. In ''giving'' her to Artemis while keeping her alive by the subterfuge of the goat, the father, in the person of Baros-Embaros, is going to be able, when the time comes, to ''give'' his daughter as a wife to a husband. To take the step that makes a *gunē* out of a *parthenos*, there will be no need to confuse the boundaries between the savage and the civilized, murder and bloody sacrifice, beast and human. Everything is finally lodged in its proper place. To the extent that the girl plays the bear, the goat plays the girl, Baros plays Agamemnon, and Artemis plays her role as a sanguinary power, the goddess can keep the girl and the husband can receive her.

A cock-and-bull story, a crazy tale, or a narrative full of instruction and wisdom? In the proverbs mentioned earlier, the expression *Embaros eimi*, ''I am Embaros,'' is said, according to certain authorities, by those who have lost their reason and gone mad, and according to others, by those who are reflective and wise. The staging of the ritual in its mimetic procedures also lends itself to this twofold interpretation. It is a *paidia*, a game, a childish ploy; but it is also and at the same time, in Greek eyes, a serious and solemn engagement. Plato, we will see, says exactly the same thing about such play.

[5] [I. Bekker, *Anecdota Graeca* (Berlin, 1814), 444. For a discussion of the various sources for the ''bear'' at both Brauron and Mounychia, see William Sale, ''The Temple Legends of the Arkteia,'' *RhM* 118 (1975): 265–84. Ed.]

3. PLAYING THE BEAR AT BRAURON

Last year we presented the documentation of the *arkteia* in the sanctuary of Artemis at Brauron: archaeological facts, inscriptions, texts, and iconographical representations. We have taken up certain elements again from new perspectives: the *krokōtos*, the saffron-colored robe, and its feminine, juvenile, and seductive meanings; weaving, as women's activity, sometimes associated with footraces in a prenuptial context; the value of the offering of fabrics and vestments to Artemis on the one hand and, on the other, to Iphigenia; the symbolic relation of clothing to a person's age and status; its place and functions, as a marriage gift, from the woman to the man, and from the man to the woman.[6]

Several points remain problematic. Age, first of all. All the testimony agrees on the prenuptial character of the ritual: before marriage, the little girls of Athens, to appease the goddess, must have worn the *krokōtos* and imitated the bear. This ceremony concerns little girls who, more than five years old, have not passed the age of ten. The period from five to ten years seems too early for a cultic practice whose object is preparation for marriage. The few texts that indicate the age of feminine puberty situate it around thirteen years, even if, according to Aristophanes, it is at seven years that a little girl could have been normally deflowered (*Thesm.* 480).

Nevertheless, we must not forget that the "growth" whose entire process is controlled by Artemis as Kourotrophos—from conception and formation of the embryo in the belly of its mother to the development of the child after its birth, its "nourishment," and its progressive maturation[7]—this growth contains phases through which the little girl must successively pass in order to reach a full femininity. On the lower limit of five years, an indication given by Plato may be illuminating. In *Laws* (794aff.) he observes that from three to six years, all children, boys and girls, must be raised together. But when they have reached the age of six, "the separation of the sexes takes place, the boys having to be raised with boys, and girls only with girls." If, to take part in the Brauronia, the girls must have passed the threshold of five years that marks the moment when the paths of growth bifurcate for boys and girls, this is because one of the functions of the ritual is to consecrate the disjunction of the sexes. On the other hand, in the representations that, on the *krateriskoi* analyzed by Lily Kahil, show little girls running, nude or clothed, we can observe, as she did herself, that there are two very distinct categories of age: little ones with a wholly childish appearance and bigger ones, already depicted as adolescents. Beyond five years is the rupture with boys of the same age; from five to ten is the passage from one state of asexual or slightly sexual

---

[6] [See *Annuaire du Collège de France* (1981–82): 419. Ed.]

[7] See Paul Demond, "Remarques sur le sens de *trephō*," *REG* 91 (1978): 358–84.

childhood to a condition already of a little *parthenos*. On this point, again a remark of Plato is relevant (*Laws* 833c–d): among the various forms of running, he notes, one must first distinguish those of males, according to whether they are children (*paides*), adolescents (*ageneioi*), or adults (*andres*): then those of females, who are divided into two categories: "For those who are not of the age of puberty, they will exercise naked; but from thirteen years on until their marriage, they will compete dressed in a suitable costume." The appearance on the *krateriskoi* of two sorts of "runners," some naked and some clothed, must express, at the level of the rite, an opposition of the same type between a nonpubertal state and the entry into a femininity that opens out, at its end, onto marriage.

Another problem. On one of the two *krateriskoi* now in Basel, published by Lily Kahil, two characters are depicted, a woman and a man, carrying, it seems, a mask of a bear. Is this, as some have thought, an illustration of Kallisto and Arkas? The connection with Brauron is very remote. Is this a depiction of Artemis, the goddess bear? Impossible, because the goddess is represented on the same vase, drawing her bow alongside Leto and Apollo. Are these the priestess and her assistant, as Lily Kahil, with some probability, supposes? But nowhere do we find an assistant who is so closely associated with a priestess.

The aetiological stories offer more solid ground for understanding the significance of the ritual. They form another group, as coherent as the versions of Baros-Embaros earlier discussed. At the beginning, there is again a bear. She is called *agria*, wild. But instead of remaining on her own territory, she comes as a regular visitor to pass the time in the deme of Philaides, with the result that she is "tamed" and becomes familiar with men whose company she shares; the text says *hēmerōstheisan autēn tois anthrōpois suntrophon genesthai* (*suntrophos*, in the proper sense, means to be raised or nourished along with). In other versions, the bear is "offered" to Artemis in her sanctuary at Brauron where, again, she is "tamed." It happens that a little girl starts to play with this bear (*prospaizein*; the word means to play, to jest, to jeer, and also to celebrate a rite or a festival). The young miss shows impudence—insolence or impudicity; the bear gets excited and scratches the little girl's face. This lack of restraint and modesty in the little girl's "game" is expressed by the verb *aselgainō*, which recalls a passage of the *Republic* (424d10eff.) in which Plato indicates that often, among the young, "it is under cover of play, or amusement, that a disdain for the laws creeps in, which is reinforced little by little, so that finally, with the last insolence [*aselgeia*], there is nothing left. Thus from the beginning, childrens' games must be subjected to a rigorous discipline."

In this ill-regulated "play" between a still-impudent little girl and a bear on the way to becoming tame, it is the animal who pays the price. The little girl's brother kills the bear with a blow of his hunting spear. Anger of Artemis.

Pestilential plague. To end it, each little girl of Athens, before her marriage, must henceforth imitate the bear and serve the sanctuary by wearing the *krokōtos* (yellow robe).

In the liminal space of the sanctuary, segregated from the boys, engaged in the process that makes them ripen into women under the control of the city and in a now-regulated game (Plato, *Laws* 802c), the little girls are going to complete the ritual course that, like the bear and following in her tracks, will make them suitable, as she is, to cohabit with a man (*sunoikizesthai andri*). Or, using the second version, we can say the same thing differently: if one wants a girl who has matured to be "tamed" for her husband just as the bear is tamed in relation to Artemis, she must, while still at an age of wildness, be constrained to "play the bear" in the goddess's sanctuary.[8]

Our analyses have led us to focus on the aspects of play, the ordered and regulated mimicry of rituals linked to the *agōgē* of the young. Here we can refer to Plato's discussion in the *Laws*. If men are marionettes whose strings the gods like to pull (644e), then our nurslings themselves (*tous hēmeterous trophimous*) must be brought to think that the "right way" is to "live out our lives through play, and playing at such pastimes as sacrificing, singing, and dancing" (803e–804a). "The essence of education [*paideias*] consists in that correct nurture [*tēn orthēn trophēn*] which best draws the soul of the child, when at play, to a love for that occupation in which he will have to have perfect [*teleion*] mastery when he grows up" (643d). A little further on, Plato directly connects play, education, and festivals (653b) when he notes that the quality in *aretē* that has been properly formed (*tethrammenon*) in the matter of pleasure and pain is what reason calls "education" (*paideia*), and he recalls that, to keep this proper education, the gods have instituted "alternations of festivals celebrated in their honor." Every young creature in fact has need of movement, shouting, leaping, and jumping, "such as dancing for pleasure and playing with others [*prospaizonta*]." But alone of all animals, humans have a sense of order and disorder, of rhythm and harmony; "It is because the gods have been given to us other men, not only to share our festivals but to grant us a sense of rhythm and harmony accompanied by pleasure through which they cause us to move by becoming our chorus leaders, linking us with one another by means of songs and dances. And to the chorus [*choros*] they have given its name from the 'cheer' [*charas*] implanted within" (653d–654a). These are the choruses that Artemis leads to educate the young, when she puts aside her quiver, bow, and arrows for the lyre, song, and dance.

---

[8] [For the most recent discussion of Brauron and Mounychia, see Pierre Brulé, *La fille d'Athènes: La religion des filles à Athènes à l'époque classique. Mythes, cultes, et société* (Paris, 1987). Ed.]

Chapter 13

BETWEEN SHAME AND GLORY: THE IDENTITY OF THE YOUNG SPARTAN WARRIOR

> You will never succeed in creating well-behaved children if
> you do not first create unruly brats. This was the Spartan
> method of education: instead of making them stick to their
> books, teach them first to steal their supper.
> —Jean-Jacques Rousseau, *Emile*

WHAT BECOMES of the ideal of heroic honor that inspired epic warriors to face death when, with the emergence of the city-state, participation in political life becomes one of the essential, or even constitutive, elements of *aretē*, human excellence? What happens when the common interest of the group begins to take precedence, in the estimation of virtue, over prestige of birth or the brilliance of great individual deeds, imposing itself as a criterion of true value?

In military terms, the contrast between the figure of the Iliadic hero and that of the citizen-soldier is so strongly marked as to be self-evident.[1] The famous example of Aristodemos at Plataea, as it is transmitted to us by Herodotus, shows that for the hoplite, on campaign in the service of his country, the individual exploit, extraordinary as it may be, and even if it leads to a heroic death on the battlefield, has no value if it deviates from the collective discipline of the phalanx (Herod. 7.231 and 9.71). The prize for *aristeia* goes to the one who best contributes to the common victory by keeping his place in the ranks during combat next to his companions-in-arms. To be "the best," one must surpass the others, all the while remaining with them, making common cause with them, being like them.

More generally, one wonders how, in a competitive, agonistic, "face-to-face" society, in which the old aristocratic values remain dominant, the ancient model of heroic honor, still prized and celebrated, can be made to harmonize with the norms of civic morality, in the search for *kleos*, for glory.

This paper was given at Princeton University in 1986, and in an abridged form at an international conference in 1987 in Geneva on the theme "Norms and Deviances." It appeared in its entirety in *MÉTIS* 2 (1987): 269–300, and was republished as "Entre la honte et la gloire: L'identité du jeune Spartiate" in *L'individu, la mort, l'amour: soi-même et l'autre en Grèce ancienne* (Paris, 1989), 173–209. Translated by Deborah Lyons.

[1] Cf. Marcel Detienne, "La phalange: Problèmes et controverses," in *Problèmes de la guerre en Grèce ancienne*, ed. J.-P. Vernant (Paris and The Hague, 1968), 119–42.

One way to approach the resolution of this problem would be to examine the educational system instituted by the cities in order to train the young to become full-fledged citizens, and at the same time to open up for them the official path of *timai*, honors. If we choose Sparta as our field of inquiry, it is because this case seems to us exemplary in its singularity. For the ancients themselves, Sparta has the reputation of being a city where the sense of honor is systematically developed, from the earliest age, by the constant practice, public and institutionalized, of blame and praise, of sarcasm and glorification, but where, on the other hand, the individual is trained from childhood to submit himself entirely and in all things to the interests of the state. Xenophon sums up well this double orientation of the Lacedaimonian *agōgē*, in which each one enters into war against the others to surpass them, while acting together to best defend the city. This duality of objectives, which one might think should have posed some problems, does not seem in his eyes to imply the slightest contradiction. He writes, "In this way is established the type of rivalry, [*eris*], which is most agreeable to the gods, and the most civic [*politikōtatē*] (that which most befits the citizens). It sets the standard for what the good man [*agathos*] ought to do. Each of them [*hekateroi*] exerts himself on his own behalf separately [*chōris*] in order always to be the best, and to be able when necessary to defend the city, each for his part [*kath' ena*], with all his power" (*Rep. Lac.* 4.5). The remark with which Xenophon follows this discussion, however, does not incline us to share his optimism about the claimed natural convergence between the individual quest for honor and the total devotion of all to the public good. Xenophon continues with these words: "It is also necessary for them to maintain themselves in good physical condition because, on account of this rivalry, wherever they meet, they come to blows with their fists" (4.6; cf. 4.4).

The problem is complicated by two characteristic features of Greek *paideia*. It aims to make of the young person an adult, which implies a transformation, a true change of status, the access to a new condition of existence. By inculcating simultaneously in the young concern for personal glory and civic consciousness, it gives them what they previously lacked, which by nature belongs exclusively to the adult who with full rights carries out all the activities associated with his status as a citizen. In this sense, until he has crossed the threshold from adolescence into adulthood, the young person is considered a different sort of being, and is treated as such. This otherness shows itself as much in the code of conduct imposed on him as in the code of ethics deemed appropriate to his age. The honor of the young must distinguish itself from that of the adult, inasmuch as it is designed to lead to a different goal.

From this follows a second aspect of *paideia*. Because it constitutes a veritable integration of the young, a sort of progressive initiation into public life, it takes the form of an organized system of trials to which the youth is subjected, and which he must undergo from beginning to end in order to become himself, that is to say, in order to acquire the social identity that he did not formerly possess. Throughout the probationary period, to show that he is worthy of one day entering into the citizen-body, the young man is put in the way of all the dangers, abuses, and degradations that threaten the honor of the good man and that risk delivering him up to public scorn (*oneidos*) and infamy (*atimia*). From the familiarity he thus acquires with the various forms of the "shameful," from his proximity to them, he will gain the capacity to overcome them, to keep himself away from them, and to adhere to true honor and glory.[2]

On this point, Plato could not be more precise. His remarks constitute a preliminary to a reflection on the educational system of the young at Sparta which is all the more precious since the philosopher evidently has in mind the Lacedaimonian *agōgē* when he lays out, in the *Republic*, the education that the future guardians in the ideal city ought to receive (*Rep.* 3.413c–414a). A kind of winnowing operation is to be carried out among them to discover which ones will be most apt to remain faithful to the maxim that ought ever to inspire them: to do in all circumstances what is best for the city. To obtain this result, "it is necessary to test them from childhood, engaging them in those actions most likely to make them forget this principle and to lead them into error, then to choose those who remain mindful of it and whom it is difficult to trip up, and on the other hand to reject those whom it is not (413c–d)." But it is not enough to measure in this way their resistance to forgetfulness and to seductive error. One must also brutalize them, submitting them to painful labors, hard sufferings, and merciless battles, in which their behavior can be observed. Finally, bringing into play the fascinating powers of a kind of magic, they must be

> submitted to a third type of test, that which consists in binding them with spells
> and watching them compete among themselves; and just as one places colts amidst
> noise and confusion to see if they are fearful, one must carry our warriors, when
> they are still young, into the midst of terrifying objects, then throw them in the
> midst of pleasures and test them with no less care than one tests gold in the fire,
> to see if they resist the seductive enchantments and maintain their demeanor in all

---

[2] Cf. Plato, *Laws* 635b–c. It is clear, observes the Athenian in the dialogue, that if one accustoms the young from childhood to flee suffering and pain, one exposes them, when they are confronted in adulthood with inevitable troubles, to becoming the slaves of those who have been trained to withstand them. That which is true of danger and suffering is no less true of pleasure: "If, from the time of their childhood, the citizens are used to living without the greatest pleasures, if they do not exert themselves to resist them and to do nothing shameful, they will suffer, following the path that leads them to pleasure, the same fate as those who give way to fear; they will become slaves in another, even more dishonorable way, to those who are able to remain strong in the middle of pleasures, who are masters of the art of using them, as completely evil such men can sometimes be" [translation adapted from Taylor (Princeton, 1961)].

circumstances, to see if they are such as they must be to show themselves the most useful to themselves and to the city (413d–e).[3]

Plato is a philosopher. In this text, he presents a theory of education, as the Greeks conceived it, as training for the young and selection of the best by means of a series of tests adapted to the psychology of their age and corresponding to the needs of a perfectly just city. The young are not yet capable of possessing the knowledge of that which is honorable, beautiful, and good. One can only inculcate in them a right opinion, and verify the extent to which, in each of them, it is solid, stable, and rooted. There are three ways in which right opinion can be modified or effaced, according to which one is a victim of a theft (klopē), which steals it from one, of violence (bia), which turns one aside from it, or of a spell (goēteia), which blinds one to it (Rep. 412e–413d).[4] The paideia therefore institutes three different types of trials to evaluate the constancy and steadfastness of the young in their attachment to honor and the public good. The trial of theft comes first: the very passage of time, weakening memory, threatens to steal from the future guardians the maxims that ought to direct their action. Childhood and adolescence are times of play, of amusement, of carefreeness, and also of credulity about the fables told by the poets as well as the lies purveyed by the sophists. To discover those who are prone to forgetfulness and error, the educational program does not plunge them into study, into the sciences or philosophy. The young are not yet ready for these disciplines. On the contrary, in this period it assigns them to amusements and festivities, choruses, dances, songs, and contests. While observing them in these playful activities one may distinguish those who, amid the games and the laughter, never cease to remember and to hold to right opinion. There follows the trial of violence. One imposes on the young a regime marked by painful effort (ponos), suffering (algēdōn), and combats (agōnes). This harsh, brutal, and savage existence, with its nakedness, blows, and pain, reveals those who are not ready to adapt and survive in difficult conditions by abandoning their sense of honor, their dignity, and their concern for the public good. Finally there is the trial by spells. The young need to be placed in a setting that seems at times to present them with real danger, with terrifying creatures and horrible faces, and at times offers them all the seductions of pleasure, all the temptations of sensuality. In arousing the fear that exposes the weakness of the coward, in exciting the desires that reveal the depravity of the shameless, the educational mise-en-scène selects those who, resisting

---

[3] On the necessity of training the young to resist not only fear and pain, but even "desire, pleasures, and their terribly seductive blandishments," cf. Laws 1.633c9–d3, and the development that follows.

[4] Of course, when a false opinion leaves our minds, and we are in one way or another undeceived, it is with our assent. On the other hand, in the case of a true opinion, its loss occurs in spite of us, by means of theft, violence, or sorcery.

both fear and lubricity, and, as befits the man of honor, keeping decency and self-control in all circumstances, will show themselves "the most useful to themselves and to the city."

If the first type of test, leading to forgetfulness and error, relates directly to the Platonic theory of knowledge and to the relationship it establishes between right opinion and knowledge, the other two are closely linked to the practices of the *agōgē* at Sparta. The trial of the young by violence, which imposes on them the harsh, spare, and precarious existence of the outcast, finds its best commentary in the remarks of the Lacedaimonian Megillos in the *Laws* (633a–d), in which he discusses the four types of "invention" instituted by Lycurgus, in order to give the young training that will make them accomplished warriors by the time they reach adulthood. Along with the common meals (*sussitia*), the physical exercises (*gumnasia*), and the hunt, Megillos insists on the importance of the fourth invention. This is the "hardening against pain which we practice in many forms, in fistfights with one another, and certain thefts which always involve many blows; and then that marvelous exercise of endurance, the *krypteia*, in which they march barefoot in winter, sleep on the bare ground, going without servants, wandering by day and night all over the whole territory (633b–d)." The *krypteia*, the fistfights of which Xenophon speaks and some of which we know were ritually organized each year at Platanistas, the blows (*plēgai*, associated with a theft, like the stealing of cheeses under the threat of the whip at the altar of Orthia)—these are certainly typically Lacedaimonian elements that make up the second type of test by violence to which the *Republic* refers. It is therefore tempting to relate the third type of trial, so enigmatic by virtue of its use of *goēteia*, a spellbinding procedure or act of fascination, to the evidence that the excavations of the British school have given us for the initiation rites of young men at the sanctuary of Artemis Orthia. Of particular significance is the use of masks, some horrible and terrifying, some grotesque and comic, associated with dances of which some are terrifying and others indecent, lascivious, and obscene.[5] The same polarity found in Plato's educational *goēteia* reappears in these ritual games: on the one hand, a mimetic of the terrifying; on the other, a mimetic of sensuality and pleasure.[6]

What does this detour through the *Republic* add to our understanding of the

---

[5] R. M. Dawkins, ed., *The Sanctuary of Artemis Orthia at Sparta*, (London, 1927).

[6] In a passage of the *Laws*, the Athenian interrogates Clinias the Cretan, and Megillos the Spartan, about the measures that have been taken in their system of education, to let the young taste pleasures rather than fleeing them, "so that, far from teaching them to flee suffering, they throw them into it, using the persuasion of honors to force them to triumph over them. Where does one find, in your laws, a similar regulation with regard to pleasures? What are the arrangements that render your citizens equally courageous in the face of pain and pleasure?" Megillos answers, "To tell the truth, although I could enumerate the laws having to do with pain, as for pleasure, I could not give large and obvious examples, although I could do so on smaller points" (634a–c1).

status of the young at Sparta during the *agōgē*? At least this: education aims to "test" the young person, proceeding in the manner of the test by wine, which Plato wishes to apply to mature men to see if they retain their mastery over themselves or fall into drunkenness.[7] The drunken man is ignoble. It is sobriety that has value and virtue, but only those who have had the experience of alcohol can be said to be sober. In the same way, to form the feeling for honor in the young, their *paideia* must put them into intimate contact, into constant commerce, during all of the marginal phase that prepares the way to maturity, with that which the ethic of honor stigmatizes as base, indecent, and vile.

Let us now turn to the sanctuary of Artemis Orthia, in order to illuminate certain aspects of the honor of the young at Sparta. Some preliminary remarks are, at this point, indispensable. Let us begin with chronology. If we accept Boardman's early dating, which places the most ancient structures of the sanctuary—the pavement and the altar (which legend associates with the meeting of the *ōbai* of Pitana, Mesoa, Kynosoura, Limnai, and Amyclai)—at around 700 B.C.E., then the importance of the construction of the new temple about 600–590 must be stressed.[8] This date corresponds to what M. I. Finley has called "the revolution of the sixth century,"[9] with the establishment of a new constitution in which the system of the *agōgē* played a central part (cf. Herod. 1.65–66). It is at this decisive turning point in the history of archaic Sparta that the cult of Artemis Orthia must have been, if not remodeled, "resemanticized" in the cult practices perpetuated there, to respond to the functions that devolved on it in the framework of education of the young.

We note in this connection that the number of votive masks found during the excavations increases by a factor of ten from the seventh to the sixth century B.C.E., suggesting that between 600 and 550 the practice had become widespread and the different types of masks fixed.[10] It is also in the sixth century that lead figurines, of which more than 100,000 have been excavated, achieve their maximum frequency and that there appear the significant changes in the character of the offerings reported by Wace. There is perhaps no need to mention that the inscriptions on the *stelae* discovered in the sanctuary (even if they range, with only two exceptions, between the first century

---

[7] Taken up in 637b–642b, and resumed at the end of book 1 (645d–650b), the discussion on the proper use of drinking and the test of the wine (*hē en oino basanos*) in view of *aidōs* and *aischunē*, the sense of honor and self-respect, concludes, after the parenthesis of 666a–667b, in the long development of 671 to the end of book 2. The most important passage for us is 671b7–d3.

[8] J. Boardman, "Artemis Orthia and Chronology," *ABSA* 58 (1963): 1–7.

[9] M. I. Finley, "Sparta," in Vernant, *Problèmes de la guerre*, 143ff.

[10] "For the grotesque masks we may note that the series may not in fact begin before 600," writes Boardman, "Artemis Orthia and Chronology," 6.

B.C.E. and the third century C.E., the period in which the *paidikos agōn* had already taken on the form of a spectacle) highlight the complete integration of the cult into the system of the *agōgē* with its age-classes, contests, and trials.

Next, let us consider the masks, of which seven types have been distinguished by C. Dickins: (1) old women; (2) unbearded youths; (3) bearded warriors; (4) so-called realistic portraits; (5) satyrs; (6) gorgons; and (7) caricatures.[11] Whatever the reservations raised by this classification, in examining these seven types one observes first that a sharp dividing line separates two kinds of masks and clearly sets them in opposition. On one side, the figures of men, adolescent or mature, bearded or unbearded, representing warriors in their ''normal'' aspect as *kouroi* and *andres* (including the so-called realistic portraits in this group); on the other, figures that, contrasting with the regular models of the young man and the adult, present a varied range of departures or deviations expressing ugliness, old age, monstrosity, horror, and the grotesque. There are wrinkled and toothless crones, like sinister nurses, witches, or Graiai, satyrs more laughable than disturbing, gorgons with their terrifying faces, and finally the various forms of grotesques, whose faces are ugly, deformed, and caricatured. The three most important categories of masks, those represented in the greatest numbers, and almost exclusively after 550, are: (1) the adult warrior (the ideal product of the *agōgē*); (2) the grotesque (showing the manifold variations on the model virile adult); and (3) the old woman (marking the furthest distance, the greatest possible otherness, on the triple grounds of sex, age, and status).

There seems to be a comparable polarity at work in the series of lead figurines representing men. They are, for the most part, combatants of the hoplite type, or archers, or musicians, standing or moving figures. But there are also some represented naked, leaping and cavorting with disordered gestures, quite far removed from the carriage and posture of a warrior in the phalanx. Similar observations may be made for the human figures cast or modeled in terracotta. Some, ithyphallic, touch on the obscene and the grotesque. In this category may also be included several ivory intaglios.

The votive masks and those figurines that echo them pose the problem of the relationships among dances, disguises, and ritual practices at the sanctuary of Orthia. The essential points have been made by Bosanquet, Dawkins, Pickard-Cambridge, and others. There is no need to rehearse the relationships they have justly emphasized between the masks of Orthia, the names of certain competitions, and the evidence of Aristophanes, Pollux, and Athenaeus on the many masked or mimetic Laconian dances.

It is, however, worth answering the general objection formulated by several scholars. These vulgar dances, so they maintain, these comic and sometimes

[11] C. Dickins, ''The Masks,'' in Dawkins, *Sanctuary*, 163–86.

obscene mimes, have neither the seriousness nor the solemnity required for the education of the future Equals. They are rather of the type reserved for the helots, in order to distance them, by the disgust and contempt they inspire, from the young people destined to become citizens. They maintain that when Plato in the *Laws* (816d2–e10) rejects for the education of the young all forms of dance that do not imitate noble and beautiful movements, but simulate vulgar and ugly postures in a trivial fashion, when he forbids any free person to learn to mime in dance anything touching on the ridiculous and indecorous, whose execution he leaves to slaves and foreigners exclusively, the philosopher is taking direct inspiration from the Spartan model. His testimony prevents us from supposing that the cult of Orthia, in its pedagogic function, could have had a place for buffooning masquerades and incongruous gesticulation.

To accept this point of view would be to renounce from the outset any understanding of the presence of masks at the sanctuary and their role in the sphere of the *agōgē*. The educative ideal of Plato is one thing, the institutional realities of Sparta are another. When Aristophanes evokes the *dipodia*, the *mothōn*, and the *kordax*; when he presents in the *Lysistrata* the young Lacedaimonian woman worn out by gymnastic exercise, from "thumping her buttocks with her heels while jumping" (*Lys.* 82), following the entrechat-technique known as the *bibasis* (Pollux 4.1–2); when Pollux, Athenaeus, Hesychius, or Photius mention the "terrifying" Spartan dances (*deimalea*), in which one mimes all sorts of animals (*morphasmos*) or simulates the satyrs' fear (*hupotroma*) or the indecent dances (*lambroteron, kallabis, sobas*), the violent and paroxystic ones (*thermaustris, turbē, turbasia, sikinnoturbē*), or the masked and mimed ones (*barullicha, kurittoi, deikēlistai*), nothing allows us to suppose that these practices were the object of any kind of prohibition for the citizens or that their instruction was excluded from the collective games of the *agōgē*. On the contrary, for some of them, the connection is explicitly established, if not with Orthia, at least with Artemis and her cults.

Moreover, to be convinced that the elite of young Greeks did not necessarily find this type of exhibition so very inappropriate, nor consider these dances so unworthy of them, one need only read, in Herodotus (6.129), the story of the behavior of Hippocleides of Athens, on the day when Cleisthenes of Sicyon was to choose from among all the suitors (whom he had lodged for a year, the better to size them up) the one most worthy to marry his daughter. The young men, from all the cities of Greece, show off their "musical" competence, each one trading taunts with the others. The Athenian undertakes to dance. He asks for a table on which to perform. He executes first the mimetic Laconian dances, then the Athenian. Finally, putting his head on the table, he "gesticulates" with his legs in the air. Scandalized and disgusted by this indecent "gesticulation," Cleisthenes announces to the young man "that he has danced away his marriage.''[12] To gesticulate is *cheironomeō*; gesticulation is *cheiro-nomia*. Thus in the long passage that he devotes to the pyrrhic dance, which, he explains, all Lacedaimonians must learn starting at the age of five to pre-pare them for war, Athenaeus indicates that, even if by his time it has taken on a more moderate and suitable character, this dance with its rapid, jerky, and violent movements is nonetheless related to the satyric dance called the *sikinnis*. And then, he promptly gives us another, indicative for the pyrrhic dance: *cheironomia*, gesticulation (Athen. 14.631c).

It is worth adding that if the author of the *Deipnosophistes* on the one hand connects the *gumnopaidikē*, because of its grace and solemn character, with tragic dance and the *emmeleia*, and on the other hand associates the pyrrhic dance, because of its quick rhythm and lively character, with satyric dance and the *sikinnis*, he links the *hyporcheme* practiced by the Spartans, boys and girls alike, to comic dance and the *kordax*. Like the *kordax*, the *hyporcheme* is diametrically opposed to the dignified and the serious; it is full of joking around, vulgar and unbridled, if not licentious (Athen. 14.630e).[13]

Plato furnishes us with indirect proof that this dance had a place in cult that was in certain respects privileged. In his classification of dances, he distin-guishes two opposed forms of *orchēis* (*Laws* 814eff.) The first, serious and dignified, imitates the beautiful; the second, frivolous and vulgar, mimics the ugly. ''Good'' dance itself is subdivided into two categories: the warlike, sim-ulating and stimulating *andreia*, in other words the pyrrhic; and the peaceful, expressing *sōphrosunē*, which is the *emmeleia*. Both of these are approved, and together they contribute to the formation of the good citizen, while all kinds of vulgar and frivolous dance are condemned. There is, however, some-thing ''left over,'' a type of dance that can no more be placed in the category of the vulgar than it can be admitted into one of the two forms of serious and dignified dances.

All the Bacchic and other similar dances, in which, under the name of the Nymphs, Pans, Sileni, and Satyrs, one mimes, as they say, drunken men, and in which one carries out purifications and initiations—this entire genre is difficult to classify as peaceful or warlike, nor in any other way one might like. The best way to define them would be, in my opinion, to set them apart from both warlike and peaceful dance, and to declare that this is not a genre of dance which befits the citizens; then, giving them no further thought, to turn our attention to the warlike and the peaceful types of dance, which, beyond any doubt, are ours. (*Laws* 815c–d)

[12] Herod. 6.129–30; Athen. 14.628d; Plut., *De malig. Herod.* 867b.

[13] In *De salt.* 10–11, Lucian notes that at Sparta ''the young people, all in a line, execute figures of every kind in time to the beat. Sometimes these are warrior figures, sometimes, a moment later, dance figures associated with Dionysos and Aphrodite. The song they sing while dancing is ac-tually an invitation to Aphrodite and the Erotes to frisk about and dance with them.''

These dances, because of their place in the cult and their religious implications, are situated at the margin of the moral and aesthetic criteria on which Plato intends to base his dichotomy between good and bad dances, compelling the philosopher to put them in parentheses, in order to remove them without having to justify his condemnation. But these are precisely the ones that continue to be practiced at the sanctuary of Orthia and in many other cult places. The embarrassment they cause Plato constitutes a precious piece of evidence. It permits us to measure, if we were tempted to forget it, the distance that separates the theory of a philosopher, with his project of the ideal *paideia*, from the reality of the Spartan *agōgē*, with its ritualized behaviors at the altar of Orthia.

But let us move on to the fundamental problem. If these votive masks recall those that were actually carried in the course of the masquerades or mimetic dances, what connection do these practices have with Artemis in her function as *kourotrophos*? What place, what role must one grant them in the "training" that aims to transform the young into full-fledged citizens, making each of them, at the end of a marked-out course of trials, a *Homoios*, an Equal among Equals?

After the work of Jeanmaire, Brelich, and Vidal-Naquet, one might be inclined to answer that these masks—satyrs, gorgons, old women, grotesques—express the belonging of the young to that realm of the wild where they remain, under the patronage of Artemis, until they have made the transition, with the *hēbē*, into the world of adults.

That there is some truth in this interpretation I will not dispute. But it seems to me that it leaves many things unclarified and on several points creates problems. Is not the role of Artemis, by means of the *agōgē* to domesticate the young, to acculturate them into finished adults? What do the "normal" masks have to do with this? Rather than a mistress of wild nature, Artemis ought to be interpreted, it seems to me, as a power of the margins, intervening at the borders of the wild and the cultivated to authorize the passage from the first to the second, without irrevocably jeopardizing their necessary—and fragile—distinction.[14] If this is so, does one not run the risk of oversimplifying, posing the young and the adult as two completely inverse figures, of which one represents the wild, and the other the civilized? In his way of life, his appearance, his conduct, the young man is effectively presented, according to the body of

[14] Cf. Pierre Ellinger, "Le gypse et la boue: I. Sur les mythes de la guerre d'anéantissement," *QUCC* 29 (1978): 7–35; "Artemis" in *Dictionnaire des mythologies*, ed. Yves Bonnefoy (Paris, 1981), vol. 1, p. 70; "Les ruses de guerre d'Artémis," in *Recherches sur les cultes grecs et l'Occident*, 2, Cahiers du centre Jean Bérard, 9 (Naples, 1984), 51–67; J.-P. Vernant, *Annuaire du Collège de Frarnce* (1980–81): 391–405; (1981–82): 407–19; (1982–83): 443–57; *La mort dans les yeux*, which appears in this volume as "Death in the Eyes: Gorg., Figure of the *Other*," above, chap. 6.

evidence that has come down to us, as an antihoplite, the opposite of the war-
rior-citizen adult.[15] But his status is more complex, and does not define itself
only by its distance from or its contrast with the small group of *Homoioi*. His
selection at birth by the Elders at the *leschē*,[16] by the nurses during the test of
the pure wine,[17] the education reserved for him, his admission at the age of
seven into the ranks of an *agelē*, his belonging between the ages of fourteen
and twenty to various age-classes subjected to the hard discipline of the
ephebeia[18]—all this places him among the elect in Lacedaimonian society,
chosen from the start, distinguished and perfected throughout the duration of
the *agōgē*, in order to become, if he shows himself continually worthy, that to
which he has been destined, and which opposes him to a multitude of "others," an authentic Spartan. In this sense, he stands out from the beginning
from the mass of all those who, excluded from the *agōgē* and kept away from
the altar of Orthia, will never be able to lay claim to the status of citizen and
will remain all their lives in the subordinate and despised status of helot. The
young man, then, occupies an intermediate position between the helot and the
full citizen. He is not the incarnation of the "wild"; while growing up, he
remains at the border between two contrasting states. In comparison to the
helots, these sub-men, these quasi-bestial beings, he is close to the *Homoioi*
whom it is his vocation, one day, to join.[19] But in comparison to the *Homoioi*
to whom he is opposed as long as he has not yet been "trained" to be exactly
like them, he is close to the helots, with whom he shares certain aspects of the
base and the wild.

It is an equivocal, ambiguous status, one that oscillates, swings, and

[15] Cf. Pierre Vidal-Naquet, "Le chasseur noir et l'origine de l'éphébie athénienne," in *Le
chasseur noir: Formes de pensée et formes de société dans le monde grec* (Paris, 1981), 161ff.,
trans. Andrew Szegedy-Maszak under the title *The Black Hunter: Forms of Thought and Forms
of Society in the Greek World* (Baltimore, 1986), 106–28.

[16] "Offspring was not reared at the will of the father, but was taken and carried by him to a
place called Lesche, where the elders of the tribes officially examined the infant, and if it was
well-built and sturdy, they ordered the father to rear it, and assigned it one of the 9,000 lots of
land; but if it was ill-born and deformed, they sent it to the so-called Apothetai, a chasm-like place
at the foot of Mount Taygetos, in the conviction that the life of that which nature had not well
equipped at the very beginning for health and strength was of no advantage either to itself or the
state" (Plut., *Lyc.* 16.1–2) [trans. B. Perrin].

[17] "The women used to bathe their new-born babes not with water, but with wine, thus making
a sort of test of their constitutions. For it is said that epileptic and sickly infants are thrown into
convulsions by the strong wine and loose their senses, while the healthy ones are rather tempered
by it, like steel, and given a firm habit of body" (Lyc. 16.30) [trans. B. Perrin].

[18] On the organization of the age-classes, by which the youth becomes sucessively *rhōbidas,
promikkiddomenos, mikizomenos, propais, pais, melleirēn, eirēn*, see K.M.T. Chrimes, *Ancient
Sparta: A Reexamination of the Evidence* (Manchester, 1949), chap. 3, "The Ephebic Organization," 84–136.

[19] According to the testimony of Theopompus, the helots behave "in an extremely rude and
savage manner [*pantapasi omōs kai pikrōs*]," *FGrHist* 115F13 Jacoby (= Athen. 6.272a).

changes its meaning according to whether it is placed at one or the other of the two extreme poles of Spartan society, which itself, as we know, comprises a whole series of intermediate ranks.

Compared to the helots, the border between adolescents grouped in the *agelē* and the grown men reunited as members of the common messes of the *sussitia* grows faint. Young and old men in this context make up the two complementary aspects of the same social body that opposes all that is not it. Compared to the *Homoioi*, the border with the helots tends to blur. The young must, to mark themselves off from the citizens, put on the traits of "otherness" that place them outside the citizen-body, outside its norms, on the margins of honor and civilized life.

We now understand better that the masks at times embody the model with which the young must identify, and at times, in the form of the savage and the grotesque, the horrible and the ridiculous, those extreme areas of alterity one must have explored in order to detach oneself entirely from them; at times even, in the form of the Gorgon mask, that ultimate, radical form of the Other, that threat of chaos and death, which one must be able to look in the face in order to become a man.

The slippages and ambiguities in the status of the young Spartan are reinforced by the fact that at no time in the course of the *agōgē* does *aristeia* appear as a stable state, permanent once attained. It constitutes an ideal pole, an exigency all the more imperative because it is always potentially linked to its opposite. The threat of disgrace and dishonor constantly hangs over the heads of all. For the young Spartan, nobility is not a quality he possesses from birth but the prize for a victory, which he must continually reaffirm if he wishes its value to be recognized. Just as in the *agōgē* the adolescent must endure a series of probationary trials to obtain the right to an adult career of honors, *timai*, the Spartan can at any time in the course of his life be excluded, and in his failure, as a "trembler" or a bachelor, fall back beneath the threshold that defines him as an authentic member of the city.[20] Only the helot, all the more because even he, in certain cases, can elevate himself above his own condition,[21] finds himself, at least in principle, constrained by status and nature not to break through the boundary that separates the Equals, the "Similar Ones," from the whole

[20] For the shame attached to the term *tresas*, see Herod. 7.231.4–5. On the dishonorable status of the *tresantes*, confined to a painful and unhappy existence, see Plut., *Lyc.* 21.2; for their exclusion from the magistracies and their civic degradation, see Thuc. 5.34.2; Plut., *Agesil.* 30.2–4. On the disgraced character of the bachelor, the scorn reserved for unmarried men, and the humiliations they had to undergo, see *Lyc.* 15.2–4.

[21] On the participation of helots in the Spartan armies, not only as personal servants for each hoplite, but as auxiliaries, or even, in cases of need, as hoplites themselves, and on the status of *neodamodeis* (emancipated helots), see Pavel Oliva, "Heloten und Spartaner," *Index* 10 (1981, pub. January 1983): 43–54.

inferior mass of "Others." Not only must he wear highly visible marks of his indignity inscribed on his person, exhibiting his congenital inferiority in some way to the eyes of all. He must also, as Ducat has perceived,[22] internalize that degradation to the point of feeling himself incapable, when asked, of pronouncing the words, singing the songs, or carrying out the movements of dance—in short, of adopting the customs that properly speaking are the privilege and characteristic of the fully human man, the full citizen.[23]

In the space of which Artemis is patron, the young man is not, in the course of his development, reduced to the same state of degradation. He does come close, however—his cropped hair makes a contrast (Plut., *Lyc.* 16.11), like the bonnet branding the helots (the *kunee*),[24] with the head of hair that the Spartan at the end of the *ephebeia* has the right and the duty to wear long and uncovered.[25] His naked feet, the prohibition against the tunic that touches them (*chitōn*), the single cloak (*himation*), worn all year round, in all seasons, the filth (*auchmēros*) with which he is covered, for want of baths or other care (Plut., *Lyc.* 16.12–14) like the animal skins (*diphthera katōnakē*)[26] the helots

---

[22] J. Ducat, "Le mépris des Hilotes," *Annales* 6 (1974): 1451–64.

[23] Cf. Plut., *Lyc.* 28.5: "They say that, at the time of the Theban expedition into Laconia, the helots who were taken prisoner having been asked to sing the poems of Terpander, Alcman, and the Laconian Spendon, refused saying their masters would not allow it."

[24] On the *kunee* or *kunē*, the cap of dogskin or of the skin of a wild animal, as the distinguishing mark of a servile, inferior, and shameful condition, see Ducat, "Le mépris des Hilotes." According to Myron of Priene (*FGrHist* 106F2 Jacoby = Athen. 14.657d), "they force the helots to wear a dogskin cap." For the same custom, at Athens, for slaves, see Aristoph., *Wasps* 445f., and for the poorest peasants, *Clouds* 268. This type of headdress is also attributed to barbarians, like the Milyans: Herod. 7.77. Already in *Il.* 10.33f., Dolon, wearing a *kunee* of weaselskin, "looks like riff-raff," *kakos*, just as Laertes in *Od.* 24.231, with a *kunee* of goatskin on his head, would make one think he was a slave, were it not for his build and bearing.

[25] "Lycurgus ordered those leaving the ephebeia to wear their hair long with the idea that in this way they would appear larger, more noble, and more terrifying." Xen., *Rep. Lac.* 2.3; cf. also Herod. 1.82; Plato, *Phaed.* 89c; Plut., *Lyc.* 22.1; *Lys.* 1.2. To the opposition youth/adult, marked by the contrast between the shaved head and long hair, corresponds the opposition helot/ citizen, marked by the contrast between the *kunē* and the uncovered head. A detail that is significant in this connection is found in the three different traditions of the foundation of Tarentum, which followed the plot of the Parthenia (cf. Pierre Vidal-Naquet, "Esclavage et gynécratie," in *Le chasseur noir*, 278f.). The Parthenioi, these "sons of girls" whose fathers were not really men, whether because they were the "the tremblers," or the "young," or perhaps because they were helots—three categories that in some way overlap—decided to stage an attack against the citizens of Sparta, at the festival of the Hyakinthia, on the signal one of them would give. This signal, according to Antiochus, was "the moment when Phalanthos [one of the conspirators] took off his *kunē*. The free citizens who made up the *demos* recognized one another by their hair" (Strabo 6.3.2.13–15). The same detail is found in Ephorus's version: "the Parthenioi thus made common cause with the helots; these conspired against their compatriots and agreed among them that a Spartan cap thrown into the agora would give the signal to all for the attack" (Strabo 6.3.3.19–22).

[26] As Ducat, "Le mépris des Hilotes," 1455, notes, the texts concerning this "uniform" of shame, in Sparta and other cities, have been assembled by Jacoby (*FGrHist* II B382–83, com-

are obliged to wear, aim to make the body "ugly," to devalue the person, to give him a sordid and nasty appearance. Two characteristic examples of this phenomenon may be mentioned. There is the description of Laertes in the *Odyssey*—with his sordid rags (*aeikea heimata*), his skin cap (*kuneē*), his filth (*auchmeis*), he could be taken for a slave (*Od.* 24.227f.). Second is the form of dress imposed on the *tresantes*, the tremblers, as a sign of their disgrace and a mark of a status that brings them as close to the young as to the helots. "They had to resign themselves to going around filthy [*auchmēroi*], and in humiliating costume, wearing patched coats of somber color, and shaving only a part of the beard, leaving the rest to grow." How should we interpret this half-shaved beard? Should we think—in the strong sense—that one cheek was shaved and the other bearded? Or, in the weak sense, that they let their beard grow on both cheeks, but only by half? In this way, without being unbearded like young men, they are also not fully bearded like old ones. A passage of Herodotus that Anne Carson recalls proves unambiguously that we must understand the custom in the strong sense and that in imposing this obligation on the "tremblers," the intention was to disfigure their faces, imprinting on them the visible mark of disgrace that affects the person. In book 2.121, Herodotus

---

menting on 115F176). Connecting the *katōnakē*, worn by rural dependents at Sicyon, with the dress of the Lacedaimonian helots, Pollux (7.68) notes that this costume, obligatory for certain categories of "inferiors," had as its purpose "that they would feel ashamed to go down into the city." The opposition between the *chlaina*, the woolen mantle that was a sign of civilized status, and the *katōnakē*, made from a skinned animal, a mark of "savagery" or "rusticity," is especially clear in Aristoph., *Lys.* 1150–56. Lysistrata addresses the Athenians to remind them that the Lacedaimonians had helped them get rid of Hippias and the tyranny. "Don't you know that the Laconians, when you were wearing the slavish cap [*katōnakē*], came in arms . . . , that they gave you back your liberty, and in place of the *katōnakē*, had your people take up once more the wool mantle [*chlaina*]." Cf. as well *Eccles.* 721–24. On the *diphthera*, another brutish and unwoven garment, as the mark of inferior status, whether juvenile, servile, rustic, or barbarian, cf. Aristoph., *Clouds* 68f. and *Wasps* 445. Thus there are overlaps among the dress of the youth, the slave, the goatherd, the barbarian, the Scythian, and others: it is always a matter of being distinguished instantly by one's appearance from the citizen and man of the city. Cf. Theog. 54ff., together with the remarks of Françoise Frontisi-Ducroux in "L'homme, le cerf, et le berger: Chemins grecs de la civilité," *Les Temps de la Réflexion* 4 (1983): 72–73. On the Scythian use of the *baitē*, the *sisura*, or the *sisurnai*, garments of animal skins, cf. Herod. 4.64 and 109. For the slippage and overlapping in figurative representation between the image of the young ephebe and that of the "barbarian," cf. François Lissarrague, *Archers, peltastes, cavaliers: Aspects de l'iconographie attique du guerrier,* Thèse de 3ème cycle, Ecole des Hautes Etudes en Sciences Sociales (1983), 205–10, published as *L'autre guerrier: Archers, peltastes, cavaliers dans l'imagerie attique* (Paris and Rome, 1990), 170–72. Noting the strangeness of the hairstyle of the Abantes of Euboea (long hair, like adults at Sparta, on the back of the head, but shaved, like the young, in front), Denise Fourgous finds here one of the signs of a marginality that connects them all at the same time to certain barbarian peoples, Kouretes, and the Athenian adolescent during the ephebeia. Their abnormal coiffures and the long robes they wear convey, as Fourgous writes, "the indeterminacy of the ethnic, cultural, and sexual status of the these people who oscillate between Greeks and Barbarians, civilized and wild, masculine and feminine." "Gloire et infamie des seigneurs de l'Eubée," *MÉTIS* 2 (1987): 5–30.

relates how one of the thieves of the treasure of Rhampsinites succeeds in recovering the corpse of his brother and accomplice whose head he had cut off to thwart his identification. He inebriates and puts to sleep the watchman whom the king had charged with watching over the dead body. But before he makes off with the body, to mock the guards as a form of vengeance on them, he shaves their right cheeks, *epi lumēi*, as an insult. *Lumē* and *lumainomai* are the terms designating the ill-treatment one inflicts on the living or the dead to dishonor and do them outrage.[27]

The helots, when they served in the army, did not generally have the right to hoplite uniform; as light-armed (*psiloi*), they had at their disposal only short swords, poniards, and daggers (*encheiridion, xuēlē, drepanon*):[28] the arms reserved for the young during the *ephebeia*.[29] In other respects, the comparison is no less instructive. Both helots and the young were subjected to harsh and incessant labors, *ponoi*. Those imposed on the helots belong to the general category of measures taken to preserve their *atimia*, their dishonor. But if one believes Xenophon, from the time of the *agelē* the little boy too is trained to go around with an empty stomach; as for the adolescent, he had to tolerate constant labors without any rest (*Rep. Lac.* 2.5; 3.2). For the helots and the

---

[27] Plut., *Agesil*. 30.4. Filth and rags are also the lot of the young. The difference consists in this: the young have shaved heads while the citizens wear long hair; the "tremblers" must go around with half-beards (which adds to the ridicule and distinguishes them from real elders) while the citizens, with their chins and cheeks shaven, are completely unbearded. Added to this is the fact that at Sparta, the young bride on the day of her wedding also has her head shaven, which distinguishes her at the same time from the *parthenos*, the virgin with long hair, and from her husband, no less endowed with hair than the young girl before her marriage.

[28] On these short weapons, implying a means of combat entirely different from that of the hoplite confrontation, suited instead to close fighting, ambush, surprise attack, and the slaughter of the enemy in hand-to-hand combat, cf. for example Herod. 1.12; Thuc. 4.110.2; 3.70.6 (on the *encheiridia*). The *xuēlē* is glossed by Hesychius as a short sword, which some call the *drepanon*. In the *Anabasis* (4.7.16), speaking of the warlike Chalybians, Xenophon compares the weapons his men use, which slit the enemy's throat before cutting off his head, to the Spartan *xuēlē*. In 4.8.25, he mentions the case of a Lacedaimonian, exiled for having, as a child, killed another child with his dagger, *xuēlē*. *Encheiridia* and *drepana* are often associated with weapons of the *psiloi*, light infantry, and the Carian and Lydian barbarians (Herod. 4.92 and 93). In the battle in which Onesilos opposes the Persian general Artybios on horseback, it is Onesilos's squire, a Carian, who severs the horse's hocks with a blow of the *drepanon* (Herod. 5.111–12).

[29] On the stelae at the sanctuary of Orthia commemorating the victory of a youth in the *paidikos agōn*, along with the name of the victor there is a small iron sickle affixed to the stone, at the same time a dedication to the goddess and a sacred recompense consecrating the success of the lucky contestant. This little sickle, the *drepanon*, has often been interpreted as an agricultural implement, evoking Artemis as the goddess of fertility. The connections, stressed by many texts and confirmed by Hesychius, among *drepanon, xuēlē*, and *encheiridion*, shows that it is rather a weapon, one of the short curved blades like the *machaira* (cf. Plut., *Lyc.* 19.4) used by the young, particularly in the *krypteia*, to slaughter the ephebes by surprise. Plutarch specifies that the initiates sent into the country to carry out this throat-cutting (*aposphazō*) had no other weapons on them than the *encheiridia* (*Lyc.* 28.2). I have remarked in the preceeding note on the connection between *encheiridia* and *drepana*.

youths, however, the end result of this life of *ponoi* is reversed. For the former, as for a donkey carrying its burden or an ox plowing a field, it is the manifestation of a subhuman state, of a nature made for servitude. For the latter, it is a temporary test. It is in the course of this test that what constitutes for the helots the definitive indication of their *atimia*, their opprobrium, becomes the indispensable condition for the young to enter into a future of honors and glory.[30]

The same is true for the whip. For the Greeks, the free man and the citizen could not be beaten. The helot was submitted to beatings, without reason or justification, at the whim of his masters, less to punish than to show and convince him that he was born for the whip.[31] The whip also accompanies the future citizen of Sparta throughout his career as a youth. On the horizon of his early childhood, alongside the *paidonomos*, there loom the *mastigophoroi*, the whip-bearers (*Rep. Lac.* 2.2). The young are chastised with the whip whenever they make a mistake, to teach them to obey, to respect what is above them: their leader, their elders, the law. But to whip the elite of the freeborn young, to treat so infamously those who are being prepared for the highest ranks of the state, is from the Greek point of view more than a paradox or a logical contradiction; it is shocking.[32] There is no lack of stories, more or less fabulous, that claim that the matrons whip the still-unmarried boys while making them run around an altar (Clearchus of Soli in Athen. 13.555c), or that the young men had to parade naked every ten days in front of the ephors, and that those judged too fat, soft, or flabby were flogged with blows of the whip, the others being heaped with praise (Ael., *Var. hist.* 7). Several more reliable witnesses, like Xenophon, Pausanias, and Plutarch, give more precise and, within their limitations, more instructive information. They retain essentially two occasions entailing the flagellation of the young. In the first place, the boys are whipped if caught in the act of stealing. This is not done to punish them for having violated a prohibition, or to teach them to respect that to which they have no right, as one would do with a helot. On the contrary, they are whipped for having allowed themselves to be caught, for not having successfully fulfilled the role of thief that they, as youths, are obliged to take on.[33] It is on the orders of the *eirenes* that the famished youths, like beasts of prey, wild animals, slip into the *sussitia* to steal their nourishment without being

---

[30] For the helots, see Myron of Priene, *FGrHist* 106F2 Jacoby (= Athen. 14.657d). For the young, Xen., *Rep. Lac.* 3.3.

[31] Myron of Priene, *FGrHist.* 106F2 Jacoby (= Athen. 14.657d).

[32] Cf. Phil., *Vit. Ap. Tyan.* 6.20: "Aren't the Greeks ashamed to whip publicly those who will one day become their leaders, or to have as leaders men who have been publicly whipped? . . . You do the gods of the Greeks an injustice if you attribute to them the responsibility for the whip in the formation of liberty."

[33] Xen., *Anab.* 4.6.14–15; Isoc., *Panath.* 12.211.

seen, taking to eat what each adult had brought as his contribution to the citizens' common mess.[34] In this regard, the young surpass the helots, if not in bestiality, at least in wildness. Living on what they steal, they are tested for wiliness and dissimulation as much as for vigor, speed, and sangfroid. The whip does not punish their crime of thievery and its lowness; it denounces the indignity of failure, the clumsiness or timidity of those who are not able to acquire, as is expected of them, the dangerous qualities of a predator. For the helot, the punishment of flagellation with its disgrace reminds him that he must keep to his place. As for the youth, he is subject to this infamous treatment as long as he has not adopted that ferocity, that cunning, that brutal determination he needs in order to be accepted one day into the ranks of men.

In the second instance, the young are whipped at the altar of Orthia. Theft seems, at least originally, to have played a role on this occasion as well. The text of Xenophon (*Rep. Lac.* 2.9) suggests a ritual *agōn* between two groups of young men. The first, in ambush at the altar, stakes its honor on stealing the greatest possible number of the cheeses that have been placed on the altar.[35] The second beats the robbers with great whip-blows in order to hold them off.[36] Victory—and with it, glory—goes to the one who succeeds, in spite of the blows, in stealing from the goddess a greater number of votive cheeses than his companions. In this context, unlike the former one, the whip does not punish, by stigmatizing his worthlessness, the clumsy thief incapable of getting away with his theft. It acts instead as an obstacle to overcome, a painful and dishonorable test he must agree to face in order to get, along with the stolen booty, the recompense of lasting fame. Lycurgus's plan, in instituting this practice at the altar of Orthia, was, as Xenophon explains, "to show that brief suffering can lead to the joy of lasting glory" (*Rep. Lac.* 2.9). One must add, and Xenophon does not fail to note it, that the swiftest, most adroit, and most daring young men—those best suited to thievery—are precisely those who will receive the fewest blows. If the whip threatens all equally, it strikes home above all on the soft and the slow—the bad thieves. In order to play the outlaw, the best policy is to adopt the roles of sly Fox and ferocious Wolf, two animals who have thievery in the blood. Thus we see that in both of these cases, the same traits of cunning and speed enable the young man to prevail.

Neither Pausanias, nor Plutarch, nor any other ancient author picks up this

---

[34] Xen., *Rep. Lac.* 2.6–9; Plut., *Lyc.* 17.5–7; *Inst. Lac.* 12.237–e.

[35] On the *bōmolochia* in connection with the ambush at the altar, cf. Françoise Frontisi-Ducroux, "La *bomolochia*: Autour de l'embuscade à l'autel," *Recherches sur les cultes grecs et l'Occident* 2, Cahiers du Centre Jean Bérard, 9 (Naples, 1984), 29–49.

[36] At the sanctuary of Artemis at Samos, we find a similar scenario of ritual theft of food by a group of young boys hiding out in a sacred place. Choruses of boys and girls have the obligation of bringing sesame and honey cakes, which the segregated youths must steal in order to feed themselves (Herod. 3.48). The connection is made by H. J. Rose, "Greek Rites of Stealing," *Harvard Theological Review* 34 (January 1941): 1–5.

tradition of the theft of cheeses from the altar. The whipping is presented by these witnesses as a test of endurance (the *karterias agōn* mentioned in one of the contest inscriptions, of which the *bōmonikoi* mentioned in six others were perhaps the victors), imposed on all the young during or at the end of the *ephebeia*. The ceremony had a sufficiently dramatic and impressive character, by virtue of its oddity, for a theater to have been constructed in the Roman era in front of the altar, from whose tiers a huge audience was permitted to watch the spectacle. According to Pausanias (3.16.7–9), it is the priestess of Artemis Orthia, holding in her hands the *xoanon* brought back by Orestes from foreign lands, discovered by Astrabakos and Alopekos, who directs and orders the flagellation. The idol, made of wood and small in size, is light; but if it happens in the course of the ritual trial that the whippers, moved by the beauty of one of the adolescents or intimidated by the high birth of another, hold themselves back, the *xoanon* becomes heavy and the priestess complains to the floggers that she is bending under the weight of her charge. Is it not the function of Orthia, as her name indicates, to "raise the young upright on their feet"[37] when she is satisfied, to make them grow tall, light, and slender, their bodies maturing without growing thick and heavy?[38] The whip must spare no one. The contest is not a sham, nor are the blows distributed for laughs. That it is a test of endurance, of steadfastness, is something of an understatement. Plutarch explains that even in his time, "one saw many young men die under the blows at the altar of Orthia" (*Lyc.* 18. 1–2). Like the young man who preferred to let his entrails be torn out rather than reveal the little fox he had stolen and hidden under his cloak, the ephebes had to show enough strength of spirit to tolerate pain unto death. "They were torn by the strokes of the whip [*xainomenoi mastixi*] all day long at the altar of Artemis Orthia, frequently to the point of death," Plutarch adds, "which they endured, cheerful and proud [*hilaroi kai gauroi*], competing for the prize awarded to the one who would last the longest, under the greatest number of strokes. And the one who wins is held in particular repute. This competition is called the *diamasti-gōsis*, and takes place every year" (*Inst. Lac.* 40.239d).

Described thus, the ceremony has taken on an unequivocal significance. The victor is no longer the one who steals the most cheeses while dodging the whip. It is the one who, under the whip, offers himself without flinching to the hardest blows. Victory, glory, and (if the contest marks the end of the *ephebeia*) entry into the adult world—all these are obtained at the price of a public treatment whose ignominy is normally reserved for helots, and whose infamy could be immediately read on their bodies from the scars the whip's talons had left inscribed on their torn flesh.[39]

---

[37] Callim., *Hym. Art.* 128ff.; schol. ad Pind., *Ol.* 3.54; *Etym. Mag.* 631.2ff.

[38] Xen., *Rep. Lac.* 2.5; Plut., *Lyc.* 17.4–5.

[39] Note that the verb *xaino*, to tear or scratch, is the same word used in the aetiological accounts

How can one make sense of this paradox? The key words here are *hilaroi* and *gauroi*. To laugh under the lash, to make sport of its blows, to make it a point of honor to ask for more, to derive pride from ignominious treatment, is to invert the meaning of the whipping. It is to show oneself beyond humiliation and shame, beyond their reach, distinct from those who submit to the whip in passivity and shame as a punishment designed for them and befitting them. Winning the ordeal of the whip turns the youth into an adult, not only because it shows the exceptional courage he has acquired in the *agōgē*, but because it confirms the break with that long period of maturation in which, still close to the helot, he was subject to the whip. In triumphing over this ordeal, in defusing its charge of ignomiby by changing it into an exploit in a contest of bravery, the young man assures his victory over the helot, from whom he is now forever distinguished. In this sense, this test brings to mind another, equally strange. During the *krypteia*, the ephebes have to kill helots, but not by facing them in battle. Dispersed and hidden by day, armed only with daggers, they attack by night, slaughtering by treachery those they take by surprise on the roads, or exterminating the strongest and the best of them, in the fields.[40] To cover one's hands with the blood of the helots, not honorably as befits an adult, a citizen, or a hoplite, but like an outlaw or a wild animal, this of course shows that the helots are in reality inferiors, that their elite can be overcome even on their own territory, and by using their own weapons and methods. In addition, and most importantly, it creates a barrier that from now on cannot be crossed, breaking with all the connivances that once connected one's status with theirs, taking the decisive leap and landing on the other side.[41]

Masks, disguises, dances—all lead to similar observations. The ugliness of the faces, grotesque, ridiculous, and horrible, the lowliness of the vulgar, unbridled, and licentious dances—this is the lot of the helots. They do not need to mask themselves with ugliness or to mime lowliness; it sticks to their skin. When they are exhibited in public, drunk on unmixed wine, incapable of controlling themselves, "singing and dancing ridiculous and vulgar songs and dances" (Plut., *Lyc*. 28.4–5), they are offering their true nature as a spectacle; their undignified mime reveals the truth of their being. Moreover, even when no Spartan is there to watch over and castigate them, they are incapable of "singing the poems of Terpander or Alcman" that every Spartan knows by heart. In their innermost hearts, they feel themselves too different from the *Homoioi*, too inferior even to conceive of aping their customs.

---

of the *arkteia* at the sanctuary at Brauron, of the scratches made by the bear on the face of the impudent little girl.

   [40] Plut., *Lyc*. 28.3–8. Cf. also Plato, *Laws* 633b with the scholia; Heraclides of Pontos, *Fragmenta Historium Graecorum* (Paris, 1873), vol. 2, 210.

   [41] These complicities between helots and youths are particularly clear in the episode of the plot of the Parthenioi, Strabo 7.3.2 and 3. See above, n. 25.

What for the helot is a permanent state, the normal shape of existence, the youth experiences as a probationary period, a preliminary phase through which he must pass in order to detach himself from it entirely. In his liminal position, the youth simultaneously learns "cultivated" behavior—the songs, speech, and ways of talking by which the true *Homoioi* recognize each other[42]—and at the same time, its reverse, marked by deviance, anomaly, ugliness, baseness, vulgarity, and savagery. Moreover, he pushes these characteristics to the limits of caricature, grotesquerie, and horror, not to assume them definitively, making them his own, but to simulate them briefly in a ritual game, a ceremonial masquerade. Thus he experiments simultaneously with the other and the same, with difference and similarity, in their extreme forms and their greatest incompatibility. The result is that exception and rule, foil and model, shame and glory, ranged side by side, are reconciled and confronted at the same time and found more clearly distinguished. Could not the *agōgē*, with the rigors of its regime, lead the youth, like the helot, to interiorize his disgrace, to experience his inferiority of status as an innate baseness, an irremediable shortcoming? Indeed, he is methodically trained to recognize his state of subjection, to obey all those—and they are legion—who have authority over him, who keep him under constant observation, and who may punish him at any time. Above him in the social hierarchy, the *bouagos*, the *eirēn*, the adult, the old man, not to mention the magistrate, all impose on him a domination that throughout the *agōgē* keeps him in a state of profound inequality and virtual servitude. The youth must feel respect and admiration, show diffidence, reserve, and modesty, and demonstrate complete submission toward his superiors. But his consciousness of his inferiority remains tied to a probationary period of tests, during which, in his own eyes, he is not yet himself. This goes along with a spirit of competition systematically developed in all respects, an attitude of permanent rivalry. The character of the youth is thus formed inversely to that of the helot. For the passivity of the one, his resigned acceptance of an innate dishonor, is substituted in the other the fierce and tenacious will to leave behind a temporary state of humility and baseness, to reverse his status, to get his own back by crossing over to the side of those who embody all powers and honors. The habit of submission in the *agōgē* is designed to foster a resolution to do better than those to whose rule one submits, one day to surpass the elders in exactly those things that cause fear and respect when one is young. At the Hyakinthia, the Spartans were divided into three choruses, according to age. The first two groups, elders and grown men, proclaimed in song their valor and their past or present exploits. The third group, that of the youths, proclaimed in the face of their elders their confidence that they would one day be "much better" than those to whom they were commanded to make themselves "equal."[43]

---

[42] Plut., *Lyc*. 12.6–8 and 19.1.

[43] Plut., *Lyc*. 21.2. Some of those who were "not counted among the *Homoioi*" but who none-

The borderline position of the young Spartan, between the helots and the *Homoioi*, means that we must qualify every detail of the picture, to balance each affirmation with its contradiction. We have said that each youth, during the *agōgē*, is continually under the gaze of others, spied on, controlled, judged, and punished by the *paidonomos*, the *bouagos*, the *eirēn*, the adults, the elders, and all his fellows. There was no time or place at which the culprit would not encounter someone ready to reprimand or punish him.[44] The eye of the city, multiplied, is constantly on him. At the same time, he is forced to assume a course of concealment, dissimulation, and secrecy, which culminates in the *krypteia*—not to be seen, to steal furtively, to slip unnoticed into gardens and banquets, to hide during the day so as to attack at night, never allowing himself to be caught, preferring death to the admission of a theft, even if that theft is part of an obligatory role.

We find the same tension and ambiguity in the issue of rivalry. Each one wishes to surpass the others, to win the prize, to be the best in a battle in which, often, as at the Platanistas, no holds are barred. One must, then, personally distinguish oneself in the never-ending contest for glory and honor. But at the same time, one trains the young, we are told, "not to wish to, nor even to be able to, live for themselves [*kat' idian*], but always to maintain ranks like bees clustered around their leader," to give everything for their country, to have no other existence than in the group, through and for the city (Plut., *Lyc*. 25.5). This ambivalence as far as rivalry is concerned—every man for himself, all for the team—shows itself precisely in the furious battle between the two *moirai*, the two competing groups of ephebes at the Platanistas: "In fighting, they use their hands and kick with their feet; they bite and gouge out the eyes of their opponents. Man fights against man in the way in which I have just described, but it is as a group [*athrooi*] that they charge violently, punishing in order to make each other fall in the water" (Paus. 3.14.10.)

They are trained to total obedience by the habit of disobedience, under orders, to the rules that define good conduct in adult life. In order to survive alone in all sorts of situations, they do not hesitate "to use audacity and trickery [*tolman kai panourgein*]" (Plut., *Lyc*. 17.4), "to do wrong [*kakourgein*]" (Isoc., *Panath*. 12.214), like scoundrels and outlaws, the better to internalize respect for the law.

---

theless were energetic in spirit, whether they were helots, *neodamodeis, perioikoi*, or *hupomeiones*, reacted like Cinadon, when faced with the subservient and humiliating situation in which they, like the young, were kept. After his arrest, when the ephors asked him what had been the goal of his conspiracy, he answered, "Not to be the inferior of anyone in Sparta." As this was an answer befitting a youth, but not a helot or anyone else of similar status, there was no choice but to have him and his accomplices make the rounds of the city under the lash of the whip (Xen., *Hell*. 3.3.5–11). In a passage of the *Politics* treating "cities in which honors are shared by only a small number," Aristotle draws a connection between Cinadon, a strong personality "who had no part in the honors," and the Parthenioi, sons of the *Homoioi*, caught in a conspiracy, having been sent to colonize Tarentum (5.7.2.1306b).

[44] See, e.g., *Lyc*. 17.1.

Are they indeed left to their own devices, free to give way to all the impulses of youth, as Isocrates claims? According to him, Spartan education is based on the complete *autonomia* of the young (*Panath.* 12.215). Or are they on the contrary never left without direction or leadership, never deserted by their leader, as Xenophon states (*Rep. Lac.* 2.11)? According to him, Lycurgus made sure that in Sparta, contrary to the practice in other cities, the young were never allowed at any time to live without a master and according to their own desires, *autonomoi* (*Rep. Lac.* 3.1). From the age of seven, the Lacedaimonian is enrolled in an *agelē*. From then on, he lives in a group, a flock, a *boua* (Hesychius, s.v.), under the leadership of a *bouagos*, a cowherd. Thus he experiences a herdlike existence that assimilates him to domestic livestock, to cattle but also to horses. One of the names for the youth at Sparta is *pōlos*, "colt." Nonetheless, under the sign of Lycurgus, as Jeanmaire has shown, many details of his comportment correspond to that of young wolves.[45] In this way, Aristotle tells us, wild animals fight against each other, *dia to mē agelaion einai*, because they are not beasts of the *agelē*, herd-animals (*Hist. anim.* 6.18.571b27–30), but rather live *monioi*, isolated and solitary (Lucian, *De salt.* 34; *Anth. Pal.* 7.289). Calf, colt, or wolf? More than anything else, he resembles the fox, a nocturnal animal who, unlike the wolf, conceals himself in order to attack. A gloss of Hesychius is instructive in this connection. *Sōmaskei*, "he exercises his body," becomes in Laconian, he tells us, *phouaddei*. He also specifies that the term *phouaxir* designates "the physical training of those who are about to be whipped for Orthia." *Alopekes*, foxes (and here we recall the name of Alopekos, one of the discoverers of Orthia), are called in Laconian *phouai*. Calf, colt, wolf, fox—and stag as well, or any other animal that is neither domestic nor beast of prey, but that is pursued, frightened and trembling, like those Satyrs whose fright is mimed in certain dances. With their filth, their shaven heads, their dirty tunics, and the whip that beats them, the young are near the helots, those serfs who, to borrow the expression of Theognis, "their flanks bound with goatskins, graze the fields outside the city, like deer" (55–56). There was, moreover, a Laconian dance called the *morphasmos*, in which one imitated all sorts of animals.

One last point. This marginal life of violence and trickery, this frugal, hungry, naked existence in the wilds, these deviant practices with their train of thieveries and acceptance of harsh punishments, their bloody fistfights and brutal murder of helots, form an apprenticeship in *andreia*, masculine courage, the specific virtue of the warrior. But this apprenticeship is conducted in such a way as to risk going too far and overshooting its mark. Dedicating the child exclusively to brutal violence, seeking to harden him at all costs by physical exercises and trials, as Aristotle has observed, brings him into the realm of *thēriōdes*, and keeps him there (*Pol.* 8.1338b13 and 31–38). Aristotle adds

---

[45] H. Jeanmaire, *Couroi et courètes* (Lille, 1939), chap. 8, "Sous le masque de Lycurge," 463–588, especially the section entitled "Cryptie et lycanthropie: Le couros lacédémonien."

that it is the sense of honor, *to kalon*, and not *to thēriōdes*, the savage, that ought to have priority in education. "For it is neither a wolf, nor any other wild animal that will venture to confront a noble danger; it is only the brave man, the good man [*agathos anēr*]. Those who allow children to pursue these harsh exercises too much . . . consign them to being good for the city for only one thing, and even in this one thing to show themselves inferior to others" (*Pol.* 1338b31–38). An excess of *andreia* runs the risk of resulting in *anaideia* and *hubris*, a shamelessness and unrestrained audacity. Without the tempering and softening effects of *sōphrosunē*, moderation, the kind of excellence to which the tests of trickery, violence, and brutality in the *agōgē* are directed shows itself to be perverted and deformed, taking on the form of a bestial savagery, a terrifying monstrosity.

Conversely, and to balance this tendency—especially between the ages of fourteen and twenty, an age, as Xenophon tells us, naturally given to *hubris*, to arrogance, to the thirst for pleasure (*Rep. Lac.* 3.2)—our little wildmen are forced to act like bashful virgins. They walk with their eyes lowered, their hands hidden under their cloaks, in silence, without opening their mouths, as good as can be. They are the picture of *aidōs*, modesty, surpassing even the most chaste young girl in the intimacy of her chamber (3.4). Our pack of wolves, at night waylaying the helots in the countryside in order to cut their throats, turns up in the streets of Sparta, by way of a text of Xenophon, transformed into a row of mild-mannered seminarians.

In the course of their education, the young thus experience the sense of an inherent alterity in the polar relation between *andreia* and *aidōs*; the first, by an excess of virility, turning into savagery, the second, by an excess of femininity, running the risk of ending in cowardice. Each of these two virtues, whose indispensable equilibrium is necessary but difficult to maintain, contains within it a fundamental ambiguity. *Andreia* is the absence of fear, but to accustom oneself to fear nothing, as Plato notes, means not to experience the fear one ought to when confronted with certain objects and certain actions.[46] It is to know no respect,[47] to push audacity to the point of shamelessness.[48]

---

[46] All would agree with me in calling shame (*aischunē*) the fear of seeming perverse when we do or say something that is not good. "The legislator and all men worthy of the name hold this fear in the highest regard, and while they call it modesty [*aidōs*], they give to boldness [*tharros*], which is its opposite, the name of impudence [*anaideia*], considering it to be the worst evil in both public and private life" (*Laws* 1.647a8–11). Each man ought to be *simultaneously* without fear (*aphobos*) and fearful (*phoberos*) (647b9). Connected with bravery (*tharros*) in the face of the enemy must be fear (*phobos*) of a bad reputation (*aischunēs kakēs*) in front of one's friends.

[47] Cf. Aesch., *Eum.* 516–24, "There are cases in which fear [*to deinon*] is useful. . . . What man or what city, if there were nothing under the sun which causes the heart to tremble with fear, would preserve respect for justice [*seboi dikan*]?" See also 690–91: "Respect [*sebas*] and fear [*phobos*], its sister, will keep the citizens far from crime by night and by day," and 698–99: "May all fear not be driven from the city; if there were nothing to fear, what mortal would do right?"

[48] Cf. Arist., *Nic. Eth.* 3.6.1115a7–14: "There are evils that it is noble to fear, and shameful

Aidōs is that necessary reserve without which there is no prudent virtue, no *sōphrosunē*. But by over-cultivating *aidōs*, one ends up being afraid of one's own shadow, a prude shocked by everything, a weakling. Obscenity and scatology, exhibited and mimed, have their roles to play in putting *aidōs* back in its proper place.

The entire game operates under the control and motivation of blame and praise. But even there, by excess or default, things tend to get out of balance. Too much praise of another becomes flattery, sycophancy, the deceitful blandishments of the fox. Too much self-praise becomes bragging, bravado, as when one, acting fierce and playing the he-man, mimics the ferocity of the wolf or the grimace of the Gorgon. Too much blame of another is sarcasm, invective, and insult instead of noble rivalry, invidiousness, and quarrelsomeness, no longer the admiration that stimulates, but the derision by which one cuts down to size those by whom one is surpassed. Too much blame with regard to oneself pulls one down into the category of the ugly, the vulgar, and the ridiculous, lowering oneself to the ignominious level of the helot or the beast.[49]

At the sanctuary of Artemis, the youths who put on masks to perform their dances and songs were not only selecting the figure of the accomplished warrior who, with his manly courage, constituted the ideal of the *agōgē*. They also tried on different forms of alterity so as to exorcise them through the mimicry of ritual. These ran the gamut from the excessive savagery of the male to the excessive timidity of the *parthenos*, from individual, solitary conduct to the herdlike behavior of the flock, from deviance, dissimulation, and fraud to blind obedience and the most strict conformism, from the stroke of the whip received to the victory won, and from dishonor to glory. This play of extremes defines the field of adolescence, whose furthest boundaries the youth must have explored in order to be integrated in himself, becoming in his turn an Equal (*isos*), a similar one, a *homoios* among the *isoi* and *Homoioi*.

---

not to fear, for example, dishonor; whoever fears it is honest and modest, whoever does not is shameless.''

[49] Aristotle exerts himself to make a coherent theory out of this inevitable tension in the civic ethic of honor, with its internal contradictions. Aside from actions that are absolutely evil per se (such as adultery, theft, and homicide), for all others, honor is located in each case in a just mean, in a position of equilibrium between opposing terms that lead equally to the ruin of virtue, one by excess, the other by deficiency. He writes in the *Nicomachean Ethics*, ''In the matter of honor and dishonor, the mean is magnanimity, the excess is that which one could call vanity, and the lack, small-mindedness'' (2.7.1107b21–23). He adds, ''There is also a mean in the realm of the passions . . . there too, one can be said to keep to the mean, another to go too far—like the bashful man who is frightened of everything, or on the other hand, the man who is deficient or completely lacking in shame—but the one who holds to the mean is called modest'' (1108a30–35) [translation adapted from Ostwald (Indianapolis, 1962)].

Chapter 14

ARTEMIS AND PRELIMINARY SACRIFICE IN COMBAT

WHY, under what circumstances, and according to what rules does Artemis intervene in the activities of warfare? If these questions are worth asking, it is because the virgin huntress, unlike the other *parthenos*, Athena the warrior, does not seem made for martial encounters. Her place is not on the battlefield. She does indeed carry a bow, arrows, and a quiver, like her brother Apollo.[1] Yet neither epic poetry, nor the Homeric hymns, nor lyric, nor tragedy portrays her in the guise of a warrior engaged in battle. This archer uses her arrows to strike "all the beasts raised in the forest, on the mountains" (*Il.* 5.51). "In the thrill of the hunt she shoots the arrows that bring groans . . . she sows death among the wild beasts" (*Hom. Hym. Art.* 2.5–10). The Homeric *Hymn to Aphrodite* mentions her in connection with Athena only to better distinguish them. Both goddesses are equally impervious to the power of Aphrodite, who cannot seduce them or put them under the spell of amorous desire. Athena's heart is charmed by "war and the work of Ares, struggle and combat"; Artemis herself takes delight "in killing the wild beasts on the mountain" (*Hom. Hym. Aph.* 2.5–10). If it should happen that she aims her arrows not at animals but at men, it would not be on the occasion of a military conflict.[2] The arrows of sudden death that she, like Apollo, launches against human creatures (*Od.* 15.410–18) seem, in her case, to be reserved for women alone.[3] Moreover, these are gentle (*aganoi*) missiles and the death they bring is a soft (*malakos*) one, a deliverance one can sometimes ask for as one longs for the peace of sleep.[4]

Mistress of wild animals (*Il.* 21.470), Artemis is not compared to the strongest, noblest, and fiercest among them except in mockery: she is a lion,[5]

This article originally appeared as "Artemis et le sacrifice préliminaire au combat," *Revue des etudes grecques* 101 (1988): 223–29. Translated by Andrew Szegedy-Maszak.

[1] Out of 1,451 representations of Artemis listed by Lily Kahil in the catalogue of *LIMC* (vol. 2), only 20 (nos. 1325–44) show the goddess with any weapons other than the bow and arrow or as bearing the following arms along with the bow: lance, axe, torch, shield, and helmet. However, some of these attributions are doubtful and hunters can also carry lances, as we see in the images grouped under nos. 214–17.

[2] In the Gigantomachy, where Artemis should be present alongside the other Olympians, the goddess plays secondary roles, when she is not simply represented.

[3] *Il.* 21.483; *Od.* 11.172–73, 324–25; 15.478; 18.202; and schol. ad 5.124.

[4] *Od.* 5.123; 11.172; 18.202; 20.60, 80.

[5] In the *Iliad*, the lion, the exemplary heroic symbol, is used "only to qualify warrior heroes in

but "for women" (*Il.* 21.483). When she meets Hera on the battlefield, in the only scene in the *Iliad* where she partakes in combat, Artemis shows herself to be a weakling, whom Zeus's wife disarms with the back of her hand. Hera then slaps and scolds her like a little girl who is being reprimanded: "Better for you to hunt down the ravening beasts in the mountains and the deer in the wilds, than to try to fight in strength with your betters. But if you would learn what fighting is, come on. You will find out how much stronger I am when you try to match strength with me" (*Il.* 21.485–88) [trans. Lattimore]. Reduced to tears, compared to a dove being chased by a hawk, Artemis flees to take refuge, trembling with terror, at the knees of her tender father, far from the world of heroic warfare where she does not belong.

Nonetheless, without going as far as Kern in making her the exemplary goddess of war,[6] some scholars of Greek religion have noted Artemis's place in the rituals preliminary to combat and in the rites of thanksgiving to deities who have guaranteed victory; thus they have seen her, on the same level as Athena, as "a warrior goddess, if ever there was one."[7]

We find a deity playing a role in warfare that nothing in her character seems to prepare her for; if we are to make sense of this, the simplest solution is to connect it directly to her nature as a *kourotrophos*, who supervises the training of young men and oversees their apprenticeship in the practices of the hunt, of which the art of war is an extension. Patron of the *agōgē*, the goddess joins her peers in ruling over the gymnasia of which she is sometimes called "queen" (Eur., *Hipp.* 229), and where youths practice the different skills of combat.[8] Military training and supervision of the youth, therefore, comprise two intertwined aspects of Artemis's *kourotrophia*. As Lonis explains, "the two combine to raise, mold, educate, and discipline the future soldiers, from the cradle to the battlefield."[9]

It can, on the other hand, be conjectured, as Brelich does,[10] that initiation programs had to include ritual battles between groups of young men from neighboring cities. Such contests would take place at Artemis's festivals in common sanctuaries located on the border between the two states. These ritual

---

their attitude to combat." Annie Schnapp-Gourbeillon, *Lions, héros, masques: Les représentations de l'animal chez Homère* (Paris, 1981), 39–40.

[6] Otto Kern, *Die Religion der Griechen* (Berlin, 1926): vol. 1, p. 106.

[7] R. Lonis, *Guerre et religion en Grèce à l'époque classique* (Besançon, 1979), 201.

[8] In the *Hellenica*, Xenophon recalls how Agesilaus was gathering and exercising his troops at Ephesus: "And here was another sight to warm the heart—the soldiers with Agesilaus at the head of them, coming back from the gymnasia with their garlands and then dedicating them to Artemis. For where you find men honoring the gods, disciplining themselves for war, and practicing obedience, you may be sure that there everything will be full of good hopes" (3.4.18) [trans. Warner (New York, 1966)].

[9] Lonis, *Guerre et religion*, 209.

[10] Angelo Brelich, *Guerre, agoni, et culti nella Grecia arcaica* (Bonn, 1961). See especially 83–84 for the most general statement of his hypothesis.

struggles could have turned into real border skirmishes and continue as open warfare between the two communities.[11]

However, in setting up what seems to be a self-evident logical continuity between Artemis's role as *kourotrophos* and that of a goddess of war, we not only run the risk of effacing differences and oppositions. Indeed, we are necessarily led to misunderstand what, for the historian of religion, constitutes the essential problem that no interpretation can afford to ignore: the unique place Artemis occupies on the battlefield, and the specific nature of her action in this realm. Our analysis of this question follows the lines established by Pierre Ellinger, who emphasizes that the links between Artemis and warfare appear less in normal conflicts than in what is called wars of total annihilation, where the prize is no longer the victory of one city over another but the survival of an entire human community.[12]

To put it bluntly, the intervention of Artemis in war does not, to our eyes, look military at all. Artemis does not fight; she guides and rescues. She is Hegemone and Soteira.[13] She is invoked as a savior in critical situations, when the conflict does not oppose two states in the agonistic model of Greek competition but rather involves the survival of a city menaced by utter destruction. Artemis goes into action when one of the combatants violates the limits set either on the use of violence during battle or on the treatment of the defeated party afterward. In such excess and all-or-nothing stakes, war goes beyond the civilized boundaries within which rules of military engagement are maintained and veers abruptly into savagery. In such "extreme" cases, when the goddess brings salvation as a reward to those she protects—usually the side that is directly menaced—her methods do not depend on superior force, physical or military. She acts indirectly, through a supernatural manifestation that disrupts the normal procedure of battle.

Sometimes she blinds people so that as they march, they find themselves lost, distracted, disoriented, with their path confused or obliterated (by fog, darkness, or snow) and the scenery rendered unrecognizably strange. They

---

[11] The best example is obviously that of the sanctuary of Artemis Limnatis and of the role the mythic traditions of the Messenians and Spartans attributed to her in the origins of the conflict between these two warring parties. But we should also consider, as Brelich does, the war between Eretria and Chalcis over the Lelantine plain, between Argos and Sparta over the Thryeatid, between Phocians and Thessalians around the temple of Artemis Elaphebolos in the pass of Hyampolis, and the attack of Chios against Erythraea on the day of the festival of Artemis Strophaia.

[12] Pierre Ellinger, "Le gypse et la boue: I. Sur les mythes de la guerre d'anéantissement," *QUCC* 29 (1978) 7–55; "Artemis," in *Dictionnaire des mythologies*, ed. Yves Bonnefoy (Paris, 1981), vol. 1, pp. 70–73; "Les ruses de guerre d'Artémis," in *Recherches sur les cultes grecs et l'Occident* 2, Cahiers du Centre Jean Berard, 9 (Naples, 1984), 51–67; "Recherches sur les 'situations extrêmes' dans la mythologie d'Artémis et la pensée religieuse grecque," thesis for the Doctorat d'État defended at the Ecole des Hautes Etudes en Sciences Sociales, 4 vols. (1988).

[13] For the collected references to the cults of Artemis Hegemone and Soteira, see L. H. Farnell, *The Cults of the Greek States* (Oxford, 1896), vol. 2, pp. 576, 585–86, notes 67 and 123.

can also be struck with mental confusion, so that, upset and panicked, they are no longer able to recognize the enemy as he is, to determine his nature or the number of his troops; at the extreme, they can no longer distinguish friend from foe and begin to slaughter one another in the belief that they are fighting the enemy. To others, by contrast, Artemis can offer a kind of super-lucidity. She may guide them, invisible to the enemy, by secret paths, or at night may show them the way to follow, even though the route is completely dark. Occasionally she can illuminate their minds with a sudden inspiration by suggesting an effective ritual act, or she may prompt a clever maneuver, a deceptive diversion that sows confusion in the enemy's ranks and paralyzes his superior force, thereby reversing a military situation that had seemed hopeless.[14]

There are so many examples, both in legendary traditions and in historical accounts (often mixed together), and they are so detailed, that they cannot be disregarded; they must be examined for important evidence on the unique role assigned by the Greeks to manifestations of Artemis in armed conflict. Taken together, these texts emphasize the close analogy between Artemis's position in relation to war and her role in the hunt. In the two cases, what concerns Artemis and causes her to intervene is the uncertain boundary between savagery and civilization, the boundary whose fragility is marked by both war and the hunt.[15]

Pierre Ellinger has expertly sorted out the elements that concern Artemis's role in "Phocian Despair," with its "total" sacrifice to Artemis Elaphebolia, that is the means to an unexpected victory, and in other episodes in the war between the Phocians and Thessalians. To these we must add items from the Athenian record. First is the Persian War when the survival of Athens was at stake. "When the Persians and their followers came with a vast array to blot Athens out of existence," says Xenophon, "the Athenians dared, unaided, to withstand them, and won the victory. And while they had vowed to Artemis that for every man they might slay of the enemy they would sacrifice a goat to the goddess, they were unable to find goats enough; so they resolved to offer five hundred every year, and this sacrifice they are paying even to this day" (*Anab.* 3.(2) 11–12) [trans. Brownson].[16] In fact, every year on the sixth day

[14] Cf. L. Piccirrili, "Artemide e la metis di Temistocle," *QS* 13 (1981): 143–56.

[15] Cf. "Death in the Eyes: Gorgo, Figure of the *Other*," above chap. 6, and *Annuaire du Collège de France* (1980–81): 391–405; (1981–82): 407–20; (1982–83): 443–57.

[16] Cf. Plut., *De malig. Herod.* 27 (*Mor.* 862c): "And they say that the Athenians promised Artemis Agrotera that they would sacrifice a goat to her for every barbarian killed; and then, after the battle, when the immense number of the dead became apparent, they passed a resolution asking the goddess to release them from their vow on condition that they sacrificed five hundred goats every year" [trans. Pearson-Sandbach]. A slightly different but parallel version appears in Ael., *Var. hist.* 2.25: "The Persians were vanquished and the Athenians sacrificed three hundred goats to Artemis Agrotera; they do this in fulfillment of Miltiades' vow."

of the month Boedromion,[17] the Athenians commemorated their victory at Marathon; under the direction of the polemarch,[18] they sacrificed goats to Artemis at her temple outside the walls at Agrai, where she was thought to have gone on her first hunt after arriving from Delos.

The goddess also showed her favor once again with regard to the Greeks at Salamis. "The 16th day of Mounychion," Plutarch says, "the Athenians consider sacred to Artemis, because on that day the goddess shone as a full moon for the Greeks who were victorious at Salamis [*epelampsen hē theos panselē-nos*]," (*Mor.* 349f). It is this nocturnal illumination, this salvific light in the darkness, that is recalled in the flat cake ringed with small torches (*amphi-phōn*) that was offered to Artemis on the 16th of Mounychion, the precise day on which the ephebes honored the goddess with a procession, a sacrifice, and a regatta.[19]

Next comes the civil war between the democrats led by Thrasyboulos and the Thirty and their followers. Diodorus's account corresponds to that of Xenophon. According to the latter, the weather had been fine until a sudden snowstorm that began during the night forced the Thirty to abandon their plans to besiege Phyle and to cut off the supply route. "The gods are with us," the democratic leader later announces. "During fair weather they provide a storm when we need it" (Xen., *Hell.* 2.4.14). Diodorus goes somewhat farther. According to him, during the snowfall, the soldiers of the Thirty were disturbed by noises whose origin they could not understand, and they thought that enemy troops were approaching. "The tumult called panic seized the camp, which had to be struck" (Diod. 14.32.3). The snow and the confusion are contrasted with the supernatural radiance that guides Thrasyboulos's democrats, who march away from the roads so as not to be discovered. "They were making their way on a moonless night in bad weather when a flame appeared before them and led them flawlessly to Mounychia, where it left them. In this place the altar of the goddess Phosphoros still stands."[20] From this Light-Bearer came salvation for the democrats and for Athens.

These Athenian stories need to be compared with other traditions. According to Pausanias, during the second Persian War some of Mardonios's soldiers

---

[17] On the reasons for making the 6th of Boedromion the commemorative anniversary of Marathon, as if that were the day on which the battle had taken place, see H. W. Parke, *Festivals of the Athenians* (London, 1977), 54–55.

[18] Arist., *Ath. Pol.* 58: "The polemarch is charged with sacrifices to Artemis Agrotera and Enyalos. He organizes the funerary games and sacrifices for those who died in the war." Cf. also Pollux, 8.91, and Phil., *Vit. Soph.* 2.30.

[19] Athen. 14.645a–b; Pollux, 6.75; Philoch., *FGr Hist* 328f86 Jacoby; Phot., s.v. *amphiphōn*; Suda, s.v. *anastatos*; *Etym. Mag.* 95.1.

[20] Clem. Alex., *Strom.* 1., ch. 24, 163, 1–4; he concludes, "May the Greeks therefore learn to believe in our traditions when they say it is possible for almighty God to guide [*proēgeisthai*] the Hebrews by night with a column of fire because he led the way for them [*kathēgēsamenos autois tēs hodou*]."

who had made a raid into the Megarid wanted to rejoin their leader at Thebes. "But by the will of Artemis, night fell when they were en route; they mistook the path and plunged into the mountain." Imagining in the deepening gloom that they were shooting against their enemies, they exhausted their arrows against a rock whose echoing seemed to them like human groans. The next morning, at daybreak, the hoplites of Megara were easily able to massacre the archers who no longer had any arrows. As a sign of gratitude, the Greeks had built a statue of Artemis Soteira. The same thing happened in the case of the Gauls, who in 279 B.C.E., under the leadership of Brennos, attacked Delphi (Paus. 10.23.5). Cicero and Pausanias agree that their retreat took place in a snowstorm, while the Phocians, who knew the country, were able to descend to attack them unexpectedly by using roundabout paths through the snow. But this time again, the confusion produced by the snow that obscured the routes and blotted out shapes is duplicated by a mental confusion.

> The disturbance [of panic] broke out among the soldiers in the deepening dusk, and at first only a few were driven out of their minds; they thought they could hear an enemy attack and the hoofbeats of the horses coming for them. It was not long before madness [agnoia] ran through the whole force. They snatched up arms and killed one another or were killed, without recognizing their own language or another's faces or even the shape of their shields. They were so out of their minds that both sides thought the others were Greeks in Greek armor speaking Greek, and this madness from the god brought on a mutual massacre of the Gauls on a vast scale. (Paus. 10.23.5) [trans. Levi]

The darkness of bad weather or panicked frenzy can cause confusion, that is, a blurring of limits, an obliteration of boundaries; the same effect can be produced by a military strategy, if it is inspired by the goddess. According to the account of the battles that were fought around the sanctuary of Artemis at Hyampolis, the Phocians took the advice of their seer, Tellias of Elis, and used chalk to whiten the bodies and weapons of six hundred (or five hundred) elite troops. These men waited until the full moon to attack in the middle of the night. On seeing the approach of these pale phantoms lit by the moon, the Thessalians were terrified. Herodotus tells us that they thought "this was something other than what it was, a prodigy" (teras, 8.27). "They thought this apparition of the night to be too supernatural to be an attack of their enemies" (Paus. 10.1.11). Taking advantage of the confusion, the Phocians followed Tellias's instructions to the letter: to kill anyone they saw who was not whitened. The same stratagem that serves to disguise the Phocians, by making them more visible than normal at night and blurring the line that separates human from divine, also clearly reveals to them, as though it were daylight, the identity of their enemies, recognizable at night by the very darkness of their forms. There is a similar effect in the case of a ruse (sophisma) immediately credited to Artemis by those who put it into practice. During an invasion by the Sicyonians, the Hyperasians judge themselves incapable of meeting them in battle. Therefore they collect all the goats in the country, group them together, and attach small torches to their horns, like those that decorate the *amphiphōn* of Artemis. When night falls, the torches are lit. "The men of Sicyon, believing that allies of the Hyperasians had arrived to help them in the battle, and that the light of the flames came from fires lit by the auxiliaries," turned around and went home without fighting. Pausanias adds, "At the place where the fairest of the she-goats, the one that led the others, lay down, the Hyperasians built a sanctuary to Artemis Agrotera, in the belief that the ruse for their struggle with the Sicyonians could only have come from Artemis" (Paus. 7.26.1–5) [trans. Levi].

At Athens, when the city was endangered, deliverance had to be obtained by promising Artemis that one goat would be sacrificed to her for each barbarian killed in combat; a goat slaughtered for every Persian soldier cut down. At Aigaleia (which was then called Hyperasia, its new name being derived precisely from its rescue by the goats), due to the trick inspired by Artemis, all the goats of the country are mobilized; by carrying multiple lights in the middle of the night, they look like a company of warriors who have come to aid the Hyperasians and whom the enemy imagine they see before them, ready for battle at daybreak.

II

But let us leave these stories, where fantasy always has its place, and turn our attention to ritual. There is one custom that is definitely attested for Sparta and that, according to some texts, was also in use in other cities like Athens; it seems to raise, in somewhat different terms, the question of Artemis's role in warfare. It is this goddess, in fact, invoked as Agrotera, to whom a goat would be sacrificed in front of all the troops before any battle. Unlike the stories we have just examined, this rite is no longer a matter of an extraordinary intervention by the goddess in an "uncommon" or scandalous conflict, whether it be a war of extermination or a battle between wholly unequal sides. Instead it is a living custom, a required obeisance to the goddess, a general rule of conduct: for an army to go confidently into battle, the signs on the victim sacrificed to Artemis had to be favorable. The kind of explanation we used earlier does not seem to work here.

We should, however, look closer. To determine the status of this sacrifice to Artemis as a prelude to battle and to understand its symbolic functions and values, we must situate it in relation to other military sacrifices from which it clearly differs. In this regard, the most illuminating text is the passage in the *Constitution of Sparta* where Xenophon recounts the rules that govern the departure of a Spartan king and his army for war (13.2ff.). The slaughter of a goat to Agrotera (according to a custom, as specified by *Hellenica* 4.2.20) is the subject of a separate description (13.8).

The preceding paragraphs dealt with sacrifices (*thusiai*) whose purpose is to open for the army the path of the military campaign outside Laconia, so that the religious tie that attaches the soldiers to the city might remain unbroken for the entire journey. These sacrifices take place, in both space and time, at the points of passage, where the gods must be asked if the way is clear and if they authorize the action. First the king sacrifices in his own home to Zeus the Guide and to the Dioscuroi; then, at the border, before it is crossed, to Zeus and Athena; lastly, in foreign territory when the campaign is underway, he sacrifices, each time it is required, at dawn, just before the new day begins, to ascertain whether it will be favorable or not. And during the whole expedition the army is in some way led by sacrificial fire, which was taken from the royal altar in Sparta prior to departure; it is always kept burning by the fire-bearer (Purphoros), who marches in front of the army to open the way, followed immediately by the flock of animals that will be future sacrificial victims.

To this set of homogeneous and coherent practices, Xenophon adds, while neatly setting it apart, a ritual said to have been instituted by Lycurgus for matters of "armed combat." It involves the slaughter of a victim by cutting its throat (*sphazein*, unlike *thuein* in the other rites). The victim is precisely described: a goat, whose ambiguous place at the edge of domestication consecrates it particularly to Artemis; its blood, spilled during the actual sacrifice, does more than the blood of other victims to evoke that of the warriors who will lose their lives on the battlefield. Among the omens delivered to Cleambros and the Spartans before the battle of Leuctra, foretelling that they would lose and leave many of their men behind, Pausanias recounts the following: he begins by describing the general custom that on campaigns outside of Laconia the Spartan kings were accompanied by herds of small livestock (*probata*) to provide favorable signs in sacrifice. "To lead these herds [*hēgemones*] they had some goats the herdsmen call *katoiades* [i.e., going before the sheep]." And here is what happened just before the battle of Leuctra: "Some wolves attacked the herd; they did no harm to the sheep but killed all the *katoiades*" (Paus. 9.13.5). A wolf's attack on an army's herd is not a unique event. What makes this episode disturbing and gives it a premonitory tone is the selective quality of its killing, in which the sheep, the usual sacrificial victims, are spared; the slaughter is concentrated exclusively on the *katoiades* goats, intended for the goddess (herself Hegemone), so that not a single one escapes. They symbolize the Spartan soldiers destined for death, just as at Athens the promise to sacrifice to Artemis as many goats as there were Persians killed in battle presaged the fate of the barbarian troops.

Both the circumstances and the procedure of this preliminary sacrifice underscore its specificity. It is performed in front of the troops, at a definite time that both Xenophon and Plutarch mention explicitly and that is confirmed by all the sources we have. It takes place not at a predetermined time of day, but "when the enemy is already in sight" and the two armies, in battle order, face each other before launching the attack.[21] This is a critical moment in a situation that is liminal in every respect. The battle is readied, on the point of beginning; the wait, before the charge is sounded, is for the sacrifice to Artemis to yield favorable omens. The sacrificer—the Spartan king, the Athenian polemarch, sometimes assisted by a seer and sometimes replaced by him— usually performs the ritual in front of the troops, in the border area, the no-man's-land separating the two armies. The psychological tension is at its highest at this moment when everything is poised on the brink to shift from the orderly and harmonious formation of the phalanx to the bloody confusion of the fighting, from the safety of standing shoulder to shoulder with one's mates to the danger of encounter with the enemy, from life to death. Everyone is torn between hope and terror.[22] Though no longer in the tranquil world of peace, the men have not yet entered the terrible realm of combat. Everything depends on Artemis. The goat that is slaughtered in her honor decides and releases the attack. The goddess must approve and almost guarantee that, as battle is engaged, the good order of the hoplites in their ranks does not transgress a boundary and plunge into the savagery either of massacre or of rout. Located on the margins of the savage and the civilized, Artemis presides over the crucial moment, as the young men begin an action that might blur the distinction between the two worlds. In order to make the move without jeopardizing this necessary distinction, it is essential to define the limits of each world, and to accentuate the distance between them more strongly than ever so as to keep them separate—all this at the very moment, whether it be in warfare or in hunting, that the danger of confusing the two is greatest.

It is worth noting that both Xenophon and Plutarch, in describing the sacrifice that precedes a murderous assault, are careful to emphasize its character as a peaceful, serene, and lustrous ritual, which imbues the subsequent attack with the qualities of order, calm, and joy. Xenophon: when the goat is killed, all the flutists present must play their instruments; every Spartan must be wearing a wreath (rather than the helmet the situation seems to require); the order is given to polish their shields to make them shine better; every young man (*neos*) must have his hair well-combed and must be calm and radiant with joy (*phaidros*, *Rep. Lac.* 13.8). Plutarch: "And when they had formed the phalanx and the enemy was at hand, the king sacrificed a she-goat, ordered all the men to crown their heads, and commanded the flutists to play the song of Castor. He then led off the marching paean, and to the music of the flutes the men advanced into danger, in an orderly fashion, without a gap in the ranks

[21] Xen., *Rep. Lac.* 13.8; *Anab.* 6.5.8; *Hell.* 4.2.20; 6.10; 6.5.18; Plut., *Lyc.* 22.4; *Aristid.* 17.7–8; *Phoc.* 13.1.

[22] Cf. Albert Henrichs, "Human Sacrifice in Greek Religion," in *Le sacrifice dans l'antiquité*, Entretiens sur l'antiquité classique (Vandoeuvres-Geneva, 1981), vol. 28, 215–16.

. . . peacefully and joyfully [*praōs kai hilarōs*] . . . without fear or excessive zeal [*oute phobon oute thumon pleonazonta*]'' (*Lyc.* 22.2–3).

Moreover, the sacrificer, his assistants, and all who take part in the rite stand ahead of the front lines, often exposed to the enemy's arrows and sometimes even to actual attack, but they are obliged to stay in place, without weapons, without defending themselves, without exchanging blows. So long as the goat sacrificed to Artemis does not show the requisite signs, nothing that directly refers to the violence, blood, and murder of war is allowed into the sacrificial area. At the same time, the whole company of soldiers must wait at rest, as harmless and as immobile in their ranks as if they were on parade. The most striking example of this is unquestionably that of Pausanias before the battle of Plataea. He maneuvers his troops until, at daybreak, he is face to face with Mardonios, who has put his men in battle array. Pausanias halts his advance and commands that every man take his position for combat. Plutarch says

> When he performed the sacrifice but did not receive favorable omens, he commanded the Spartans to lay their shields at their feet and to stand still, looking at him, without defending him against the enemy, while he sacrificed again. Just then the enemy horsemen charged, and some of the Spartans were struck by their arrows. . . . The situation was critical, but the soldiers' discipline was extraordinary. They did not attempt to repel the enemy that was approaching; waiting for the signal from the deity and from their commander, they let themselves be hit and killed at their posts. Some authors say that when Pausanias was sacrificing and praying a little forward of the line, a squadron of Lydians suddenly fell upon him, striking and scattering all those taking part in the sacrifice; since they were unarmed, Pausanias and those with him fought back with rods and whips. (*Aristid.* 17.7–10)

The men surrounding Pausanias have come to assist him in the sacrifice and are without their weapons; in order for the ritual to proceed normally, they are reduced to defending themselves against the invaders with the whips and staves that had been used to lead the sacrificial animals to their place. Lined up and standing in battle order, the entire army is immobilized, exposed without being able to retaliate against the enemy's assault. It is only after Pausanias has called on Cithaeronian Hera and the other gods of Plataea that the victims provide favorable signs and the seer predicts victory. ''Immediately the order was given to the army to go against the enemy, and the phalanx suddenly looked like a spirited animal that rears up in readiness to defend itself'' (*Aristid.* 18.2). The story is the same in the account in Herodotus that is Plutarch's source: the Spartans offer sacrifice with the intention of beginning battle against Mardonios; they are unable to obtain favorable omens; many of their men die and even more are wounded by the Persian arrows raining down on them, but the omens do not improve. Then Pausanias offers a plea to Plataean Hera. ''Just after Pausanias's prayer, the omens given to the Spartans in their sacrifices became favorable [*egineto ta sphagia chrēsta*]. When they finally changed, the Spartans too attacked the Persians'' (Herod. 9.61).[23]

Thus, on the threshold of battle, before launching the attack, every precaution was taken to put the whole army in order, in the most civilized condition of warfare.

The young men acquaint themselves with such civilized order in the gymnasia and, more generally, throughout the *agōgē* whose patron is Artemis. Within war, civilized order is located between two extremes from which it is equally removed and each of which, in its own way, represents the same fall into chaos and savagery. To enter danger calmly (Xenophon), tranquilly, and joyfully, without a troubled spirit (Plutarch), the young man has to have been trained since childhood to shun both terror and excessive rage. Panic and *furor* produce the same effects: they both debase warrior practices by reducing a military confrontation, kin to the *agōn* of the stadium and gymnasia, to the level of bestial violence, blind frenzy, without rein or rule. The panic Artemis sometimes likes to inflict brings the army back, as we have seen, to a state of complete confusion. Ally cannot be distinguished from enemy, self from other. In fury and madness the contagion of killing spreads. Killing becomes internecine, citizen slaughtering citizen, one friend another, a relative his kin. Blind and depraved, war becomes fratricidal butchery, generalized murder.

In its extreme form, when the warrior is outside himself, possessed by Ares, maddened by *lussa*, the condition of *furor* does not merely blur the order of battle but also erases the boundaries between the two sides and even between mortals and immortals; it breaks the sacrosanct barrier that usually prevents men from attacking the gods. In book 5 of the *Iliad* (5.85–86), after Athena has infused Diomedes's spirit with *menos* and *tharsos*, the hero springs so fiercely into the battle that it is impossible to say which side he belongs to, whether he is allied (*homileoi*) with the Trojans or with the Achaeans; he is like a river in spate, which overflows its banks and spreads into farmers' fields

---

[23] We find the same pattern again when Agesilaus, in an expedition against the Acarnanians, ravages their country. Caught in a narrow pass, his army is harrassed by the enemy occupying the heights: "While he was making the sacrifice [*esphagiazeto*] the Acarnanians kept up the continuous pressure. Hurling stones and javelins they came in close and inflicted a number of wounds. Then Agesilaus gave the order; the men in the age group 20–35 ran forward from the other hoplites, the cavalry charged, and Agesilaus himself followed them up with the rest of the army." Xen., *Hell.* 4 (6).10 [trans. Warner (New York, 1966)]. When the Athenians sent Phocion to Euboea against Philip as a general with a small army, there is also a marked contrast in attitude between the sacrificial phase preliminary to combat and the unleashing of the assault: "When the enemy advanced against him, Phocion ordered his men to stand to arms, but to remain quiet until he had finished sacrificing [*sphagiasētai*]. In this way a long time elapsed, possibly because the omens were unfavorable [*dusierōn*] but alternatively, because he wanted to draw the enemy closer to his position. . . . But at this moment, the sacrifices were completed, the Athenians burst out of their camps, routed the attackers, and cut down most of them as they strove to escape among the entrenchments" (Plut., *Phoc.* 13.1 and 4) [trans. Scott-Kilvert (New York, 1973)].

without any regard for dikes or breakwaters. When Ajax is in his fury, he too confuses the lines of the opposing armies. Somewhat later, Athena endows Diomedes with his father's strength, three times greater than his own, and removes from his eyes the mist that has covered them up to now "so that he might be able to distinguish between a god and a man" (*Il.* 5.125–31). Maria Daraki has provided a fine analysis of the epic formula *daimoni isos*, when it is used to describe a warrior who is enraged, attacking by himself, led astray by a *hubris* that makes him break every norm and, most particularly, blinds him to the distinction between human and divine.[24] On the battlefield, the *daimoni isos* seems the incarnation of that Ares whom Athena (who represents the more intelligent and controlled aspect of war) describes as insanely angry, *mainomenos*, and *alloprosallos*, one who goes from one to the other (*Il.* 5.831; cf. 595). The inability to stay firmly on one side is linked to the "frenzy" of Ares *mainomenos*, not just in the specific case that gives rise to Athena's rebuke when Ares chooses to fight for the Trojans after having committed himself to supporting the Greeks. Zeus too calls Ares *alloprosallos*; for Zeus, Ares is the most hateful of the gods, because he has inherited from his mother Hera an untamable *menos*, completely out of control, always seeking strife and warfare (*Il.* 5.889–91). It is frenzied recklessness that turns Ares— and Diomedes—into an *alloprosallos*; it becomes impossible to say which side he is fighting for or against, because his only aim is slaughter. Similarly, when Pindar's poetic song seamlessly blends one theme into another, he will say in its praise that its headlong rush drives it from one subject to another: *thunei ep' allot' allon* (*Pyth.* 10.84).

Already in epic, the threat of a descent into savagery takes the form, during war, of the warriors' excessive rage; in the time of the *polis*, this same danger is clarified and controlled by the order of the hoplite formation. Because it is so typical, the case of Aristodemos will suffice as an example. At Plataea, where he was killed, all agreed that he had shown outstanding courage. Nonetheless, the Spartans denied him an *aristeia* because, in his fury, possessed by *lussa*, he had left his position in the line (Herod. 9.71). Neither terror nor frenzy, but steadfast calm, disciplined order, constant self-control—these are the goals of the military training for young men. Thanks to such qualities, the Greeks triumph over the barbarians who are "by no means inferior in valor or strength, but lack instruction [*anēpistomenes*] and tactical skill [*sophiēn*]" (Herod. 9.62). More generally, in regulating the use of violence, murder, and massacre according to the model of a religious ceremony and the pattern of a competition, Greek warfare civilizes a type of activity that is always verging on savagery, which it nevertheless strives to avoid.

It is this savagery, hovering in the background of war, that the presence of

[24] Maria Daraki, "Le héros à *menos* et le héros *daimoni isos*: Une polarité homérique," *ASNSP*, ser. 3, no. 10 (1980): 1–24.

Artemis on the threshold of battle both recalls and aims to avert. The goat sacrificed to her shares with her an ambiguous, pivotal position. The goat symbolizes beforehand the human blood that the brutality of battle will cause to be shed, and at the same time diverts the threat onto the enemy; the goat sacrifice also protects the army, now in battle array, from the danger of falling into either the confusion of panic or the horror of a murderous frenzy.

At the meeting point of the two sides, at the critical moment in a liminal situation, the *sphagē* permits or forbids attack on the enemy, and so it involves the boundaries between peace and conflict, life and death, the splendor of youthful manhood and the blood-soaked corpse. The sacrifice also marks the limit between civilized order, where every soldier has a place and an assigned task to fulfill, and the realm of chaos, given over to pure violence, as among wild animals who know neither law nor justice and among whom "fish and wild beasts and winged birds devour one another" (Hes., *WD* 276–78).

It can happen that war, or battle, transgresses the norms of regular conflict, and its insertion into the cultural order causes some kind of problem for one reason or another. Then the preliminary sacrifice of a goat to Artemis before battle is projected in the Greek imagination in the phantasmic form of a hideous slaughter, a sacrifice that is extreme, deviant, corrupted, verging on murder. It is as if, to neutralize the danger, Artemis must first receive an offering in the symbolic figure of an innocent human victim, ignorant of the battlefield, an offering that sums up everything the clash of battle conceals in the way of unjust violence and savage brutality. On the horizon of a *sphagion*, ritually slaughtered before battle, is silhouetted, in myth, the figure of the young virgin, ignorant of marriage, immolated in honor of Artemis.[25]

---

[25] The need to sacrifice a young virgin to Artemis at the beginning of an expedition or before undertaking a battle in order to ensure its success, as Agamemnon did with Iphigenia at Aulis (or according to other versions, at Brauron), is expressed again in the stories about Agesilaus when he was about to embark on his expedition to Asia (Plut., *Agesil.* 6.6–11) and about Pelopidas on the eve of the battle of Leuctra. During the night preceding the combat, Pelopidas has a dream: if he wants to vanquish the enemy, he is bidden to sacrifice a red-haired virgin. Since the order seemed strange and criminal to him, he informs the seers and generals of his vision. The seers counsel him to obey and, to bolster their advice, they recall the ancient examples that, by the success they achieved, validated the grounds for these human sacrifices. By contrast, they add, "when Agesilaus was setting out on an expedition from the same place and against the same enemies as Agamemnon, he had the same vision when he lay asleep at Aulis, in which the goddess Artemis demanded that he sacrifice his daughter, but he was too tender-hearted to give her up, and thus ruined his expedition, which ended unsuccessfully and ingloriously. Others took the opposite view, and argued that such a barbarous and impious sacrifice could not be pleasing to the powers above. . . . While the Theban leaders debated this problem and Pelopidas in particular was at a loss what to do, a filly suddenly broke away from a herd of horses, galloped through the camp, and stopped at the very spot where the conference was taking place. The other spectators admired above all the color of her glossy mane, which was a fiery chestnut. . . . But Theocritus the prophet, with a sudden flash of understanding, cried out to Pelopidas, 'The gods are with you! Here is your victim. Let us not wait for any another virgin, but take and slaughter the gift the god

Inversely, in a standard war between Greek city-states, violence directed at a *parthenos*—sexual violence followed by the victim's suicide—leads inevitably to the defeat of the guilty army, marking its military enterprise with the stain of *hubris* and lawlessness. The rape of a young girl is enough immediately to throw a military expedition onto the side of savagery, to cut off those who take part in battle from the cultural order that war endangers but of which it is nevertheless a part. In the formulation of Pierre Ellinger, rape is to the community of *parthenoi* what savage warfare, a war of annihilation, is to the civic community.[26] In both cases, following similar patterns, Artemis is involved from the outset.

---

has provided for you' '' (Plut., *Pelop.* 21.1–5, 22.1–4) [trans. Scott-Kilvert]. Usually, the human victim to be slaughtered as a condition of victory is a *parthenos*, like Iphigenia sacrificed to Artemis, Makaria to Kore, or the daughter of the Messenian Aristomedes to the gods below. When it is a male, however, it is a question of a *pais* or *neos*, like Menestheus, whose youth disqualifies him from the world of war, which is reserved for those complete men, the adults or young men who have already crossed the threshold of adolescence and are ripe for marriage, even if it is not yet consummated: cf. Eur., *Phoen.* 944–98. [Menoikeus vs. Haimon. Ed.] Between *parthenoi* and certain animal victims (goat, doe, filly, even bear) there can be equivalences, slippages, or even substitutions.

[26] Pausanias reports the Lacedaimonian version of events that accounted for their conflict with the Messenians and justified their final victory: ''It was in the reign of Phintas that the first quarrel took place. . . . On the frontiers of Messenia there is a sanctuary of Artemis Limnatis in which the Messenians and the Lacedaimonians alone of the Dorians shared. The Lacedaimonians say that their *parthenoi* came to the festival and were raped by Messenian men. . . . They add that the maidens who were violated killed themselves out of shame'' (4.6.1f.). A just return for this outrage: the same situation, but inverted, in the conflict between Sparta and Thebes. In 371 B.C.E., during the battle of Leuctra in Boeotia, the resentment of the daughters of Skedasos, violated by the Lacedaimonians, and the curse they pronounced against Sparta before killing themselves are not without relevance for the victory won by Epaminondas. An oracle made clear, in effect, that ''the Lacedaimonians were destined to be defeated at the spot where stood the monument for the virgins, who are said to have killed themselves because they had been violated by certain Lacedaimonians'' (Xen., *Hell.* 6 [4].7) [trans. Brownson]. ''Leuctros was the person,'' says Diodorus, ''for whom this plain was named. His daughters and those of a certain Skedasos as well, being maidens, were violated by some Lacedaimonian ambassadors. The outraged girls, unable to endure their misfortune, called down curses on the country that had sent forth their ravishers and took their lives by their own hands'' (15.54.3) [trans. Sherman]. Pausanias gives the detail that before the battle: ''Epaminondas sacrificed with prayers to Skedasos, implying that the battle would be to avenge them no less than to secure the salvation of Thebes'' (9.13.5) [trans. Jones]. Cf. also Plut., *Pelop.* 20.5–8, and *Amat.* 3 (*Mor.* 773b8–774d8): ''It is said that before the battle, Pelopidas, one of the generals of the Theban army, troubled by the presages he deemed ill-omened, saw Skedasos in a dream, who exhorted him to take courage for he told him that the Lacedaimonians were coming to Leuctra to pay their debt to him and his daughters.''

PART FIVE

Theory

Chapter 15

HISTORY AND PSYCHOLOGY

IN ORDER to look at the relations between history and psychology, for purposes of discussion I will adopt the psychologist's perspective. A partisan, even partial point of view, but essential for three reasons. First, not being a historian, I would not be able to speak in the name of history. Second, it seemed to me that the organizers of this seminar would want to find out from nonhistorians just how they situate themselves today in relation to history. What enrichment do they expect to derive from it in their own fields of specialization? What questions are they tempted to put to the discipline of history in the context of their own researches? Added to these circumstantial motives is a third and fundamental reason that insists on the significance itself of the alliance between history and psychology, which can be observed in many respects. Some recent facts, among others, highlight this convergence of the two disciplines. In 1961, a historian, M. Madrou, published a work entitled *Introduction à la France moderne: Essai de psychologie historique.* One year earlier, in 1960, a psychologist, M. Barbu, published in London a book with the title *Problems of Historical Psychology.* The same year, a psychiatrist, M. Van den Berg, brought out a work in Holland that has recently been translated into French as *Metabletica ou la psychologie historique* (Paris, 1962). Thus, in the space of two years, a psychologist, a psychiatrist, and a historian, independently and without knowledge of each other, all placed their works under the sign of a historical psychology. Yet it should also be recalled that at the Ecole des Hautes Etudes, there has been an ongoing center of research for comparative and historical psychology, founded and led by our colleague, the psychologist Ignacy Meyerson.

What is the meaning of this convergence between history and psychology? The fact that historians are looking at the psychological dimension of the facts they have to study is not a new phenomenon. It would be difficult to find historians who in the past have not made some reference to psychology, whether explicit or implicit. Already in Thucydides, who has been called the father of history, the core of historical explanation is said to reside in the idea

This essay was originally delivered as a lecture for historians and published as "Histoire et psychologie" in *L'histoire, science humaine du temps présent*: xxve Semaine de Synthèse (Paris, 1965), 85–94. It was later included in the volume *Religions, histoires, raisons* (Paris, 1979), and is used here by the kind permission of Editions la Découverte (formerly Maspéro). Translated by Froma I. Zeitlin.

of *kata to anthrōpinon*, that which is according to human nature. For the Greek historian, human nature is a kind of abstract model, distilled from the analyses of the sophists and defining the psychology of *homo politicus* just as, at the end of the nineteenth century, another abstract model would set up the psychological outline of a *homo economicus*. Recourse to the psychological dimension is therefore nothing new in the study of history. What has been modified, however, is the place and role of this psychological factor in historians' research. In the past, the psychological has been a principle of historical explanation. To interpret institutions, works, and the interrelations of human acts, the historian had gladly turned to a psychology of man, considered as a constant, evident, and universal given. For the historian of today, the psychological no longer constitutes a principle of intelligibility, a self-evident norm to be imposed. Rather it has become one aspect among others of historical material, one of the dimensions of the subject, a problem that needs to be accounted for in the same way as all the rest of the data. In a history, moreover, that puts the emphasis on economic transformations and social evolution, the historian today finds a place for research that concerns the changes of mentality in human agents. Hence the perspective of history has been modified. Nevertheless, the novelty does not come from the fact that history appeals to psychology, but from the fact that it uses a different psychology differently. Perhaps one could say, simplifying in the extreme, that we have passed from a psychologizing history to historical psychology, conceptualized as one of the branches of historical research. History has tended to greater and greater specialization (history of techniques, economic and social history, history of institutions, law, religion, art, and science) and at the same time aims to make itself into a general history of man and civilizations.

The situation is entirely different when it comes to psychology. This time a historical perspective and the introduction of a temporal dimension into the study of interior man constitutes a radical innovation in the state of the field. These factors mark a turning point, a rupture, not only with the past practices of the discipline, but also with the general orientation of the majority of psychologists working today. Behavioral psychology, Gestalt psychology, and psychoanalysis all concur at least in that, in different forms, they remain tied to a traditional conception of an immutable human nature. By the methods they use (founded on direct observation or experimentation), and by the very conditions they impose on psychological inquiry by limiting their subject to contemporary man, the great majority of psychologists, a priori and without even being fully conscious of it, avoid any reference to a potential history of psychological functions. Those who reject this presupposition of fixity and admit the possibility of a transformation in human activities (from forms of feeling and perceptive organization to intellectual operations and large complex functions like the person or the will) feel themselves closer in this respect to the historians. Refusing to speak of man in general, they, like historians, pay attention to what men really were at a given moment, in a given place. Again like the historians, they are struck by historical distances, by everything that separates ancient Greek man in his behavior and interior world from the man of the Renaissance and the man of today, the Western model from that of the Chinese, Indian, or African. Human experience varies according to civilizations, and within these, according to historical periods. The psychologist must therefore always situate the various types of human behavior that are the subject of his study in a historical context, and, in order to follow the development of different states of the same psychological function over time, he must, to the greatest possible extent, date these phenomena with precision. What shows up very quickly in the course of this work is the inadequacy of the chart of psychological functions in current use, if one tries to apply it to men of other periods and cultures. In this respect, the psychologist experiences the same feeling of ''difference'' as an ethnologist does, when he arrives at a territory and finds that, in order to understand the institutions and behavior of archaic peoples, he must abandon many of his ideas and even the interpretative framework he had brought with him from the West. When the differences are applied to distance in time rather than to the distance between two cultures, the danger for the psychologist, as for the historian, is to fall into the error of anachronism and to project onto the man of the past ways of feeling and forms of thought that are proper for contemporary man. This is why studies like that of Lucien Fèbvre on sensibility in history are of interest to psychologists, and more generally, so are the remarks of the same author on the links between the two disciplines in an article in the *Encyclopédie* entitled ''History and Psychology.''

Still another factor relates the researches of comparative psychology to the historian's procedures. If, as Marc Bloch thinks, history finally has no object other than man, if the historian, like the ogre, is always in quest of human flesh, it still remains true that the material on which he works does not place him in the presence of living men, but gives him access only to mere traces, to those documents preserved, such as written texts, archival pieces, figural representations, and other different orders of *Realia*. The historian is thus perfectly aware of the necessarily intermediate and indirect nature of his method. To get to the man, he must make a long detour through his works. He must patiently collect the various products of human activity at a given moment of time, interpret them, replace them in the historical series to which they belong, and situate them in the larger context of their particular culture. This is a salutary lesson for the psychologists who might let themselves be deceived by the mirage of some immediate knowledge of man, and who would trust in the exclusive virtues of so-called direct observation.

Thanks to the work of historians, the psychologists also understand better how artificial the opposition is between the individual and the group, between the psychological and the social. Because of his training, the historian knows that the psychology of an individual character can only be explained by a study that shows him engaged, and variously engaged, in a whole hierarchy of groups, each having its own physiognomy. The psychological and the social thus appear inseparable from each other. The social factor cannot just be superimposed later on the psychological, nor can it be thought to construct it from the outside. It is one of its dimensions just as, inversely, there is a psychological dimension in every social phenomenon. As for the category of the individual, it is itself a historical product. We see it being elaborated and taking shape in the West in the course of a long and complex history that is at once social and psychological.

Still, whatever the contacts and influences may be, historical psychology should not be considered a branch of history. It is an autonomous discipline with its own subjects, problems, and methods. The adoption of a historical point of view does not appear to the psychologist as something to be borrowed from history but rather as an internal necessity of his field, linked to the fundamental nature of human psychology. For him, reflection about history can only be fertile if it opens out on a critical reexamination of the theoretical bases on which his discipline rests. The case of Meyerson and his work seems exemplary in this regard. Although he had done a good deal of history and had often spent time with historians, it was his actual experience in the areas of medicine, psychopathology, physiology, and animal and experimental psychology that led him to broaden the conceptual framework of his research and to refound its methodological principles when it came to human psychology. The traits that effectively define human as opposed to animal psychology imply a certain turning of psychology toward a new field of investigation. This set of characteristic features consists of: first, a systematic organization of various kinds of behavior; second, the orientation of mental activities, as of everything that is done or made, toward a product capable of being transmitted and preserved; and last, the significant nature of various human creations, in which form and matter are as inseparable as signifier and signified. As convergent phenomena, these traits finally lead us to the conviction that there is no such thing as pure mind. The mind of man is in his works. It cannot be separated from them; it can only be reached through them. Authentic human behaviors that constitute the material of an objective psychology of man will therefore be whatever he has continued to create and transform throughout his history. In the different types of works he has constructed, man has expressed whatever of the properly human he bore within himself; in producing these works, he is himself formed and constructed. Therefore all the documents on which the historian works also are of concern to the psychologist, but he looks at them differently and asks different questions of them.

First, the psychologist takes them, not in a raw state, but as already elaborated by historians: dated, interpreted, put into place in a well-defined historical series. In this respect, therefore, psychology is dependent on history. In each sector in which psychology conducts its investigations, it presupposes that the historical work has already been done. Dependent by right on historical research, psychology also comes afterward in fact. Historical psychology was born in the last twenty years, at a moment when the scientific status of history was already firmly established. It is thus understandable that, when the logic of their own discipline had led them to face problems of historical psychology, the historians turned to models of traditional psychology. In a general way, they used concepts and an interpretative frame of reference borrowed from American social psychology or cultural anthropology rather than from the new psychological discipline that was in the process of elaboration.

Other factors having to do with the differences in perspective between the historian and the psychologist have, no doubt, operated along the same lines. The historian of a given period wonders about what people of that time were like and therefore conducts his inquiry in a synchronic way. He searches in the attitudes, behaviors, and systems of values that belong to various spheres of social and spiritual life for those resemblances and convergences that would allow him to define a kind of communal psychology. Then most often he resorts to notions such as mentality, group psychology, vision of the world, or sometimes cultural model and basic personality. The psychologist too is mistrustful of concepts he finds too global, too general; they do not tell him much more than something about the "spirit of an age." What he is looking for, however, are differentiated aspects of mental functioning. He will not speak of mentality, but of particular functions like memory, imagination, person, or will. Moreover, in each of these functions he will distinguish different levels of elaboration and multiple aspects. If he treats perception, it will be to consider in part certain subjects that lend themselves to precise analysis: perception of colors, perception of forms. If he does research on memory, it will be to discern various types of memorization, to define their practical conditions of use, their fields of application, and the place they have in a system of the self. There are, in effect, many forms of memory, linked to particular techniques of remembering, practiced in social milieus for well-defined purposes. Some of these do not yet imply a properly temporal dimension or a reconstruction of an individual past of subjects or even a consciousness of the past as past.

This attitude of the psychologist, no longer global and absorptive but "discriminating," goes together with research that is conducted not so much in a synchronic as in a diachronic mode. The interest for psychology in historical study stems precisely from the fact that, in the great psychological categories, which today are presented in relatively unified form, such an approach allows researchers to discern the multiple strata and the various aspects and levels that rightly belong to different historical layers. The psychologist attempts to date the various states of elaboration of a function, to find the moments when they are formed with new mental techniques and more complex types of activities, and to discover when, as a result, a given function is enriched, transformed, and reorganized.

Historians, of course, are not satisfied simply to speak of a collective psychology or attitudes that are specific to a particular group. They also strive to set up a balance sheet of the mental equipment used by men in the past. This inventory of intellectual tools that are characteristic of a particular period and a particular society requires close attention to the facts of vocabulary and language, the various modes of symbolic expression, and the forms of organization of space and time. Repertories such as these are very valuable for the psychologist. Nevertheless, on this point the psychologist is once more likely to prove more demanding: on the one hand, he will want to specify in detail the subject of research; on the other hand, for each of the areas of experience he chooses, he will have to extend the field of investigation. To take one example, let us consider the problems of time. The historian will be interested especially in the instruments used to measure time, in systems of punctuation that, for a group of men, define the chronological framework of their existence; he will try to appreciate the depth of their temporal horizon. Through the cycles of social life, he will try to clarify the rhythms of time or even of various human times, their continuous or discontinuous aspects, the linear and irreversible nature of their course or, inversely, the periodic return of the same temporal phases. The psychologist cannot limit himself to the study of time conceived as a framework of successive events. He looks to see how the various types of temporal experience are organized. In his analysis, he must also distinguish differentiated structures of time with their specific mode of elaboration: multiple forms of overcoming the past and of the consciousness of the past, the category of the present along with the particular qualities it assumes in a certain civilization (for example, in Greece, the real-life present as *kairos*), and lastly, the series of different behaviors oriented toward the future, ranging from diverse forms of expectation to activities designed to provide a grip on the future, to master it, or in some way to integrate it into the present.

This field of inquiry then adjoins very broadly the area of instruments used to measure and order time. It extends to all institutions, all works, all types of behavior that, in a given society, imply some use of a temporal perspective. It is through the practice of all the types of activities that contain temporal aspects that the human experience of different dimensions of time is constructed, enlarged, and specified, and finally, in our contemporary societies, systematized and unified. When it comes to the history of how the past is elaborated, this kind of study will have to take account, among other elements, of religious data—myths of origins and memory; rites of foundation, inauguration, and return to the primordial—and of juridical facts such as those concerning testimony and administration of proof. Finally, it will have to include the birth of history, the development of the kind of historical thinking that will have played a decisive role in giving the past its existential status and objective dimensions. In the same way, how are we to approach the study of the category of the future, in ancient Greece, for instance, without finding a place for the problems posed by divination, for political practice with all it implies about prevision and calculation as well as being a wager about a hazardous and opaque future, and finally, for juridical and religious procedures that, in diverse forms, actually engage one self with another for some time to come: oaths, contracts, treaties, and so forth?

These brief remarks will perhaps help to explain an apparent paradox. The psychologist will resort less to the works of historians interested in collective psychology than to those works of specialized history that bear on the development of languages, techniques, economy, law, religion, arts, and sciences. These are the works he will most readily consult to search out his material, because he needs studies that assemble into sufficiently extended historical series those facts with enough relation to one another to be included in the psychological history of the same function. The authentic behavior of man, we said, is what he has made and constructed throughout history. Those products of human activity that make up the aggregate of cultural facts are available to the psychologist's analysis already classified and grouped into large categories of works, constituted into differentiated series, and arranged chronologically. Moreover, historians have already identified the significance itself of these works. Equally significant, such diverse elements as a utensil, a language, a rite, a juridical institution, or a work of art, like all human products, should not only be described from the outside by the specialist, but should also always be deciphered and interpreted. The psychologist's task is not to graft a ready-made externalized psychology onto the conclusions of specialized historians. He must rather relate the works, their structures and meanings, to various psychological functions and situate them in a table of mental organization. The psychologist's originality consists in a new perspective on the works studied by historians that will consider them from the viewpoint of a history of functions. The psychologist starts from a particular function as it appears today. In its complex organization, this function seems to reveal a series of hierarchized activities. The psychologist therefore transports himself into the past. He undertakes to confront the actual image of this function in those documents he gets from historical sources. Through these documents he seeks to find out to what extent activities of the same order were practiced, what forms they assumed, and whether or not the works were organized into an architecture of the whole. His first task is therefore to pinpoint in the context of a given culture the various types of works and institutions that are likely to concern the history of this function or some particular aspect of it. Correlatively, starting this time not from works in order to connect them to the same function but rather from a function in order to search for it in works, the psychologist will ask whether they correspond to it or not, or to what extent and on what level they correspond to it as works in a particular society at a particular historical moment. He then operates by a series of oscillations that send him back from the works to the functions and from the functions to the works.

In the historian's perspective, psychological history has been presented as part of a whole, as one element juxtaposed to others. The psychological was placed alongside the technical, the economic, the social, the political, and so forth. It had in some sense its own sphere of existence, requiring a new branch of specialized history: the history of mentalities or of collective psychology. For the psychologist, on the contrary, psychological history (in the sense of the German *Geschichte*) has to be conducted from within each of the areas explored by the different specialists. The psychological no longer seems external to the works but rather is present in each and every one of them. The reason is that the psychological history of a human group (in the sense, this time, of *Historie*) does not unfold alongside and, so to speak, parallel to a history that is technical, economic, social, religious, and so on; it is worked out in them and through them. In this sense, the psychologist can make Marx's celebrated formula his own according to which all of history is only a continuous transformation of human nature.

Chapter 16

GREEK RELIGION, ANCIENT RELIGIONS

IN FOUNDING a chair of Comparative Studies of Ancient Religions, the Collège de France has simultaneously maintained a tradition and introduced a new subject. With regard to the maintenance of a tradition: almost a century has now passed since the first Chair of History of Religions was set up at the Collège, a chair that was occupied uninterruptedly until recent years. Undoubtedly then, as now, there were specialized scholars who in their fields—China, India, the classical Near East, Egypt, the Semitic world, Islam—were faced with problems of religious history, but these were approached in the context of a particular civilization. To found a Chair of History of Religions was, on the contrary, to deal with a body of religious facts—no matter in what form—as one special field, a sphere of reality sufficiently comprehensive, explicit, and independent to be capable of being viewed, in the evolutionistic outlook of the period, as a sequence incorporating its own continuity, coherence, perhaps even its own conclusion. It also meant that religious phenomena were granted the status of an ordinary subject of knowledge, open like any other to scientific investigation.

This dual approach had theoretical implications and political reverberations, as is very clearly evident in the inaugural lecture given in 1880 by Albert Reville, the first to hold the chair. In this we can catch the echoes of debates that not only set historians and theologians against each other in the field of interpretation of sacred texts, but that divided French society in general. Albert Reville was concerned with defending the history of religions on two fronts: against those who already called his chair one of irreligion, and against those who saw it as one of superstition. This line of defense, no matter how out of date it may appear today, was not the result of circumstances alone. It was related to a more basic point of view concerning the very direction of the new course of studies. For although the Church was uneasy about a history of which the purpose was to put all religions on the same plane, it is nonetheless true that religious studies arose and developed in the West within a context

This text was originally delivered as Vernant's inaugural lecture of the chair of Comparative Studies of Ancient Religions at the Collège de France on December 5, 1975. It was published in French as "Religion grecque, religions antiques," in *Religions, histoires, raisons* (Paris, 1979), and in English as "Inaugural Address at the Collège de France, 5th December 1975," in *Social Science Information* (= *Information sur les Sciences Sociales*) 16 (1977): 5–24. The translation, by H. Piat, is reproduced here with some minor revisions and a few bibliographical notes by the kind permission of *Social Science Information.*

both dominated and circumscribed by Christianity. It was through the religious categories formulated by the Christian tradition that historians contemplated religion and, as was remarked by Albert Reville's two successors—his son Jean first in 1907, and later Alfred Loisy in 1909—it was tempting to arrange religious facts in terms of Christianity as a point of reference and a destination and thus along the lines of gradual evolution. The study of this subject would then, through the selection of topics and chosen fields of research, evolve as if spontaneously in a system of the Hegelian type. Christianity would thus be the consummation of what other religions, elsewhere or formerly, had inadequately adumbrated.

A man of the stature of Ernst Cassirer is a good instance of this. In his *Philosophie der symbolischen Formen*,[1] he explains how in order to unravel the meaning of a ritual as widespread as sacrifice, it should be examined at the point when sacrifice to the gods becomes a voluntary sacrifice of God, with the spiritual and introverted values ascribed to it by Christianity. It is when this transformation is attained that sacrifice unveils its religious truth and reveals the office it has always and everywhere performed, which puts it at the very heart of the practice of the cult. It is through sacrifice that the increasing affinity of a human being, an individual, and a divine absolute is established in a relationship in which reciprocity should also be commensurate with the tension between the two.

This influence exerted by Christianity on a whole stream of religious sciences, which tended to pull into its orbit the general facts of worship, had its counterpart. At the turn of the same century (the *Année sociologique* was founded in 1898) the team of scholars grouped around Durkheim, of similar evolutionist outlook, approached the problem from the opposite point of view. The team assigned the origin of social development to religion, or rather to the wider and more general category of the sacred that they substituted for religion. Within this nebula of the sacred are found those elements, intermingled to a greater or lesser extent in the beginning, which separately or together will give rise to complex social institutions as well as to elaborate religious systems. The preeminence in Durkheim's opinion of the sociology of religion as the subject containing the seeds of all other social phenomena leads inexorably to the great importance attached in this field to the so-called primitive religions.

But between the opposite ends of this chain, stretching between Christianity as viewed by the historian and the primitive cults from which the sociologist takes off, lies a vast religious terrain, varied and multifarious, as highly organized on the level of thought as on that of institutions. Without going so far as to say that this terrain has been neglected by the religious sciences, it must

---

[1] (Berlin, 1925); trans. R. Manheim, under the title *The Philosophy of Symbolic Forms* (New York, 1955).

nevertheless be acknowledged that it has often been explored less for and by itself than in its relation to that which it was not. Let us take as an example Greek religion in the archaic and classical periods. It is a world that must be penetrated, but the approaches are indirect and difficult because it differs religiously so very much from our own. To start with, we have no key, no conceptual grid that need merely be fitted to it. The framework of interpretation has to be constructed and continually adjusted during the very course of research. In this field, however, attempts at understanding have hitherto been mainly directed along two lines. At times, in the wake of Father Lafitau who, as early as 1724, saw a link between Greek religion and the idolatry of American savages, efforts have been made to trace in the Greek pantheon, its rites and mythology, the vestiges of magical practices and a primitive mentality. At other times research tended to be directed toward what, in a polytheistic system, seemed to lead to a universal and unified concept of the divine, or to foreshadow, in the mysteries and sects, a religion of individual salvation.

As for those scholars who, rejecting the dual and contrary facileness of survival and prefiguration, decided to keep strictly to Greek facts, they have carried out as philologists and historians the indispensable task of collecting, restoring, and carefully arranging various kinds of documents of religious significance. Nothing can be achieved without their help. Interpretation, however, seems to need other methods of approach. The help of a whole group of variegated studies is required to determine the very questions to be asked. In fact, in the positivist and narrow historifying outlook in which this line of research was inevitably entrenched, the pantheon could not fail to appear as a mere conglomeration of gods, an assemblage of unusual personages of diverse origin, the products, in random circumstances, of fusion, assimilation, and segmentation. They seem to find themselves in association rather by virtue of accidents of history than by the inherent requirements of an organized system, demonstrating on the intellectual level the need for classification and organization, and satisfying exact functional purposes on the social level.

With regard to the myths, while their study according to the rules of good historical criticism has avoided fanciful, arbitrary, and anachronistic interpretations, it has been thought sufficient to prepare an index card for each of them—presumed date of birth and curriculum vitae—by locating the site of each one's first appearance, its development, and its permutations, according to one or another testimony. The profusion and diversity of Greek myths, their richness, have seemed to debar treating them as a whole system with its own vocabulary and general framework, its own rules and inherent constraints. No one has wondered if the variants, rather than appearing to be the result of pure accident or the whims of individual fancy, might not be an ordained arrangement in which divergences, disparities, and contradictions become as meaningful as congruities and accordances.

A scattered and heterogeneous pantheon, a mythology of bits and pieces: if this was the polytheism of the Greeks, how could these men, whose exacting rigor in the realms of intellectual consistency is extolled, have lived their religious life in a kind of chaos?

Merely to put this question implies broadening it by comparing the Greek case with other religious systems that are at the same time different enough and sufficiently similar for such a comparison to be possible and worthwhile. We refer to those polytheistic and national religions, lacking the universalist vocation, that developed in the great civilizations of the past; urban civilizations in which the growth of cities imparted in varying forms a similar type of complexity to the social organization; scriptural civilizations in which religious thought found expression in and through texts that in various ways are linked to writings of different kinds—literary, politico-administrative, scientific—sometimes mingling, sometimes conflicting with them.

Analogous cultural levels, homogeneity of documentary sources, similar types of polytheist religion; comparison becomes imperative. There is more to it. Following Karl Jaspers, historians of civilizations have pondered the causes and significance of an amazing phenomenon. At about the same period (between the seventh and second centuries B.C.E.), profound changes took place in the traditional religious worlds of civilizations as far apart as China, India, Persia, Judaea, and Greece. Confucianism, Buddhism, Zoroastrianism, Jewish prophecy, and the philosophical search for the absolute in Greece were all breaks with the past, innovations, and their comparative simultaneous emergence is intriguing.

In an inquiry published recently in the journal *Daedalus*,[2] it was suggested that all these phenomena should be regrouped under the heading of a search for the transcendent. Let us rather put it that we are confronted with a series of religious mutations that differ considerably here and there. In order, however, to understand these mutations in their manifold forms and aspects, in order to determine what novel dimensions they introduced in the sphere of religion, we must start from the base from which they sprang—those polytheistic systems closely enough related for the reforms to take place in a sort of chain reaction, yet sufficiently varied for the cleavages never to overlap and for the reshaping to accentuate, on the whole, the divergencies.

Comparative study of the polytheisms of antiquity thus leads to questioning not only the idea that an essence of religion exists, which would be banal, but that there is any continuity in religious phenomena. Have there not occurred, in this as in other spheres, turning points, breaks, advents that have conferred on the religious fact in man and in society a content, a status, a function it did not previously possess? If we consider the case of Greek polytheism, the idea of god did not refer to any special person, nor even to any individualized

----

[2] Vol. 4, no. 2 (1975).

agent, two categories that had not yet clearly emerged. A god is a power that represents a type of action, a kind of force. Within the framework of a pantheon, each of these powers becomes distinct not in itself as an isolated object but by virtue of its relative position in the aggregate of forces, by the structure of relations that oppose and unite it to the other powers that constitute the divine universe. The law of this society of the beyond is the strict definition of the forces and their hierarchical counterbalancing. This excludes the categories of the all-powerful, the omniscient, the infinite. The relationship of these gods to the world is not exactly transcendent nor immanent. The interplay of the sacred and the profane, as appears from the vocabulary and the rite, does not obey the rules of a mere duologue. There are various forms and degrees of the sacred rather than a single sacred-profane antithesis. The mixing of religions with social life at its different levels, its links with the individual and his life and afterlife, do not lend themselves to an exact definition of the sphere of religion.

This reluctance to fit into the structures to which we are accustomed is what makes the comparative study of polytheistic systems so interesting. It is also what obliges us to change and vary the angle of attack compared to traditional scholarly methods. The work of scholarship essential for reconstituting religious facts in all their authenticity is incapable by itself of elucidating them. Other branches of learning such as religious sociology and historical psychology are needed. In other words, the research of the specialist, without abandoning its identity, must become one of religious anthropology. The continually repeated perusal of the texts of myths, the careful deciphering of the structures of the pantheon, the exact interpretation of rituals, should not be separated from an inquiry of dual dimensions which would concern, in the first place, the social roots and status within the group of the various kinds of beliefs and believers, and in the second, the psychological world, the mental categories of ancient religious man. At this point I cannot refrain from voicing my debt to the two masters who trained me: Louis Gernet, a Hellenist but also a sociologist, and Meyerson, a psychologist, but a historian-psychologist cognizant of all forms of human conduct, observing them not in the artificial surroundings of the experimental world, but as they have come down to us in history in the form of documents in that vast laboratory built up from all the facts of civilization.

I am bound to add that if I have been able to undertake the work to which I have applied myself, it is due to the changes that have taken place during the last thirty years in the field of religious studies. The sociology of religion no longer devotes most of its energy, as at the dawn of the century, to primitive peoples. It grapples with the great contemporary religions. Research into the prevalence, mode, and scale of religious practice according to social environment, the correlations between religious attitudes and behavior in other areas of social life, the attention given to deviations, heterodoxy, sectarian phenom-

ena, and messianisms as well as to conformity, have allowed the better discernment of the relations between the social and the religious. At the same
time, the need for a specific method of classification of religious systems, and
the lack of an appropriate model in this domain, have become more clearly
realized.

Take the case of Max Weber, for instance, who from the Hellenists' point
of view has an exemplary importance. His construction is the most systematic
and fullest attempt to formulate a comparative sociology regarding religion.
By the juxtaposition of a series of dichotomies such as transcendence-imma-
nence, asceticism-mysticism, intra- or extraworldly orientation, the different
religious systems range between two opposite poles: at one pole, we have
Calvinism, which for him represents Christianity at its most extreme, in its
most rigorous and purest form, its religious rationalization brought to comple-
tion. At the other pole we have Buddhism. Somewhat like the antiworld that
the Pythagoreans invented for their purposes and in their desire for symmetry,
Buddhism is the absolute opposite of the preceding model. In Calvinism we
have transcendence and an intraworldly asceticism; in Buddhism immanence
and an extraworldly mysticism. But in the checkerboard pattern formed by
these various typological combinations, there is no square in which to enter
Greek religion. It hardly appears as a religion at all. In Weber's view, Hellas
takes pride of place as the ideal city in social and political history but is relegated to the wings and does not come onto the stage of religious history. By
what criterion does one deny the authenticity, granted to other creeds, of a
religion that for more than a thousand years had its followers and its devotees?

With regard to ethnologists and anthropologists there has been just as much
change. Grappling with archaic cultures, they have not only exorcised in their
own field the phantoms of totemism, mana, and the primitive mentality that
still occasionally haunt the peaks of Olympos, but in company with Claude
Lévi-Strauss have suggested a method of interpreting myths and an overall
conception of mythical thought that compels Hellenists to get down to some
serious rethinking and to speculate on what exactly Greek mythology is.
Where should it be placed in relation on the one hand to oral narratives of
archaic societies and, on the other, to various genres of writings that we have
inherited from the Greeks? What is at stake in this debate is fundamental: to
what extent is there a type of thought that can be termed mythic in general?
Can rules of transformation be propounded that will allow us to pass from one
mythology, such as that of Greece, to another, such as that of the Amerindi-
ans? In other words, under what conditions is comparative mythology valid
and how far can it be applied?

As for historians, they no longer study the general history of religions. Con-
centrating as they do now on a specific religious area—one particular civilization at one particular period—they could not fail to become aware, like us,
of the peculiar character of religious worlds and the difficulties of interpreta-

tion in language and thought when moving from one system to another. Nor, on the other hand, could they fail to recognize the need to compare these differing religious patterns. With many of them, in the Collège and in other institutions, we have long cooperated for the purposes of research that would be meaningless if specialists in religions other than Greek did not take part and did not feel equally involved.

Our research in fact presupposes cross-checking and collating on all levels. It is impossible today to indulge in global comparisons, looking down from a great height on religious worlds in order to identify general characteristics in the light of more or less vague similarities. Comparison should, from the outset, be rooted in one of the religious systems with its particular configurations, and should be continued from inside each religion with which comparison would seem to be rewarding. Indeed, this is the method followed in our research on divination. We did not seek to define divination in general nor to disclose the full range of divinatory techniques used all over the world. Our starting point was the problems that oracular practice raises for the Hellenist on two planes. What part does divining play in the processes of decision making as defined within the city structure? And what intellectual procedures were followed in the interplay of questions and answers? For instance, was the consultation conducted according to a model of the binary type or did it depend on a logic of ambiguity?

Comparison with the great scriptural civilizations such as China and the Sumero-Babylonian world does not only throw light on the vast differences in social status and intellectual procedures between the oracular dialogue of the Greeks and those divinatory techniques that treat their subject as symbolic shapes that it would be the duty of the diviner to decipher in the same way a scribe reads the signs of an ideographic script. The difficulties, the *aporiai*, of Greek divination that have been observed as plain facts when this case alone was taken into consideration are also clarified once this type of divining finds its place in a much larger body in which it merges, but from which it is distinguished by a series of interdependent characteristics and convergent variations. These are significant to the very extent that they acquire value as signs that, in comparison to other patterns, define a special status.

Comparison is thus the affair of specialists, and the comparatist is, first, a man of one religion. For the endeavors of specialists to converge, however, for the same orientation to emerge, each specialist must be capable in his field of widening his usual perspective and of taking account of all the facets of the religious phenomenon involved. The word "multidisciplinary" is fashionable today. Rather, however, than gathering the representatives of established subjects around a table, each with a specific goal, method, and language, it would be preferable to persuade historians of religion, through comparative study, to think in a multidisciplinary manner themselves; to approach religious facts with which they are familiar from a new angle that would make it possible to bring them into line with those of other cultures, and to decide on a joint direction of research and a common set of problems. Whenever a question was raised in the course of our research, such preliminary exchanges of opinion on the way in which a problem arises in various religious contexts have not only widened all our horizons but have influenced the view each had of his own field. They have occasionally even put in doubt interpretations that seemed only too well-founded. Each project, each team working together on it, thus takes on a slight tinge of joint adventure in which open-mindedness, intellec-tual empathy, and friendship, quite apart from competence, have always had and will always have their place.

This is why, if the responsibility of teaching entrusted to me weighs all the more heavily on my shoulders so that I can only hope not to be too unworthy of my predecessors, nevertheless the honor accorded me by my election is less concerned with what could fittingly be called my person than with this frontier post, this center of a crossroads where I find myself, the point of focus where, through me, many divergent and radiating strands are collected and woven together.

A question will be asked. Why should Greece be the starting point in under-taking this comparative work? In theory, there is no answer: it just happened like that. In fact, if we consider the trend in Greek studies since the last war and the place of Greece in the domain of religious comparatism, several very different reasons can be discerned. The first and most important is to some extent a negative one. Greek religion is the only one that cannot be integrated into the three-functional model—sovereignty in its dual juridical and magical aspect, martial force, fertility—that Georges Dumézil has been able through comparatism to recognize in all the religions of the Indo-European peoples. Dumézil's enterprise provided us not only with a methodological model; it also reestablished religious comparatism. This had been in danger of being invalidated due to the excesses of the Max Müller school of comparative my-thology, to Frazer's generalizations, and more recently to the hazardous ex-trapolations of the Groebener and Frobenius school of cultural history. The evidence that there are specific concordances between the religions of such separate peoples as Indians, Indo-Iranians, Italiots, Celts, Teutons, and Scan-dinavians, draws its strength from the combination of and counterbalancing between two factors: on the one hand, the scrupulous exactitude of historical and linguistic investigation; on the other, the full awareness of the systematic nature of religious phenomena. If comparison is possible, it is because the pantheons, mythologies, and rituals imply an architecture, involve an inter-locking body of concepts, convey an ideology, and offer an exact and coherent analysis of men, objects, their relations, and the social and cosmic equilib-rium.

Dumézil's comparatism is aware of the ideological variations that separate one people from another, but it is basically concerned with the omnipresent scaffolding that our shared Indo-European inheritance represents for us all— the vestiges of a common origin in the religious sphere like those existing on the linguistic plane. The strength and relevance of this comparatism is thus the result of its restriction to the religions of historically related peoples. It is less a question of comparing religious systems that are foreign to one another than of discovering from the divergent branches the tree from which they all sprang. In this sense, the misfortune of Greek religion, an orphan cut off from its Indo-European roots, barred from the terrain of interpretation with which it should be possible to reconcile it, gives the Hellenist his opportunity. Starting from this isolated case, he can develop an all-encompassing comparatism.

For instance, the Greek concept of sovereign power ignores the polarity of the Indo-European principle of sovereignty, with its two complementary aspects: ordered and juridical, violent and magical. Comparison cannot therefore be made on this plane in which Greece would be merged in a generality. The Greek myths of sovereignty, however, in recounting how in the world of the gods supremacy is achieved, exercised, and maintained, with which weapons and which allies and against which opponents, raise general problems regarding the relations to be established and preserved between power and order, and between power and disorder. It would seem that to be able to establish order it was necessary to overcome and absorb the power of what preceded it, of the primordial and chaotic. Also involved are the relations between power and the various types of know-how that the sovereign must recruit for his own sale in the spheres of order and disorder. Each of these questions tends to direct us to one or another civilization, setting us on paths that may not intersect. We have followed some of them, emphasizing, like Haudricourt, the contrast between peoples for whom power is primordial, any order presupposing an originative power, and those who, on the contrary, think religiously in terms of order, the most effective power being that which has no need to make itself felt.

Similarly, insofar as the Greek pantheon does not include this trifunctional keystone of Indo-European religions, we need not seek a single model that would reveal the secret of the system by linking it to theologies of the same type. We have to identify in the pantheon the manifold structures and to detect all forms of grouping in which the gods are habitually associated or in opposition. It is a complicated system of relationships in which each god is part of a variegated network of association with other gods; it surely has the function of a classificatory system, applicable to the whole of reality—to nature and to human society as much as to the supernatural world. It is, however, a system in which the main structures do not exactly coincide and which has to be followed along its several lines like a table with a number of columns and many entries. These pantheistic structures are the subject of research, not the deities in isolation. Their variety offers a wide prospect of possible comparison, especially as each of them is located and functions on several levels. The Hermes-Hestia couple, for instance, represents not only the complementary nature of two divine powers, the immovable goddess of the hearth and the mobile god of transitions, exchanges, and movements; this theological structure is also an intellectual one. It is a conception of space as a center and an enclosure, and of movement as the possibility of passing from any one point to another, to which this couple in their contrasts and their essential fellowship give definition. Furthermore, the divine couple and the mental category are not lost in the stratosphere of ideas. They have their place in the workings of institutions. They organize and regulate matrimonial practices, the rites of descent, and the contrast between masculine and feminine tasks. They distinguish between two kinds of economic goods, those lying stored with Hestia in the enclosed space of the dwelling and those that roam the open sweep of the country with Hermes. Each facet of any analysis in which religious structures, categories of thought, and social practices overlap closely is apt to initiate a process of comparison.

This freedom conferred on the comparatist by the special status of Greek religion is augmented by several features that the progress in classical studies has emphasized or singled out, and that are not without significance to our undertaking. Greece, as you well know, is primarily the seat of inceptions. As Mme. Jacqueline de Romilly remarked in this very place, Greece was the starting point in all spheres: social life, political institutions, forms of thought. Paradoxically, the recent decipherments of Linear B, by resurrecting a Mycenaean Greece which preceded Homer's testimony by five centuries, has not reestablished historical continuity nor diminished the quality of abrupt emergence of a particular type of civilization. On the contrary, the separation between the Mycenean past and the Greece of city-states familiar to us has been accentuated. It is no longer possible for us today to reconstruct a prehistory of Greece starting from a tribal community or even a previous matriarchal society. Archaeological research—and I am thinking here particularly of the work of Anthony Snodgrass—has confirmed this. It has demonstrated not only a pushing back of all aspects in the dark age of Greece, but a cleavage so profound that what emerges at the end of the ninth and the beginning of the eighth centuries is a sudden spurt in a fresh direction, the beginning of a new system.

How does this affect religion? Nilsson's classic theory of a Minoan-Mycenaean religion that lived on in Greek religion has to be considerably amended. Continuity is certainly evident in the sites of worship and in the names of deities appearing on the tablets, some of which, such as Dionysos, are those least expected. But this is not the point. The relationship between the social and political forms of organization characteristic of Greece and religion is too intimate for the advent of the former not to have involved profound changes in the latter. Without going as far as to state with Herodotus that Homer and Hesiod established the figures and capacities of the gods and specified their relations, the fact is that in the eyes of the Greeks they gave the pantheon and the mythology their canonical form. Even in the heroic legends in which memories of the Mycenaean past have had the good fortune to be most faithfully preserved, discrepancies are still apparent. In literary tradition, the heroes are situated in a world and a period that are not quite that of Greece. They do not belong to the Iron Age. Above all, the heroes are a religious category that is the focus, from a particular date onward, of an organized cult, depending on both worship of the gods and funerary cults, and they can only be conceived of within the framework of the civic religion. Moreover, the essential elements of worship—the temple with its outside altar, the great cultic statue of the deity, the religious calendars, the organization of funerary space, the Panhellenic games as they functioned after their foundation at Olympia in 776, Apollo's preeminence at Delphi—were all not in existence prior to the eighth century. Even a sacrificial rite as old as the Bouphonia of Athens (the archaism of which aroused the wit of Aristophanes, who saw it as being an example of the old-fashioned stuff from an earlier age) cannot have existed before the founding of the city because of its dedication to Zeus Polieus, its connection with the Prytaneion committee, and its vindication in myth.

These circumstances seem sufficient to discourage the call for retrospective comparatism. We shall therefore not attempt to explain Greek sacrificial rites—the principal act of worship—by comparing them, as Karl Meuli and Walter Burkert did, with what can be but dimly perceived in the hunting rituals of paleolithic times, even in the light of existing rites among the hunting peoples of Siberia. Our purpose is entirely different. We wish to apprehend the nature of sacrifice in the meanings, values, and functions it implied for the Greeks of the archaic and classical periods. This ambition presupposes that sacrifice be resituated within the religious system of which it constitutes one element, and that the system itself be restored to its right place within the general body of the civilization to which it belongs. Taking a gamble on synchronism—which is warranted by the circumscribed historical nature of our subject—no longer leads comparatism through the stages of a hypothetical genesis, but instead directs it toward the comparison of analogous and dissimilar patterns, by relating the Greek case to sacrifice as practiced in other religious systems, forming part of other civilizations. It can readily be seen how our approach differs from the method followed by Hubert and Mauss in their admirable *Essai sur la nature et les fonctions du sacrifice*.[3] They start from an overall pattern, an outline, in which the successive events of sacrifice—entry, culmination, exit—have a universal significance because they fulfill the requirements of a rite, the eternal function of which is to establish the double movement in the relationship of the sacred and profane through the medium

[3] Published in *Année Sociologique* 2 (1899), it was reprinted in Marcel Mauss, *Oeuvres* (Paris, 1968), vol. 1, 193–307, as "Les fonctions sociales du sacré."

of a victim. We follow the reverse procedure and take our departure from a specific sacrificial conformation, the particular characteristics of which have been studied with maximum care. In our opinion, a general theory of sacrifice is shown to be all the more untenable by the fact that Mauss's model cannot quite apply to the Greek case. As Jean Rudhardt observes, the ritual gestures do not tear either the sacrificer or the participants away from their family or civic group, nor from activities that one could hardly call profane, but that are, shall we say, ordinary—the normal activities of an individual living among his fellow men. On the contrary, the sacrifice usually integrates the performers of the rite in the groups they are part of and trains them for their occupations, both public and private.

Our analysis, therefore, should deal with sacrifice from two points of view, two angles of approach, which for us differ but which are all one to the Greeks. On the one hand, we have the ceremonial feast at which the gods invited are present and communication is established between earth and heaven by the smoke and odorous fumes given off by the burning of the offering on the altar; on the other, we have the rituals of slaughter and cookery and the preparation of a meal of meat under rules that make the consumption of meat in the course of daily life a lawful, even pious act. We have to focus our analysis on the practical details of this cookery: the choice, preparation, management, and slaughter of the victim; the carving according to rules that allow the setting aside of the internal and vital organs, the big bones with the pelvis and tail, the meat finally cut up in a manner to ensure equal sharing; the different ways of cooking—what is burned in toto for the gods, what is grilled on the altar fire, what is boiled in a cauldron; the destination of the various pieces, edible or inedible, for religious purposes or not; consumption on the spot, the right to take the meat away or to sell it. It is from this body of detail, at once ritualistic and mundane, that a theology of sacrifice can be formulated, the outline of which is clearly revealed to us by the myths of its foundation.

Greek sacrifice differs from Vedic sacrifice in that the latter is a prototype for the act of creation, which brings forth and binds the universe together in its totality. Much more modest, Greek sacrifice recalls Prometheus's act, which alienated man from the gods. In a ritual that seeks to join the mortal with the immortal it consecrates the unattainable distance that henceforth separates them. Through an alimentary code it seats man in his proper place, between beasts and gods, midway between the savagery of animals who devour each other's raw flesh, and the immutable felicity of the gods who know nothing of hunger, pain, and death because they feed on nectar and ambrosia. This concern with exact delimitation and careful allocation brings sacrifice in ritual and myth into close conjunction with cereal agriculture and marriage, which, together with sacrifice, define the special situation of man. In the same way that man, to survive, must consume the cooked flesh of a domestic animal sacrificed according to rule, he must also nourish himself on *sitos*, a cooked meal obtained from properly cultivated domestic plants and, for his family line to continue, he must beget a son by sexual union with a woman whom marriage has taken from her primitive state to be domesticated by establishing her in the conjugal home. Owing to this need for balance in Greek sacrifice, the sacrificer and the god, although associated in the rite, do not as a rule intermingle; they are kept at a distance, neither too close nor too far apart.

That this powerful theology, indissolubly linked to a social system in its way of setting up barriers between man and what is not man, of defining his relations with what is above and below man, should be found on the level of dietary procedures explains why the peculiarities of diet among Orphics and Pythagoreans, on the one hand, and of some Dionysiac practices, on the other, have real theological significance and express wide divergences of religious approach. Vegetarianism, abstention from the eating of flesh, is a refusal of the sanguinary sacrifice, which is likened to the murder of one's kin. *Omophagia*, the *diasparagmos* of the Bacchants—that is, the devouring of the raw flesh of an animal hunted down and torn apart alive—is the reversal of the normal values of sacrifice. But if one circumvents sacrifice from above by consuming only absolutely undefiled food or by existing on odors only, or if one subverts it from below by destroying, through the removal of the barriers between men and beasts, the distinctions between them imposed by sacrifice, it becomes possible to attain a state of total communion that can be taken just as easily as a return to the tender familiarity of all creatures in the Golden Age or as a descent into the chaos and confusion of savagery. It is in any event a question of establishing, either by individual asceticism or by collective frenzy, a type of relationship with the deity that official religion, through its sacrificial procedures, denies and bans. It is equally true that through inverted methods with contrary implications, the customary separations of sacrificer, victim, and deity become confused and blurred and finally disappear. Analysis of sacrificial cooking thus leads to plotting, as in a diagram, the more or less remote positions, comparatively closely associated or far apart, of the various sects, religious undercurrents, or philosophical attitudes at variance not only with the proper forms of worship but with the institutional structure of the city and all it implies regarding man's status when he is socially and religiously in harmony.

From this standpoint, comparison needs be made in the first place with Vedic sacrifice with the same type of dietary regulations, the same values of cooking in both its technical and metaphorical implications, and the same role of the allocation of food according to rules. In Hinduism, however, the refusal of sanguinary sacrifice, instead of finding itself as in Greece clearly outside the sacrificial system with no possibility of symbiosis, is actually in continuity with it. It extends it as much as it goes beyond it. Sacrifice and the renunciation of sacrifice are interrelated and transform each other in turn through the interplay of reciprocal processes. The purpose then of comparative research will be to discover the characteristically specific differences that will allow us to understand this basic divergence of attitude. A number of points immediately attract our attention. The creative value of Vedic sacrifice, which attempts not to confine man in his small world but rather to ensure the permanence of the universal order and the proper functioning of the cosmos, finds a guarantor in the cosmogonic myth of *Puruṣa*, primordial man, who is at one and the same time the first sacrifice, the dismembered sacrificial victim, and the result of the sacrifice; that is to say, the whole world: heaven, air, earth, gods, beasts, and men, born from the immolated parts of *Puruṣa*'s body. Hindu sacrifice thus at the outset expresses the process of identification of sacrificer, victim, and gods with each other that Greek sacrifice objected to and rejected and that manifested itself in paroxysmal and aberrant practices. The two strategies therefore differ from the beginning. An Indianist, Charles Malamoud, could state that the course of conduct in Vedic sacrifice is to make the only valid offering—oneself; then to retrieve oneself after having created a substitute. In Greek sacrifice, man has no need to retrieve himself as he has not offered himself to the world beyond: he has put himself in the right relationship to it. In India, cremation of the corpse during the obsequies is the culmination of the sacrificial rite. In the flames of the pyre that consumes his body the individual offers himself, with no substitute this time, in a sacrificial oblation. But the renouncer also obeys this logic. He acts on the same lines and follows through to the end what has been implied in the internal mechanism of the sacrificial rite. The renouncer has extinguished all sacrificial fires on which the victims were burnt in order to turn his fires inward, to burn or be cooked from within by offering himself as a sacrifice on the flames of the Veda. The renouncer therefore has no need to be burnt after his death so that he may rejoin the gods and enter the cycle of reincarnation once more. Having already been burnt while alive, he has become identified with the universal Self. He has broken the pattern of the creativity of action of which sacrifice is the model and the consequences of which continue in a chain from one life to the next. As Malamoud again states, to renounce is to raise one's *tapas*, one's inner heat, to such a high temperature that fusion of the deity, the sacrificer, and the victim is achieved. By projecting oneself beyond sacrifice, one attains its values, instead of, as in Greece, taking the opposite course.

Second, in a hierarchical society with a system of castes—*varna*—differentiated by status and occupation, and not a homogeneous body of citizens all on the same plane and entitled, if undefiled, to make sacrifice, it is the responsibility of one of the *varna*, the Brahmins, to supervise the proper conduct of the sacrificial process so that the ritual order, the *dharma*, will continue on earth. The Brahmin sacrifices for himself as head of his household, but also for the others, since he has the qualifications for so doing. This religious vocation of the Brahmin, which both separates him from and connects him to the other *varna*, is why, within the society of castes governed by *dharma*, the witness to the renunciation of sacrifice should be (as Biardeau has observed) in the first place and as a rule, the Brahmin, that is, the expert in sacrifice. It is this same Brahmin who in the course of his life, after having been head of his household, the sacrificer and the sacrificator, and with his family line assured by descendants, is able on the threshold of old age to free himself from his ritual obligations and enter a new state of life, first as a forest dweller, then as a renouncer in the literal sense—alone, deprived of hearth and home, living on wild and raw food or on alms. Specialization of the sacrificial function in a society of hierarchical castes goes hand in hand with specialization of the different religious roles played by the Brahmin at various stages of his life. This is unthinkable in Greece. The unison of the civic and religious spheres in which the individual has his being implies that if he is not within the structure of sacrifice and part of it, he can only be outside and alongside it. He can never be at any higher or lower stage that the system may comprise.

My final contrast concerns the place of and the part played by the individual in these sacrificial worlds, and the type of individualization that occurs. In India, paradoxically enough, the individual is in some respects more powerfully delineated, but it is in a hollow way, a negative fashion, and in the shape of religious experience suitable to the renouncer. In order to be, the individual must have severed all ties that were part of him previously and that, by his own desire, bound him to others, to society, to the world, and to his own acts. The affirmation of the individual takes place on a plane and in such ways that the fulfillment of oneself can equally be conceived as total emptiness, the abandoning of everything that constitutes the singularity of the being in his relations with the world. In Greece, the sacrificer, as such, remains solidly included in the various domestic, civic, and political groups in whose name he carries out the sacrifice. This integration into the community, and especially into its religious activities, gives such steps toward individualization a completely different style: they occur in a social framework in which the individual, as he begins to emerge, appears not as one who renounces the world, but as a person in his own right, a legal subject, a political actor, a private person in the midst of his family or in the circle of his friends.

Comparative research therefore brings face-to-face two models sufficiently diverse for the general appearance of sacrifice to seem entirely different, yet also homogeneous in that we can pass from one to the other by the series of transformations that influence common features at various levels of the civilizations concerned.

Greece, as has been said, is the seat of inceptions. In fact, is there another instance in history that has seen the emergence in the course of a few centuries of so many new intellectual pursuits—philosophy, history, demonstrative science—and when whole areas of human experience previously included in the religious sphere—law, politics, economics, art—shook themselves free? Hellenists have traced these developments in the evolution of vocabulary, concepts, and the plastic arts. In addition, since World War II, in the company of Fränkel, Snell, Dodds, and others, they have undertaken the task of retracing the history of inner man—his mental framework, his sensibilities, his participation in the group, his recognition of himself and his actions. The specialist of Greek religion who hopes to be enough of a historian and comparatist to refrain from applying psychological categories of another period and another place to his documents therefore finds the terrain already cleared for him by the philologists. Similarly, in his attempt to break away from the partitioning of classical studies with each one carving out his own isolated field in the realms of Greek culture, he joins up with those students of antiquity who acted as pioneers in choosing another angle of approach, covering all aspects of the social life of the group in order to grasp the connections—whether with regard to economic facts, like Moses Finley, facts of law, like Louis Gernet, facts of religion, like Henri Jeanmaire, or facts of history and historical thought, like Arnaldo Momigliano.

Among the inceptions that altered the whole of Greek civilization, one has been brought to light by Milman Parry which since then has been considered from many points of view to be of major importance in the problems today facing research on Greece. This is the transition from oral poetry, and in a wider sense oral culture, to a written literature. All scriptural civilizations have experienced a transition like this but it happens in Greece at a relatively late date so that the change takes place in a way before our very eyes. Whether like Milman Parry we agree that Homeric epic in its formulary style provides us with evidence of a work of wholly oral composition in which improvisation calls into play an exceptional verbal and rhythmic memory and relies on a vast store of traditional themes, phrases, versified data, and whole verses previously conceived; or instead we take Homer as a bard who indeed composes his poetry orally but who already entrusts an assistant with the task of writing down his song; or third, on the contrary, we see the works as the first example in textual form of oral poetry, Homer having made use of a phonetic script in the eighth century for the purposes of literary composition—no matter what our attitude, the oldest Greek texts we possess, epics, hymns, theogonies, ancient lyrics, all belong to the period of the transition from the oral to the written word.

The mythologist, therefore, is led to follow two lines of research simultaneously: comparison of mythic narratives as presented in the oral tradition, and comparison with all other kinds of literary works produced by the Greeks. It may be that the prevailing concept of myth will consequently be put in doubt, although the main problem is less one of comparing the myth as a whole with what is not myth than it is of circumscribing exactly the disparities between various types of discourses: disparities in vocabulary, patterns of construction, syntactic links, narrative methods, and techniques of collating semantic values by use of a text. It is a question of situating a work such as that of Hesiod in relation, on the one hand, to an oral narrative, and on the other, to a philosophical or historical text, as well as to the version of the same myth in one of Pindar's odes, in a tragedy, or in the scholarly recension of the sort of historian termed a mythographer.

The nature of our information obliges us never to dissociate completely in any myth the various underlying codes that analysis identifies from the textuality of the narrative in which the myth is recounted to us. And this concentration focused on different levels of the text will also be concerned with intertextual phenomena. Like any other text, a myth in written form is destined to be made public and is therefore more open to critical attack in that, thanks to writing, the author acquires a much greater independence vis-à-vis his public than in the case of oral composition. In the latter the demands of communication compel the singer—if he wishes to be listened to—to comply most carefully with the expectations of his audience. In written mythological tradition the existence of this sort of confrontation is not expressed in the form of a refutation or in argumentative discussion, but by meaningful variations. These may occur either in the actual narration, the order of sequence being open to alteration, inversion, or suppression, or in the way traditional verbal constructions are employed, as when Hesiod reproduces Homeric conventions but with slightly varied form. As a result, these disparities, even though small, have the impact of a differentiation of meaning. They serve to set at a distance what is evoked in order to dissociate it from the original.

The Greek terrain, therefore, is one that most strongly incites the mythologist to grapple with the overall problems of myth on the textual level. To what extent does it constitute an explicit form of expression using language otherwise than in dissimilar kinds of literary discourse and subject to a specific logic? How do codes and narrative structures interlock in the text? More exactly, in what manner does the text make simultaneous use of a multiplicity of different codes and so combine them that the same semantic conformations, the same networks of contrasts and similarities, are displayed? How, in some instances, is the text able to create an impression of dissociation, of the infraction of these codes, or even, as in the case of tragedy, their systematic disarrangement by means of what Pierre Vidal-Naquet, in his study of the *Oresteia*, terms interferences, which through overlapping semantics and metaphorical assimilations establish connections, coincidences, and fusions between such usually separate or contrasting spheres as are normally those of sacrifice, the hunt, and murder?

Behind these technical questions others can be descried: should Greek myths be taken as a classificatory framework, a system of categories, or an intimation of a certain type of knowledge of the real? To what extent do myths express general rules of the workings of the mind; to what extent are they linked to a specific culture? In dealing with these questions the Hellenist has no other recourse than to conduct his investigation at several levels by differentiating between the forms and modalities of mythological discourses—and each level directs his comparison into different channels.

He may in the first place scrutinize a text as a whole, systematically composed and elaborated by one author; for example, Hesiod's *Theogony*. He will handle it as a single work in regard to which it does not suffice merely to note the general design and the cohesion of its parts, but which requires that analysis should be able to account for the minutest details of the text. He may also, depending on the topic chosen, establish a vast corpus embracing all versions of various related myths no matter what their date or who their author, and then enlarge this corpus to include information provided by other, nonmythological sources in the same culture regarding facts involved in the myths, their classification and taxonomy in the Greeks' habitual representation. This is how Marcel Detienne went to work regarding the mythology of aromatics and honey, and how together we handled myths of crafty intelligence.

Finally, as an experimental exercise, one could place oneself at the highest level of abstraction by constructing general models to try out to what extent and in what conditions this framework can be applied, leaving no loose ends, to groups of myths that at first sight appear to have no link with each other. For instance, recent remarks of Claude Lévi-Strauss indicate that the theme of forgetfulness by its association in myth with misunderstanding and indiscretion—that is, with a lack or an excess in communication with others—should itself be interpreted as a lack of communication with oneself. Along these lines one may attempt to formalize the forms and degrees of communication in all spheres: between men and gods, between men by verbal exchange, exchange of women, exchange of goods; sexual exchange and the communication of life by procreation of children; communication between each generation and the following one, fathers transmitting their titles and functions, the sons succeeding to the status of their fathers in due course and subject to circumstances; and lastly, communication with oneself. Looked at within this framework, the parallels established in Greek myth between facts that appear heterogeneous to us become clear: bastardy, when there is no direct line of descent, lameness, when one limps and cannot walk straight, stammering, when the tongue limps and one does not speak straight to direct the thread of one's discourse, and forgetfulness, when one stumbles over an order that cannot be brought to mind. At this level, it is possible to extend comparison to every kind of myth—to compare Greek and American myths as one would those of related civilizations. The only problem is to find out if this framework is not too generalized to continue to be relevant or whether, in order to adhere to texts, it should be made more precise than a simple dichotomy—the excess or lack of communication—by substituting a ladder with numerous rungs, the sequence and complexity of which vary from one area of communication to another and, no doubt, from one culture to another.

Let us now consider how comparison works at the most concrete of the three levels we have identified: the reading of a text like Hesiod's *Theogony*. To begin with, the field is more circumscribed. Comparison will concern works of the same kind in civilizations with which the Greeks were in actual contact: the Babylonian poem of creation, the Hurrite theogony in the cycle of Kumarbi, the Hittite song of Ullikumi, the Phoenician cosmogonies. The study of parallelisms, with respect to the whole and to detail, will merge with a historical investigation to locate the channels and dates of transmission and to follow the progression of influence. The problem will then involve what has been borrowed by one culture from another and the way in which these adopted elements have been reinterpreted and remodeled, as well as the changes in semantic values resulting from their inclusion in a different mythic tradition.

The middle level is what we have decided to explore this year in the seminar to be devoted to comparative research on the myths and gods of crafty intelligence. Comparison in this case can cover all levels in succession. We shall consider first to what extent a god such as En-ki in the Sumero-Babylonian pantheon has a status analogous to that of Greek deities defined by their *mētis*: whether he represents the same kinds of shrewd action and the same sort of wily knowledge. We will then have to classify and arrange in order the various types of narratives that dramatize the adventures of crafty intelligence, how it acted, and its successes and reversals. In this typological attempt, comparison with African oral tradition, so rich and varied, may well be the most fruitful.

Finally, at the most abstract level, we will be faced with generalized models that have been suggested for the interpretation of the personage of the *trickster*, the deceiver, who has been portrayed sometimes as the mediator, sometimes as the violator of interdicts, and sometimes as a marginal person, in the position of liminality in the Victor Turner sense.

It is therefore by following numerous and fairly dispersed paths, with no systematic preconceptions, like exploring an experimental field for which there is as yet no complete theory, that we shall test on the texts the tools available to us for understanding the functioning of what Louis Gernet called the mythic imagination (or "lunacy," as he sometimes would affectionately put it), and what today is called symbolism.

In our lectures I shall approach this problem from an entirely different angle, not that of mythic but that of figurative symbolism, the way the heavenly powers are represented through the plastic arts in religion.

For at least two reasons Greece is of special interest in this respect. First, while the Greeks were cognizant of all forms of representation of the supernatural—unworked stone, beams, pillars, objects of all kinds, animals, masks—they accorded almost canonical value to anthropomorphic depiction. For what reason? What are the religious implications of the special status granted the human body as a mirror of divine power? What godly aspects is the human figure, more than any other, able to represent? Second, the human representation of gods led in Greece to the movement from the symbol to the image. The archaic anthropomorphic idols are not images. They are not portraits of a god. They reveal to us through the medium of the human body divine values that brilliantly illumine the idol, that transfigure it by directing on it, like a beam of light from on high, those shining blessings that derive from the gods—beauty, youth, health, life, power, grace. For the idol to become an image it is not enough that, released from ritual, it should have no other function than to be looked at and that it should be transformed, in the eyes of the city, into nothing but a spectacle. Instead of merely introducing into the visible world the presence of an invisible god, the idol should also, by expert imitation of the external forms of the body, suggest to the eyes of the beholders a representation of the god's appearance. This is a decisive development that finds full expression in the Platonic theory of *mimēsis*, defining all images produced by all forms of art, not only in the plastic arts but in music and literature, as imitations of the appearance. The symbol hypothesizes two contrasting spheres—the natural and the supernatural—between which, however, communication is occasionally established by an interplay of connections, the supernatural even forcing its way into the natural to "appear" in the form of those dual realities of which one side is revealed while the other stays facing the invisible. The image is not of the order of an apparition. It is an appearance, a semblance. As the fruit of an imitation it has no other reality than this similitude with what it is not. Its appearance is a pretense. In the face of the paired natural-supernatural, visible-invisible, it introduces a new dimension, another aspect—the fictitious, the illusory, that which in the eyes of the Greeks defines the nature of *muthos* as fiction, as when they wanted to debase it by contrasting it with the discourse of demonstration-*logos*. The symbol presupposes two levels, nature and supernature; contrasting levels, but by a play of correspondences, communication is sometimes established between them, the supernatural irrupting into nature to "appear" there in the form of those double realities of which one face can be seen, but the other remains turned toward the invisible. The image is not of the order of an apparition: it is a seeming, a simple appearance. Fruit of an imitation, it has no other reality than this similarity to that which it is not.

Then and then only do the parts fall into place, the parts that in Western tradition join to mark the boundaries of the major realms of experience and the patterns of thought that apply to each of them—the sphere of knowledge with reasoning and concept, the fields of art with imitation and image, and of religion with forms of symbolic expression.

Comparative research into the rite, the myth, and the shape of the gods, thus leads to a major problem of history: how is the area of knowledge defined in our culture and where are the borderlines of religion drawn? This means that those categories by virtue of which we endeavor to apprehend religious facts in their various aspects are themselves involved in our research. The investigation in which they serve as tools turns back toward them and designates them as the real subject of the inquiry. This is an uncomfortable situation but it undoubtedly throws light on one of the underlying incentives of our work. In launching into an antiquity of which the last links with us appear to be dissolving before our very eyes, in seeking to understand an extinct religion from within and without by comparison, it is that in the end, we are asking questions, like anthropologists, about ourselves.

Chapter 17

A GENERAL THEORY OF SACRIFICE AND THE
SLAYING OF THE VICTIM IN THE GREEK *THUSIA*

FROM the last decades of the nineteenth century until the middle of our own, the history of religions took on the task of constructing a general theory of sacrifice. Today we are more prudent than we used to be. Now we are more concerned with complexity, especially with the diversity of ritual practices, whereas before we had instantly labeled them with the same term, borrowed from the Latin, and had lumped them together into a single arbitrary category. This procedure, whose origins, motivations, and incentives Marcel Detienne has recently investigated,[1] would have to fulfill a certain number of conditions if it were to be legitimated. There is one condition at least that Hubert and Mauss singled out and attempted to satisfy in their *Essai sur la nature et les fonctions du sacrifice*,[2] an essay that stands as the model of a unified general theory because of the information it contains, its wide range of views, and its systematic method.

To speak of sacrifice, we must be sure from the outset that this concept corresponds to an exact object, which is strictly defined and characterized by traits that unequivocally distinguish it from related religious phenomena. As its name indicates, Hubert and Mauss observe, sacrifice is a consecration. But not every consecration is a sacrifice (extreme unction, for example). In the sacrificial rite, consecration radiates outward beyond the consecrated object to reach one personage in particular, whose role is fundamental, if we are to devise a physiognomy of sacrifice, and that is the sacrificer. By furnishing the divinity with the consecrated object, the sacrificer expects the ceremony to

---

This text originally appeared as "Théorie générale du sacrifice et mise à mort dans la *Thusia* grecque," in *Le sacrifice dans l'antiquité*, Entretiens sur l'antiquité classique, 27, Fondation Hardt (Vandoeuvres-Geneva, 1981), 1–21. The appended Greek text has been omitted, and the interested reader may consult the volume for the transcription of the discussion that followed among the participants. The second part of the text was translated by some students (now unknown) at Michigan State University for a conference organized by William Tyrrell, who has assented to its reuse, and the whole has now been completed and revised by Froma I. Zeitlin. Permission to publish has kindly been granted by the Fondation Hardt.

[1] Marcel Detienne and J.-P. Vernant, eds., *La cuisine du sacrifice en pays grec* (Paris, 1979), 24–35; trans. Paula Wissing, under the title *The Cuisine of Sacrifice among the Greeks* (Chicago, 1989).

[2] Published in *Année Sociologique* 2 (1899), it was reprinted in Marcel Mauss, *Oeuvres* (Paris, 1968), vol. 1, pp. 193–307, as "Les fonctions sociales du sacré."

produce a transformation as a result of the sacrifice and to bestow on him a new religious quality. One of sacrifice's distinctive features, therefore, is the fact that it plays among three terms, with the consecrated object serving as the intermediary between the sacrificer and the divinity. In this sense, the sacrifice can be distinguished from direct forms of contact between men and gods, such as the one that aims to effect a blood alliance. Finally, sacrifice must not be confused with simple offerings. Consecration in sacrificial rites always implies the destruction of the object—consumed by fire if it is a vegetal oblation, its throat cut and its body immolated if a living creature is involved. No sacrifice without mediation, no mediator who is not in some sense a victim.

But is it sufficient to have staked out, like a surveyor, the boundaries within which sacrifice should be inscribed? A new question seems to arise immediately. Does the figure of sacrifice remain constant when the relations among the three partners implied in the sacrificial schema are highly modified from one civilization to another or from one case to another within the same culture? And is it identical when they are organized according to different patterns? When transformation occurs, does not the relative placement of the actors (sacrificer, victim, divinity) change in new situations? On the other hand, can a sacrificial outline be constructed as an abstract model without taking into account a whole series of variables: (1) nature of the victim, which can be a wild beast, a domestic animal, a human being; (2) modalities of immolation; and (3) postsacrificial practices according to whether the victim is, wholly or in part, assigned as human food, or, on the contrary, is forbidden for consumption?

In other words, the question to ask is whether a ritual scenario, even if it occurs in one place or another in apparently similar forms, does not assume different, even contradictory, religious meanings according to the context in which it is found. An understanding of sacrifice presupposes that each type of ritual be resituated in the religious system of which it is a part and that this religious system itself be treated in the context of the civilization as a whole to which it belongs. Investigations of sacrifice should, therefore, be engaged from the start in the very specific limits established for a religion and a society. Their task would be, not to introduce a general theory of sacrifice, but to lead to a comparative typology of different sacrificial systems.

To illustrate these overly general views, we have chosen to investigate how the victim is put to death in the case of the *thusia*, the Greek sacrifice meant for human consumption. There are several reasons for this choice. First, the factual: all the available evidence tells us that it is impossible to conceive of an animal sacrifice without putting the victim to death, and that this immolation seems to constitute an irrefutably brutal fact whose meaning is too univocal to lend itself to discussion. Second, for theoretical reasons. During recent years, two types of research have taken up where older theories left off. It can be said that two scholars, a Hellenist, Walter Burkert, whose work extends that of Karl Meuli, and an anthropologist-philosopher, René Girard, have vastly increased the interest in these problems about sacrifice by renewing their approach.[3] Their differences in orientation and method are immediately apparent. Nevertheless, they agree on the idea that the fundamental feature of the sacrificial rite is a scenario in which the victim is slain and that the victim's ritual murder constitutes the entire ceremony's center of gravity. Is this interpretation absolutely new? In our opinion, the theory of Hubert and Mauss also assigns a central place and decisive role to the slaying of the animal, even though they treat sacrifice from another point of view, emphasizing its use of an intermediary as a technique for connecting the two usually separated spheres of sacred and profane (an interpretation justly criticized, in the case of ancient Greece, by Jean Rudhardt in 1958).[4]

The question we want to pose about the *thusia* is to find out whether this act of putting to death does not assume meanings, values, and functions that may differ according to the context and symbolic organization of the ceremony.

II

There is a central dramatic moment in the sacrificial scenario: the slaying of the animal. If one accepts a general theory of sacrifice, such as the one described by Hubert and Mauss, this moment constitutes the ritual's apex. Let us take the Greek sacrifice of an ox as an example. In this case, the animal's spine is struck with an ax, severing its cervical vertebrae and permitting the person performing the slaughter to cut its throat with a *machaira* (knife) so the blood can gush out. In Greece, this instant, during which "the soul departs from the bones" (*Od*. 3.455), is punctuated by the *ololugē*, the women's ritualist yodel-like cry, which marks the intensity of religious emotion (*Od*. 3.450–52). Prior to this climactic point in the ritual, everything has been set up to wrest the victim, as well as those performing the sacrifice, away from the profane world to which they belong. A perfect animal was chosen, one kept free from the yoke and preserved from undue contact with the hardships of daily toil. The sacrificial beast was adorned and crowned with headbands, and then, accompanied by flute music, it was led with great pomp to the altar where it was sprinkled with lustral water. The animal has in a sense followed an ascending curve that elevates it little by little from the profane to the sacred. The peak of the curve is marked by the animal's death and hence is the climax of the consecration, the point of maximum and definitive worship. As long as the animal lives, its body remains linked to the profane world. Through death, the animal's most sacred element—its life—disappears into the beyond, the

[3] Walter Burkert, *Homo necans*, trans. Peter Bing (Berkeley, 1983); René Girard, *Violence and the Sacred*, trans. Patrick Gregory (Baltimore, 1977).

[4] *Notions fondamentales de la pensée religieuse et actes constitutifs du culte dans la Grèce classique* (Geneva, 1958), 295–96.

"elsewhere," and passes to "the other side of the veil"; henceforth it belongs to the sacred domain. Man, still bound to the sphere of the profane, may dispose of the body, for even though sanctified, the animal's remains do not contain the fully sacred power that would make it untouchable to mere mortals. The man performing the sacrifice has also followed a curve similar to the victim's; he has been raised toward the sacred, but not to the same heights, because he has not accompanied the victim in death. He can therefore return to his starting point at the end of this trajectory with rejuvenated forces and a new vitality. If the sacrificer himself were engaged in the ritual up to its final stage, he would, just as the victim does, find death and not life.

Thus the sacrifice seems like an operation that permits man to approach the sacred domain, to touch it without losing himself in its grasp. His strategy depends on a kind of ruse: entry into the sacrifice only on the assurance that he can return from it. He remains under shelter: the gods take the victim instead of the immolator. This act of substitution, however, shows that the ritual's logic is sustained by a necessary final consequence of the procedure: the act of slaying. Because consecration, when fulfilled, destroys by its intensity whatever it uses, the person performing the sacrifice can only be consecrated indirectly, in a subdued and oblique manner through a shock-absorbing intermediary. Thanks to the victim's mediation, sacred and profane worlds make contact and intermingle yet remain distinct entities.

If this pattern is valid, the key to the sacrificial mechanism lies in the murderous violence imposed on an animal. The brutal destruction of a life, offered as a substitute for one's own, is the only means by which man may enter the sacred world without also leaving the profane.

Violence and murder are thus found at the core of sacrifice. For the moment, let us accept this model, at least as a temporary hypothesis, of a collective behavior that uses the murderous act for religious ends by displacing its violence and directing it toward an animal promoted to play an intermediary role between men and gods. What information do Greek myths provide on this subject? What do they tell us about the manner in which legendary accounts were articulated within the ancient *polis*? What functions were effectively assumed by the ritual practices to which these myths refer?

First, in the Promethean foundation myth of sacrifice, violence and murder are passed over in silence. The son of Japet brings a large living ox before men and gods; when it is dead, he cuts it up and divides it into two parts. There is no account of butchery and slaughter. This omitted statement is most revealing: the essential element of the ritual lies precisely in what Hesiod leaves out—that is, the incidence of murder at the climax of the sacrifice. Mythical discourse in this case proceeds by censorship or camouflage in relation to the ritual's practical reality. Formulated in this way, the hypothesis stated above seems difficult to uphold. Why?

In effect, this hypothesis presumes the existence within the social order of "reality" or "truth" as defined by what man does. Conversely, it also assumes a rhetorical illusion: what one tells in relation to what one does. The distance between the candid nakedness of the practice and the fallacious masquerade of discourse is a measure of that part of the ideology governing social consciousness.

Unfortunately, this splendid dichotomy between practice and discourse, between the doing and the telling, crumbles on closer inspection. In its general unfolding and in the details of its sequences, Greek sacrificial practice reveals the same negative attitude and the same wish to deny violence and murder as those found in the silence of myth. One could object by asking: what about the slaying? Quite briefly, the sacrificial ceremony might be precisely defined as follows: the sum of procedures permitting the slaughter of an animal under such conditions that violence seems excluded and the slaying is unequivocally imbued with a characteristic that distinguishes it from murder and places it in a different category from the blood-crime that the Greeks call *phonos*.

Let us recall only a few points. It is not enough for the animal to be led of its own accord from beginning to end, without a leash, under no coercion and of its own volition. The animal is expected in some manner to give consent to the blow it is about to receive, either by a movement of the head or a shiver in the body. In an extreme situation, the animal will throw itself voluntarily into the sacrificial fire. The instruments that too clearly evoke murder and bloodshed in the Greek imagination, such as the *machaira*, are left unseen: they are hidden in a basket beneath the grains of barley that will be sprinkled over the victim when it reaches the altar. In this sense, the silences of myth no longer translate as a form of censorship used to hide the ritual's true objective. They seem rather to accord with common practice and to correspond to the specific gestures whose import they underline and whose intentions they make explicit.

Furthermore, if we depart from the categories of speaking and doing to examine the one of seeing, a new order of relationships can be observed. In the repertory of sacrificial scenes found on vases, not one of them presents the slaying and death of the victim. The images are silent when the ax falls and the throat is cut. When the *machaira* is brandished, it is only exposed as an instrument to cut up the remains according to an orderly procedure. One never notices the knife at the moment of slaughter because blood is never represented as flowing from the victim's neck at the moment of death. Jean-Louis Durand writes: "The act which paves the way to death in the throat of the beasts is never represented."[5] In the images as in the myths, "death and sacrifice are without exception kept separate." Renewed censorship or excessive inhibition? Are we to assume revulsion on the part of those painters when they had to expose, in all its brutality, the decisive moment that separates the often

---

[5] "Bêtes grecques," in Detienne and Vernant, *La cuisine de sacrifice*.

represented early sequence of the *pompē*, where the animal, very much alive, is being led to the altar, from the later sequences, also represented, where the beast is transformed into a mass of flesh, in edible meat, where it is cut in pieces, suspended from branches, placed on tables, driven into the spits (*obe-loi*), put up to boil in pots, and roasted over a fire?

If this were really the case, how are we to account for the explicit depiction of horror when it is precisely at its highest pitch, when it is no longer an ordinary animal but rather a human being who is to be sacrificed like a beast? Here any apparent reticence or any entreated repugnance disappears: the painter relentlessly, and in the crudest manner, represents the knife sinking into the unfortunate victim's throat, whose blood gushes over the ground or the altar. "One sees Polyxena's blood spurt, but not that of pigs and sheep," notes Durand.[6] In one instance we find inhibition and dissimulation, in the other cynicism and exhibition. One cannot help but conclude that in the imagery the two ways of representing the slaying both complement and oppose each other: the presence and absence of blood are the distinctive markers that emphasize the distance between the sacrificial animal, whose meat will be ritually consumed, and its opposite—a ruthless murder, an ungodly act of violence fraudulently disguised as a sacrifice. The gap revealed by the different handling of images aims to show that a human being is neither a good meal nor a good sacrifice. Properly speaking, there is no human "sacrifice" which is not also a deviant or corrupted sacrifice, a monstrous offering.

If within the operation that jointly offers an animal's life to the gods and transforms its body into food for human consumption, myth, imagery, and ritual are uniformly bound so as to "neutralize" violence and murder, then the interpretation of sacrifice is to be found in only one of two possible directions. If we follow the first, we are required to comment on the institution itself, that is, on the social phenomenon in its entirety, as claimed first by myth, and to affirm that sacrifice is "ideological" in terms of both its parts and its totality. The key to this vast, collective activity, around which the entire political and religious life of the city gravitates, would, in the final analysis, reside in the capacity of sacrifice to conceal its real object, to cover up its practical truth. Through the behavior it actualizes as much as through the glosses it provides through myth, sacrifice would become what Meuli called "a comedy of innocence." It would aim to veil the human participants' awareness of the very nature of the act they are actually in the process of making a reality: violence and murder.

But if we refuse to impose a meaning on sacrifice contrary to the one explicitly given to it by the Greeks, we must also refuse the opportunities offered by a recourse to the notion of ideology. Consequently, if we follow the second direction, we will have to determine the reasons that allow this orientation to

[6] Ibid., 138.

produce a coherent theory of Greek sacrificial practice. This theory must encompass the meaning and range of a strategy that, at all levels of the slaughtering process, systematically bypasses the moment of death. If the ritual remains silent, one can ask in the same argument what is proclaimed by the
image and the myth. What is the nature of this social truth that the Greek
imagination seeks to establish by overt and falsifying omission in order to
acknowledge the contrast between murder and violence on the one hand and
sacrifice on the other?

Two solutions are available. The choice of the first, based on an ideological
exegesis, lends itself from the start to a claim that brings out clearly its equivocal and uncertain character.

Indeed, there existed in the Greek world, on the margins of the official
religion, individuals who looked like magi and groups with the character of
brotherhoods or sects, which refused to perform sacrifices. They extolled a
"pure" life-style that distinguished them from ordinary men, one of whose
chief rules was a vegetarian regime, that is, the abstinence from all the meats
that could only be obtained through the intermediary of sacrifice. These forms
of religious behavior, aberrant with respect to the norm, claimed that by side-
stepping the sacrificial act they could establish a closer contact with the divine,
a proximity not recognized by the official religion and rejected as a form of
impiety. In order to condemn sacrifice in all its implications in terms of man's
relation to the gods, to replace it with a wholly different religious concept,
which, together with vegetarianism, allowed a different means of access to the
divine, these marginal groups, like the Pythagoreans and the Orphics, assimilated sacrifice to murder. They denounced murderous violence in the sacrificial rite, which they saw as analogous to the harm one would inflict on a family
member. They effaced the boundary between sacrifice and murder, between
domestic animal and human being, a boundary the sacrificial institution had
worked to build. No intellectual ambitions were at stake. Their aim was not to
use rational analysis to strip sacrifice of the ideological adornments that
clothed it. Instead, these groups proposed a different type of religiosity that
did not depend on sacrifice. They extolled an experience and approach to the
divine that implied, as a preliminary condition, the disqualification of bloody
sacrifice. This sectarian refusal to engage in the official religious game and to
recognize the difference it established between sacrifice and murder, domestic
animal and human being, found its foundation and its end in the desire to
efface another boundary, to erase another distance—the boundary that separates men and gods. In order to allow men to become divine, sacrifice was
rejected as murderous and ungodly, its symbolic organization dismantled. But
what evidence authorizes us to take the word of these marginals rather than
that of the representatives of the official cult to get at the truth behind the
sacrificial act? If we cling to the notion of ideology, we could also say that the
assimilation of sacrifice to murder is no less "ideological" for the Greeks than

the contrary position. Both are equally religious strategies that confront each other, the first through the symbolic construction of a sacrificial system (that is, the differentiation between sacrifice and murder), and the second through the deconstruction of such a system (that is, through the identification of sacrifice and murder).

An initial conclusion can now be reached: the concept of ideology is not an operative element in Greek sacrifice. Its pertinence is minor in the sense that, with this as a point of departure, one cannot discriminate between the real and the illusory within a social reality.

We must therefore proceed differently. Without projecting our own convictions on these Greek omissions, we shall allow to be heard what they kept silent about as much as what they enunciated. The omitted and the enunciated become two sides of a single discourse whose coherence, once demonstrated, must be taken seriously. Whatever may have been the origin of sacrificial practices in the remote Indo-European past, whatever their social functions and religious values may be in other civilizations, the essential point here is to understand what the Greeks, as Greeks, made of it. How did they organize gestural patterns and mythical commentaries in order to construct an entirely original symbolic system? Such a system not only established a link with the gods, hence respecting the inaccessibility of the sacred world; it also established a social link within the profane world according to a particular model—the political community. Lastly, through the consecrated nourishment of sacrifice, such a system rooted each and every participant in the rite in his proper place, assigned the status of man defined between beasts and gods.

In a study written in 1975, I stated:

> Greek sacrifice differs from Vedic sacrifice in that the latter is a prototype for the act of creation, which brings forth and binds the universe together in its totality. Much more modest, Greek sacrifice recalls Prometheus's act, which alienated man from the gods. In a ritual that seeks to join the mortal with the immortal it consecrates the unattainable distance that henceforth separates them. Through an alimentary code it seats man in his proper place, between beasts and gods, midway between the savagery of animals who devour each other's raw flesh, and the immutable felicity of the gods who know nothing of hunger, pain, and death because they feed on nectar and ambrosia. This concern with exact delimitation and careful allocation brings sacrifice in ritual and myth into close conjunction with cereal agriculture and marriage, which, together with sacrifice, define the special situation of man. In the same way that man, to survive, must consume the cooked flesh of a domestic animal sacrificed according to rule, he must also nourish himself on *sitos*, a cooked meal obtained from properly cultivated domestic plants and, for his family line to continue, he must beget a son by sexual union with a woman whom marriage has taken from her primitive state to be domesticated by establishing her in the conjugal home. Owing to this need for balance in Greek

sacrifice, the sacrificer and the god, although associated in the rite, do not as a rule intermingle; they are kept at a distance, neither too close nor too far apart.

That this powerful theology, indissolubly linked to a social system in its way of setting up barriers between man and what is not man, of defining his relations with what is above and below man, should be found on the level of dietary procedures explains why the peculiarities of diet among Orphics and Pythagoreans, on the one hand, and of some Dionysiac practices, on the other, have real theological significance and express wide divergences of religious approach. Vegetarianism, abstention from the eating of flesh, is a refusal of the sanguinary sacrifice, which is likened to the murder of one's kin.

Omophagia, the *diasparagmos* of the Bacchants—that is, the devouring of the raw flesh of an animal hunted down and torn apart alive—is the reversal of the normal values of sacrifice. But if one circumvents sacrifice from above by consuming only absolutely undefiled food or by existing on odors only, or if one subverts it from below by destroying, through the removal of the barriers between men and beasts, the distinctions between them imposed by sacrifice, it becomes possible to attain a state of total communion that can be taken just as easily as a return to the tender familiarity of all creatures in the Golden Age or as a descent into the chaos and confusion of savagery. It is in any event a question of establishing, either by individual asceticism or by collective frenzy, a type of relationship with the deity that official religion, through its sacrificial procedures, denies and bans. It is equally true that through inverted methods with contrary implications, the customary separations of sacrificer, victim, and deity become confused and blurred and finally disappear.[7]

This interpretation still seems valid, but we would like to enhance its justification by means of a special case. There exists an Athenian ritual that exemplifies the institution's nature and that clearly brings out many of the internal tensions within Greek sacrifice. This particular sacrifice is called the Bouphonia, and in it the Greeks have in some sense overtly dramatized the paradox of a self-negating slaughter, abolishing itself when transposed to a ritual, and transcending itself so it may enter into culture and found the religious, civic, and human order. The term Bouphonia means "murder of the ox" and hence from the outset already calls in question the division between murder and sacrifice. The victim chosen is a yoked ox rather than a beast that was spared the yoke. By sacrificing a faithful working companion, a creature that is, broadly speaking, a member of the household like a relative or domestic slave, the boundary that normally separated humans from animals was blurred. We know that in Greece wild beasts were not normally sacrificed. They were killed without scruple like enemies in the hunt. The meat, therefore, from this ritualized slaughter—sacrifice—belongs exclusively to domes-

---

[7] *Leçon inaugurale au Collège de France* (Paris, 1976) (reprinted in *Religions, histoires, raisons* [Paris, 1979], 22–23), translated as "Greek Religion, Ancient Religions," above, chap. 16.

tic species: pigs, goats, sheep, and cattle. These animals, however, are not situated on the same level. If certain Pythagoreans refused to eat any of them, other members of the sect were less intransigent and differentiated between, first, cattle and sheep, which are too close to men to slaughter without committing a crime, and second, pigs and goats, distant enough to be put to death without fear of pollution. At the summit of this hierarchy of domestic animals, the plough ox occupies a totally separate position. It is so close to man, so integrated into his universe, that the ox is situated outside the ordinary sacrificial sphere. To sacrifice a plough ox is already in itself anomalous and threatens to subvert the whole ritual and its internal logic. Thus an immolation of this kind of victim is likely to be interpreted by the Greeks as a testing of the validity of sacrificial practice. Through the extremes of its content and its borderline status, the sacrifice of a plough ox functions as a touchstone for the equilibrium of the entire system. Aetiological myths that recount the origin of things and explain the circumstances of their foundation also serve to reveal symbolic operations enacted in ritual that transform the violence of murder into a pious participation in civilized life. Meat, too, as Plutarch shows, undergoes the same process that at the end of the ritual transforms a piece of raw, bloody, and impure flesh, newly cut from the victim, into fully human nourishment, thereby binding together those who eat the sacrifice through a common form of cultivated food.[8]

The most valuable passage on this subject, because it is the fullest and most detailed, is found in the second book of *De abstinentia*. This passage in Porphyry, borrowed from Theophrastus, has been extensively commented on by Jean-Louis Durand from a perspective akin to our own.[9] Without recounting every detail of his analysis, we would like to add a few remarks to Porphyry's text, eloquent enough in itself, that relate directly to our problem. (The translated text is appended to the end of this piece.)

(1) Relying on what Theophrastus reports of the foundation of the Athenian Bouphonia, Porphyry's aim is to show that "men must neither soil the altars of the gods through murder, nor must they touch such food [animal meat] any more than the body of their own kind [alimentary flesh thus being assimilated to anthropophagy]." The practice, still preserved in Athens, would have a didactic value (*paraggelma*), although in actual fact, the lesson revealed in Theophrastus's account goes in exactly the opposite direction. Not only is a plough ox sacrificed each year on the Acropolis to the greatest god of the pantheon, Zeus Polieus in his function as the city's divinity, but all the citizens, in order to conform to Apollo's order given through the Pythian oracle, are obliged to communally partake of the victim's flesh. The paradox goes even further. If there is indeed a murder at the beginning of the story, with a

[8] Plut., *Quaest. Rom.* 109, 289e–f; cf. Detienne and Vernant, *La cuisine de sacrifice*.
[9] "Le corps du délit," *Communications* 26 (1977): 46–61.

victim (the ox), and a culprit (the murderer)—a stranger called Sopatros of uncertain status, who, after having acted on his own in a fit of rage, finds himself guilty and subsequently goes into exile—at the end of the story with the official institution of the rite and the legal procedure for judging the murder, all the participants in the ritual suddenly disappear. First, the murderer vanishes, because once Sopatros has acquired citizenship on his return to Athens, there is no longer a guilty party. Second, the victim's body: "the ox is put back on its feet in the course of the same sacrifice that had taken its life," and thus there is no more victim. Thirdly, the feeling that a crime was committed is lost, because the Pythia orders the ox's flesh to be eaten, "without any scruple." Finally, the instruments are likewise disposed of: the murderous ax is "forgotten" by the text when it recounts the final judgment on the participants, just as it eliminates the man who used it to strike the animal, while the knife is sent to the bottom of the sea with whatever else is felt to be guilty.

(2) Through its silences, affirmations, and semantic ploys, the text proceeds to efface both the murder and the crime according to the same narrative progression, which, starting from a prepolitical situation (i.e., a kind of social confusion), constructs the city of Athens, with its plowed land, town, acropolis, religious rites and priesthoods, communal feasts, law, and status of citizenship.

(3) In primordial times, when the ox is assassinated by an outsider to the society in a moment of subjective anger, the animal is neither eaten nor sacrificed. Its bones are not burned for the gods. How could they be? In those "ancient times" animals were not offered in sacrifice, but only those cakes and types of cereal dough that the ox himself would devour at the altar. An eater of cakes, excluded from sacrifice, forbidden for human consumption, the ox in this primordial era is not yet truly separated from man. Once dead, it is buried by its assassin, who gives it the same funeral honors as a man would receive. It is only at the foundation of rituals, when men, for their part, have authentically become citizens, that the ox is alienated from them and allowed to fall into the category of animals to be sacrificed and eaten. Through this gap, the animal's status, especially that of an edible animal, undergoes a metamorphosis. At first, in its proximity to man, the ox has no place in the dietary code. It devours and tramples the grains it ought to be helping to make grow for men, and the crop, whose first fruits are reserved exclusively for the gods, it turns into animal fodder. When buried in the earth, like a man, it hides in its belly the barley seeds it has swallowed, thus blocking the normal growth of the grain. At the end of the narrative, the ox, placed in its position of sacrificial victim, is gutted of its meat, and becomes sacrificial food for human consumption once it has been stripped of its bones, which are piously burned over the altar for the gods. It is filled up, this time, with straw—the true animal food—and not with barley. Finally, it is hauled back on all fours, stuffed with hay, as if it were alive, and harnessed to a cart. On every level, therefore, its dietary vocation is confirmed in the context of religious life and organized

politics. A provider of meat for men and of bones and fat burned for the gods once it has been ritually slaughtered, the animal, now associated with agricultural labor, appears also as a producer of grain. This is the grain that has been cooked three times and that, together with the cooked meat of domestic animals slaughtered according to the ritual, establishes man in the place that, according to the Greeks, constitutes the space of human civilized life, in a two-fold distance from beasts and from gods.

If the act of slaying lies at the heart of the *thusia*, it resides there like a subversive threat that is repeatedly conjured away. It is a defect against which care is taken to construct and organize the delicate balance of a rite which embeds life in death. It admits that we must slaughter animals in order to eat, yet at the same time it aims to banish acts of murder and savagery from what is human.

· · ·

Porphyry, DE ABSTINENTIA
Book 2.28.4–2.30

28. For we are not bound to stain the altars of the gods with gore. Humans should not touch such victuals just as they do not touch the bodies of their own kind. But the precept which is preserved still at Athens should be kept in each of our lives.

29. In antiquity, as I said before, humans sacrificed grain to the gods, not animals, and they did not use them for their own nourishment. At a public sacrifice in Athens, one of the oxen coming in from the fields is said to have eaten some of the meal in honeyed oil and the incense and to have trampled all over the rest. A certain Diomos or Sopatros, not a native but someone farming in Attica, became enraged at what had happened. He seized an ax that was being sharpened nearby and struck the ox. The ox died. When the man recovered from his anger and realized what he had done, he buried the ox and went of his own accord into exile in Crete as one who had committed impiety. Then the rain stopped falling, and the grain no longer grew. Delegates were sent by the state to Delphi to inquire of Apollo. The Pythia responded that the exile in Crete would redeem these conditions: avenge the murder and resurrect the dead in the same sacrifice in which it died, and things would be better for those who tasted the dead and did not hold back.

A search was undertaken, and the man responsible for the deed was discovered. Sopatros reckoned that he would be released from the unpleasantness of being polluted if they all did these measures in common. He told those who came to him that the ox must be slain by the city. Since they were at wit's end over who would be the slayer, he offered them this possibility: if they made him a citizen, they would share the murder with him. Agreement was reached on those terms. When they came back to the city, they arranged the affair in the way in which it remains today.

30. They chose girls to bring the water. They fetched the water used for sharpening the ax and knife. After sharpening, one man administered the ax, another struck the ox, and a third cut its throat. They next skinned it, and everyone tasted the ox. Afterwards, having sewn up the hide of the ox and stuffed it with hay, they set it up again with the same stance as when it was alive and yoked it to the plow as if ready for work. Assembling a trial for murder, they summoned all who had participated in the deed to defend themselves. The water fetchers charged that the sharpeners were more to blame than they. The sharpeners said the same about the ax-administrator, and this one of the throat-cutter, and this one of the knife which, being without a voice, was condemned to murder.

From that time to the present always during the festival of Zeus Polieus on the Acropolis at Athens those mentioned above perform the sacrifice of the ox in the same way. Having placed meal in a honeyed oil and cakes of ground barley on a bronze table, they drive around it selected oxen. Whichever takes a taste is struck. The families of those who perform these rites exist today. Those descended from Sopatros, who struck the ox, are all called Ox-Smiters. Those descended from the one who drove the ox around are called Prodders. Those descended from the slaughterer they named Carvers because the feast came from the distribution of the meat. They filled up the hide, whenever they were brought to court, and threw the knife into the sea.

Translated by T. Taylor (Oxford, 1913)

Chapter 18

SPEECH AND MUTE SIGNS

DESCARTES'S well-known dictum about "good sense" could just as well be said of divination—that it is the most widely distributed commodity in the world. Throughout the course of human history, there is no society that in its own way has not known and practiced it. In inviting historians of the great civilizations of the past to compare the various oracular techniques of different societies, our purpose was to examine jointly the various forms assumed by this divinatory intelligence. But were we then not running the risk of repeating the work of documentation that others have already done so well?[1]

In reality, our project was both less vast and more ambitious. Our claim was not to present a quasi-exhaustive chart of those divinatory norms catalogued by specialists in diverse civilizations. We intended instead to take some pertinent cases for comparison to attempt to reply to two fundamental questions we thought were raised by divination, if we approached it in its dual dimensions as a mental attitude and a social institution. What, on one hand, can be implied about the nature of the intellectual operations that take place during the stages of an oracular consultation; what defines the logic of the system that is activated by the seer in order to decipher the unseen and answer its consultants' requests? In short, what type of rationality is expressed in the game of divinatory procedure, the apparatus of oracular techniques and symbolisms, and the classificatory frameworks used by the seer to sort out, organize, manipulate, and interpret the information on which his competence is based? On the other hand, what position and function does a particular society assign to oracular knowledge? Because prophetic science is practiced on occasions when a choice, or important choices, need to be made and because it determines decisions, both public and private, how far does its field of application extend and what are the areas of social life subject to its authority? Where on these levels are we to situate the relations of the seer to other figures such as the king, priest, and judge, who, in their roles, also have a power of decision?[2]

This piece, "Parole et signes muets," originally appeared as the introduction to a collective volume entitled *Divination et rationalité* (Paris, 1974), and is reproduced here with the kind permission of Le Seuil. Translated by Froma I. Zeitlin.

[1] See especially the series of studies assembled in two volumes by André Caquot and Marcel Leibovici, *La divination* (Paris, 1968).

[2] These are the kinds of questions posed by A. Adler and A. Zempleni in their investigation of divination among the Moundang of Chad: "The question to be asked is what is the nature of the intellectual procedure that it [divination] implies and what is there in it of knowledge that it puts

It might have been presumed in advance that these two types of questions were interdependent. In societies in which divination is not, as it is in our own, considered a marginal, even aberrant phenomenon, where it constitutes a normal, regular, often even obligatory procedure, the logic of oracular systems is no more foreign to the mind of the public than is the incontestable value of the seer's function. Divinatory rationality in these civilizations does not form a separate sector, an isolated mentality, contrasted with modes of reasoning that regulate the practice of law, administration, politics, medicine, or daily life; it is coherently included in the entire body of social thought and, in its intellectual processes, it observes similar norms, just as the seer's status in the functional hierarchy seems very closely linked with those other social agents responsible for collective life. Without this dual approach that integrates divinatory intelligence into ordinary mentality and the seers' functions into the social organization, divination could not fulfill the role ascribed to it by functionalist anthropologists: an official instance of legitimation that, at a time when choices are fraught with consequences for group equilibrium, offers decisions that are socially "objective," that is, independent of the desires of the parties at issue and benefiting from a general consensus of the social body that puts this type of response above dispute.[3]

Our agenda was then to investigate the reasons for this consensus in cases where they could be most clearly observed. Relying on certain civilizations where divination held the tightest grip, both in its extent and in its high degree of elaboration, the idea was to show how the seer's symbolic operations and the mental system underlying them could have imposed both their kind of rationality on the intellectual plane and their legitimacy on the social one.

II

Given this perspective, the question might have been whether the Hellenists were in the best position and the best equipped to launch the investigation and set out a program of research. The status of divination in ancient Greece appears uncertain and ambiguous in all respects. If the forms of oracular consultation, practiced in one or another place, were very diverse, we do not have documents at our disposal that in either number or exactitude are comparable to those we can find, for example, in the Chinese and Mesopotamian worlds.

---

into play. . . . Since it is, above all, a social institution meant to guide the choices of individuals as well as of the community in order to make all kinds of decisions . . . we must examine its relations with political and religious powers." *Le bâton de l'aveugle: Divination, maladie, et pouvoir chez les Moundang du Tchad* (Paris, 1973), 12.

[3] Cf. E. E. Evans-Pritchard, *Witchcraft, Oracles, and Magic among the Azanda* (Oxford, 1937); G. Park, "Divination and Its Social Contexts," *Journal of the Royal Anthropological Institute* 93 (1963): 195–209; V. W. Turner, *The Drums of Affliction* (Oxford, 1963); Gluckman, Max, ed., *The Allocation of Responsibility* (Manchester, 1972).

Most of all, we are not dealing with organized systems, with a body of doc-trines recorded in treatises. We do not even have precise information about the functioning of that oracle par excellence, the one whose renown and prestige eclipsed all others and whose authority, starting from the eighth century, was established over the entire Hellenic world: the oracle of Delphi. Were the questions prepared and submitted in advance or formulated on the spot at the moment of the consultation? Were they always expressed in the form of an alternative, of a choice between two solutions, as seems to have been the rule at Dodona, or could they assume different forms according to the individual case? In what sense, on the other hand, was the Pythia inspired? If she proph-esied in a true state of trance, the sounds and words she uttered in her delirium, if they were to be intelligible, ought to have been submitted for translation to a college of priests, a body of "prophets" whose task it was to interpret and edit the response of the oracle. If, on the contrary, the Pythia replied directly to the consultant, one might suppose she spoke calmly and that the presence of the god whose breath inspired her manifested itself in her without, however, disorienting her words or her mind. Were these responses given in prose or in verse, recorded in writing or transmitted orally? Were they explicit and clear, as certain documents lead us to suppose, or enigmatic and ambiguous, as the entire literary tradition declares? Since it seems finally indisputable that cler-omancy always occupied a place at Delphi, what was the association between consultation by lot and inspired divination? Was it a question of two indepen-dent techniques, each used by separate personnel, or of two moments, two levels of the same oracular practice? Did the Pythia begin by "shaking" and consulting the lots before prophesying out loud just like certain African vi-sionaries, also possessed by spirits (such as the *na sa iwa so* discussed by Retel-Laurentin in this collective volume), who use "mechanical" or "alea-tory" procedures to support the revelations they then transmit in words? So many questions remain that Hellenists today still cannot answer with any de-gree of assurance and that affects any full interpretation we might hope to offer of the Delphic oracular scenario and its intellectual components.[4]

Furthermore, the deficiencies in our information are due, at least in part, to the fact that the place of the seer in Greece is not so rigorously fixed, nor is the authority of divination so firmly established, as in other civilizations. In the Homeric world organized around great noble families and royal houses, the seer is a professional, a *dēmiourgos* who is summoned to the household when needed, just as one calls a carpenter, doctor, or bard and who, like them, puts his technical competence at the disposition of the public (*Od.* 17.382–85). In some sense, he remains a stranger in the house, where he resides for a time in service, a guest who is never wholly integrated into the family group. If, dur-

---

[4] Cf. P. Amandry, *La mantique apollinienne à Delphes: Essai sur le fonctionnement de l'oracle* (Paris, 1950); M. Delcourt, *L'oracle de Delphes* (Paris, 1955).

ing the archaic period, seers are marginal in the sphere of domestic life, they also do not comprise an organized body with institutional structures and norms. Even if there are *genē*, lineages of seers, like those of singers, they are not grouped into brotherhoods whose status, on a scale of functions and honors, would be clearly and univocally defined. Their competence, moreover, like that of all other demiurges, is limited. They do not hold the privilege of a knowledge that would give them a sort of intellectual monopoly in the group by making them the repositories of a vast system of knowledge, inaccessible to the common run of men and indispensable for collective life. Even when we come to the territory of their particular skills, seers sufficiently resemble other personages for there not always to be a clear line of demarcation between their respective roles. In some ways their role verges on that of the priest who, in fulfillment of his sacrificial tasks, is called on to interpret the signs displayed by the flames, smoke, and entrails. When seers exercise their art for curative ends, by revealing ancient buried sins in order to purify them, they move into an area where they meet up with the physician. Last of all, there are the bards, who with divine inspiration are capable, like prophets, of seeing beyond appearances into the invisible, singing as if everything past and future were present in the here and now.

In the classical period too, in other forms, these fluctuating and somewhat marginal facets of divination are just as evident. Under the city's rule, all important communal decisions—whether they concern the political domain and are taken in the assemblies, or whether they apply to the administration of law and are adopted in the court precincts—all of these, from now on, put a similar mechanism of choice into play. The options from which to choose become the object of an explicit confrontation in the course of public and conflictual debate. They take the form of opposing speeches which, if victory is to be won, must succeed in convincing the audience through argument and a refutation of the contrary proposal. Decision making thus relies on verbal procedures of discussion that derive from a rationality that could be called rhetorical or dialectical; it is based on a logic of persuasive argument, wholly alien in its principles and spirit to the divinatory mentality. In the context of the *polis*, divination, whether exercised privately or on the occasion of certain official functions, can only have a minor and accessory role. From this point of view, it is noteworthy that in classical Greece we find oracular activity concentrated for the most part around the great sanctuaries, whose Panhellenic character relegates them to the margins of the city. They are outside the institutional framework that defines the civic community and that, with free discussion and the right to vote, makes each of its members a fully participating citizen in all the processes of decision concerning public affairs.

What the city-states expect from the oracle when they dispatch a delegation of *theōroi* for official consultation is, in almost all the known cases, a matter of counsels or prescriptions of a religious sort: foundation of cults, seers, and heroes; regulations for sacrifices, offerings, and dedications; management of sacred domains; purificatory procedures for murders, suicides, or major sacrileges and pollutions; measures to take and rituals to institute in expiation of a natural calamity or of an epidemic; and in time, consecration, through the oracle's consent, of an institutional or legislative reform. Whatever conjunctions there may have been at various moments between divination and politics (e.g., when collections of oracles, real or fictive, were used by Spartan kings and Athenian tyrants as instruments of their personal projects and ambitions), they each belong to different levels of social practice. They are too sharply divided and the opposition too marked between their kinds of rationality for the conflict not to be openly expressed in the reflections of those who, in their intellectual activity, entered into the same territory of knowledge in more or less direct competition with oracles and seers. These are, first of all, of course, sophists and philosophers, but they are also historians, doctors, and wise men. In professing to teach the art of rhetoric that could give the power to win the decision on any debated question, what else did the sophists finally claim, if not to substitute a secular technique for an oracular type of procedure, one wholly different but equally efficacious, which, in the sectors where it was applied, corresponded to a similar final result?

Divination is not only challenged and, as it were, repressed by the *polis* at the institutional level in the rules of exercising power and administering justice. It becomes the subject of dispute in theoretical terms about different forms of thought. These were worked out by those new types of intellectuals we see appearing in Greece from the sixth to the fifth centuries, and who, in the fourth century, through the schools they founded for dispensing their instruction, are led to claim, for themselves, their disciples, and the informed audience to whom they address themselves, the privilege of acceding to true knowledge. Some of them draw the conclusion, in fact, that they are, at least by right, the only ones qualified to advise rulers or even to take their place and personally direct affairs of state.

In the picture we get of Greece, these conflicts of competence and confrontations of rationality within the same culture confuse the clear image of divination that emerges when the words of an oracle are accepted without question. Nevertheless, these disputes have the advantage of drawing attention to the most often misunderstood aspect of the problem. In its official and institutionalized forms, divination always implies an appropriation of more or less advanced knowledge by a restricted group of specialists—a knowledge the gods themselves guarantee. What then is the attitude of the social body toward the keepers of a knowledge that, at its extreme, lays claim to omniscience? What position is assigned to them in the game of competing influences and powers? Their competence may vary to a greater or lesser degree according to the case, but in what ways do we find it channeled into certain sectors? How is it subordinated to and used by those who resort to another kind of prestige and authority? The fundamental question that emerges from an investigation, like ours, into divinatory practice is finally one of the relations between Knowledges and Powers in "traditional" ancient or archaic societies.

Two studies in this collective volume are more specifically concerned with these problems, even though they approach them from different angles. For the first, it is a matter of defining the status of divination in a thinker like Plato, who represents both the triumph of the new philosophical rationality and what Louis Gernet called "an imperialism of the intellectual."[5] Plato is convinced that his knowledge makes him one of the chosen, a *theios aner*, a divine man, who is called on to revive in another form the mythic figure of the King-Magician, certain that his mastery of religious secrets and his possession of superior faculties equip him to govern in sovereignty over his peers. From this point of view, it would seem that divination no longer has its place, that it is condemned on all levels, banished now from power by the process itself that excludes it from knowledge. Yet matters are far less simple. To the extent that divination is a technique claiming to apply human reason to the interpretation of signs sent by the gods, Plato sees it as illusion and error; politicians can only be taken in by these chicaneries. But to the extent that divination is not about signs and does not involve intelligence, when it is just a matter of inspired words, then it implies the gods taking charge over men. In this case, divination is shown, of course, to be unreason and madness, but it is a divine madness, which, in default of that true knowledge only the philosopher can bring to rulers, allows politics in some way to be implanted in the world beyond, anchored in a universe other than that of sensible existence and material interests. If this is a domain that respects the philosopher's victorious rationalism, it is also scrupulously conservative in the area of religious practices to which divination belongs, and it does so because it recognizes in the irrational a kind of trace left there by the world of ideal Forms.

It is not sufficient, then, just to disqualify divination in Plato on the plane of rational knowledge or to substitute philosophy when it comes to the exercise of power. Divination must also be retrieved and reintegrated in its anthropological and political system, channeled, and above all, displaced to the realm of "intermediate" reality that, being neither that of the intelligible nor that of the sensible categories, cannot refer back to truth without also belonging to error.

The problem of the repression of divination in the Roman Empire in the fourth century of our era, which is treated later in this collective volume, is in some sense the reverse. We are no longer dealing with the figure of the philosopher, who, in his picture of the ideal city where only Knowledge qualifies for sovereignty, was compelled to find a place for divination, even though it still had to be excluded from true knowledge. We are in the presence of an emperor whose power also claims to be total and absolute, like that of the philosopher-

[5] *Anthropologie de la Grèce antique* (Paris, 1968), 428.

king, but in another way, guaranteed by the gods and inscribed in the cosmic order. If the Empire persecutes and forbids divination in all its forms and treats it just like magic, it is not because it is false or because it has links with the irrational. Rather, it is because it can jeopardize the state through its very efficaciousness. Because it stems from the same type of rationality as that invoked by the power to establish and confirm political legitimacy, it may interfere dangerously on any occasion, even a minor one, where it appears. Plato condemned private divination and only accepted it to the extent that, when exercised for public use, it was conducted in this framework, under the control and in the interests of a state whose organization and ends were fixed by reason. In divination, the Empire represses an enterprise that is all the more pernicious because it is the one most closely connected to the public interest. If it finally forbids even the most harmless consultation, carried out on purely personal and private grounds, if it makes it a crime against the state and an offense of treason, this is because, by its very principles and orientation, divinatory procedure is practiced on a territory that touches on the foundations of power. To scrutinize the future and decipher celestial signs is to gain access to that secret zone where one can read the life and death of the emperor, the destiny itself of the Empire, because these are figured there in written form for all time. The repression of divination in the Theodosian code is not essentially due to religious motives, to Christian influence, since pagan emperors had already done it. Repression answers to the needs of state. It is the totalitarian character of power that makes intolerable the organization of a form of knowledge that bears, not on abstractions, but on the real course of events, and whose internal logic impels it, when faced with power, to make itself into total knowledge. Christianity only further justified the state's repression by adding the support of a religion that rejected all oracular practices as the Devil's work and condemned in divination a "curiositas" deemed impious with regard to a future over whose providential paths God and only God can rule.

On this point, it is tempting, for purposes of comparison, to refer to the conclusions of a study conducted in a wholly different context by Adler and Zempleni on divination among the Moundang of Chad. What interested them was how the Moundang handled the oracular procedures of Kindani, based on geomancy, so as to diminish their importance. In restricting its forms, the Moundang found a way of averting the threat to their social order if the appropriation of knowledge should become too complete. "Moundang society," they observe, "thus avoids a knowledge whose unlimited extension would require an all-knowing and all-powerful subject, served by a class of priests and wise men who would claim for themselves a part of this omniscience and omnipotence. . . . It certainly looks as though Moundang society has found it useful to guard against a knowledge which would take advantage of the privilege of truth in order to dictate what group decisions ought to be."[6]

---

[6] Adler and Zempleni, *Le bâton de l'aveugle*, 213.

III

Knowledge of particular events, careers of individual lives that aspire to total knowledge[7]—it is this double ambition that sustains divinatory intelligence and gives its procedures a paradoxical character. Divination is concerned with sequences of particular facts that require consultation precisely because of their aleatory nature. With the procedures it applies to them, divination handles these facts according to a general logic that leads to the exclusion of chance from the frame of events. The idea is to suppress the uncertain and unpredictable in relations of temporal succession by interpreting them on the model of structural relations of homology and correspondence that can be noted and located in a segment of space. To decipher these spatial configurations, divination retains and isolates certain objects that are given the symbolic values of a microcosm: tortoise shells, viscera of sacrificed animals, figures traced haphazardly on sand, areas defined and directed according to certain rules, visible parts of the sky, aspects of the face and body, and combinations of dice, shells, or cards.[8] And, from the internal agency of these objects or collections of objects, which it takes as small-scale reflections of the total cosmic order, divination infers secure conclusions about events whose outcome, whether desired or feared by the consultant, is always, by definition, uncertain at the start. If the omniscience claimed by the seer were to be fully realized, it would eclipse the function itself of divination, its practical purpose, as well as the chancy character of events, for the consultant does not expect the oracle to predict a future that is already inexorably fixed. Rather the oracle is to indicate, in a particular instance, what one must or must not do in order for matters to turn out to one's advantage and for the most favorable outcomes to be realized. Divinatory systems are thus founded on equilibrations, of greater or lesser stability, between opposite poles that are sustained in a kind of constant tension. On the one hand, there is the formal frame, the logical structures, and a grammar activated with a view to a complete and rigorous codification of the event or the specific fact; on the other, there is the multiplicity of concrete situations in all their diversity and variability, about which someone has come to question the oracle and which the response must allow to be modified in the direction desired by the consultant.[9]

[7] Cf. the remarks of R. Bastide on divination as a science of events in "La connaissance de l'évènement," in George Balandier et al., eds., *Perspectives de la sociologie contemporaine: Hommage à Georges Gurvitch* (Paris, 1968), 159–68.

[8] Cf. J.-P. Vernant, "La divination: Contexte et sens psychologique des rites et des doctrines," *Journal de psychologie* (1948): 299–325.

[9] As an example of a rigorous analysis of a formal system that regulates the combination of figures used in a type of learned divination, such as Arab geomancy, see R. Jaulin, *La géomancie: Analyse formelle* (Paris, 1966). On the problems posed by applying this formal framework to concrete situations on which the seer must speak, on the different means used to introduce "play" into the system, such as alluding to the many figures of symbolic tales, known by heart and recited

On this level too, the Greek case is instructive by its particularities and also perhaps because of its deficiencies and inadequacies from the perspective of divinatory logic. The Greeks valorized oral divination; rather than techniques of interpreting signs or aleatory procedures like the throw of the dice, considered by them to be minor forms, they preferred what Crahay calls the oracular dialogue, in which the deity's word replies directly to the questions of the consultant. This preeminence of the word as a means of communication with the world beyond is in keeping with the fundamentally oral character of a civilization in which not only is writing a recent phenomenon by comparison to the Near East and China, but, in its entirely phonetic character, it extends the spoken language and is aligned with it. The reason is that writing reproduces sounds instead of using graphic signs to display the realities themselves, and this too is the aim of speech in its own way. In this context, the written word acquires an import that is altogether new. It is no longer the specialty of a category of "wise men," who, because of it, deploy a privileged means of access to knowledge of the real, a technique that permits both the symbolic expression of things in their essential qualities and the deciphering of the universe. Writing becomes an instrument of divulgence put at the service of what is now a common culture. It publicizes and allows everyone to see all facets of knowledge that the word had previously reserved for closed and privileged groups. The development of a written literature replaces the traditional forms of oral expression and in the Greek world goes together with advancements in political, historical, medical, philosophical, and scientific thought, advancements that sanction the rupture with a divinatory mentality. In some sense, divination itself is then attracted into the field of the new rationality of discourse. By contrast to the interpretation of signs or procedures of technical divination that require the services of a specialized seer, the god's oracular word, once formulated, is, like every other word, accessible to each individual. In order to understand it, there is no need for a particular competence in divination; it is sufficient that whoever piously comes to consult the oracle has the same qualities of sane reflection, levelheadedness, and moderation that characterize the good citizen and, with the addition of shrewdness and acuity, serve political ends. In the different explanations the oracular response elicits, it can even become the object of the same kind of argumentative debate used in assemblies and law courts. No text is more vivid in this respect than the story of the "wooden wall" recounted by Herodotus (7.140–45).

Before the invasion of Xerxes' Persian armies, the Athenians sent a dele-

---

by the seer, some of which will prove relevant in the course of the consultation, and resort to historical data that can be used by analogy to find a solution in a particular case submitted for divinatory inquiry, cf. R. Bastide, "La connaissance de l'évènement," 161–62. More generally, on the "ruses" of the seer that allow him to adjust his code "to the more or less specific information he has about the situation of his consultants," cf. Adler and Zempleni, *Le bâton de l'aveugle*, 129ff.

gation of *theōroi* (envoys) to consult at Delphi. Before they had even made any inquiries, the Pythia foretold catastrophes to come. Dismayed, the *theōroi* decided to solicit a new consultation and to beg, as suppliants, for a more favorable response, threatening to remain in the temple where they were until they died. The Pythia agreed then to prophesy again: "Zeus grants to Trito-geneia [Athena]," she declared, "that only a rampart of wood will be invincible, and it will help you and your children. But await not the cavalry and land army which are coming in a mass from the continent, nor be still; withdraw, turn your backs; a day will come again when you will meet the enemy face-to-face." To these words of comfort the Pythia added an allusion to Salamis, a point to which, along with Herodotus, we will have occasion to return. The *theōroi* carefully edited the response they received before going back to Athens. And here is how the Greek historian presents the sequel to this affair of the oracle, which is also an affair of state:

> When they had returned and had made their report to the assembly of the people, and many opinions were expressed to explain the oracle, and two especially were opposed; some of the older men said that, in their opinion, the god specified that the Acropolis would escape disaster, for in earlier times the Acropolis of Athens was fortified with a "thorn-hedge"; they therefore supposed that this was "the wooden wall"; others, on the contrary, said that it was the ships the god meant, and they urged that everything should be abandoned in favor of the immediate preparation of a fleet. Now those who insisted that the ships were the "wooden wall" were embarrassed by the last two verses the Pythia had uttered: "O divine Salamis, you will bring death to women's sons / When the corn is scattered, or the harvest gathered in." Because of these two verses, the opinion of those who identified ships and "wooden wall" was strongly contested, since the soothsayers [*chrēsmologoi*] took these words in the sense that, if the Greeks were to prepare for a naval battle, they would be defeated in the waters of Salamis. Now there was at Athens a man who had newly arrived in the ranks of the first citizens; his name was Themistocles, son of Neocles. This man disputed the accuracy of the soothsayers' interpretation. If the prophecy, he observed, really referred to the Athenians, the god, in his opinion, would not have used, as he did, such a mild term: "Unfortunate Salamis," he would have said, and not "divine Salamis," if the inhabitants were doomed to perish in the waters of this island; but for whoever rightly interpreted the oracle, it was the enemies the god had in mind and not the Athenians. Themistocles therefore advised them to prepare for a naval combat, understanding in this sense that it was the wooden wall. The Athenians, when he disclosed this advice to them, judged it preferable to that of the soothsayers, who did not want them to consider naval combat or even, to put it briefly, to mount any resistance, but advised them to abandon Attica altogether and seek a home elsewhere.

Herodotus adds that already in the past, in circumstances where it was not a question of interpreting the oracle but of how best to use the public funds that came from the silver mines of Laurion, Themistocles had succeeded both in having his views prevail in the assembly and in directing Athenian policy in a way to ensure its victory, that of maritime supremacy. This is the same type of political intelligence, the same clear-sighted shrewdness deployed by the man of state to decipher the obscure words of the oracle, think up a strategy suitable for the circumstances, and find the appropriate arguments to convince the *démos* to decide in his favor. It is highly significant that Themistocles, according to Herodotus, had had the opinion of the soothsayers against him, who, although not seers and certainly not exegetes of the state, still, in comparison to a man of politics, look just like specialists in interpreting oracular texts. If the soothsayers are finally defeated, it is because the discussion about the oracle not only takes place in broad daylight, in public, as required for a problem of common interest, but because it appeals to the same order of argumentation as every other question debated in the Assembly and because the decision that marks the end of an oracular consultation at Delphi, its practical conclusion, is, in this last case, fixed by a majority vote of the citizens.

This convergence between the god's word in the oracle and the human word in the Assembly, both stemming from the same type of intelligibility, is expressed in a particularly striking way in the analogy between the formulas used for posing questions to the oracle and those for composing the decisions of a circumstantial kind decreed by the people in the Assembly. The oracle is not asked to predict the future, to announce what is to come; it is questioned before embarking on the course that seems best, in order to know whether it is licit or forbidden and, in cases where it is forbidden, to find out what suitable action can be taken to have some chance of getting access to it. What is expected, therefore, from the god is not a prediction that would actualize the event in some way before it comes about, but a guarantee, an agreement on the brink of an undertaking, attesting to the fact that it is not going to contravene the invisible order instituted by supernatural powers. To make its object as specific as possible, this inquiry about what the gods permit or advise on the occasion of a definite project naturally tends to be formulated in terms of a comparison between two contrasting options that are submitted to the god for his decision as to which of the two will guarantee the maximum advantages. The oracle is asked in which of the two situations being considered success is more likely and the best results obtainable. What is expected from the oracle, therefore, is that it fix an order of preference between possible choices, by taking account, in its judgment, of factors that human intelligence cannot evaluate. The situation in the debates of the Assembly is similar. There again it is a question in a given situation of estimating, in the face of two opposite points of view, the advantages that can be reasonably counted on for each of them, and thus judging which of the two it seems reasonable to prefer

over the other. The decrees do not say "the city decides or orders that . . . ,"
but "it has pleased the council and the people," i.e., "the Council and the
people have considered it best, it seemed preferable to them to. . . ." And it
is the same formula once again that Herodotus uses in the controversy between
Themistocles and the soothsayers on the alternate interpretations of the oracle
about the "wooden wall": the Athenians judged his advice "preferable" to
that of his opponents.

In oracular practice, such as was actually exercised in the classical period,
the response itself of the god seems to have slipped into the binary model
suggested by the question. The reply resolves a dilemma and indicates clearly
which of the proposed options ought to bring the best results and prove the
most useful. On this ground of the "preferable" and in the area of practical
counsels and of prescriptions that are most often of a religious kind—those
defined as the ordinary competence of divination—there is no trace of the
equivocal or ambiguous in the oracle's response.

But there exists another "model" of divination, attested throughout all of
written literature, from Herodotus to the philosophers and including the tragic
poets, that should not be considered an artificial creation just because it probably originated in an oral tradition passed down from the archaic age to popular circles.[10] In this "theoretical" representation of divinatory activity that
the *polis* seems to have made very early on, the words of the inspired prophet
and of the oracle no longer have value only as advice, encouragement, or
admonition on the threshold of action: they imply a true omniscience, founded
on the gift of double sight and on a direct contact with the invisible and the
beyond. This suprahuman knowledge confers on its possessor the power of
encompassing a totality of time at each and every moment, and of seeing, as
though before his eyes, everything that was and will be. Conceived in this
way, divination is directed at a coming event (or sometimes at a past event,
also unknown to the living, when its consequences still weigh on today's and
tomorrow's existence); it is, in the proper sense, a pre-diction of the future,
the formulation of a destiny for both individuals and groups. Divination thus
seems to be bound up with a conception of destiny it already knows in its own
way, the implications of which regarding the relations of human time and
divine omniscience the philosophers will undertake to sort out. In the perspective of a predictive divination, fate is inscribed in and plays on two different
planes at the same time. On the plane of human existence, it is discovered
little by little, as it happens, through the vicissitudes of events whose apparently incoherent succession only takes on meaning and becomes intelligible at
its end, when all is definitively accomplished. On the divine plane, the reverse
is true: each one's fate is sealed from the start, irremediably established before
birth because indeed the ultimate meaning that only the end of death can assign

---

[10] See P. Amandry, "Oracles, littérature, et politique," *REA* 61 (1959): 400–13.

to a man's existence was already his, in the eyes of the gods, for all time and was, from the beginning, included in his fate, and fixed there forever. It is this secret significance of destiny—inscribed, from the gods' outlook, from birth, accessible from the human viewpoint only after death—that the word of the oracle is thought to reveal in the course of life itself. In its prophetic function, divination is represented therefore as an irruption of divine immutability and omniscience into the inconstant flux of human existence. But if the oracle really possessed the power to announce the future, to reveal fate as clearly as, in practice, it dispenses advice and admonition, what would disappear would be the radical ignorance of the future that defines the human condition and distinguishes it from the gods. This is why, as the famous formula of Heraclitus indicates, the oracle in reality does not tell the future any more than it hides it; it only signifies it (*sēmainei*). It allows it to be seen by hiding it; it lets it be divined by means of an enigmatic word, of a "spoken" that functions like a sign, but an obscure sign, as difficult for human intelligence to decode as the events themselves about which they came to consult. The ambiguity of the oracular word reintroduces into mortal time this fundamental opacity, this necessarily hazardous character of previews and projects that it is divination's task to attenuate, if not to abolish.

In the context of an oracular dialogue like the one the Greeks knew, the divinatory word seems therefore to diverge according to whether one turns to the concrete practice of consultations or one examines the theory, more or less explicit, by which that society claimed to justify its divinatory procedures, and the theology it constructed out of the prophetic function. To the extent that the word of the oracle is clear, that it unequivocally resolves a dilemma, it comes to support human enterprises in determining, together with the consultants, the order of preference in the field of possible choices; to the extent that it reveals the future in advance as something irremediable, it is, on the contrary, obscure and ambiguous; it is generally only understood too late, when the event itself is responsible, alas, for our enlightenment.

As an adjunct technique of decision, divination operates, on the one hand, according to a binary logic of choice between two options, one that, on another level, is similar to that which sophists and rhetors use when they confront each other with words to gain the ear of the tribunal and assembly with their proposals. On the other hand, like a formulation in advance of an irrevocable destiny, it acquires the value of a sign, like a presage, but a sign that is enigmatic and, at its extreme, as impenetrable as the future itself. In each of these two cases, divination, in its oral form, did not lead to a continuous and methodical reflection about the sign (this was left for philosophers), or to an elaboration of a code of decipherment, a body of decoding techniques, that would permit a systematic interpretation of different classes of signs (for the Greeks, reflection about signs was essentially conducted starting from and as a function of language).

IV

This series of negatives has led us to turn, as a counterproof, to the historians of ancient societies that, in contrast to Greece, can be characterized as great civilizations of writing. These scholars report parallel conclusions about the examples of China and Mesopotamia, which differ from each other in so many other respects. These cultures display the interdependent links between the invention of the graphic sign, its extreme valorization as an intellectual instrument reserved for a body of ''learned'' specialists, the grip it maintains as a social tool of codification in the service of power, and the powerful development of a divinatory thought that functions like a true semiology, a general science of signs. In interpreting presages on the model of a decipherment of signs of ideographic or pictographic writing, divination not only aspires to predict the future; it claims to decode the universe as if it were a matter of a text wherein was inscribed the order of the world, a tablet on which the gods had traced out individual destinies. By contrast to Greek data, where divination is, above all, oral and where science is contrasted from the start with divinatory mentality, the attention given in the great scriptural civilizations to graphic combinations and symbolic configurations directs the progress of rationality, even as far as scientific procedures, along the same path that divination had previously opened up.

The difference is no less striking with forms of rationality appropriate to the procedures of technical divination used by the Nzakara of the central African republic, treated in the last essay of this volume on divination. In formulating their questions in terms of a dilemma, the Greeks, as we have seen, tried to obtain replies from the oracle that were as univocal as one might hope for in the mode of oral expression, so they could determine as clearly as possible which option to choose in preference to another. In order to enlighten their consultants, the seers of Nzakara, the *ba sa iwa*, themselves engage in a dialogue with *iwa*, the oracular power, and they pursue it in having recourse, more systematically than did the Greeks, to interrogatory practices of a sort such that the reply can only obey a strict logic of the alternative: wood when rubbed rises or not; ashes or powders stick or do not stick; the axe falls on one side or the other. There is never a third term. The art of the seer does not consist therefore in deciphering signs or of interpreting words that are obscure to a greater or lesser degree; he must first master the sacred techniques that compel *iwa* to speak without any ambiguity; then he must be capable of conducting the interrogation to its end, to question the god thoroughly and according to the rules. The competence of the seer presupposes that he knows the repertory of questions that allow him to make an inventory of the entire group of invisible forces that threaten to disturb the normal course of human life. His role is to auscultate the consultant's situation down to the minutest details with a diagnostic founded on a chain of yes or no responses. He proceeds therefore like a doctor who examines his patient from head to foot and who seeks to discover, for each part of the body, whether it does or does not present the symptoms that are in the inventory of the medical science of which he is the repository. This divinatory logic, one will observe, conforms in its rigorous binarity to the mentality of the Nzakara who, at all levels and moments of social life, proceed in their intellectual operations with chains of antinomies.

We could not hope to summarize or comment on the analyses of Africanists or Sinologists like those one will read here, and there is nothing to add to the work of Jean Bottéro on Babylonian divination, which by its breadth, exactitude, and originality, constitutes a complete overview that would have justified publication as a book. We can only thank the authors who collaborated here, without whom we could not even have undertaken this comparative study on the role of the word, writing, and "mechanical" techniques in the different forms of divinatory rationality. It is the quality of these contributions that gives our work value. To our thanks addressed to the authors, we would like to add our appreciation for those numerous others who were kind enough to participate in one way or another in our effort of communal research.[11]

[11] The following contributed papers to this volume: Léon Vandermeersch, "De la tortue à l'achillée"; Jacques Gernet, "Petits écarts et grands écarts"; Jean Bottéro, "Symptômes, signes, écritures"; Roland Crahay, "La bouche et la vérité"; Luc Brisson, "Du bon usage du dérèglement"; Jeannie Carlier, "Science divine et raison humaine"; Denise Grodzynski, "Par la bouche de l'empereur"; Anne Retel-Laurentin, "La force de la parole." The following collaborated in our inquiry by presenting reports and participating in discussions: A. Adler, "La divination chez les Moundang"; P. Amandry, "La divination en Grèce: Le consultant devant l'oracle"; R. Bastide, "Problèmes de divination; connaissance de l'évènement"; J.-P. Brisson, "La divination dans le monde romain"; M. Cartry, "Le système divinatoire chez les Gourmantché"; R. Jaulin, "Problèmes de géomancie"; J. Maître, "Astrologie et société dans la France contemporaine"; D. Sabbatucci, "La divination africaine: Problèmes et perspectives"; R. Schilling, "La divination à Rome: Traditionalisme et rationalité"; P. Verger, "Système de divination par Isa chez les Yoruba."

Chapter 19

THE INDIVIDUAL WITHIN THE CITY-STATE

1. THE STARTING point of my research is the distinction established by Louis Dumont between two opposite forms of the notion of the "individual": the individual outside the world and the individual in it.[1] The first finds its model in the Indian who, in renouncing the world, chooses independence and uniqueness. He must break with all social ties and cut himself off from life as it is lived here and now. In India, renunciation of the world is a condition for the individual's spiritual development. One must break off from all the institutions that form the warp and weft of collective existence, abandon the community to which one belongs, and withdraw to a place of solitude defined by its distance from others—from their conduct and their values. According to the Indian model, the emergence of the individual does not occur within the social framework: it implies that one has left it.

The model of the second type is modern man, the individual who affirms and lives his individuality, which is posited as a value within the world. This is the worldly individual: each one of us.

How does this second type of individuality come about? For Louis Dumont, it is derived from and dependent on the first. When the first seeds of individualism appear in a traditional society, they always do so in opposition to that society and in the form of that first type of individual who is exterior to the world. Such, he asserts, is the course of Western history. From the Hellenistic period onward, the sage, as human ideal, is defined by his place in opposition to mundane life: attaining wisdom means the renunciation of the world and separation from it. In this sense and on this level, Christianity in the first centuries after Christ does not break radically with pagan thought, but continues in a similar pattern. The accent, however, is displaced: the Christian individual exists in and through his relationship to God, that is, basically through his orientation away from the world and the consequent devaluation of worldly existence and its values.

This English text, translated by James Lawler, was presented as the Lurcy Lecture of the University of Chicago in 1986. It has been revised and edited by Froma Zeitlin, who translated the notes added to the French version, "L'individu dans la cité," published first in the collective volume *Sur l'individu* (Paris, 1987), 20–37, and again in *L'individu, la mort, l'amour: Soi-même et l'autre en Grèce ancienne* (Paris, 1989), 211–32.

[1] Louis Dumont, *Homo hierarchicus: Essai sur le système des castes* (Paris, 1966); *Homo aequalis: Génèse et épanouissement de l'idéologie économique* (Paris, 1977).

1.1. Worldly life, however, becomes progressively contaminated by the ex-traworldly. As Louis Dumont demonstrates, the extra-worldly slowly pene-trates and invades the whole social field. "Worldly life," writes Dumont, "will be conceived as the ability to conform entirely to a supreme value; the extraworldly individual will have become the modern individual within the world. Here is the historic proof of the extraordinary power of the original disposition."[2]

This stark, systematic view of the conditions that allow the individual to emerge by disengaging himself from social constraints through the practice of renunciation has been further elaborated by Dumont. He studied a particular civilization, ancient India, and first applied this view only to societies he calls hierarchical or holistic, those with a caste system in which each person has a true place only as a function of the whole and with respect to the whole. The human being is completely defined by the position he occupies within the so-cial group, by his position in a hierarchical ladder made up of separate and interdependent levels. Dumont later widened his view to include all societies, even those in the West, and he produced a general theory of the birth of the individual and of the development of individualism.

2. I would like to explore the validity of this general explanation by looking at how matters were represented in archaic and classical Greece, the Greece of the city-states, between the eighth and fourth centuries B.C.E.

2.1. But first, two series of remarks are in order. The first concerns religion and society in ancient Greece; the second, the notion of the individual.

Greek polytheism is a religion of the intraworldly type. Not only are the gods present, not only do they function within the world, but cult rites and ceremonies have as their aim to bring the worshippers into the cosmic and social order over which the divine Powers preside. The diverse aspects of this order correspond to the different modalities of the sacred. In this system there is no place for the figure of the renouncer. The closest are those we call the "Orphics," and these remained on the margins throughout the whole of antiq-uity. They never became an official religious sect (within religious practice). They never even became a well-defined religious group that might have com-plemented the official cult or given it an added dimension by introducing the perspective of salvation.

Moreover, Greek society was egalitarian, not hierarchical. The city defines those who compose it by placing them in a group on a single horizontal plane. Whoever lacks access to this plane is excluded from the city-state and from society (and at its limit, from humanity, like the slave). But each individual,

---

[2] *Essais sur l'individualisme* (Paris, 1983). The chapter "De l'individu hors du monde à l'in-dividu dans le monde," 33–67, originally appeared in *Le Débat* 15 (1981).

if he is a citizen, is, at least in principle, able to fulfill all the social functions, with their religious implications. There is no priestly or warrior caste. Each and every citizen, since he is able to wage war, is also qualified to accomplish the sacrificial rite, as long as he does not bear the mark of some pollution. He can perform the rituals within his own household or in the name of the larger group if his status as magistrate authorizes it. It is in this sense, then, that the citizen of the classical *polis* belongs not to Dumont's *Homo hierarchichus* but rather to *Homo aequalis*.

In an earlier study I compared Indian and Greek sacrifices with respect to the individual's role within each type. In order for the Indian ascetic to exist as individual, he must cut himself off from all those social ties which hitherto had bound him to others, to the world, to himself and to his own acts by his own desire. As I wrote before:

> In Greece, the sacrificer, as such, remains solidly included in the various domestic, civic, and political groups in whose name he carries out the sacrifice. This integration into the community, and especially into its religious activities, gives such steps toward individualization a completely different style: they occur in a social framework in which the individual, as he begins to emerge, appears not as one who renounces the world but as a person in his own right, a legal subject, a political actor, a private person in the midst of his family or in the circle of his friends.[3]

2.2.   Now for the second order of remarks. What does "individual" mean? And what does "individualism" mean? Michel Foucault uses these terms to distinguish among three different notions that can be associated but whose links are neither constant nor necessary.[4]

(a) The place afforded to the private individual and his degree of independence with respect to the group of which he is a member and to the institutions that govern him.

(b) The valorization of private life with respect to public activities.

(c) The intensity of relations, with respect to the self, by which the individual takes himself in his different dimensions as an object of preoccupation and concern; the way he orients and directs toward himself his efforts of observation, reflection, and analysis; the concern for the self and also the elaboration of the self, the formation of the self using all the mental techniques of attention directed toward the self, self-examination, self-testing, taking one's own bearings, so to speak, self-clarification, self-expression.

---

[3] "Greek Religion, Ancient Religions," above, chap. 16.

[4] *Le souci de soi* (Paris, 1984), 56–57, trans. R. Hurley, under the title *The Care of the Self* (New York, 1986), 42–43.

It is clear that these three notions do not overlap. In a military aristocracy, the warrior becomes a separate individual through the uniqueness of his exceptional valor. He is not in the least concerned with his private life or self-analysis. Conversely, the intensity of relations with the self may accompany a disqualification of the values of private life and even a rejection of individualism such as we find in monastic life.

For my part, I would like to propose a somewhat different classification within the perspective of historical anthropology. I freely acknowledge that it has a certain arbitrariness, but it does allow us to see more clearly some of the problems involved.

(a) The individual, *stricto sensu*. His place and role in his group or groups; the value accorded him; the margin of movement left to him; his relative autonomy with respect to his institutional framework.

(b) The subject. When the individual uses the first person to express himself and, speaking in his own name, enunciates certain features that make him a unique being.

(c) The "ego," the person. The ensemble of psychological practices and attitudes that give an interior dimension and a sense of wholeness to the subject. These practices and attitudes constitute him within himself as a unique being, real and original, whose authentic nature resides entirely in the secrecy of his interior life. It resides at the very heart of an intimacy to which no one except him can have access because it is defined as self-consciousness.

If, in order to understand better these three levels and their differences, I were to risk comparing them to literary genres, I would say schematically that the individual corresponds to biography, in the sense that by contrast to epic or historical narrative, it is based on the life of a single character; the subject corresponds to autobiography or memoirs where the individual himself tells his own life story; and the "ego" corresponds to confessions or a diary in which the inner life, the unique subject of a private life—in all of its psychological complexity and richness, and its relative opacity or incommunicability—provides the material for what is written.

From the classical period onward, the Greeks were familiar with some forms of biography and autobiography. Momigliano has recently studied the evolution of these forms and concluded that our idea of the individuality and character of a person originates with their production.[5] However, not only did the Greeks of the classical and Hellenistic periods lack confessions and diaries—their existence was unthinkable—but, as Misch observes and Momigli-

---

[5] "Marcel Mauss e il problema della persona," in *Gli Uomini, la società, la civiltà: Uno studio intorno all'opera di Marcel Mauss*, ed. Riccardo di Donato (Pisa, 1985); "Ancient Biography and the Study of Religion in the Roman Empire," *ASNSP*, ser. 3, no. 15 (1985), reprinted in A. Momigliano, *On Pagans, Jews, and Christians* (Middletown, Conn., 1987), 159–77.

ano confirms, the characterization of the individual in Greek autobiography allows no "intimacy of the self."

3. Let us begin with the individual. There are three ways to delimit his presence in Greece:

(1) The individual valorized as such, in his singularity.

(2) The individual and his personal sphere: the domain of his private life.

(3) The emergence of the individual within social institutions that, by their very functioning, afforded him a central place from the classical period onward.

3.1. I will take two examples of the "extraordinary" individual from the archaic period: the warrior hero (Achilles); and the inspired seer, the divine man (Hermotimos, Epimenides, Empedocles).

More than his status and titles within the social body, what characterizes the hero is his unusual destiny, the exceptional prestige of his exploits, the conquest of a certain glory that is his alone, and the survival through the ages of his renown within the collective memory. Ordinary men vanish as soon as they die into the dark oblivion of Hades; they disappear, *nōnumoi*; they are the "anonymous," the "nameless." Only the heroic individual, by assenting to face death in the flower of his youth, sees his name perpetuated and glorified from generation to generation. His exceptional figure remains forever inscribed at the center of communal life. For this to happen, the hero has to isolate himself, even oppose himself to his own kind; he has to cut himself off from his peers and his commanders. Such is the case of Achilles. But this distance from the group does not make him one who renounces, who abandons worldly life. On the contrary, by pressing to its furthest extreme the logic of a human life dedicated to a warrior ideal, it carries the worldly values and social practices of the warrior beyond their ordinary limits. By his strenuous, rigorous life, his refusal to compromise, his insistence on perfection even unto death, the hero brings a new dimension to usual norms and group customs. He founds a manner of honor and excellence that goes beyond ordinary honor and excellence. He confers a radiance, a majesty, and a solidity on those vital values and social virtues that lack these in the normal course of living. But now they have been sublimated and transformed by the ordeal of death and are no longer susceptible to the ruin that threatens all worldly things. Yet it is the social body itself that acknowledges this radiance, majesty, and solidity, assimilating into its own institutions these glorious qualities and ensuring them honor and permanency.

The magi. These too are individuals separate from the common pursuit of mortals. They have their own way of living, their rules, and their exceptional powers. They practice exercises I hesitate to call "spiritual"—control over respiration, concentration of the breath so as to purify it, to detach it from the body, liberate it, and dispatch it to the beyond; "re-memoration" of former lives; escape from the cycle of successive reincarnations. Such are the godly men, the *theioi andres*, who rise above their mortal existences while still alive and achieve the status of imperishable beings. These seers are not renouncers, even if in their wake a school of thought will arise whose members propose to flee the here and now. On the contrary, precisely because of their unique natures and the distance that keeps them apart from the group, these figures play a special role in periods of crisis in the seventh and sixth centuries B.C.E. They function like *nomothetai*, lawmakers, such as Solon, in order to purify communities of their pollutions, calm revolts, arbitrate conflicts, and promulgate institutional and religious ordinances. The city-states must have recourse to these "extra-ordinary" individuals in order to regulate public affairs.

3.2. The sphere of private life. From the most archaic forms of the city-state, at the end of the eighth century B.C.E.and already in Homer, the domains of public and private, of common and individual, are marked. Each domain is defined with respect to the other and is dependent on the other: *to koinon* and *to idion*. Communality includes all activities and practices that must be shared; they are not the exclusive privilege of any individual or group of nobles, and in order to be a citizen, one must take part in these activities. The private domain is that which is not shared, and concerns each individual alone.

The configurations of what is common and what is private, as well as their respective boundaries, have a history. In Sparta, the education of the young (*agogē*) and the banquets (*sussitia*, compulsory meals partaken together) remain in the common domain: these are civic activities. In Athens, where the emergence of a purely political sphere within the city operates on a more rigorous level of abstraction (the political here is the sharing of certain powers among all the citizens: commanding, deliberating, deciding, judging), the private domain—that which concerns each person for himself—will assign to domestic life the education of children, and banquets at which one entertains guests of one's choice. The group of relatives and friends defines a zone in which private relationships between individuals can develop, assume more depth, and acquire a greater degree of emotional intimacy. The *sumposion* becomes popular as early as the sixth century. Meeting together at home after dinner to drink and converse together, to enjoy one another's masculine company and that of courtesans, and to sing elegies under the auspices of Dionysos, Aphrodite, and Eros—all these activities signal the appearance of a freer and more selective interpersonal exchange within social life. Each individual's tastes are taken into consideration in order to achieve a certain pleasure, a pleasure controlled and shared with regard to the law of "drink and be merry." Florence Dupont describes it this way: "The banquet is the place and means for the private citizen to attain pleasure and fulfillment, while its parallel, the Assembly, will be the place and means for the public citizen to attain freedom and power.''[6]

Funeral practices and monuments attest to the growing importance of the private sphere over the public domain, where we see emotional ties binding an individual to his loved ones. Until the end of the sixth century in Attica, tombs are generally individual. They continue the ideology of the heroic individual and his exceptional nature. The grave stele gives the name of the deceased and is addressed to each and every passerby. The engraved or painted image, as well as the funerary *kouros* on the tomb, figures the deceased in his youthful beauty as an exemplary representative of the social values and virtues he incarnated. But from the last quarter of the fifth century, the custom of family tombs emerges. This custom arises parallel to and separate from the public funerals performed in honor of those patriotically fallen in combat during which the deceased's individuality is submerged in the common glory of the city. Henceforth the funerary steles associate the deceased individual with the surviving members of the household. The epitaphs celebrate the personal feelings of love, regret, and admiration of husbands and wives, parents and children.

3.3.   But now let us leave the private sphere to enter the public domain. We see there a series of institutions that bring about the emergence of the private individual in some important aspects. I will take two examples: the first concerns religious institutions, the second, the law.

The mysteries, such as those of Eleusis, exist alongside civic religion. They are celebrated, of course, under the official patronage of the city. But they are open to whoever speaks Greek, whether foreigner or Athenian, woman or man, slave or free. Participation in the ceremonies, up to and including complete initiation, depends on each person's own decision and not on his or her social position or function within the group. Moreover, what initiates expect from their experience, their ritual enthronement, is a better lot for themselves individually in the other world. Thus there is a freedom of choice to proceed to initiation, and a uniqueness, once one leaves, of a posthumous destiny others cannot claim. But as soon as the ceremonies are completed and the consecration obtained, nothing in the initiate's dress, demeanor, religious practice, or social behavior distinguishes the initiate either from the mode of his or her former existence or from that of the uninitiated. The person in question has acquired a sort of intimate confidence, and is religiously changed within by the familiarity acquired with the two goddesses. The initiate remains socially unchanged, the same as before. Individual involvement in the mysteries never at any moment creates an extraworldly individual, detached from this life or civic ties.

[6] *Le plaisir et la loi* (Paris, 1977), 25.

And now another manifestation of religious individualism: from around the fifth century onward religious groups spring up that take their initiative from an individual who founds them. These groups meet together in his presence in a private sanctuary, dedicated to some divinity. The members wish to reserve the privilege of celebrating a particular cult together with the aim, as Aristotle says, "of performing sacrifices together and of meeting with one another" (*Nic. eth.* 1160a19–23). The worshippers are the *sunousiastai*, associates, and they make up a small closed religious community; they enjoy getting together to practice their rites where, in order to participate, each one must request entry and must have been personally approved by the other members of the group.

The individual here, by choosing his god and a form of unique religious practice, and by being accepted into the small community of worshippers, now enters into the cult organization, but the place he occupies is not extraworldly or outside society. In the appearance of this new type of organization in religious life we see the beginnings of more easygoing and relaxed relations between private individuals. This kind of association is quite different from the predetermined and even programmed religious roles determined by civic status. We now see something we might call "social selectivity."

But it is especially in the legal system that we see the private individual emerge from the very heart of public institutions. Let us look at two examples: criminal law and the testament.

From blood revenge between families—the vendetta, with its procedures of compensation and arbitration—to the establishment of courts of law, the passage from a prelegal state to a legal system brings about the notion of the individual criminal. The individual henceforth appears as the subject of the offense and the object of judgment. There is a rupture between the prejuridical notion of crime and that of the law—between crime viewed as a *miasma*, a contagious and collective pollution, and crime understood as committed by a single person, which has various degrees of seriousness corresponding to the different courts where it may be tried (the crime was perhaps "justified," or committed "unintentionally," or of "one's own free will," or "with premeditation"). Indeed, it is precisely the individual who must answer, within the judiciary system, when it comes to examining the degree of relation between him and his crime. This juridical history has a moral counterpart: it involves notions of responsibility, personal culpability, and worth. There is also a psychological counterpart: it poses the problem of circumstances, constraints, and deliberate or spontaneous planning, which all figure in the subject's decision. One must also take into account the underlying motives of his actions. These problems will find an echo in Attic tragedy of the fifth century. The constant questioning of the individual agent is characteristic of this literary genre, the scrutiny of the human subject face-to-face with his action, the relationship between the dramatic hero in his singularity, to what he has done and decided, for which he bears the burden of responsibility and which nevertheless go beyond him.[7]

The last will and testament also provides evidence for the social advancement of the private individual. Louis Gernet has carefully analyzed the conditions for and the modalities of its appearance.[8] At first, in the case of adoption *inter vivos*, the private individual, as such, does not play a role. It is up to the head of a family, if he has no children, to adopt a relative so that his household does not come to an end and his patrimony is not distributed after death among his collateral kin. The practice of testamentary adoption follows along the same lines: it is always a question of the household whose maintenance must be ensured. What matters is the *oikos* and not the individual. But conversely, from the third century onward, as an extension of the *donatio mortis causa*, the practice of making a will, properly speaking, is instituted. It becomes a strictly individual affair, allowing for the free transmission of possessions according to the written desires of a particular subject, which must be respected. He is seen as master of his decision with regard to all that he possesses. Henceforth there is a direct and exclusive link between the individual and his wealth, whatever its form—inherited and acquired, movable and nonmovable goods. Everyone now has property, a financial worth.

4. The subject. The use of the first person in a text can have very different meanings according to the nature of the document and the form of its enunciation. It may be a king's edict or proclamation, a funerary epitaph, an invocation of a poet who stages his own appearance at the beginning or in the course of his song as inspired by the Muses or possessed of a revealed truth, a historical narrative into which the author intrudes in person to give his opinion, or a self-defense or self-justification in the "autobiographical" speeches of orators like Demosthenes and Isocrates.

The discourse where the subject expresses himself in saying "I" does not therefore constitute a tightly defined category, nor does it have univocal import. If I retain this term, however, it is because in Greece it corresponds to a type of poetry—broadly speaking, the lyric—in which the author, by using the first person, gives the "I" a special kind of confidence that expresses a sensibility that is his or her own and endows it with the general significance of a model or poetic *topos*. By making their personal emotions, their present state of mind, into the major theme of communication with their public (friends, fellow citizens, and *hetairoi*), the lyric poets confer a precise verbal form and a firmer consistency on the indecisive, secret, intimate, and personal subjec-

---

[7] [Although in real life, women did not participate in judicial procedures, in tragedy we find them demonstrating a similar self-scrutiny in the same setting of the ongoing debate between personal responsibility and exculpability. Ed.]

[8] "La loi de Solon sur le testament," in *Droit et société dans la Grèce ancienne* (Paris, 1955), 121–49.

tivity that resides within us. By formulating what we experience individually in the language of the poetic message, this innermost emotion is incarnated and acquires a sort of objective reality. But one must go further. Affirmed, sung, and exalted, the subjectivity of the poet questions established norms and socially recognized values. It also serves as a touchstone for individual evaluations: the beautiful and the ugly, the good and the bad, happiness and misfortune. Archilochus claims that man's nature is diverse. Each person enjoys something else in his heart (frag. 36 Lasserre). Sappho echoes the same sentiment: "For me, the most beautiful thing on earth is whatever one loves" (frag. 16 Lobel-Page). There exists then a relativity of communally held values. In the last resort, the criterion of values falls to the subject, the individual—what he or she has personally experienced—and this is what forms the substance of the poem.

Another element must be emphasized: alongside the cycles of cosmic time and the order of social time and in opposition to these, there emerges a time that is lived subjectively by the individual: unstable, changing, but leading inexorably to old age and death. It is a time to which one is subjected, with its unforeseen and capricious reversals and the anguish of its irreversibility. Within himself (or herself), the subject experiences this personal time under many different guises: as regret, nostalgia, anticipation, hope, and suffering, as the memory of lost joys, of those presences that are gone. In Greek lyric the subject feels and expresses himself (or herself) as that part of the individual over which he or she has no control, that which leaves one powerless and passive, and which nevertheless, is, in the poet, life itself—the life one celebrates: *one's* own life.

4.1. The ego. The Greeks of the archaic and classical periods have, of course, an experience of their ego and their person, just as they have of their bodies, but that experience is organized differently from our own. The ego is neither bounded nor unified; it is an open field of multiple forces, as Hermann Fränkel argues.[9] Most important, this experience is turned outward, not inward. Individuals seek and find themselves in others, in those mirrors reflecting their image, each of which is an *alter ego* for them—parents, children, friends. As James Redfield observes with respect to the epic hero: he only sees himself in the mirror others hold up to him.[10] The individual is projected and objectified in what he accomplishes, in what he actually carries out. These are the activities and undertakings that allow him to grasp himself, not in their potential but in their actuality (*energeia*), and that never exist as such in his

---

[9] *Dichtung und Philosophie des frühen Griechentums* (Munich, 1962), trans. Moses Hadas and James Willis, under the title *Early Greek Poetry and Philosophy* (Oxford, 1975), 80. Cf. also Bruno Snell, *Die Entdeckung des Geistes* (Hamburg, 1955), 17–42, trans. T. Rosenmeyer, under the title *The Discovery of the Mind* (Oxford, 1963), 1–22.

[10] "Le sentiment homérique du Moi," *Le genre human* 12 (1985): 104.

consciousness.[11] There is no introspection. The subject does not make up a closed, interior world he must penetrate in order to find himself—or rather to discover himself. The subject is extroverted. Just as the eye does not see itself, so the individual must look elsewhere to apprehend himself. His self-consciousness is not reflexive, folded in on itself, and contained. It is not internal, face-to-face with itself: it is existential. Existence is prior to the consciousness of existing. As has been often noted, the *cogito ergo sum*, I think therefore I am, has no meaning for a Greek.[12] I exist because I have hands, feet, and

[11] Cf. J.-P. Vernant, "Catégories de l'agent et de l'action en Grèce ancienne," in *Langue, discours, société: Pour Emile Benveniste*, ed. J. Kristeva, J.-C. Milner, and N. Ruwet (Paris, 1975) (reprinted in *Religions, Histoires, Raisons* [Paris, 1974], 85–95).

[12] Cf. Richard Sorabji, "Body and Soul in Aristotle," in *Articles on Aristotle*, ed. J. Barnes, M. Schofield, and R. Sorabji (London, 1979), vol. 4, pp. 42–64, especially paragraph 4, entitled "The Contrast with Descartes." Also in the same volume, see Charles H. Kahn, "Sensation and Consciousness in Aristotle's Psychology," 1–31. Kahn stresses "the total lack of the Cartesian sense of a radical and necessary incompatibility between thought or awareness, on the one hand, and physical extension, on the other." See too Jacques Brunschvig, "Aristote et l'effet Perrichon," in *La passion de la raison: Hommage à Fernand Alquié*, ed. Jean-Luc Marian (Paris, 1983), 361–77. He notes (375): "One can hardly propose that Aristotle, as psychologist and moralist, could have thought that the actual being of the producer is the work itself (even only in one sense) and that the function of Socrates, as Michael of Ephesus puts it, is 'nothing other than Socrates himself in action.' My function (but also my friend, my debtor, my child, my reflection, my shadow) can very well be '*something of me*,' my projection, my expression, my objectification or my 'extraneousness'; it seems crude and absurd to say that *it is I*, that I am there where it is, that it is my being. . . . My relation to myself is not assimilable to any relation that I can have with any object whatsoever. Everything that is an object for me is in principle other than me. I will suggest, to conclude, that there is a sort of 'epistemological obstacle' (let us say 'Cartesian,' for short) which must be gotten rid of, if we want to understand a certain number of Greek ideas. It would be interesting in more than one regard to pick up the traces of a kind of paradoxical *cogito* in Greek thought which could be formulated as follows: I see myself (in my function or in some of the other projections of myself enumerated above), therefore I am; and I am there where I see myself; I *am* that projection of myself which I see." In the same vein, see Gilbert Romeyer Derbey, "L'âme est en quelque façon tous les êtres (Aristote, *De anima*, T8, 431b21), *Elenchos: Rivista di studi sul pensiero antico* 8 (1987): 364–80. "If the soul is the being to which the world is given," he concludes, "what is important to know is how the soul is given to itself. This problem of subjectivity is not present as such, in Aristotle; nevertheless an indication of book 12 of the *Metaphysics* can help to elucidate this point. Divine thought, as one knows, is 'thinking about thinking,' which amounts to saying that the divine *nous* (mind) is in itself its own object and thinks itself directly. On the contrary, however, human sensation or knowledge are 'always of something else' [*aei allou*] and 'of oneself over and above that' [*hautēs en parergōi*]. The soul grasps itself then in addition, on top of it all, so to speak, and this result can only come about through the grasp of another being, by the apprehension of the world. In short, the soul can only be itself in being, in some sense, all the other beings. . . . If divine thought is thought of itself alone, human thought is thought of oneself and of things, or rather of oneself in relation to things; the soul is not what it will be in Descartes, a *mens pura et abstracta*, or even already in Plotinus—that which is discovered by 'taking everything else away.' Consciousness therefore slips only furtively into philosophy; we are well on the road that leads to Cartesianism, but Aristotle did not take a single step along this path." In emphasizing the intellectual transformation that Descartes's *Dioptrique* brought to the field of vision and perception in general, Gérard Simon notes: "As a

feelings; I exist because I walk and run, because I see and feel. I do all these things and I know that I do them.[13] But I never think my existence through the consciousness I have of these sensations. My consciousness is always dependent on the outside: I am conscious of seeing such and such an object, of hearing a certain sound, of suffering a certain pain. The individual's world has not taken the form of self-consciousness, of an inner universe that defines each person in his radical originality. Bernard Groethuysen sums up the special nature of the ancient individual in a succinct but precise formula by saying that self-consciousness is the apprehension of self in a "he," and not yet in an "I."[14]

4.2. But you are bound to ask, how do you deal with those texts of Plato in which he writes: "What constitutes each of us is nothing other than the soul. . . . The being which is in truth each of us, and which we call the immortal soul, goes away after death to join the other gods" (*Laws* 954a6–b4)? In the *Phaedo*, Socrates, on the verge of death, addresses his listeners in these terms: "What I myself am is this Socrates who converses with you [*ego eimi houtos Sokrates*] not that other Socrates whose body will soon be before your eyes" (115c). And speaking with Alcibiades, the Platonic Socrates addresses his listener: "When Socrates speaks with Alcibiades, he does not speak to your face, but to Alcibiades himself. And this Alcibiades is the soul" (*Alc.* 130c).

The affair seems settled. What Socrates and Alcibiades are, what each individual is, is the soul, the *psuchē*. We know how this soul, which departs after death to join the divine beyond, made its appearance in the Greek world. It originated with the magi I discussed earlier. They rejected the traditional notion of the *psuchē*, the double of the deceased, a strengthless phantom and a vague shadow vanished into Hades, and tried through practice of breath control and purification to gather the soul that was dispersed in all parts of the body so that, once isolated and unified, it might be separated from the body at will in order to travel into the beyond. The Platonic conception of a soul, which is Socrates, finds its point of departure, its "initial formulation," in these exercises of escape from the body and the world and flight toward the

---

result, sensations ceased to be preconstituted, that is, as possibilities offered by the world and awaiting the agent capable of actualizing them. Henceforth, the problem of apperception could no longer be resolved by passing over it, nor could its place be taken by the host of faculties which gradually elaborated the sensibles already potentially in things until complete intellection was attained. It became impossible to treat perception in the third person: for the first time the soul becomes a subject par excellence." "Derrière le miroir," *Le temps de la réflexion* 2 (1981): 328.

[13] Cf. Arist., *Nic. eth.* 1170a29–32: "If he who sees perceives that he sees, and he who hears, that he hears, and he who walks, that he walks, and in the case of all other activities similarly there is something which perceives that we are active, so that if we perceive, we perceive that we perceive, and if we think, that we think; and . . . to perceive that we perceive or think is to perceive that we exist" [trans. R. McKeon (Chicago, 1947)].

[14] *Anthropologie philosophique*, 2d ed. (Paris, 1980), 61.

divine, the goal of all of which is salvation through renunciation of earthly life.

All this is true. Still, we must clarify an essential point. The *psuchē* is truly Socrates but not Socrates' "ego," not the psychological Socrates. The *psuchē* is in each of us an impersonal or suprapersonal entity. It is *the* soul in me and not *my* soul. This is true first because this soul is defined by its radical opposition to the body and everything relating to it. Thus excluded is anything having to do with our individual particularities, with the limitations specific to physical existence. Next, this is also true because this *psuchē* is a *daimōn* in us, a divine being, a supernatural force whose place and function in the universe goes beyond our single person. The number of souls in the universe has been forever fixed; it remains eternally the same. There are as many souls as stars. Thus each man at birth finds his soul, which has already been there since the beginning of the world. It is in no way his and it will go on, after his death, to become incarnate again; it may become a man, or an animal, or a plant if it has not previously purified itself enough to rejoin the star to which it is attached.

The individual soul therefore does not convey a man's individual psychology but rather the aspiration of an individual subject to become one with the all, reintegrated into the general cosmic order.[15]

This *psuchē*, of course, already has a much more personal content in Plato and even more so afterwards. But this gesture toward the psychological comes about through mental practices undertaken in the city and oriented toward this world.

Let us take memory as an example. The Pythagoreans and other magi performed memory exercises, not in order to take hold of personal time, that fleeting time of personal memories—as with the lyric poets—or to set up a temporal order, as the historians will eventually do. Rather, they do so to remember the series of all previous lives from the beginning, so that they may "join the end to the beginning" and escape the cycle of reincarnation. This memory is the instrument that allows their exit from time, not its reconstruction. It is the Sophists, by founding a completely utilitarian mnemnotechnics, and it is Aristotle, by linking memory to the sensible part of the soul, who will create an element of the human subject and of his or her psychology.[16]

But above all, something else will be decisive in finally rounding out the inner "ego," giving it consistency and complexity: I refer to all the different behaviors that will connect the *daimōn* soul, the divine soul, immortal and suprapersonal, with the other parts of the soul that are linked to the body, its needs, and its pleasures: *thumos* and *epithumia*. This intercourse between the

[15] Cf. J.-P. Vernant, "Aspects de la personne dans la religion grecque," in *Mythe et pensée chez les Grecs: Etudes de psychologie historique*, 10th ed. (Paris, 1985), 368–70.

[16] "Aspects mythiques de la mémoire et du temps," in Vernant, *Mythe et pensée*, 10th ed., 107–52.

noetic, impersonal soul and all the rest has an orientation and a goal. It is a matter of making the inferior submit to the superior in order to achieve, in oneself, a state of freedom analogous to that of the citizen within the city. In order for man to master himself, he must control that desiring, impassioned part that the lyric poets exalted and to which they surrendered. Through self-observation, through self-imposed exercises and trials, and through the example of others, man must come to grips with himself in order to be his own master, as befits a free man in society whose ideal it is to be a slave of no one, neither of another nor of himself.

This continual practice of moral *askēsis* comes about, is developed, and has meaning only within the framework of the city. Moral training and civic education that prepare you to live the life of a free man go hand in hand. As Michel Foucault correctly states, "moral *askēsis* formed part of the *paideia* of the free man who had a role to play in the city and in his dealings with others; it had no need of separate methods."[17]

Even when, with the Stoics, the ascetic practice that aims at mastering oneself and at the same time remaining free with respect to others, achieves a relative independence in the first centuries of our era as an exercise for the self, it never compels one to leave the world. Techniques of listening and of self-control, of self-imposed trials, and of recollection of all that happened during the day, will tend toward the formation of specific procedures that revolve around "the concern for the self." This "concern" goes still further; it no longer leads only to domination over appetites and passions, but to an "enjoyment of the self," free of desire and trouble. Yet even so, it is never a question of abandoning the world or society. Speaking of Marcus Aurelius and of the kind of inner-anchorite he aspired to be, Foucault notes: "This activity devoted to the self . . . constituted not an exercise in solitude but a true social practice."[18]

4.3. When and how will this "concern for the self," as it appears in late paganism, create a new sense of the person in the history of the individual in the West? When will these traits assume their characteristic features and originality? The turning point occurs between the third and fourth centuries of our era. A new style emerges in collective life, in relations with the divine, and in one's experience of oneself. Peter Brown has shed important light on the conditions and consequences of this mutation. It occurs on three planes: social, religious, and spiritual. I will recall here only those elements of his analyses that directly pertain to the inner dimension of individuals, to the consciousness they have of themselves.

[17] *L'usage des plaisirs* (Paris, 1984), 89, trans. R. Hurley, under the title *The Use of Pleasure* (New York, 1985), 76.
[18] *Le souci*, 87 (*Care of the Self*, 51).

We must first emphasize the very rapid disappearance of the "model of parity," which still had force during the age of the Antonines. Citizens were still equal among themselves and equal with respect to the gods.[19] Society, it is true, is not of the hierarchical type, as in India, but more and more, in the countryside and in the cities, human groups tend to choose exceptional individuals. These people are above the ordinary in the way they live, as if marked with a divine stamp, and their function is to make secure the link between heaven and earth and to exercise a power over men that is not secular but spiritual.

With the rise of the holy man, the man of God, the ascetic, and the anchorite, a kind of individual appears who separates himself from the common herd and disengages himself from the social group only in order to set out in quest of his true self, one strung between the guardian angel who pulls him upward and the demonic forces below that mark the lower boundaries of his personality. The search for God and the search for the self are two dimensions of the same solitary ordeal.

Peter Brown speaks of the "dogged concern" given here to self-consciousness: "dogged" because it entails implacable and prolonged introspection and a vigilant and scrupulous examination, which mistrusts inclinations of the will and free choice. Its aim is to scrutinize these and to determine to what extent they remain opaque or have become transparent to the divine presence. A new form of identity takes shape at this moment: it defines the human individual by way of his most intimate thoughts and secret imaginings, nocturnal dreams, sinful drives, and the constant obsessive presence in his innermost heart of all forms of temptation.[20]

Here is the point of departure for what we perceive as the modern self—the modern individual. But this break with the pagan past also has a continuity. These are not men of renunciation. In their quest for God and the self, for God in the self, they kept their eyes on the ground. By taking advantage of a heavenly power which deeply marked their persons, within and without, they were unanimously recognized by their contemporaries as true "friends of God," and were thus qualified to accomplish their mission here on earth.

Augustine is a good witness to this turning point in the history of the individual when he speaks of the abyss of human consciousness, *abussus humanae conscientiae*, and wonders at the depth and infinite diversity of his own memory, at the mystery of what he is: "This then is my spirit, it is myself. What am I, then, my God? A changing, multiform life of immense, prodigious size." As Pierre Hadot writes: "Instead of saying: the soul, Augustine affirms: I am, I know myself, I will myself. Each of these acts mutually implies the

---

[19] Peter Brown, *The Making of Late Antiquity* (Cambridge, Mass., 1982), 35ff.
[20] Ibid., 90ff.

others. . . . Christianity needed four centuries to attain this self-consciousness."[21]

The new meaning of this person, then, was tied to a different, more intimate relationship between the individual and God. But there was certainly no flight from the world. Peter Brown, in the same book in which he points out the breadth of the changes affecting the structure of the self in the Roman fourth century, also notes that by this new value accorded to the supernatural, "far from encouraging flight from the world, men became all the more involved in it by creating new or reformed institutions."[22]

The Augustinian man who, in the dialogue with God, can say "I," is certainly far removed from the citizen of the classical city-state and from the *homo aequalis* of pagan antiquity. But the distance is that much greater and the gulf even more profound from the one who renounces the world and from the *homo hierarchicus* of Indian civilization.

[21] "De Tertullien à Boèce: Le développement de la notion de personne dans les controverses théologiques," in *Problèmes de la personne*, ed. I. Meyerson (Paris, 1973), 133–34.

[22] Brown, preface to the French edition of *Making of Late Antiquity*, trans. Aline Rousselle, under the title *Génèse de l'antiquité tardive*, 6.